Staf Hellemans, Jozef Wissink (Eds.)

Towards a New Catholic Church
in Advanced Modernity

Tilburg Theological Studies
Tilburger Theologische Studien

edited by/herausgegeben von

Prof. Dr. Erik Borgman
Dr. Dr. Claudia Mariéle Wulf
Prof. Dr. Henk Witte

Volume/Band 5

LIT

Towards a New Catholic Church in Advanced Modernity

Transformations, Visions, Tensions

edited by

Staf Hellemans and Jozef Wissink

LIT

Bibliographic information published by the Deutsche Nationalbibliothek
The Deutsche Nationalbibliothek lists this publication in the Deutsche
Nationalbibliografie; detailed bibliographic data are available in the Internet at
http://dnb.d-nb.de.

ISBN 978-3-643-90204-7

A catalogue record for this book is available from the British Library

©LIT VERLAG GmbH & Co. KG Wien,
Zweigniederlassung Zürich 2012
Klosbachstr. 107
CH-8032 Zürich
Tel. +41 (0) 44-251 75 05
Fax +41 (0) 44-251 75 06
e-Mail: zuerich@lit-verlag.ch
http://www.lit-verlag.ch

LIT VERLAG Dr. W. Hopf
Berlin 2012
Fresnostr. 2
D-48159 Münster
Tel. +49 (0) 2 51-620 320
Fax +49 (0) 2 51-23 19 72
e-Mail: lit@lit-verlag.de
http://www.lit-verlag.de

Distribution:
In Germany: LIT Verlag Fresnostr. 2, D-48159 Münster
Tel. +49 (0) 2 51-620 32 22, Fax +49 (0) 2 51-922 60 99, e-mail: vertrieb@lit-verlag.de

In Austria: Medienlogistik Pichler-ÖBZ, e-mail: mlo@medien-logistik.at

In Switzerland: B + M Buch- und Medienvertrieb, e-mail: order@buch-medien.ch

In the UK: Global Book Marketing, e-mail: mo@centralbooks.com

Table of Contents

Staf Hellemans & Jozef Wissink, *Introduction*　　　　　　　　　7

Part I: Projecting the New Church

Staf Hellemans, *Tracking the New Shape of the Catholic Church in the West*　　　　19

Anthony J. Carroll, *A Catholic Program for Advanced Modernity*　　　51

Peter Jonkers, "*A Purifying Force for Reason*". *Pope Benedict on the Role of Christianity in Advanced Modernity*　　　79

Ton Meijers, *Reform with Continuity. Religious Freedom and Canon Law*　　　103

Henk Witte, "*Ecclesia, quid dicis de teipsa?*" *Can Ecclesiology Be of Any Help to the Church to Deal with Advanced Modernity?*　　　121

James Sweeney, *Catholicism in Britain: A Church in Search of its Way*　　　147

Part II: Ministering the New Church

Stefan Gärtner, *Individual Pastoral Care in Late Modernity. An Essential Matter for the Church*　　　179

Kees de Groot, *How the Roman Catholic Church Maneuvers through Liquid Modernity*　　　195

Willem-Marie Speelman, *Liturgy of Real Presence: From Books to Communication*　　　217

Monique van Dijk-Groeneboer, *Reaching out beyond the*   241
Fortissimo's? Youth, Church, and Religion

Jozef Wissink, *Mission and Modernity. Reflections on the Mission*   257
of the Church in Advanced-Modern Society

List of Contributors   275

The authors wish to thank Michelle Rochard for the correction and improvement of the English, Jan Wijnhoven for the final formatting of the manuscript, and the School of Catholic Theology of Tilburg University for granting publication subsidies

Introduction

Staf Hellemans and Jozef Wissink

It is a truism that everything is changing very fast. The Catholic Church – that self-styled champion of tradition and steadfastness – is no exception. It is not only affected and challenged by changes from the outside world. The Church itself is promoting all sorts of changes. As a result, a new Catholic Church is emerging in the West, one that is, in many respects, very different from the Church before 1960. This book aims to describe this new Church-*in-the-making* (its new frame of mind, its new position in society, its new internal functioning) and to treat some basic issues the Church has to deal with (e.g., how to imagine the Church in advanced modernity, how the Church can attract youth and adults, rebuild local communities, refashion liturgy, rethink pastoral guidance and mission). The book is the result of an interdisciplinary endeavor by philosophers, sociologists, and theologians working at the School of Catholic Theology at Tilburg University in the Netherlands, reinforced by two researchers from the Heythrop Institute at the University of London. Consequently, the book addresses the evolution and prospects of the Catholic Church in the West, above all in Western Europe.

The book has a systematic objective: to describe the crucial changes in the Church after 1960, to determine what the new shape of the Catholic Church in the West is/will be, and to suggest some proposals of how the major problems arising out of this new situation for the Catholic Church might be taken up. This is not the first time in history that the Catholic Church has been forced, due to radical changes in society, to re-invent itself. This was also the case after the French Revolution and the Napoleonic period abolished absolutism and the old unity between church and state. It took the whole first half of the 19th century to establish a new church formation. This ultramontane mass Catholicism was well, though critically, embedded in the first modernity and was in manifold ways retailored in the following decades. It collapsed in the 1960's and 1970's – we take the year 1960 as the watershed date – as a result of another wave of radical social changes, the transition to what we call 'advanced modernity' or 'late modernity'. This transition forced the Church once again into a complete overhaul. How the remake should be done was and is, however, heavily contested. At first, at the Second Vatican Council (1962-1965) and in the years thereafter, a strategy of religious liberalism striving to forge a partnership with the modern world seemed to prevail. Afterwards, a conservative policy was launched. We want to avoid being stuck in such an ideological approach. Our aim with this book is, instead, to transcend an all too partisan view and to get an overall picture of the longer term. The remaking of the Church should not be reduced to the execution of a plan or strategy, either well- or ill-conceived. It is far more complex, involving a myriad of initiatives, the outcome of which is, to a high degree, unintended. A broader perspective is also needed because a new church formation is not built in a couple of years, but in a time frame of many decades. Indeed, the new Church is still in the making. Yet, we also think that the remaking has, by now, progressed to an extent that the outlines of the new Church are beginning to become apparent.

Projecting the new Church

In the first chapter, sociologist Staf Hellemans attempts to flesh out the lead idea of the book: the systematic interpretation of the whirlpool of changes and conflicts in the past decades in terms of a transitional period, in which the old church formation, ultramontane mass Catholicism, is being dissolved and the making of a new church formation, choice Catholicism, has begun. The proposal of a transition to a new Church implies raising at least two questions. First, what does this new Church look like? Some basic characteristics of the new Church will thus be described: the prevalence of choice, the trend towards a minority church without enforcing power, the evolution towards a delocalized and flexible church organization, the predominance of experiential religion in an event church, the religionization of the Church and the transformation into a multicultural world church. Hellemans insists that these are characteristics that are consonant with advanced modernity, notwithstanding the alienation felt and the critique given by the Church. Second, how strong and impactful might this new Church be? Three alternative scenarios are envisaged: a strict church (sect), a liberal church (fellowship), or a major minority church. The conditions for realizing the last scenario are explored, leading to the conclusion that it will be highly difficult for the Catholic Church to remain a vigorous major church in the West.

What will be decisive is whether the Catholic Church, in presenting the religion of the Christian God, will still be perceived by many people as having relevance for living a good and fulfilled life. In the past, Christianity was highly relevant: it was woven into the very texture of society and captured both the dreams and fears of the people. Will the future Church be able to do the same? Philosopher and theologian, Anthony Carroll, SJ, inspired by Charles Taylor and continuing the programmatic line of thinking of the Vatican II constitution *Gaudium et Spes*, sets himself the task of delineating a Catholic account of and vision for advanced modernity. The project has both a retrospective and a prospective part. Against secularist views that hail Enlightenment rationality and science as the only progenitors of modernity and denounce religion as their opposite, Carroll stresses the central role of Christianity in the genesis of modernity, not only of Protestant Christianity (which is more accepted), but also of Catholicism. The intimate link between Catholicism and modernity means that the Catholic Church can be, in the contemporary world, a valuable dialogue partner.

The Church provides resources of meaning, solidarity, and hope that are in short supply in other programs of modernity, resources that can help tackle the major challenges and problems with which advanced modernity and the people living in it are confronted: personal well-being, the collective building of normative consensus, the handling of the issue of inequality, dialogue with other cultures. According to Carroll, by entering and fostering mutual learning processes, both advanced modernity and the Catholic Church have much to gain.

Adding to Carroll's proposal of a Catholic program for advanced modernity, philosopher Peter Jonkers explores the intellectual strategy that might enable the Catholic Church, now fallen back to the status of a minority church, to be valued, nevertheless, as a viable and pertinent interlocutor in the public arena. As a case in point, he analyses the ideas put forward by Pope Benedict XVI and confronts them with the secular approaches of Rawls and Habermas. According to Jonkers, Benedict follows a double line of reasoning: he acknowledges the accordance between Christianity and Enlightenment, while at the same time pointing to the incompleteness of the Enlightenment. The latter's restricted interpretation of reason precludes addressing adequately major problems like radical pluralism and scientific reductionism and may even end in a perversion of reason (as, potentially, in genetic engineering). The Church can act here as "a purifying force". On the one hand, it is attached to reason and places itself under the criticism of reason in order to avoid religious pathologies like fundamentalism. On the other hand, as a wisdom tradition geared to existential knowledge and to the promotion of the good life, it broadens reason and guards this power against reductionist rationalities as well as against pluralist evaporation. Jonkers concludes, together with Pope Benedict and in line with Carroll, that the great religions, among them (Catholic) Christianity, are relevant for advanced modernity and that they should, more particularly, be welcomed as indispensable and correcting forces in the public arena of advanced modernity.

As said in the opening lines, 'change', 'transformation', 'renewal' is everywhere present in advanced modernity, and also in the Catholic Church. The Church is not only proposing programmatic changes to the late modern world (see Carroll and Jonkers), but is also implementing internal changes. Canon lawyer Ton Meijers presents a study of how internal changes are perceived and justified by the Catholic Church. He takes religious freedom as an exemplary case. In the 19th century, several popes condemned vehemently the introduction of a civil right to religious freedom by liberal governments as a road to religious relativism and indifferentism. However, in the Second Vatican Council, specifically in the constitution *Dignitatis Humanae*, religious freedom was embraced as a fundamental human right. Since then, the popes have repeatedly reclaimed this human right for the Church against encroachments from the state or from anticlerical and anti-Christian movements. How does the Catholic Church deal with this seemingly overt discontinuity? Meijers shows that the Church reconciles its new attitude towards religious freedom with older views through a twofold strategy: by refusing to condemn the old viewpoints and formulations and, moreover, by inserting them in the new documents. In particular, the old prime argument for objecting to religious freedom – the moral obligation to seek the divine truth – has not been abrogated, but is being upheld in the new view as a crucial mediating link. This manner of reasoning is clearly at work in the phrasing of *Dignitatis Humanae*. A careful insertion of the old in the new can equally be detected in the new Code of 1983. Canon 748 on religious freedom thus refers not only to *Dignitatis Humanae*, but also – and verbally! – to canons of the old 1917 Code. The same procedure is again used in the new teaching on mixed marriages. Meijers calls this propensity towards harmonization of new views with old ones 'reform with continuity'. He thus makes explicit how the Catholic Church self-legitimately copes with and even invokes internal changes.

From the perception by the Church of internal changes, we next move to the changing perception by the Church of itself. Theologian and ecclesiologist Henk Witte reviews the history of the leading ecclesiological metaphors in the last two centuries. Since ecclesiological metaphors express the self-understanding of the Church, they serve as a good entrance to assess how the Church is affected by and responding to modernity. From before 1800 until 1960, the Church preferred to view and to present itself as a 'societas perfecta', as a church that had at its disposal all the means to exist self-sufficiently. The model was directed against the confinement policy of, first, the absolutist state and, later, the liberal nation states. At the same time, it expressed metaphorically the ideal of ultramontane mass Catholicism. Because the stress on the institutional and visible dimensions of the Church was felt increasingly as one-sided, it was complemented in the first half of the 20th century with the model of the mystical body of Christ. In the 1960's and 1970's, in a time that the Church was rethinking its relation with modern society in partnership terms, 'sacramentum mundi' and, above all, 'people of God' came to the fore as new leading models. Since the middle of the 1980's, with heavy insistence from the Vatican, 'communio' has taken over the lead role as the ecclesiological, self-reflective model. Though every institution likes to present itself nowadays as an informal group of like-minded people, the model also expresses the wish for church unity in a time of pluralism and potential discord and harbors, at least potentially, a Trinitarian vision of God who loves to dialogue with humankind. Witte thus gives full weight to the link between the changing position and the changing self-understanding of the Catholic Church within modernity.

In the preceding contributions, we met in advanced modernity a Catholic Church that is changing (Hellemans), programming change (Carroll and Jonkers), legitimizing change (Meijers), and reflecting change (Witte). In the chapter provided by sociologist and practical theologian James Sweeney, CP, we look at conscious projects of change, designed to bring about church renewal and revitalization. To keep the survey within manageable proportions, Sweeney focuses his history on one country, Britain. The British trajectory is similar to that of most Catholic churches in Western Europe: being a fortress church before the Council, it opened itself with great enthusiasm in the 1960's and was forced to find a new balance afterwards. In contrast, however, to the Netherlands, the British Catholic Church did not fall prey to endless conflicts between progressives and conservatives. Consciously set-up renewal projects constitute, of course, only one particular portion of the sweeping changes that are traversing the Catholic Church. But the chronological review of these renewal attempts by Sweeney allows us to follow the post-conciliar evolution of the Church upon the heels, so to speak. It also adds some valuable conclusions. First of all, the amount and variety of the renewal attempts are immediately striking. It invalidates the generally held outsider view that the Catholic Church resists any change whatsoever and is 'only' upholding old views and structures. Second, the evolution of the renewal attempts is informative with regard to the road taken into the new church formation: the impact and the memory of the Second Vatican Council are fading and all efforts are now directed towards the revitalization of a declining Church in what is seen as a threatening environment. According to Sweeney, the post-conciliar era, taken in a strict sense, is now over and we are moving "beyond the Council" "into unchartered territory".

Ministering the new Church

The lead idea that a new Catholic Church is emerging in advanced modernity is explored further in the second part of the book. While the first part deals in more general terms with how the Catholic Church is affected by and is responding to change, the second part focuses on some important sectors of the Church: pastoral care, church development, liturgy, youth work, and mission. What can be said about the ways the new Church is and should be organizing and performing its ministry for a population that is no longer 'at home' in territorial parishes and can no longer be regarded as being church members 'from the cradle to the grave'? Looking over the chapters, two major desiderata are being raised by the authors again and again: the call to individualize and to differentiate ministry, and the need to reach out towards people at the margins of and outside the Church.

For practical theologian Stefan Gärtner, the new situation implies the need for a profound overhaul of the way pastoral care is designed and delivered. The pre-1960 model of standardization, in which all persons were treated in a more or less uniform way as a homogeneous category of 'believers' (as, for example, in funeral rites), no longer applies. In a time of individualization, the individual with his or her unique biography, living in a highly demanding 'risk society' (Beck), must be the starting point for ministry. Above, we spoke of the need for the Church to demonstrate to people that religion is the *conditio sine qua non* to allow one to live a fulfilled life and that the Church is crucially important in helping to reach this goal. In his contribution, Gärtner translates this ideal in a view on pastoral care wherein the pastor guides, case by case and within a Christian framework, the processes of identity building by the individual. Contemporary and future pastoral care should "not only connect the various fragments of one's life to a coherent life story, … but also demonstrate the role that the Gospel can play in this process". This is, for sure, no easy task. Because biographical orientation is so crucial for individuals in late modernity and because it is so difficult to give individual pastoral care – religious life guidance – it should, according to Gärtner, be given special priority in the Church.

Sociologist and theologian Kees De Groot takes up the issue of the new forms (in plural) of local church organization. Here again, the crumbling of the old standard-model, in this case, the organization of the Church locally as an all-embracing and uniform 'parish civilization', is obvious. According to De Groot, in advanced modernity – which he, following Zygmunt Bauman, prefers to call 'liquid modernity' – the Church has become a hybrid organization. Indeed, the Church nowadays organizes and provides services for different kinds of persons and target groups and it combines, in doing so, different types of organizations (mutual support groups like the parish core communities, service delivery agencies like the parish professionals for locals and the chaplains and spiritual counselors in prison, army and hospitals, campaigning bodies such as the new ecclesial movements). Being immersed in 'liquid modernity', the Church has thus become a network organization. The problem, though, is that the Church tends to continue organization styles and thought patterns that are inherited from 'solid modernity', taking mass Catholicism from before 1960 as the norm. De Groot concludes that the Church should support neither exclusively solid forms (for example, parishes) nor exclusively liquid forms (for example, new ecclesial movements), but should rather keep an open eye for all the forms in which God presents Himself in the contemporary world.

While Gärtner and De Groot emphasize the need for more differentiated pastoral care and forms of church organization, liturgist scholar Willem-Marie Speelman reminds us of a second, complicating problem when ministering to the 'individualized individuals' (Luhmann) in advanced modernity: the lack of openness on the part of the individuals. His analysis of the post-1960 liturgical and ritual celebrations leads him to conclude: "My diagnosis is that there is no real communication in advanced modernity because people are not open to transformation." To prove his point, he first goes back in history. In the Middle Ages, especially since the Gregorian Reform of the 11th century, the liturgy became more clericalized and standardized, thanks to the increasing use of (Roman) liturgical books. In the 20th century, with the rise of electronic media, the center shifted from book to practice to communication. The reform of the liturgy in the Second Vatican Council effectuated this change, yet is confronted with major problems. Indeed, communication is a two-way process. It demands a porous and vulnerable Church that is giving presence to the Presence of the Lord – this point corresponds to the de-standardizing drive in advanced modernity, mentioned above. But it also demands openness for this Presence from the side of the individuals. Individuals, however, according to Speelman, tend to remain enclosed within the walls of their 'buffered selves' (Taylor). The Church, for its part, has no other option than to offer, in a balanced communicative approach, the Real Presence of the Lord, in the hope that a transformative relation with the participants becomes established.

In addressing the difficult question of whether and how today's generation of young people and the Catholic Church might meet in advanced modernity, sociologist Monique Van Dijk-Groeneboer takes up the same issue as the one raised by Speelman, but this time in a non-theological way: how to reach and open up people. Building on surveys she conducted, she distinguishes four groups amongst today's youth: church committed 'fortissimo's', church festive 'legato's', religion seeking but church alienated 'spirituoso's', and non-interested 'tranquillo's'. By way of conclusion of this first part and referring to the 'legato's' and 'spirituoso's', she rejects the idea that contemporary youth is no longer open to religion. She then turns to the Catholic Church. In its declarations, the Church still places great value in church commitment by young people. Consequently, it spends a lot of effort on reaching youths. Next, taking the Netherlands as an example, Van Dijk-Groeneboer reviews the concrete ways in which the Church tries to mobilize today's youth. It appears that a great many initiatives are taken: on the national level (e.g., Dutch Catholic Youth Day), on the diocesan level (e.g., gatherings in the lead up to confirmation), and on the parish level (especially youth choirs). However, nearly all mobilizing initiatives are directed towards the 'fortissimo's'. Van Dijk-Groeneboer thus ends her contribution with a plea for putting more energy in addressing the other three categories of young people.

The last chapter of the book, provided by practical theologian Jozef Wissink, continues to analyze head on, from a theological viewpoint, the second great desideratum: the need to reach out to people other than the core members of the Church. Its overriding importance is nowadays acknowledged by the Church itself and treated under the term 'mission'. Before 1960, mission was understood as the evangelization of the Third World or as the preaching of mission retreats in the parishes in the West. After 1960, it took on a new meaning, pointing to the 'new evangelization' the Catholic Church is calling for in times of secularization. The theological groundwork had already been laid at the Second Vatican Council. The need for mission was afterwards highlighted by papal encyclicals like *Evangelii Nuntiandi* (1975) and *Redemptoris Missio* (1990). On the ground, many initiatives – at many levels (parish as well as diocesan), by religious congregations as well as by new ecclesial movements – have been undertaken. Wissink develops a scheme to systematize the bewildering array of activities and pleads for a dialogical missionary attitude that avoids the pitfalls of both indoctrination and mere listening. It is clear that the Catholic Church as well as theological and missiological thinking are only at the beginning of what appears to be an enormous and crucial undertaking. Indeed, if the Catholic Church wants to remain a major church, it will have to stabilize its membership and audience by attracting a substantial portion of outsiders.

Convergences and divergences

In order to draw some lines of convergence and divergence among the contributions, it seems useful to start from the distinction between the three possible future scenarios that was made in the chapter by Hellemans. The first possibility mentioned is that of the Catholic Church becoming a sect. The meaning of 'sect' is determined by three characteristics: a) small in number, b) highly demanding, and c) having a marginal position in society. A sect is a subculture, a counter-culture. The second possibility is that the Church could also evolve into an equally small, yet liberal fellowship, going along with the dominant culture. In the third scenario, the Church would also become a minority, yet remain vigorous and recognized by many people as an important voice and resource. In short, in this last form, the Church will still have a substantial membership and a tangible societal influence.

The other authors react to this picture from the perspective of their own disciplines and from their theological standpoints. In their articles, one can discern a theological evaluation of the three scenarios: the third scenario is clearly wished for by everyone, while the first and the second are not really taken into account. Dreams of a revival of mass Catholicism are nowhere stated, probably because none of the authors believes that it is still feasible. In any case, we have seen no tendencies towards nostalgia in any of the authors. Perhaps the painful experience that ecclesiastical power is as liable to abuse as political or economic power has made our hopes for the Church more modest. We seem to feel at home in the checks and balances that are associated with the position of a minority church in advanced modernity. But if we have to be a minority church, then we hope that it will be a vital church that is open to the questions of the people and of our culture.

Another remarkable convergence is that the contributions from the Netherlands and Great Britain are breathing the same air. The cultural setting has great likeness and also the position of the Catholic Church in society is about the same. It is true that there has been less polarization and less controversial appointments of bishops in Britain, but for the rest, the resemblances are striking. Furthermore, the resemblances seem, with time, to grow rather than to diminish.

The attitude towards our modern culture is differently appreciated by the authors, but none seems to reject our advanced-modern culture completely, nor is there an overall optimism about it. Some authors stress with greater emphasis the positive side of advanced modernity. Anthony Carroll, for instance, enumerates some points where the Church should be learning from our culture. Kees de Groot pleads against a one-sided option for old and trusted 'solid' forms of church organization. Other authors emphasize or treat more negative aspects of modernity, developments that block the receptivity of religion. Speelman interprets post-modern individuals as "buffered selves" and advises the Church to offer them "her real presence" – and through it – the Presence of the Lord in the moments when a buffered self falls apart and the person appears in his/her vulnerability and finiteness. In the setting of pastoral care, Gärtner gives more or less the same advice. Jonkers shows how Joseph Ratzinger/Pope Benedict is critical towards scientific positivism or ironic relativism, while at the same time seeking dialogue with other strands of modern thinking in order to make the claim plausible that faith is not unreasonable. The other authors do not show a preference with regard to the pros or the cons: they keep each other in balance.

Some issues for further research

The first question is about the theological evaluation of the three possible outcomes. In theology, the word 'sect' carries mostly negative associations. The Church has a universal mission: it reaches out for all people, all nations, all cultures, and all religious mentalities. When, in the 4th and 5th centuries, the Donatists wanted to close the Church for ordinary sinners, Saint Augustine kept the gates open for them. He stated that we should bear and tolerate one another and let the ill weeds grow up together with the wheat. Being small can never be a goal for the Catholic Church. On the other hand, the Church should avoid becoming salt without taste. One could think of a culture so hostile towards the Gospel that making accommodations would imply succumbing to this culture. Indeed, there are times that the heart of faith is in danger. In these times, the Church should not give in. In Israel, this occurred in the time of Ezra and, again, in the time of the Maccabees. For Christianity, one can mention the times of persecution, e.g., under Nero, Hitler, and Stalin. Thus, we should not demonize the concept of 'sect', but we should articulate why our time and our culture should not be interpreted as so bad as to believe we have no option other than the sectarian one. Possibly, the debate on the evolution of the Catholic Church in this direction is more a question of how one evaluates our culture theologically than of internal dogmatic differences. In any event, also from a dogmatic perspective, further reflection is necessary.

The concept of Church as fellowship should not be demonized straight away either. It is true that the Church is not a debating club; it is a dialogical community. This means that intellectual openness and honesty to take all questions seriously should be fostered. And, because the Church is or should be a community of love, the frankness of the brothers and sisters should be present. These are all values that we associate with the image of fellowship. These are also the strong points of liberalism. However, the weak point of liberalism is that it often lacks a sense of mystery and is sometimes prepared to sacrifice the heart of religion to the logic of reason or to the trends of a culture. We should be more critical than liberals, not less.

The point we want to make, therefore, is that our evaluation of the three scenarios, of the different outcomes of the transformation process in which the Church is involved, depends on our theological evaluation of our culture. This means that practical theology is in great need of developing a theological hermeneutics of our culture. Connected with this is the question of the role of progressives and conservatives in a vital minority Church. We should not identify the appeal for change in the Church with the influence of liberals and progressives. Conservatives also change the Church, though this is mostly hidden from their own eyes. In the 19th century, for example, the conservative neo-Thomist theologians were more active in changing Catholicism into a mass movement than their liberal counterparts. We think that for the development of a vital minority Church, the most important factors are not those that oppose conservatives and progressives, but factors like spirituality, being energetic and inspiring, transparency of governance, etc. Further reflection on this point is also needed, both for progressives and for conservatives.

Part I

Projecting the New Church

Tracking the New Shape of the Catholic Church in the West[1]

Staf Hellemans

1. (How) will the Catholic Church remain a major church in the West?

The topic I want to raise is the future of the Catholic Church in the West –
and I will only speak about the West. Since the 1960's, Catholicism and the
Catholic Church have been experiencing difficult times in most Western countries. The number of religious personnel and of practicing Catholics is declining. The far-flung and exceptionally strong network of Catholic organizations
has been dismantled to a large degree. The penetrating Roman Catholic subculture, which was still vigorous in the 1950's, has evaporated. Diminishing numbers, less and less powerful organizations, the erosion of a pronounced subculture – it is fair to say that after 1960 a whole world, an encompassing religious
civilization, has passed away (see, e.g., Gabriel & Kaufmann 1980; Lambert
1985; Hervieu-Léger 2003; Dobbelaere, Billiet & Voyé 2011). In most Western
countries, there is, at present, no indication that the downward spiral will end
anytime soon. Consequently, the question emerges whether the Catholic Church
will remain a major church in the future. Indeed, it is not only the Catholic
Church that is affected. The gloomy prospect of marginalization also threatens
the other big churches in the West: Anglican, Lutheran, Reformed, as well as
the Orthodox churches. The breakdown of all these churches would certainly
constitute a development of world historical importance.

However, our analysis should not stop at tracking only the passing away of
past structures, forms, and behavior. To get an informed picture of the present
developments, let alone of future trends, we need to assess in the first place the
transformations that are taking place and the new forms, and, indeed, the new
formation, that Catholicism is assuming at the present time. We have to ask
what are and what will be the new characteristics of the new Catholic Church in
the making, and how the Church fits in and attunes itself to the context of advanced modernity. Only thereafter is it possible to explore its possible future as
a major church, whether a new stability could be emerging, and, if so, what the
conditions are that have to be met. Needless to say, this is a risky venture.

---

1   The first version of this text was written during my stay as Visiting Research Fellow at
    Heythrop College, London in Spring 2010. It was presented at the conference, "Reading the
    Signs of the Time" at Heythrop College on June 15, 2010. I thank Jim Sweeney, Anthony
    Carroll, and Michael Kirwan for their comments and support.

The text is divided into three parts:

1. The theoretical framework: the Catholic Church as an evolving part of an evolving modernity, implying the transition, with the coming of advanced modernity, to a new church formation (sections 2 to 4).

2. The portrayal of the likely basic characteristics of the new Catholic Church in advanced modernity (section 5).

3. An exploration of the conditions and the chances of the Catholic Church to remain a major church in the West in advanced modernity – which is, of course, the trickiest issue (sections 6 to 8).

2. The theoretical framework: religious modernization and the transition towards a new church formation

First of all, to enable us to analyze the prospective forms of the Catholic Church in the West – and of the other major churches as well – we need to take leave of some deep-seated, but flawed, presuppositions about religion and its relation to modernity. The most fundamentally flawed presupposition is that religion is opposed to modernity. From an oppositional perspective, religion is negatively affected by, but does not partake in, modernity. This is a shortsighted view. On a deeper level, religion is as a societal domain – almost by definition – part of modernity, in the same way as politics, the economy, the arts, the sciences, or the family, are part of modernity. Moreover, religion is an evolving part of an equally evolving modernity. Just as the economy and politics have evolved from pre-modern to modern forms, so has religion (see, e.g., Luhmann 1972; Kaufmann 1979; 1989; Altermatt 1989; Gabriel 1992; Hervieu-Léger 1993; Hellemans 1997; 2007).

As a consequence, religion cannot be considered as an alien, pre-modern enclave. Instead of separating and opposing religion and modernity, we need to examine the various ways of interdependence that exist between the two – religion being a realm within modernity, and modernity being the encompassing context for religion. This does not mean that institutional religion and, more particularly, the major churches will be able to retain the same powerful positions they held in previous times. In modernity, religion also takes other forms than the highly institutionalized church form. A continuing decline of the position of the Catholic Church in the West cannot be ruled out. However, the embedding of religion in modernity also means that religion is remade anew in and by modernity and that the future of major churches is not closed off a priori. Hence, we should investigate which church modernization processes are taking place in advanced modernity, how the platform of advanced modernity is being used by the major churches to carve out new religious spaces, and what the success of these creative responses to modernity might be.

Religion, including church-shaped religion, is thus embedded in modernity and is continually remade in interaction with modernity. This is the first pillar of my theoretical framework to analyze the current evolution of religion and the churches. A second pillar is deduced from the observation that history progresses in discrete, discontinuous ways. Sometimes, the structure of society changes quite rapidly and thoroughly. At other times, change happens more smoothly. Religion changes accordingly. Thus, I interpret the history of the West and of Catholicism in the last 500 years as a series of formations, interrupted by times of upheaval. More particularly, one can distinguish three church formations that are embedded each time in their respective societal formations: (i) from 1500 to 1789, early modern Catholicism in early modernity; (ii) from 1789 to about 1960, ultramontane mass Catholicism in the first modernity; and (iii) after 1960, choice Catholicism in advanced modernity. Each church formation manifests particular structural characteristics and particular dynamics. Characteristic for early modern Catholicism, for instance, is the build up of a specific Catholic identity (sacraments and liturgy, saints and Mary, upgrading of diocesan organization and priestly formation) over and against Protestant Christianity, the better instruction and supervision of the diocesan clergy, and the close, at times threatening, connection with absolute monarchy, all of which deepened the extent and intensity of the religious monopoly of the Church in Catholic and re-Catholicized countries. Between 1800 and 1960 the Catholic masses were, to an extraordinary high degree, integrated into and mobilized by the Catholic Church – I therefore label this church formation as 'mass Catholicism'. The transition from one formation to another is always a period of crisis and of great strain and upheaval since old forms are – in part, from necessity – abandoned and new forms established. The Reformation and Counterreformation in the 16th century and the revolutionary years around 1800 are such crisis periods, closing one era and inaugurating another one. My main contention is that the present crisis of Catholicism should be interpreted as such a transitional crisis, that Catholicism is presently, under the new conditions of advanced modernity after 1960, in search of new forms and a new overall church formation. As a result, we should develop an empirical research program to analyze this transition (Hellemans 2009).

3. Ultramontane mass Catholicism

Before going into the analysis of the transition towards a new church formation in our time, let me first illustrate how Catholicism in the 19th and the first half of the 20th century was constituted anew and how deeply it was embedded in the first modernity. I label this church formation 'ultramontane mass Catholicism' because the ultramontane (i.e., papal) orientation and the high integration of the masses of the population constituted the two most characteristic components of this church formation.

The modernization of the Catholic Church was very visibly at work in the far-reaching centralization of the church organization after 1800 (Kaufmann 1979; Pottmeyer 1975; 1997). It is true that centralization had been a major aim of the papacy since antiquity, and that the Gregorian reforms in the 11th to 13th centuries and the Tridentine reforms of the 16th and 17th centuries already fostered the cause of centralization. Yet, the 18th century Church of the *ancien régime* still was, as in the centuries before, a federal body. Rome was pivotal, but the bishops had independent power, as did many priests towards their bishop. Only in the 19th century was the Catholic Church turned into the highly centralized organization we know today. The pope advanced to become the daily leader in church affairs, multiplying his interventions through encyclical letters and other statements. As an indirect consequence of the disappearance of feudal rights for local churches, bishops became fully dependent on the pope's authority and priests, in turn, on their bishop's will. The proclamation of the pope's supreme jurisdiction and of papal infallibility at the First Vatican Council in 1870 endorsed and enshrined this process of centralization. Such a far-reaching centralization process on an international scale was only possible in modern societies. On a national scale, the process was most prominently at work in the post-feudal national states – leading sometimes to totalitarian states in the 20th century. The building up of centralized organizations was also visible in other areas of life, such as in the rise of big industrial companies and of mass political and cultural organizations. The centralization process within the Catholic Church should not be considered as a pre-modern backlash but, rather, as a manifestation of modernization.

The centralized and well-oiled church organization was put to great use in another instance of religious modernization, namely, the full-fledged integration of the masses of the population. As with the centralization process, one can point here again to earlier attempts by the Catholic Church to reach and socialize all people, not only the rich and famous, but also the poor. However, it was only in the 19th century that it became possible, thanks to the resources opened up with modernity, to realize this objective of full socialization and mobilization of all the faithful. Higher levels of literacy and school education meant also better religious instruction. Religiously backed health care and welfare work were greatly extended. New interests of the population, like political representation, social and economic interest mediation, cultural manifestations, and even touristic yearnings, were also taken up by the Church and a host of side organizations – and generated what later became known as the Catholic pillar, subculture, milieu, or fortress church (Thurlings 1979; Poulat 1986; Billiet 1988; Hellemans 1990; 1993; Damberg 1997; Aspden 2002). Never before in history was the Catholic Church so intensely oriented towards the masses of the population; never before was it able to mobilize them to such a high degree. Like the socialist labor movement and other mass movements, the Catholic Church was a fitting example of mass modern society.

Other aspects of 19th and early 20th century Catholicism can similarly be interpreted as manifestations of successful religious modernization processes, for example, the widening of the entrance to the priesthood and to the religious orders, the apogee of missionary activity in the wake of colonialism, or the development of a social doctrine. In these ways, Catholicism was reconstructed anew in all respects with considerable success in many countries and regions like the Netherlands, Ireland, Britain, Flanders, the Rhineland, and North and Western France. These successful modernization processes provided the Catholic Church with a powerful position to engage with modernity. The result was a new Catholicism – steeped in modernity – and yet it was a staunchly conservative Catholicism.

4. The transition to choice Catholicism

After 1960, it was no longer possible to maintain this modern, conservative Catholic subsociety. In the 1960's and afterwards, the impressive Catholic powerhouses, that had been so compatible with the first modernity, were dismantled – and so were their large socialist, communist, and, in some cases, Protestant counterparts in a number of European countries (e.g., the Netherlands, Switzerland, Belgium, Austria, Italy, France) (Hellemans 1990; 1993). Advanced modernity, with its deepening individualization processes, was different from the first modernity (1800-1960) in that it could not be broken up into a few organized subsocieties. This initially invigorated the hopes of many to reform the ultramontane fortress Church into an open church that would cooperate with other churches and with secular movements to bring about a prosperous and just society for all (see the Second Vatican Council (1962-1965) and, in particular, the documents *Lumen Gentium, Unitatis Redintegratio, Nostrae Aetate* and *Gaudium et Spes*) (McSweeney 1980; O'Malley 2008). But they were soon to be disappointed.

The rapid decline of the Catholic Church, as was visible, for example, in the fall of church attendance, the radicalization of the cultural revolution of the sixties after 1965, the internal polarization between progressives and conservatives, and the ensuing disarray inside the Church, convinced Pope Paul VI, although reluctantly, to put on the brakes (see Coleman 1978 on the Netherlands as an exemplary case study). The publication in 1968 – the symbolic year of the cultural revolution of the sixties – of *Humanae Vitae* (the encyclical letter that condemned artificial contraception) was the first signal that the Catholic Church was returning to a conservative stance. The conservative church policy would gain more force in the following years, notably under Pope John Paul II (1978-2005). Yet, an overall return to the previous Catholic subsocieties proved to be impossible. Even with the conservatives back in charge, the Catholic Church found itself forced to reconstruct itself anew in advanced modernity, to go out and experiment with new forms of Catholicism.

The remaking of the Catholic Church in advanced modernity is still in its infancy. Many experiments have been launched, some with success (like the World Youth Days), some without success (like the current 'new evangelization' of Europe). Some tendencies already appear to be set fixed for the coming decades (for example, the crisis in the parishes and the decline in the number of priests); the future of others is uncertain (for example, the role and impact of the well-publicized 'new ecclesial movements'). In other words, it is, at the moment, very difficult to describe the structure and dynamics of the new church formation given that it is only beginning to take shape. Nevertheless, I think that after five decades of dismantling and remaking, some basic characteristics and possible trajectories are beginning to show up. It is, of course, always possible that I miss some basic tendencies or that society and religion change course.

5. Basic characteristics of choice Catholicism

Before getting in to the possible future trajectories, let us first concentrate on the characteristics that are defining the new church formation. The list is, of course, not exhaustive. Other facets could be highlighted. For example, an analysis, difficult though it is, of the ideological and theological tensions between different factions in the Church would be most welcome. Furthermore, the shortage of priests will, without changes to the recruitment policy, continue to be aggravated. This will have a major impact on the Church: lay pastors and lay people will become in charge of the daily functioning of the Church and clashes will likely occur with the fewer and fewer clergy members who, owing to their ordination, will come to occupy top positions even if they are not very qualified. Even so, I hope that the overview of what I consider to be basic characteristics will give a good idea of the new church formation in the making. In order to demonstrate that the Catholic Church is, in various ways, tuning in to and using the platform of advanced modernity to rebuild and reposition itself, the situation before 1960 will be contrasted with current developments.

5.1. Choice

I labeled the new church formation as 'choice Catholicism'. Indeed, we live in times of choice. This is true for most areas of life: place of living, partner, children, education, occupation, political view, lifestyle, etc. (see, e.g., Beck 1986; Giddens 1991). This is even truer for religion because, here, one can opt out without lasting consequences and can live without recourse to institutional religion at all. Although choice has never been absent – think of the age-old call for inner conversion in all the great religions – the sense that we have to choose ceaselessly in all areas of life has drastically increased since the 1960's. One should, however, avoid falling into the trap of a choice-ideology that celebrates our age uncritically as a high time of personal freedom and authenticity. Choice, in most cases, does not mean our decisions are made in full personal sovereignty. We are constrained by age and physical conditions, by our social-economic position (the lower, the less chances), by our former choices (for example, the choice of having children has consequences), and by the particular situation wherein choices are made. More importantly, our choices are influenced in many conscious and subconscious ways (Duyvendak & Hurenkamp 2004). In fact, following the increase in choice options, the efforts to channel our choices have been greatly extended as well: advertising and marketing agencies, electoral campaigns, or trendy art exhibitions all work hard to steer our choices. Even the various religions are doing their utmost best to affect our choices, as televangelists and the broadcasting of well-organized ceremonies exemplify. However, notwithstanding the constraints and the channeling of choices on one side, and the fallacy of ideological exaltation of individuality and the self on the other side, making choices has become a daily reality.

As indicated, choice has become particularly important in the field of religion (Roozen & Hadaway 1993, Part III; Gabriel 1996; Hervieu-Léger 1998; Hoge *et al.* 2001). First, the number of institutional religions is rising, especially since 1960 (see, e.g., Hero, Krech & Zander 2008). It is true that people choose overwhelmingly for the religion they were raised in, but this choice can now be complemented or even supplemented (through relocation, marriage, feelings of disappointment, or fresh appetites). In the United States, currently about 30% of the population change religious affiliation during their lifetime, mainly to a neighboring denomination (Sherkat 2001,1466-1467). In Europe – more secular, with lower levels of plurality, and with stronger major churches – the proportion of those who change their religious affiliation is much lower (Need & De Graaf 2005, 295-296 estimate the percentage of those who switch between major groupings (!) of denominations in the Netherlands at about 5%). Second, choice has been heightened by the rise of less institutionalized forms of religion (Heelas 2002). For people who feel attracted to religion, it is no longer necessary to turn to highly institutionalized religious settings requiring participation in a religious community. They can, nowadays, look for less obliging religious offers. Many people turn to the media. Books and the internet abound with religious and quasi-religious ideas and material. Likewise, the tourist and heritage industry provides many opportunities for explorations of any kind. For the conscious seekers, all sorts of information and meditation sessions are offered in spiritual and commercial centers and (para-)educational settings. Above all, in the last decade, there are the ever-widening circles of the "wellness" industry. Why engage in a restraining and boring community when you can, so to speak, pick the raisins out of the bread? Finally, individuals can decide to live their lives outside any form of institutionalized religion – hence the significance of the secularization issue. In striking contrast with other sectors in modernity (e.g., the market economy, the state, school education, medical care) where individual participation in institutionalized forms is nearly inescapable, or where non-commitment carries at least trenchant disadvantages for the individual, the commanding difficulty faced by institutional religions is figuring out how to get people to commit. The main reason for this difficulty can be inferred from the above: individuals who leave institutional religion do not have the feeling that their lives are negatively affected. Thus, generally, people leave religious institutions with ease and out of casualness. Since 1960, institutional religion has lost its commanding relevance. The plurality of institutional religions, the rise of non-institutional offers, and the ease of opting out all favor a state of affairs in which commitment to an institutional religion is being considered as a non-evident act of choice.

Some misunderstandings with regard to the concept 'choice' have to be addressed. The predicament of choice cannot be reduced to a couple of 'big' choices to which one remains loyal throughout his or her life. On the contrary, life, nowadays, is an unceasing concatenation of innumerable choices on a daily basis, and nearly all of them are small and ambivalent choices. These choices may add up to what seems, in hindsight, to constitute a big and permanent choice. But this is the exception rather than the rule. Choices at one moment have to be re-affirmed at the next and many are altered or withdrawn in the process. We select many of our choices without attaching future consequences to them and we often choose them because of this (for example, candle lighting in a church or participation in many a church ritual). We often also make half-hearted choices, steering between a clear yes or no, to keep our options open or to avoid confrontations. Above all, more than ever, we can always retreat from choices that were formerly made. This is not only manifest in the increasing rates of divorce, but also in the substantial proportion of ordained priests and religious who abdicate, or in the turnover rates of once enthusiastic young Catholics in the so-called 'new ecclesial movements'. One sometimes hears a Catholic high cleric embracing choice as a once-and-for-always decision of total dedication towards the Church: once the choice is made for the Catholic Church, one should and will abide. But this is not the way choice works in practice. Choice is, on the contrary, a never-ending process of muddling through a panoply of small choices, and keeping one's involvements and loyalties under the constant check of new choices.

5.2. A minority church without enforcing power

The facilitating of religious choice – especially the choice to opt out – in a context of religious pluralism and the rise of non-institutional religion engenders two direct major consequences for the Catholic Church: first, it is reduced to a minority position and needs to find new ways to attract a following; second, there is a shift in the power balance from church officials to the laity.

Before 1960, the Catholic Church enjoined a near religious monopoly in many European countries, the result of the *reconquista* policy waged by the Catholic Church in alliance with the state power against the Protestants (e.g., in the Southern Netherlands, France, or Hungary). Although there were sizeable minorities in several Protestant countries (like the Netherlands, Germany, Switzerland, the United States, and Canada) and small minorities in most other countries (like Eastern Europe), the Catholic countries set the tone – especially France, Spain, and Austria. They supported the Catholic self-image as the only true church with a divine right to religious monopoly and thus also with the right of excluding other religions (summarized in the dictum "nulla salus extra ecclesiam"). It is only after World War II, and, particularly, after 1960, that this situation was reversed. Many old as well as new religions entered the scene. More importantly, the number of Catholics and of practicing Catholics dwindled in most European countries. The Catholic Church in the West found itself, almost all of a sudden, in a minority position for which it was not prepared. However, it is fair to say that the Catholic Church is beginning to adapt (see Wissink in this volume).

Due to the lasting power of the Church in Italy and in many countries outside the West, many church officials in the Vatican and elsewhere still believe that the preservation of, or a return to, a majority or even monopoly position is the Church's 'natural' destiny. But, with time advancing, it has also become apparent that realizing this destiny will demand huge effort. It appears to be very difficult to activate the local churches on the ground in countries that had a former monopoly and to turn them into more evangelizing and recruiting constituents. The theological groundwork has already been done at the Second Vatican Council with the acceptance of religious freedom, a more positive valuation of other religions, and a broader conception of mission. From the 1970's onwards, the popes have issued several statements in which evangelization and an active attitude of going out towards non-Catholics in the modern world is propagated (see, e.g., *Evangelium nuntiandi* (1975) of Paul VI and *Redemptoris missio* (1990) of John Paul II). In theology, there is much talk about the issue – mission sciences have been re-conceptualized and topics such as outward reaching community building in a secular world or re-evangelizing the West are attracting increasing attention. In the local churches, it has taken more time, but here also a whole new series of initiatives have been taken in the last years (see Van Dijk-Groeneboer and Sweeney in this volume). As is so often the case, old (the monopolistic nostalgia) and new (an activist, outward-looking policy) are both present and mingled.

The facilitating of choices by the population and the minority position of the Catholic Church have engendered yet another crucial shift. They have reversed the internal power balance between the church officials and the fold. Before 1960, the self-confident and well-organized Catholic Church enforced, if necessary, compliance by the faithful. Leaving the Church or even objecting to the parish priest or the Catholic hierarchy often carried nasty consequences for the challenger – as is bitterly outlined by many anticlerical novels. Whether or not Catholicism was the majority religion, the hold of the Catholic Church was, in either case, equally strong since Catholics were firmly integrated into Catholic cultures and organizational networks – hence the hard labeling of the Catholic milieu as 'pillar', 'camp' or 'fortress'. Priests and hierarchy had a predilection for the metaphor 'shepherds guiding the flock', as it was both an ecclesial ideal and a reality. The dissolution of these pillars, milieus, or "parish civilizations" – to use a designation coined by Yves Lambert (1985) – brought about an end to this power differential and had, in fact, the effect of a disarmament on the part of the church hierarchy. As joining a church and participating in its activities have become a matter of choice – with a very attractive exit-option – the power balance has shifted in favor of the laity. The church hierarchy can no longer force the believers to follow the ecclesiastical instructions and norms. Those who are looking for religious imprints in their lives can easily bypass the Church. They can turn to other religious organizations or to a less organized offer. And, even if they are attracted and fascinated by the call of the Catholic Church, they can more easily evade the acceptance of the whole package or terminate what seemed for a while to be a life-long commitment. The former 'flock' and 'following' have become wayward 'fellow believers'. This reversal of the power relations in favor of the laity and of the individual believer/consumer has a crucial consequence: it makes the Church into a service organization that has to cater to a clientele that is conscious that it can always turn its head away. How the Church should respond to this power reversal is currently the source of great debate. Should the Church lower the demands and make consumerist offers for only occasionally interested, lukewarm bystanders – the liberal or mildly conservative strategy? Or should it maintain or even raise its high demands in the hope that enough committed believers will be attracted – the conservative and fundamentalist strategy? Should the Church bet on the establishment of strong community bonds or, on the contrary, forsake this in these times of individualization (see Witte in this volume)? Should it focus almost exclusively on spiritual matters? Should it continue to defend ethical positions that are not accepted by the majority of the population, including the majority of the faithful? Should it take up a favorable stance towards modernity and a corresponding public role that shares in and stresses the deep values common in both Christianity and modernity (human rights, equality and liberty, values of self-realization and personal autonomy)? Or should it make sure that a Christian counter-voice is heard against a modernity that is dangerously derailing and considered deeply anti-religious (see Jonkers in this volume)? The new situation – the power reversal – may be clear and closing the ranks may be a tempting strategy; however, how properly to respond to these challenges is not clear at all and is not decided yet.

5.3. A delocalized, flexible church organization

With the transition from ultramontane mass Catholicism to choice Catholicism, the organizational functioning of the Church is also undergoing tremendous change. We have seen that the Church was reorganized in the 19th century – in unison with other organizations like the state, big industrial companies, and left-wing political parties – as a centralized mass organization. This form of organization has become obsolete in advanced modernity and so the functioning of the Church is being devised anew again, as is the case in most other organizations.

To specify the changes, let us first look at the Church as a mass organization before 1960. The Catholic Church was, after 1800, more than ever, directed towards the rank and file. After the end of the alliance of 'church and state' (though not immediately in all states) and with the increasing importance of the middle and the lower reaches of the population – manifest in widely divergent ways such as in the extension of electoral suffrage and the rise of political mass movements, the spread of literacy and of standardized education, the beginnings of mass consumption and of mass newspapers – securing the loyalty of the bulk of the population became a concern of paramount importance, especially for a religious institution that claimed to act on behalf, and in the interest, of the whole population. At the same time, these modern developments acted as integrating carriers of the middle and lower classes into modern society. They also gave the Church the opportunity to realize, at last, centuries-old aspirations of disciplining religious as well as non-religious behavior and the mentality of the faithful. In sum, the context of modernity made a mass inclusion strategy both necessary and possible. The inclusion strategy was enacted in various ways. Access to the priesthood and to religious orders and congregations – in particular, female congregations – was widened, which resulted in a flood of new entrants, especially from the rural areas. Thanks to the dedication of the rising number of religious men and women, the number of Catholic schools, hospitals, and homes for the elderly, orphaned, and disabled was greatly extended. Above all, new, 'modern' interests of the population, like political representation, social and economic interest mediation, new cultural tastes such as theatre visits and reading, and even leisure and touristic desires, were taken up by the Church and a host of side organizations.

This uploading of the Church with old and new functions was accompanied by a strengthening and centralization of the church organization itself. As already mentioned, papal power advanced greatly in the 19th century and the pope became the effective daily leader of Catholics worldwide. A similar centralization process occurred in the bishoprics: with the loss of feudal privileges and income, priests became dependent upon the governance of the bishop who, alone, decided on the nominations of priests in 'his' parishes. The local clergy, in turn, became less bound to local power holders, not only because of their new dependence on the local bishop, but also thanks to the strengthening of the Catholic subculture and organization network of which the clergy was in charge. This brings us to the last and most important carrier of the Church as a mass organization: the mighty deployment of the parish as a 'parish civilization' (Lambert 1985). All through history, since the inception of the system in the early Middle Ages, the parish – and with it, the parish priest – had widened its appeal and workings. After 1800, the parish was, once again, greatly extended because it was the parish that took up and realized both the old and the new functions of the Church mentioned above. The refashioned ideal of a Christian society was cast in concrete terms as a world of parishes, headed by their priests and supervised by their bishops and ultimately the pope, a parish world that catered to all the needs of the parishioners, religious as well as non-religious.

After 1960, this parish-based system, which aimed at an all-encompassing and continuous integration of the whole local population into the Church and in a Catholic society, was shattered to pieces. This is not to say that the basic hierarchical structure of the Church was given up; the pope and bishops did not abandon their ambitions to maintain their hold nor did the orientation of the Church towards the masses waver. Rather, what, in fact, stopped functioning was the 'parish civilization', the local and continuous satisfaction of all the needs of the faithful under the direction of their parish priests (Gabriel 2010). Since 1960, the Catholic flock – and, in fact, all people in advanced modernity – has become delocalized, i.e., less bound to the locality they live in. Parish life is less and less defined by place of residence and more and more by choice. People are no longer content with the routine parish offer, but look around for appealing offerings in other near and far neighborhoods. Performing parishes are attracting people; non-performing ones are losing people. A typical example is the high level of attendance on big occasions, particularly on Christmas Eves, in medieval cathedrals with high liturgy and fine church music, while church attendance on an ordinary Sunday and in suburban parishes is minimal. Due to the general decline in church commitment and the rising mobility of the faithful, the old parish system is sliding into a major crisis.

The delocalization process has, moreover, a second dimension. More and more tasks are taken up by intermediary instances above the parishes, in the case of the Catholic Church, in particular, on the diocesan level (Damberg & Hellemans 2010). Before 1960, Rome and the diocesan level took responsibility for the overall design and policy of the Church and for the training and allocation of the clergy. The actual organization and 'production' of religion was done at the parish level – with some exceptions like pilgrimages, some highly reputed processions, and some occasional mass assemblies. Nowadays, an array of supra-local instances have taken over part of the business, and with time, will continue to take over an increasingly greater part: at the lower level, federations and fusions of parishes, deaneries and subdiocesan instances; at the middle level, the dioceses (diocesan curia, bureaucracy, and services); at the higher level, national conferences of bishops and their secretariats and international conferences of bishops (e.g., at the level of the EU and European continent) and synods of bishops. By far, the most important instance in this multi-level functioning is the diocese. A good indication is the number of personnel working on the diocesan level. In the territorially extended dioceses of Western Europe – thus excluding the mini-dioceses in Italy and in some other regions – the number of diocesan personnel was, from the 16th century to 1945, generally not higher than a good dozen, including the bishop and the heads of the church law tribunal and the diocesan priest seminary. After 1945, the number began to grow, first slowly, then exploding in the 1960's and 1970's. Since then, depending on the finances, the number has remained stable or continued to grow at a smaller rate, only declining a bit in the last years due to financial constraints (Damberg 1997, 162-166; Oehmen-Vieregge 2010, 28-29; Witte 2010, 151-152). The diocesan role has expanded accordingly (for some critical comments, based on the situation in Italy, see Diotallevi 2010). Due to the increasing complexity of modern society, the diocese now has to handle a range of legal, administrative, and social security issues, which it did not have to take care of before. This complexity, in combination with the demands for democratization of the Church in the 1960's and 1970's, has generated an array of advice groups and of expert and supervisory committees. The diocese is also taking over from the parishes the efforts to reach categories of people – youth, elderly, ethnic groups, etc. Fuelled by the success of papal visits, World Youth Days, Taizé International Encounters, and the like, the dioceses not only try to mobilize the faithful for national and international mass gatherings, they are also increasingly staging diocesan mass gatherings themselves: confirmation gatherings in many a diocese (for example in Haarlem, Rotterdam (since 1997), and Malines-Brussels), gatherings for sextons (since 2010) in Utrecht, inter-diocesan pilgrimages for pupils and students of the Paris region (Brémond d'Ars 2010, 116-118). The crisis of the parishes forces the dioceses to intervene incisively in the rebuilding of the parishes. The rise of lay volunteers, who assist or replace the declining number of priests, creates evermore demand for formation on a diocesan level. In sum, the process of delocalization forces the Catholic Church to overhaul completely its organizational functioning and its system of religious production. Dioceses, parishes in old church buildings (notably cathedrals), and active groups and movements (I refer again to the 'new ecclesial movements') seem to have found prominence and a new role in the process. But what will happen to the 'local' parishes and the federations or fusions of parishes? Whether the base of the church pyramid will have a future is, at the moment, not clear at all. Given the dominant role of the parish in church life so far, the failure to revitalize the local parishes would seriously endanger the Catholic Church as a major religious institution.

As is already indicated by the above, the swift changes, which are visible in every domain and aspect of life in advanced modernity, also force the Catholic Church – and the other major churches as well – to become more flexible (see Hellemans 2007,198). In the first place, the flexibility of the Church is at work institutionally. As economic firms or state organizations are ceaselessly initiating new initiatives and restructurings, so is the Catholic Church (see De Groot in this volume). It is restructuring the parishes – an enduring task for times to come. It is experimenting with the staging of new events (the papal visits, which began in trial during the early years of the pontificate of John Paul II, have by now become a standard part of papal leadership). The Church is re-organizing the formation of priests, rethinking the catechesis that is linked to the 'rites de passage', issuing new prescriptions for celebrating the Eucharist and other gatherings, etc. (see also Speelman in this volume). The flexibility is not restricted to ritual or organizational items, but covers also substantial questions. As science and a globalized culture are endlessly throwing up new, diverging, and, not infrequently, controversial interpretations (and university-based theology is an important part of the flow), the leadership of the Catholic Church is tempted and challenged to make pronouncements on a widening range of issues: to draw lines on theological issues, to speak out on new topics like medical end-of-life treatment, in vitro fertilization, or embryonic stem cell research, to make pronouncements over political and social topics, to name a few. The increasing flexibility, organizationally and substantially, has the effect that governing a church seems to come close to running a company and it becomes tempting to phrase the leading of a church in terms of efficiency and marketing (see the row over the document *Kirche der Freiheit* of 2006 in the German Protestant Church (EKD), Hermelink & Wegner 2008). Moreover, optimizing strategies might conflict with venerable traditions (e.g., discussions about the widening of the priesthood to allow women and married men) or with customs held dear (e.g., the protests against the closing of parish churches). Since everybody is aware that every decision has become contingent, it makes each and every decision debatable and, in principle, reversible (see again the issue of the priesthood). The transmission of a tradition has thus become *nolens volens* a matter of contestable 'tradition policy'. For a church like the Catholic Church that draws its self-image to such a high extent from the conviction that it is 'only' continuing the tradition that was once instituted by Christ himself, this is a highly disquieting situation (see also Meijers in this volume). The problem is by no means limited to religious liberals. It poses itself with equal if not with more force for religious conservatives since, in a contingent world, the legitimacy of their position and policy is less evident than ever.

5.4. Experiential religion in an event church

For most of Christianity's history, an ascetic life and doctrinal obedience were seen as the hallmark of a holy, Christian life. Stress on discipline and practices of mortification remained strong in 19th and 20th century Catholicism, as is exemplified in many religious orders and congregations (see, e.g., Derks 2007, 144-164 on the Dutch Women of Bethany). Alongside discipline, doctrinal obedience was regarded a prime virtue and it received even more attention after 1500 when the Catholic Church felt itself under mounting threat first from the Protestant Reformation and, after 1800, from liberal and socialist movements. In the 19th and first half of the 20th centuries, both virtues were embedded within a sprawling system of ecclesiastical norms, aimed at regulating the whole life of the faithful in minute detail.

After 1960, however, this system of discipline and obedience could no longer be maintained. In the sixties, both virtues were abruptly derogated and replaced by other values such as personal liberty, spontaneity, authenticity, and (religious) experience. This *volte-face* has aptly been labeled as 'the turn towards the subject' or 'the anthropological turn' and the concomitant society has been criticized as 'spectacle society' ('société du spectacle', Guy Debord 1967) or as 'experience-driven' or even 'thrill-seeking' society ('Erlebnisgesellschaft', Gerhard Schulze 1993). Of course, authentic life and intimate experience of God were always highly praised in Christianity (as, for example, in the work of the church father Augustine), but discipline and obedience were, up until 1960, seen as their consort values or, at least, as indispensable preconditions. What is new is that the two sets of values are nowadays generally regarded as being intrinsically antagonistic, with discipline and obedience standing on the 'bad' side of the divide. This change of valuation also affects the evaluation of the Catholic Church as an institution, since the only reason for institutional religion to exist now seems to be to serve the individual quest for a rich and authentic encounter with God. The Catholic Church and many conservative critics in its fold are vehemently criticizing this instrumental vision of the Church. Yet, at the same time, they are, like all Catholics, actively looking for and promoting authenticity and personal experience in a variety of ways. Such is the power of modernity! All rituals have been redesigned since 1960 – beginning with the Eucharist in the constitution *Sacrosanctum Concilium* of 1963 at the Second Vatican Council – to promote the active participation and experience of the participants. Medieval and early modern mystics like Eckhart and John of the Cross have been rediscovered and are, for the first time in history, widely known. Contemporary spiritual authors (for example, Thomas Merton, Henri Nouwen, John Main, Anselm Grün) are held in high esteem. Spirituality centers have been founded and courses in spirituality mounted. Celebrations on Christmas Eve and festive celebrations in cathedrals are attracting crowds, who are even traveling far for the occasion. Most spectacular of all is the staging of new types of mass events like the World Youth Days (Hepp & Krönert 2009). These events follow the format of contemporary music festivals: informal atmosphere, collective effervescence (applause, shouting, singing, and dancing), easy and mostly temporary connections with people one has never met before, the building up of peak moments and, of course, the physical presence of, and 'dialogue' with, 'stars' (the higher in the church hierarchy the better). The search for authenticity and experiential religion is, perhaps, also the deeper cause for the success, after 1960, of the 'new ecclesial movements' like *Opus Dei*, the *Catholic Charismatic Renewal, Communione e Liberatione*, the *Neocatechumenal Way,* or the *Focolari* (Hanna 2006; De Groot 2006; Sengers 2006). Dedicated Catholics on the look out for 'the real thing' find in these small communities like-minded people and an enthusing setting. In conclusion, we can say that church life is being refocused towards spirituality, ecclesial movements, and mass events. Again, the parishes seem to have no place in these. The parishes are no longer regarded as places to live religion authentically and experientially, adding to the crisis the parishes find themselves already in as a consequence of the general decline in church commitment.

5.5. The appeal of a religionized religion

Ultramontane mass Catholicism functioned as a sort of 'total institution'. It catered for all life functions, religious as well as cultural, socio-economic, and even political. As a consequence, the Church became surrounded by a belt of Catholic organizations of all sorts, making the Catholic religion and, particularly, the Catholic Church highly relevant for people's lives (cf. supra §3 and §5.3). In advanced modernity after 1960, many of the Catholic side-organizations were dismantled or drifted away from the embrace of the Church (the evolution of the Christian democratic parties and of the Christian/Catholic labor movements are typical examples). The Catholic Church thus lost the range of social functions that it performed or helped to perform before 1960. It has, as a result, been turned into a 'religionized' church, that is, a church that has been reduced to the core business of religion, relating the immanent with the Transcendent (Hellemans 2007, 108-110 and 186-194). Of course, religion, aiming as it is at life's ultimate goals and conditions, always permeates the whole of life. In contrast to the past, however, it is now up to the individual to establish links between his or her religion and non-religious organizations and life spheres. The connections are no longer, in an over-all way, pre-decided by the institutional linkages of the Church with befriended organizations. Voting behavior and reading habits of Catholics – to give two examples – have, as a result, been radically changed. The religionization of the Church has consequences for the way of approaching and drawing people in to the realm of the Church too: now the Church has, mainly, only religious means left at its disposal. It can no longer appeal to religious-minded 'secular' institutions (like kings before 1800) or Catholic organizations (like Catholic parties or labor movements after 1800) to function as lines of transmission. In advanced modernity, it is rather unlikely that the Church will, in the future, again be able to take up the former 'secular' functions it has lost (for qualifications, see §8). It will have to base its appeal almost solely on religious grounds. Thus, the questions come up: How can the Church penetrate society as a religionized church? How can the Church retain relevance?

There are, indeed, a number of possible answers to these questions (see also Carroll and Gaertner in this volume). First and foremost, religion has an intrinsic appeal, viz., surrendering to and living at one with the Holy. This is the heart of all religion. Those who get near to this heart, albeit temporarily, testify that it causes a state of rapture and that, henceforth, they long assiduously to reach this felicitous condition again. But the less religious virtuosi are also able to sense the warming and reassuring glow of the Holy. It is, therefore, imperative that the Catholic Church be perceived by the majority of a public as a good, and, if possibly, as the best, way to live a blessed life. In the preceding paragraph, we already mentioned some ways the Catholic Church is offering itself to the virtuosi and the public at large. A strong point is the long tradition of spirituality and mysticism, a tradition that is being continued and renewed in an array of spirituality and retreat centers, often linked to religious orders and congregations. Second, religion has not only a perennial calling, but also a therapeutic pertinence. Contrary to the glorious expectations of the 1960's, advanced modernity turns out to be a risky and stressful environment to live in (see, among others, Beck 1986). The bulk of the stress of coping with life is, moreover, a result of the individualization processes, which is, more than ever, heavily loaded on the frail shoulders of individual persons. They are looking out for help and they often turn to religion to try to find it. The hope of overcoming the trap of over-individualization and of getting nearer to living a fulfilled life is attracting 'individualized individuals' (Luhmann) to religion; hence, the huge, present-day interest in religious healing and religiously tainted psychotherapy (also in non-Christian forms, e.g., 'Mindfulness' and 'Kabbalah'). Religion and spirituality are perceived here by those seeking relief as 'survival mechanisms' to cope with a demanding life. Third, morals and ethics – with their customary close ties to religion – seem to have gained a new relevance in a two-fold way. In an era of choice, opting for a particular moral outlook has become an important part in the (re)construction of one's personal identity and way of life. This is all the more true for a religiously-tainted moral outlook, liberal as well as conservative. Moreover, the choice of a stringent moral and religious outlook promises for conservatives a refuge of prudence, stability, and even solidarity and prosperity in the face of what is regarded by them as libertine, unrestrained, egotistic, and chaotic modernity. Fourth, religion also functions in our society as public conscience. Religious leaders issue repeatedly declarations on matters of general interest. The Catholic Church is well-prepared for this role given that it has a tradition of Catholic social thinking on which it can draw (Boswell et al. 2000; Curran 2002). As a unified and worldwide institution, the statements of the higher ranks – popes, bishops, and conferences of bishops – are diffused by the media. As a well-organized church, it has learnt to lobby for its positions as an interest organization in the many national as well as international cenacles of political power (Böllmann 2010).

At the same time, the Catholic Church faces two severe restrictions to its outreaching capacity. First, are there still enough people interested? Without the support of the now disbanded or independent organizations like Catholic parties and Christian labor movement organizations, the Church has lost much of its former capacity for mounting popular mobilization (as was the case with, e.g., *Rerum Novarum*) and for power play and forceful lobbying (as was the case in many a school struggle and culture war). The therapeutic and identity-supporting role of religion is only appealing to a small number of people. The public at large seems to bestow upon the churches the role of public conscience only when eschewing detailed norm prescriptions and when endorsing already widely accepted human values (cf. the different reception of statements on social over against moral issues). Second, most of the religious avenues mentioned are not exclusive to the Catholic Church. The Catholic Church finds itself always in a competitive position in which it has to prove that it has a good and effective offer to bring in. It is impossible to predict the outcome of this competition.

In sum, the question remains open whether religion alone – on occasion supported by morals – is enough to retain the Church's former preponderant position in society. It seems doubtful. In the past, the central position held by institutional religion was due to the fact that it performed a number of functions. This is now possible only at the margins of society. Immigrant churches operate as repositories of homeland culture and as self-help groups for their members. Strict churches are offering a tightly knit group culture and a lot of activities – on occasion even job coaching – but at a price of high commitment for membership and segregation from the outside world. These roads are closed for the major churches. They cannot, in my opinion, compensate for the loss of the former functions with new functions or with more intense religious experiences. A more modest role in advanced modernity looks inevitable.

5.6. Part of a multicultural world church

In the slipstream of the colonization of the non-European world, the Catholic Church became a world church. Because colonization imposed Westernization by force and because ultramontane Catholicism was, at the same time, fostering Romanization, the world church was highly Western. In this way, the centripetal forces accompanying the worldwide spread of Catholicism were held in check till 1960. Since then, the de-colonization and increasing modernization of the non-Western world have changed the situation thoroughly.

The contemporary evolution of religion and the Catholic Church partakes in the broader evolution of modernity. We are, in fact, witnessing the protracted ending of Western world dominance. The economic growth of most of the non-Western world is in full swing. The now independent non-Western states are gaining more political power. The cultural share of the non-Western world is expanding (in literature, for example, authors of Asian and Latin American origin are now a standard part of the scene). The demographic weight of the non-West is increasing. A similar shift in numbers, power, and influence is also occurring within the Catholic Church. In 1900, 68% of all Catholics lived in Europe. In 1950, this number fell to 49%. The percentage dropped to 27% in 2000 and is predicted to shrink to about 20% by 2025 (for the first three figures, see Froehle & Gautier 2003, 5; for the prediction, see Jenkins 2002, 195). As a consequence, the composition of the College of Cardinals and of the Roman Curia has already seen changes, although Europeans and especially Italians are still preponderant. The Vatican II Council was still guided by a European agenda and by European cardinals. In all probability, it will likely be the last council to have been so guided in the long series of councils since the First Council of the Lateran in 1123.

The consequences of this historical shift are tremendous and are only beginning to make themselves known. First, one should not interpret the end of

European (Western) dominance in Catholicism as a shift towards a new regional/continental center of power. As the books *The Next Christendom: The coming of global Christianity* (Jenkins 2002) and *Global Catholicism: Portrait of a World Church* (Froehle & Gautier 2003) rightly indicate, there is a new type of global Catholicism in the making. Catholicism, as is the case with many other religions, is no longer presented in the garb of one specific civilization, but more and more as a 'global culture' (Hexham & Powe 1997) that leaves room for diverse translations into regional 'cultural dialects'. Historically, this comes down to a 'second universalization' of the world religions. In becoming world religions in the time of agrarian civilizations, these religions had already jumped from local/regional to 'universal' hegemony within a civilization and its periphery. This position enabled them to make the second jump to global spread around the world all the more easily in modernity (Hellemans 2007, 118-122). Specific for Catholicism is, of course, the towering position of the Vatican. As global headquarters in a globalized world, it is profiting from the dynamics inherent in the drive towards a 'second universalization' to re-affirm its central position (see Quinn 1996; 1999 and Denaux 2012 on the Roman recentralization from the 1970's onwards). Second, in accepting the need for room for the enculturation of the Catholic faith, the globalization of Catholicism has greatly fostered its centripetal forces. Yet, as a side-result, the prospect of disunity and internal conflict is also growing. The Anglican Communion is already haunted by such conflict. The same could spread to the Catholic Church too. For example, the ethical sensibilities in the West are different from most of the non-West and this causes tensions between Western liberals and non-Western conservatives (Jenkins 2002). Liberation theology originated originally in Latin America and also harbored anti-colonial (anti-Western) sentiments. Up till now, the highly centralized functioning of the Catholic Church prevented the blossoming and drifting away of culturally distinct Catholicisms – but at the price, in the West, of disaffection and of widening the cleavage between the Rome-oriented top and the bulk of the Catholic population. A liberal opening would probably diminish these effects, but in giving more leeway to the centripetal forces, more conflicts would, at the same time, presumably be unleashed between them (as is apparent in the Anglican Communion). A third item related to the advent of a multicultural world church concerns immigration. Since Catholics are many – about 1 billion worldwide – immigration to Western countries provides an influx of many Catholics. Catholic migrants might help to stop indigenous church decline. This is actually happening in the United States (with the influx of Hispanics) and in the London area (with the immigration of Poles, South Americans, and, to a lesser extent, Philippinos and Africans). Yet, immigration also generates new problems: How to integrate migrant Catholics into an ageing indigenous church (Trzebiatowska 2010)? And will the religious fervency of these immigrants last over several generations?

6.   Sect, fellowship, or major minority church?

Having outlined the main characteristics of the new church formation in the making, there is one crucial question that we have not yet tackled. How successful will the new formation be: Will choice Catholicism continue to shrink or will it find a new hold and prosper to some degree? It will be clear that this question cannot be answered here once and for all. Only time will tell. But we can try to specify the question so as to sharpen our senses for future developments. In the first place, we have to be aware that the actual transition towards choice Catholicism is not the first transition in history towards another church formation. Such transitions have occurred in the past and have also been hazardous undertakings, albeit successful ones. This was the case for the early modern era after the shock waves of the Reformation. It is also true for the Catholic revival of the 19th century, which occurred after early modern Catholicism had been brought to an abrupt end in the French Revolution and the Napoleonic period. Nevertheless, the transition to choice Catholicism manifests itself as a particularly perilous one. Although the existence of the Catholic Church as such is not threatened, its position as the dominant church in Europe and, indeed, its identity as a major church appealing to the mass of the population are at stake. In the second place, the context for the major churches in the West is more negative than in the past. We already came across a number of inhibiting developments: the suspicion towards big institutions, the rising number of competing religions, the rise of non-institutional religion, the dissolution of the former Catholic subsocieties and the concomitant loss of many functions, the ease of living one's life without recourse to (institutional) religion. Yet, we should be careful not to think in terms of a predetermined outcome. While the old form of ultramontane mass Catholicism has become obsolete in advanced modernity, we cannot automatically infer from this that no new church formation might be set up and instituted with some degree of success. After all, there is much variation between countries. Whereas the decline of Catholicism is massive in such diverse countries as the Netherlands, Belgium, France, or Spain, there are indications of a fair level of stability in Italy and the United States, and it seems to be finding a new hold in Britain. Therefore, let us first explore from a theoretical vantage point the possible future scenarios of church development.

Theoretically, the outcome of the evolution of the Catholic Church in a few decades could be imagined as one between three alternatives: a small vociferous sect, a small liberal fellowship, or a more flourishing minority church. A first possible trajectory is further decline and retreat into a strict leftover church, in what is commonly called a sect. Sect (or strict church) is here defined in a neutral way, as a religious group that is highly demanding, vigorously opposed to mainstream culture, and, thus, small and marginal in society. It must be said that a sectarian outcome is a likely scenario for the Catholic Church in many Western countries. In most of these countries, church participation continues to diminish at a stable rate. The huge overrepresentation of elderly people as well as the ever decreasing proportion of active versus nominal Catholics does not bode well either. Moreover, there is a strong tendency in the Catholic Church to withdraw behind allegedly safe, but high walls. Indications of this withdrawal are the defiant conservative stance in dogmatic and ethical positions against the more liberal sensibilities of most Catholics and of the public at large, the rigorous new priests who enter the priesthood 'against the world', the choice by Rome of uncompromising bishops, the popularity in Rome and in conservative circles of the notion of a Catholic 'counterculture' as a 'pocket of resistance' (De Dijn 2009, 202) against the tide of modernity and post-modernity.

A second possibility, which is almost the reverse of the former, is the future of a liberal fellowship movement, of a progressive leftover church. As in the strict church scenario, church participation and involvement would continue to decline and the Church would no longer be regarded in the eyes of mainstream society as an institution that matters. But instead of retreating into the bulwarks of a small strict church, a fellowship would pursue a liberal policy, stressing the autonomy of the church members and expressing 'decent', mainline views of society. The Remonstrant Brotherhood and the Old Catholics in the Netherlands and the Unitarian Universalists in the United States are examples of small liberal churches. The Church of England could also be heading in this direction – if a decline continues and conservative Evangelicals do not take over the leadership. Given the actual course of the Catholic Church, becoming a liberal fellowship seems, at the moment, less likely.

A third possible scenario is one of becoming a major minority church. In this case, the Catholic Church would continue to attract a sizeable portion of the population and to impact upon society at large. To my knowledge, the concept 'minority church' was introduced by Roger Mehl to refer to the numerically small, but not unimportant, protestant Reformed Church in France (Mehl 1965). David Millett used the concept shortly afterwards to characterize a number of smaller religious institutions in Canada, which, due to their smallness, can neither be classified as 'churches' properly speaking (like, in his eyes, the Catholic and Orthodox churches and the five major protestant denominations) nor, due to their 'churchlike' behavior, as sects or cults (Millett, 1969). My usage differs from both authors in referring to the new context of secularized societies without a majority church and in reserving the concept 'minority church' for religious groups with a substantial membership and a tangible influence (for a comparable treatment of the evolution of the Evangelical Church in the former German Democratic Republic, see Pollack 2009, 249-275).

7.   Probing the idea of a major minority church

In order to probe whether the concept of a minority church, as I mean it, has a real chance to materialize, I propose setting up a thought experiment: let us try to imagine the conditions that would foster a major church in advanced modernity. The first thing to say here is that it would be patently wrong to conceive the future Church in terms of the past church formation, namely, a big Church in charge of society, or at least part of that society, with a laity under the unshakable authority of the pope, bishops, and priests. Given the current crisis of the Church, it is tempting, especially for conservative Catholics, to conjure up such an idealized image of ultramontane mass Catholicism as the ideal for all times. But the past never returns. Thus, the minority church will be smaller in size, with fewer priests – and even more so if celibacy is upheld – and with fewer core members. It will no longer be surrounded by a belt of Catholic social organizations. It will no longer be able to force people into conformity with church rulings. The implication of all this, expressed in positive terms, is that the Catholic Church has to attract and seduce people into its realm, and it has to do so with religious means only (see also section 5.5). The Church has to become an attractive church for people who know they are free to choose otherwise. How might it do this?

7.1. Conditions

To stop the downward spiral and become an attractive and major minority church, I venture the suggestion that the Catholic Church needs to meet four conditions in advanced modernity.

First, as a religionized church, the Catholic Church will have to develop new paths – in fact, many new paths – of devotion and spirituality. Before 1960, a whole range of variegated devotions was being offered upon which people, according to their needs and tastes, could draw: veneration of saints, processions and pilgrimages, a church calendar with accompanying festivities and devotions that ordered daily life, the wide range of formulaic prayers. These old forms have lost their attraction and, therefore, need to be renewed or replaced. Some old forms can be rejuvenated – think of the success of international pilgrimage centers or the renewed interest in Gregorian-sung masses. Some alternatives have already been introduced. The staging of mass events has become, since about 1980, a systematic undertaking of the Church, first on an international scale, followed by much emulation on national and diocesan levels. As new forms of devotion and spirituality, one can also point, to the retreat and spirituality centers, to the conscious combination of tourism and religion in cathedrals and old churches, and to concerts of sacred music in churches. Nevertheless, if the Church wants to attract more people, much more needs to be done. The new or rejuvenated paths must also be organized in a more systematic way, which can only be done on the diocesan and national levels. The systematic propagation of church activities is lacking. The retreat centers, many of which are struggling to survive, need more backing. National centers for the encouragement of praying and contemplation in daily life have to be set up. There is a need for, so to speak, 'living saints', who exemplify – like the Dalai Lama in Buddhism – that sanctity and bliss are attainable in daily life via the Catholic Church, also in advanced modernity. In short, to become an attractive minority church, the Catholic Church should be transformed into a spiritual hotbed.

Second, the audience and following of Catholicism must be addressed. Nowadays, the Catholic Church is perceived, mainly due to the severe tone of its public proclamations, as targeting only those who are willing to engage fully and to accept all the Church's teachings. Such a highly demanding policy is the surest way towards a sect outcome. Such a policy contradicts the performance in the past, where part of the Church's success can be attributed to the fact that it endeavored to be a church for all people, for saints as well as for sinners. Resuming an inclusive policy in advanced modernity would mean that it would make conscious efforts to provide religion for different layers of the population, for people with different degrees of commitment: for the non-committed public at large, for the lukewarm, occasional clients, for the committed members and, last but not least, for the few, but crucial religious virtuosi. A layered offer is thus essential. Actually, there are many avenues present for the public at large – such as the lightning of candles, visits to churches, or attendance of church funerals. But a layered offer does not add up to a full-scale, comprehensive policy, and the effect is counteracted by the self-presentation by the Catholic Church as an institution that is insisting on nothing less than total commitment and dedication.

Third, the Church has to increase the influx of newcomers (who come with varying degrees of commitment). Before 1960, new members were, with a few exceptions, born from Catholic parents. What remained to be done was to instill the religion in the new generation. Over the centuries, this religious socialization has been deepened and perfected ever more. Religious socialization of born Catholics remains even today, of course, the primal route to gain new believers. But in our times of choice, a breakaway of a sizeable proportion of youngsters, both towards other religions and towards non-religion, has become unavoidable. In order to stabilize, let alone increase, its following, new believers have to be recruited from outside the Church. I already referred to the papal calls for a 'missionizing church' and to the slow, mental change on the ground (see also Wissink in this volume). A crucial part in the increase in outreaching capabilities will no doubt be played by the media. As an important international player, the Catholic Church is assured of media coverage. Wide media coverage has its disadvantages: in cases of conflicts and scandals – and there will always be some – one runs the risk of being torn down. As the child abuse scandal makes clear, the Catholic Church still has much to learn in dealing transparently and swiftly with clerical transgressions and, more generally, in coping with public critique on inner-churchly decision making and problem handling. Learning how to use wide media coverage to its advantage is of equal, if not more, importance. Our age of choice and media also presents the opportunity to gain a new following that is not already acquainted with the Catholic religion. The first thing to do here is to invest in church media (see already the website vatican.va) and to approach the general media in such a way as to make the Catholic activities and spiritual paths better known and to convey the message that the Church helps each and every person attain a richer and more fulfilled life. Sizeable portions, if not the majority, of the population no longer have firsthand experience of the Catholic Church via its parishes. They depend on mediated information. If the Church hopes to attract outsiders, it must aim to reach the public by transmitting positive messages through the media. Next, all newly interested people should be welcomed, including those – which will be the majority – who only want to sniff the Roman perfume a little. Finally, the newcomers, depending on their degree of interest and desire for commitment, are to be encouraged in a non-directive way to explore the variety of Catholic religious avenues. When a sizeable number of newcomers is willing to pass through these three stages (getting informed, being welcomed, finding fitting avenues), a quantitative stabilization of a minority church will begin to come within reach. This would, at the same time, thoroughly alter the constituency of the Church towards a mixed following, constituted in part by those who opted for remaining in the church they were born and raised in, and in part by those attracted from the outside.

Fourth, turning the Church into an attractive, big institution will demand a major reform of the way the Church is run First of all, a sufficient number of professionals have to be provided for. Unlike many small Protestant denominations whose leadership is built on a combination of self-selection and backing by the congregation, the leadership of the Catholic Church and the Catholic faithful alike have always relied on officials, trained and appointed by the Church. It is clear by now that celibate, male priests will, in the decades to come, by no means suffice to staff a church with a large following. Either the priesthood becomes opened to married men and (married) women, or lay pastoral workers will have to be brought in to do most of the pastoral work. Handing over the lower reaches of the Church to the laity could constitute an alternative, yet it carries its own risks. An almost complete handover to the laity would foster autarkic, congregationalist tendencies. What is more, as is the case with most other voluntary organizations, the Catholic Church is struggling with an ageing and declining number of volunteers who are willing to engage themselves for the good of the organization. A lack of volunteers would, just as a lack of professionals without volunteers, mean the collapse of the territorially extended organization of the Church as it has been known since the Middle Ages. In addition to the personnel problem, the running of a major church faces a second major challenge, namely, the generalized suspicion in advanced modernity towards all big institutions and organizations. Thus, in order to be attractive, the advantages of being a big institution have to outweigh the perceived disadvantages. The advantages are threefold: (i) a global church with vast organizational capabilities; (ii) a broad and diverse church with multiple offers for all people and with room for people with different persuasions; (iii) an age-old church with a rich heritage. However, these are, strictly speaking, merely opportunities that still have to be turned into real advantages. The major disadvantages include, as I mentioned already, the generalized suspicion and even aversion by the public to big institutions. But there are also the dangers of a mounting bureaucracy in the face of an ever more complex society, and of an internal paralysis between liberal and conservative church factions. How the Catholic Church should counter the disadvantages and the threats while, at the same time, capitalizing on the advantages of being a big church is not clear to me. It is also not clear whether a positive sum game is still possible at all. If not, the outcome of becoming a small (strict) sect or a (liberal) fellowship, or something in between, is unavoidable. At the moment, however, it is too early to rule out the possibility of a well-staffed church institution that is sensitive to and attractive for a large public. But becoming an attractive church also has consequences for how the Church, as a big institution, is run. Specifically, it will demand the following: more transparency in church direction and management (for example, in the appointment of bishops and in its communication with the outside world), a judicious amount of decentralization, less stress on doctrinal and moral conformity and a more favorable and detached attitude towards diversity and lay initiatives, avoiding stand-offs between different church factions, appointments of more spiritual or energetic bishops rather than of bishops who stress only obedience and orthodoxy, the provision of a fair number of professionals and volunteers, and, last but not least, more humility on the part of the institution.

7.2. A new church dynamic?

In my opinion, these four conditions have to be met, at least to some degree, in order for the Catholic Church to become an attractive, major minority church in advanced modernity. Each condition, though, does not stand on its own. Combined together, there might unfold a new church dynamic, a positive feedback loop between the major constituent parts of the new church formation, resulting in a new stabilization of the Catholic Church.

To get a better idea of what is meant by a 'new church dynamic', let us first go back to the ultramontane mass Catholicism of the 19th and first half of the 20th century. The church dynamics that gave power and stability to this church formation sprang up from three factors: 1. the integration and mobilization of a mass following that was still born in the Church; 2. the centralized church organization, staffed by well-trained religious personnel; 3. the confrontational struggle against secular and protestant 'enemies'. These three components invigorated one another. They formed a positive feedback loop: the centralized church organization took the leading role in the satisfaction of numerous religious and non-religious needs of the mass following and this mutual orientation of Church and following was strengthened by the segregation into a fortress subculture. As a result of this dynamic, ultramontane mass Catholicism remained vigorous up until the 1950's – undergoing many evolutions and adaptations along the way.

We should not rule out a priori that another similar new dynamic might also unfold in advanced modernity. I am inclined to think that the four conditions I have sketched out above could eventually ignite this new dynamic as four constituent parts of the new church formation, namely: 1. the offering of an array of paths of devotion and spirituality that is perceived, by the 'individualized individuals' of today, as helpful to cope with their lives in advanced modernity and to live a fulfilled and good life 'in the light of eternity'; 2. the offering of layers of religious activities thereby fostering a Church that caters not only to highly committed members, but also to the whole population through a welcoming attitude for all who are interested (even if only minimally interested); 3. the implementation of a conscious and systematic outreaching policy towards people outside the Church, and, in particular, the use of the media and the staging of big events in order to make the Church and its potential known; 4. the transformation of the Church from an institution that insists on total obedience and total commitment into one that is more open, more humble, and more welcoming, and staffed with enough professionals to do the job – the condition *sine qua non*. In these ways, the particularities of advanced modernity might be put to work in favor of a major minority church.

7.3. An ideal 'ideal type'

Both the probing of the four conditions or constituent parts (i.e., relevant spiritual paths for people with different degrees of commitment by an attractive, well-staffed and outreaching church) and the questions surrounding the eventual unfolding of a new church dynamic make clear that the preceding thought experiment is not to be confused with a description of the reality of the Catholic Church today or of its probable evolution (for a recent, critical analysis of the reality, see Kaufmann 2011, 98-181). The vision imagined might rather be called an ideal 'ideal type', i.e., an ideal type that sketches an ideal. Ideal types, in the tradition of Max Weber, are analytical constructs of a few complementary characteristics in pure form. Reality, on the contrary, is always messy, a muddling of many idiosyncrasies that do not add up to the pure characteristics of a clear and distinct construct. In this sense, the three possible futures of the Catholic Church that I have sketched – a strict leftover church (sect), a liberal leftover church (fellowship), and a major minority church – are all ideal types (Weber 1904, 190-212). Moreover, it is evident that the conditions that I suggest need to be met to become an attractive, major minority church, are rather heavy. My delineation of the contours of a major minority church should thus be regarded as an opportunity for the Catholic Church – as well as for the other major churches – in advanced modernity. It may, perhaps, be a remote opportunity and, in any case, one that will not easily be realized. The threat of becoming an intransigent sect or a weak fellowship is looming high.

8. Advanced modernity: benign or harsh?

In the analysis of the new church formation so far, the focus was laid on the part played by the Catholic Church: the basic characteristics of choice Catholicism, its possible trajectories, its strategic options and conditions. However, the Catholic Church, as only one side of the coin, cannot force the evolution only by itself. The other side is the evolution of modernity, of the modern context within which the Church moves. The question here is whether – without falling into the trap of predetermination – the context of advanced modernity encourages some trajectories more than others. Our exploration has led us to emphasize the difficulties for the Catholic Church to remain a major church in advanced modernity. The presupposition behind this view is that advanced modernity is, all-in-all, benign and beneficial for the 'individualized individual', and that the chances to live a good life exceed the disadvantages and problems in advanced modernity. But the possibility cannot be ruled out that this may not be the case. What if in the future advanced modernity proves to be a harsh and inhospitable environment for most people, with living conditions deteriorating instead of improving?

It has become quite well established that existential security or insecurity has an effect on one's religious behavior and attitude (see, e.g., Norris & Inglehart 2004). People who are well-off are, in general, more inclined to take a secularizing or a religiously liberal stance towards institutional religion. Secularization, interpreted as the declining force of institutional religion, has made progress in most Western countries, particularly after the Second World War, in an era of triumphant modernity, prosperity, and welfare for the bulk of the population. Religious liberalism is associated with prosperity as well. The bourgeoisie was, in the 19th century, at the heart of the movement toward religious liberalism, both in Protestantism and in Catholicism. In the 1960's, the rise of welfare and the educated middle classes facilitated the opening of Catholicism in these years. Inversely, being hindered by severe problems to live one's life – either individually due to sickness or psychological troubles or socially due to immigration, poverty, and insecurity – can drive one towards more fervor and a harder stance, as religion is promising relief. For a marginalized or destitute constituency, institutional religion is often the only major resource to which they can turn, and the only one that is also capable of aggregating and voicing their views and troubles in the public sphere. It is the most noble flag one can wave! It is no wonder that immigrants are generally becoming more religious. Liberal, detached religion will thus be attractive for well-to-do people, particularly in societies without protracted internal conflicts and with widely spread welfare and existential security. Hard, fanatic religion will have more chances in societies and among people who experience difficult living conditions.

We do not know how advanced modernity will evolve. Based on the rise of welfare and the long-lasting peace after 1945, we tend to have a benign view of the future and to regard contemporary problems – mounting pressure on individuals, environmental problems, migrant subcultures, the fourth world or the plight of people in many non-Western countries – as surmountable, temporary, or, at least, treatable. Thus, we unconsciously view the middle classes – secularizing and/or liberal – as our default option. If this presupposition turns out to be true, the further shrinking of the Catholic Church will be very probable. A sectarian outcome, if a conservative, highly demanding policy is upheld, will, in this case, be more likely. The outcome of a liberal fellowship or of a major minority church cannot be ruled out, but are – given the current church policy – less likely. Yet, advanced modernity might also turn abrasive. Welfare in the West might decline for many people if social inequality at home and competition abroad keep rising. If the welfare states begin dissolving, the churches might, once again, take up some of the functions they lost with the rise of the welfare state. Personal insecurity might rise as life becomes ever more individualized. Integration of citizens into a national and international community might fail, as multiple subcultures form and solidify. Such a hardening societal context would give fewer chances for religious liberalism than in a prosperous advanced modernity, but it would give more maneuvering room for a conservative church to establish itself again at the centre of society, either as a bigger sect or as a major, conservative minority church. However, even for those who have a predilection for religion, this is not a future to be wished for. And, given what we can say now, advanced modernity turning abrasive is also the more unlikely scenario.

9.   The uncertain future of the Catholic Church

The prospects for a vigorous Catholic Church with a large following and a high impact on society do not look good. At the moment, the outcome, in say about fifty years, of a small, sect-like church – whether one likes it or not – does seem the most likely. The unrelenting decline in numbers in combination with a retrenchment-like policy both point in this direction.

Nevertheless, the outcome has not been realized as yet. We have to remain cautious, and not only because the future always remains open. First of all, there are examples of Catholic churches that, although not without problems, remain vigorous (like in Italy and the United States). Second, we do not dispose, at present, of sound theories on churches and church development, which lowers the potential of forecasting whether a new church dynamic might start up eventually in advanced modernity. Third, migration is bringing in Catholics from the non-Western world. They could bring more vitality into the autochthon churches or, at least, halt their decline. Fourth, it is conceivable that Catholicism outside the West will make, in the future and with advancing prosperity, a turn from conservatism to liberalism – as was the case in the West in the 1960's – and that the liberal policy option will get a second chance, especially if the conservative option, which is now dominant, shows no success.

References

Altermatt, U. 1989. *Katholizismus und Moderne. Zur Sozial- und Mentalitätsgeschichte der Schweizer Katholiken im 19. Und 20. Jahrhundert*. Zürich: Benziger Verlag.

Aspden, K. 2002. *Fortress Church. The English Roman Catholic Bishops and Politics 1903-1963*. Leominster: Gracewing.

Beck, U. 1986. *Risikogesellschaft. Auf dem Weg in eine andere Moderne*. Frankfurt am Main: Suhrkamp.

Billiet, J. 1988. *Tussen bescherming en verovering. Sociologen en historici over zuilvorming*. Leuven: Universitaire Pers Leuven.

Böllmann, F. 2010. *Organisation und Legitimation der Interessen von Religionsgemeinschaften in der europäischen politischen Öffentlichkeit*. Würzburg: Ergon.

Boswell, J.S., F.P. McHugh & J. Verstraeten (eds.). 2000. *Catholic Social Thought: Twilight or Renaissance?* Bibliotheca Ephemeridum Theologicarum Lovaniensium 157. Leuven: Peeters.

Brémond d'Ars, N. 2010. 50 Jahre katholische Pastoral in Frankreich: eine soziologische Annäherung. Pp. 111-137 in W. Damberg & S. Hellemans (Hgg.). *Die neue Mitte der Kirche. Der Aufstieg der intermediären Instanzen in den europäischen Grosskirchen seit 1945*. Stuttgart: Kohlhammer.

Curran, Ch. E. 2002. *Catholic Social Teaching 1891-Present. A Historical, Theological and Ethical Analysis*. Washington: Georgetown University Press.

Damberg, W. 1997. *Abschied vom Milieu? Katholizismus im Bistum Münster und in den Niederlanden 1945-1980*. Paderborn: F. Schöning.

Damberg, W. & S. Hellemans (Hgg.). 2010. *Die neue Mitte der Kirche. Der Aufstieg der intermediären Instanzen in den europäischen Grosskirchen seit 1945*. Stuttgart: Kohlhammer.

Debord, G. 1967. *La société du spectacle*. Paris: Buchet-Chastel.

Denaux, A. 2012. Gezag en gezagsuitoefening in een vitale kerk. In S. Hellemans, P. Rentinck & J. van den Eijnden (red.). *Een katholieke kerk met toekomst*. Utrecht: 2VM (in press).

Derks, M. 2007. *Heilig moeten. Radicaal-katholiek en retro-modern in de jaren twintig en dertig*. Hilversum: Uitgeverij Verloren.

Dijn, H. De. 2009. Catholic Tradition: Custodian of Paradox. Pp. 189-204 in P.C. Beentjes (ed.). *The Catholic Church and Modernity in Europe*. Münster: LIT-Verlag.

Diotallevi, L. 2010. Diözesen und Säkularisierung in Italien. Pp. 179-213 in W. Damberg & S. Hellemans (Hgg.). *Die neue Mitte der Kirche. Der Aufstieg der intermediären Instanzen in den europäischen Grosskirchen seit 1945*. Stuttgart: Kohlhammer.

Dobbelaere, K., J. Billiet & L. Voyé. 2011. Religie en kerkbetrokkenheid: naar een sociaal gemarginaliseerde kerk? Pp. 143-172 in K. Abts, K. Dobbelaere & L. Voyé (red.). *Nieuwe tijden, nieuwe mensen. Belgen over arbeid, gezin, ethiek, religie en politiek.* Tielt: Lannoo.

Duyvendak, J.W. & M. Hurenkamp (red.). 2004. *Kiezen voor de kudde. Lichte gemeenschappen en de nieuwe meerderheid*. Amsterdam: Van Gennep.

Froehle, B.T. & M.L. Gauthier. 2003. *Global Catholicism. Portrait of a World Church*. Maryknoll: Orbis.

Gabriel, K. 1992. *Christentum zwischen Tradition und Postmoderne*. Freiburg im Breisgau: Herder.

Gabriel, K. (Hg.). 1996. *Religiöse Individualisierung oder Säkularisierung. Biographie und Gruppe als Bezugspunkte moderner Religiosität*. Gütersloh: Chr. Kaiser.

Gabriel, K. 2010. Gemeinde zwischen Delokalisierung und Relokalisierung. *Evangelische Theologie* 70: 427-438.

Gabriel, K. & F.-X. Kaufmann (Hgg.). 1980. *Zur Soziologie des Katholizismus*. Mainz: Grünewald.

Giddens, A. 1991. *Modernity and Self-identity. Self and Society in the Late Modern Age*. Cambridge: Polity Press.

Groot, C.N. de. 2006. Orthodoxie en beleving: Bewegingen in de Rooms-Katholieke Kerk in Nederland. *Religie en Samenleving* 1: 151-173.

Hanna, T. 2006. *New Ecclesial Movements: Communion and Liberation Neocatechumenal Way Charismatic Renewal*. New York: Alba House.

Heelas, P. 2002. The Spiritual Revolution. From 'Religion' to 'Spirituality'. Pp. 357-377 in L. Woodhead *et al.* (eds.). *Religions in the Modern World*. London: Routledge.

Hellemans, S. 1990. *Strijd om de moderniteit. Sociale bewegingen en verzuiling in Europa sinds 1800*. Leuven: Universitaire Pers Leuven.

Hellemans, S. 1993. Zuilen en verzuiling in Europa. Pp. 121-150 in U. Becker (ed.). *Nederlandse politiek in historisch en vergelijkend perspectief*. Amsterdam: Het Spinhuis.

Hellemans, S. 1997. *Religieuze modernisering*. Utrecht: KTU.

Hellemans, S. 2007. *Het tijdperk van de wereldreligies. Religie in agrarische civilisaties en in moderne samenlevingen*. Zoetermeer-Kapellen: Meinema/Pelckmans.

Hellemans, S. 2009. A Critical Transition. From Ultramontane Mass Catholicism to Choice Catholicism. Pp. 32-54 in P.C. Beentjes (ed.). *The Catholic Church and Modernity in Europe*. Münster: LIT-Verlag.

Hepp, A. & V. Krönert. 2009. Religious Media Events. The Catholic "World Youth Day" as an Example of the Mediatization and Individualization of Religion. Pp. 265-280 in N. Couldry, A. Hepp & F. Krotz (eds.). *Media Events in a Global Age*. London: Routledge.

Hermelink, J. & G. Wegner. 2008. *Paradoxien kirchlicher Organisation. Niklas Luhmanns frühe Kirchensoziologie und die aktuelle Reform der evangelischen Kirche*. Würzburg: Ergon.

Hero, M., V. Krech & Zander (Hgg.). 2008. *Religiöse Vielfalt in Nordrhein-Westfalen. Empirische Befunde und Perspektiven der Globalisierung vor Ort*. Paderborn: F. Schöningh.

Hervieu-Léger, D. 1998. The Transmission and Formation of Socioreligious Identities in Modernity: An Analytical Essay on the Trajectories of Identification. *International Sociology* 13: 213-228.

Hervieu-Léger, D. 2003. *Catholicisme, la fin d'un monde*. Paris: Bayard.

Hexham, I & K. Poewe 1997. *New Religion as Global Cultures*. Boulder: Westview Press.

Hoge, D. *et al.* 2001. *Young Adult Catholics. Religion in a Culture of Choice*. Notre Dame: University of Notre Dame Press.

Jenkins, Ph. 2002. *The Next Christendom. The Coming of Global Christianity*. Oxford-New York: Oxford University Press.

Kaufmann, F.-X. 1979. *Kirche begreifen. Analysen und Thesen zur gesellschaftlichen Verfassung des Christentums*. Freiburg im Breisgau: Herder.

Kaufmann, F.-X. 1989. *Religion und Modernität*. Tübingen: J.C.B. Mohr (Paul Siebeck).

Kaufmann, F.-X. 2011. *Kirchenkrise. Wie überlebt das Christentum?* Freiburg im Breisgau: Herder.

Lambert, Y. 1985. *Dieu change en Bretagne. La religion à Limerzel de 1900 à nos jours*. Paris: Cerf.

Luhmann, N. 1972. Die Organisierbarkeit von Religionen und Kirchen. Pp. 245-285 in J. Woesner (Hg.). *Religion im Umbruch*. Stuttgart: F. Enke.

Mehl, R. 1965. *Traité de Sociologie du Protestantisme*. Neuchâtel: Delachaux et Niestlé.

Millett, D. 1969. A Typology of Religious Organizations Suggested by the Canadian Census. *Sociology of Religion* 30: 108-119.

Need, A. & N.D. de Graaf. 2005. Zich bekeren en wisselen van kerkgenootschap in Nederland. *Mens en Maatschappij* 80: 288-304.

Norris, P. & R. Inglehart. 2004. *Sacred and Secular. Religions and Politics Worldwide*. Cambridge: Cambridge University Press.

Oehmen-Vieregge, R. 2010. Wandlungsprozessen in den deutschen Diözesen nach 1949: Die (Erz-)Diözesen Köln, München-Freising und Limburg. Pp. 21-48 in W. Damberg & S. Hellemans (Hgg.). *Die neue Mitte der Kirche. Der Aufstieg der intermediären Instanzen in den europäischen Grosskirchen seit 1945*. Stuttgart: Kohlhammer.

O'Malley, J.W. 2008. *What Happened at Vatican II*. Cambridge: Harvard University Press.

Pollack, D. 2009. *Rückkehr des Religiösen? Studien zum religiösen Wandel in Deutschland und in Europa II*. Tübingen: Mohr Siebeck.

Pottmeyer, H.J. 1975. *Unfehlbarkeit und Souveränität. Die päpstliche Unfehlbarkeit im System der ultramontanen Ekklesiologie des 19. Jahrhunderts*. Mainz: Grünewald.

Pottmeyer, H.J. 1997. The 'plena et suprema potestas iuridictionis' of the pope at the First Vatican Council and 'receptio'. *The Jurist* 57: 216-234 and 235-248.

Poulat, E. 1986. *L'Eglise, c'est un monde*. Paris: Cerf.

Quinn, J.R. 1996. The Exercise of the Primacy. Facing the cost of Christian unity. *Commonweal* 13: 11-20.

Quinn, J.R. 1999. *The Reform of the Papacy. The costly call to Christian unity*. New York: Crossroad.

Roozen, D.A. & K.C. Hadaway. 1993. *Church & Denominational Growth*. Nashville: Abingdon Press.

Schulze, G. 1993. *Erlebnisgesellschaft. Kultursoziologie der Gegenwart*. Frankfurt am Main: Campus.

Sengers, E. 2006. *Aantrekkelijke kerk. Nieuwe bewegingen in kerkelijk Nederland op de religieuze markt*. Delft: Eburon.

Sherkat, D.E. 2001. Tracking the Restructuring of American Religion. Religious Affiliation and Patterns of Religious Mobility, 1973-1998. *Social Forces* 79: 1459-1493.

Thurlings, J.M.G. 1979. *De wankele zuil. Nederlandse katholieken tussen assimilatie en pluralism*. Deventer: Van Loghum Slaterus.

Trzebiatowska, M. 2010. The Advent of the 'Easyjet Priests'. Dilemmas of Polish Catholic Integration in the UK. *Sociology* 44: 1055-1072.

Weber, M. 1973 (originally 1904). Die 'Objektivität sozialwissenschaftlicher und sozialpolitischer Erkenntnis. Pp. 146-214 in Id. *Gesammelte Aufsätze zur Wissenschaftslehre*. Tübingen: J.C.B. Mohr (Paul Siebeck).

Witte, H. 2010. Die katholische Kirche in den Niederlanden. Wandlungsprozesse nach dem Zweiten Vatikanischen Konzil. Pp. 139-157 in W. Damberg & S. Hellemans (Hgg.). *Die neue Mitte der Kirche. Der Aufstieg der intermediären Instanzen in den europäischen Grosskirchen seit 1945*. Stuttgart: Kohlhammer.

A Catholic Program For Advanced Modernity

Anthony J. Carroll

1. Introduction

The intention of this chapter is to present a short sketch of a viable program for Catholicism in late or so-called advanced modernity, which I call a program of Catholic Modernity. I shall do this by first outlining the basic characteristics of the framework of Catholic Modernity which I use to situate Catholicism within advanced modernity.[1] The highly contested nature of multiple discourses on modernity makes it important to locate Catholic Modernity in relation to these debates as a distinctive account of modernity in its own right. Whilst this outline of a Catholic Modernity will be necessarily brief, it will provide an account of the synchronic reading of advanced modern societies and also highlight the often overlooked aspects of the diachronic development of these societies which have emerged out of internal reforms within Catholicism.[2]

Second, I shall sketch the benefits for advanced modernity that could be derived from a Catholic Modernity. In building upon the critically positive attitude of the Second Vatican Council to modernity, I argue that a Catholic Modernity provides resources of meaning, solidarity, and hope that are in short supply in other programs of modernity. This critically positive attitude of the Second Vatican Council has not been "rolled back" in recent years to a counter-modern position as some have suggested. Rather, the theological recovery of a Christological humanism and pneumatic theology which sees the Holy Spirit as active within history and society has structured Catholic theology in the post-Vatican II era. Through the shift away from a former neo-Thomist extrinsic conception of grace towards an intrinsic conception of grace that characterises Vatican II Thomistic theology a normative orientation of Catholicism to modernity has been provided that has ushered in a structuring ecclesiological narrative, which one might characterise as a position of critical solidarity with the advanced modern world.[3] Such a continuation of this critically positive normative attitude of the Second Vatican Council explains why the Catholic Church's attitude to interreligious dialogue has developed in the way that it has over the decades which have followed the Council. This continuation will be demonstrated by considering the 2010 document of the Catholic Bishops of England

---

1   Here I am drawing on Carroll and Hanvey 2005; and Carroll 2007; Carroll 2009a; Carroll 2009b; and Carroll 2010.
2   See, for example, Reinhard 1977; 1995; and O'Malley 2000.
3   See Carroll and Hanvey 2005: 39-41.

and Wales, *Meeting God in Friend and Stranger. Fostering Respect and Under-standing Between the Religions*, which represents the normative position of the Second Vatican Council as a critical solidarity with advanced modernity.

Finally, I assess the potential gains for a Catholic Modernity from the challenges posed by advanced modernity. Taking the 'turn to dialogue' within the Catholic Church seriously it is no longer the case that Catholicism sees itself as the teacher of the world but rather as a dialogue partner with it. This paradigm shift in Catholicism means that a Catholic Modernity is itself an unfinished project which progresses through entering into mutual learning processes with the secular world (cf. Habermas, 2008).

2.   What is meant by a catholic modernity?

The idea of a Catholic Modernity was first proposed by the Canadian philosopher Charles Taylor in a lecture he gave at the University of Dayton, Ohio in 1996.[4] The lecture series was set up to give Catholic scholars such as Taylor, the opportunity to reflect on the importance of the Catholic faith for their lifetime's work of scholarship. The central idea of the lecture is that Christianity has shaped Western secular culture and that in liberating itself from Christendom, the secular humanist culture of modernity has been able to carry the core values of the gospel beyond that which was possible in the fusion of the gospel and culture that Christendom represented. Exclusive humanist visions of human fulfilment have detached human happiness from religious strictures allowing groups, such as gay people, for example, to follow their own life projects with freedom and respect. In his outline of a Catholic Modernity, Taylor seeks to follow the vision of the reform of the Catholic Church at the Second Vatican Council, which accepts a differentiation of Church and state, and rejects a fusion of the gospel with a culture that had formerly characterised Christendom.

However, as well as the gains of having moved beyond this fusion of faith and culture, most notably in a greater acceptance of mutual tolerance and difference visions of life, a significant loss has occurred. This loss, according to Taylor, is that in eliminating the transcendental horizon of human fulfilment in God, exclusive humanisms overlook the conditions which make full human freedom and compassion possible. As a result, exclusive humanisms have a tendency to aim higher than their value resources can reach. The case that Taylor uses to illustrate this point is that of the value of universal human rights and compassion which, whilst deeply embedded in the secular project of Western modernity seems to rely on a transcendental origin to this universalism such as that all humans are made in the image and likeness of God. Furthermore, the tendency of exclusive humanisms to view their horizon only within the immanent frame of historical time means that humanist projects have had a tendency to enforce their visions and so undermine the very conditions of freedom which

---

4   See Taylor 1999.

they are meant to be committed to. A lack of a transcendental horizon of eschatological time means history is all there is and all must be fulfilled in it by the secular project of modernity. The resulting haste to achieve the pure vision and the time pressure to realise this over-intensifies the self-belief of humanist projects such that persecutions, intolerance, and ideological battles have resulted in the opposite of the free and compassionate society. Such a vision of the free and compassionate society as represented by Kant's moral and political philosophy, for example, has left in its wake the bloodshed of the French Revolution, the persecutions of the Communist project, and the mass slaughter of the Jewish people in German fascism, as well as much of the gains of the separation of Christianity and culture in the modern age.

Moreover, within modern secular democracies the entropy of the resources of universal solidarity and compassion is evident as countries around the world move to protect their own citizens in times of crisis. The "spiritual lobotomy", as Taylor calls it of exclusive humanism results in a levelled down model of human fulfilment that drains resources of universal solidarity and compassion that spiritual figures such as Mother Theresa, Mahatma Gandi, and Jean Vanier inspire in others. Without such inspirational figures that go beyond the right and the just, exclusive humanisms are left with celebrities such as Bob Geldof, Bono, and the Live Aid project as the embodiment of the good society. Good as these exclusive humanist projects are they lack the resources to inspire sustainable compassion and to transcend the ordinary beneficence of modernity and point to a universal solidarity. Spiritual visions of religious traditions such as Christianity which sustain care for the poor, the sick, orphans, and the dying, can so easily go to the wall when purely immanent humanist values screen them out as illusory. The search for a new positive correlation between the advances of exclusive humanism and such a transcendental vision characterises the program of a Catholic Modernity as sketched by Taylor in his Dayton lecture.

Yet, it is obvious that for some the notion of a Catholic Modernity is an oxymoron. Anti-religious groups in advanced modernity form a strange alliance with new forms of Ultramontanist Catholicism to reject the view that Catholicism can find a positive correlation with late modernity. From the side of those anti-religious groups, Catholicism is a thing of the past and no longer a rational part of a modern world governed and understood according the laws of science. Its continued existence is due to various reactionary factors against modernity which coalesce in religions such as Catholicism and other traditionalist interest groups such as monarchists and political dictatorships. From the side of Ultramontanist Catholics, modernity is the result of original sin, a product of the sin of pride in believing we can go it alone without God and use our autonomy against the source of freedom itself.[5] This counter modern impulse has found significant embedding in some new ecclesial movements and in certain aspects of John Paul IIs and Benedict XVI's papacies, though one needs to be careful of

---

5   See Hellemans 2001; 2010: 173-192.

over-simplistic readings of this especially when one takes into account developments in church teaching concerning other religious traditions.[6] The framework of Catholic Modernity unsurprisingly rejects both these positions and advances the view on the normative basis of a legitimate reading of the Second Vatican Council that Catholicism and modernity are intrinsically connected and even require one another for healthy development. The acceptance of the legitimate autonomy of the secular realm of human freedom in *Gaudium et Spes* 59, which itself built upon the teaching of Vatican I on the "two orders of knowledge" (First Vatican Council Chapter 4 on faith and reason), grounds the position of a Catholic Modernity that human freedom is legitimately expressed in building culture and society.[7]

3. A new view of the history of modernity

In recent times, since around the 1980s, intensive debates have taken place in the humanities and social sciences about the nature and scope of modernity. These have been sometimes provoked by the deniers of modernity, the postmodernists, who have tended to see rationality as inter-twined with aspects of power that negated the legitimacy of the claim of reason to being a universal normative basis of modernity. Interventions by thinkers such as Jürgen Habermas have defended the universal claims of modernity against such postmodernist critics.[8] Other thinkers such as Ulrich Beck in his highly influential *Risk Society. Towards a New Modernity* have claimed that modernity was not over but rather undergoing a fundamental transition to what he called a "reflexive modernisation".[9] He argued that due to the breakdown in the modern class structure through global risks, such as environmental disasters, the increasing individualisation and re-organising of the relation between politics and science, the formerly differentiated and stratified modernity is being replaced by a de-differentiated and de-stratified society characterised by functional coordination and social democratisation. These social transformations led to a de-traditionalisation of family and kinship structures, a position shared by Beck's former colleague Anthony Giddens in his own social theory.[10] Not without his critics it is clear that Beck's intimations of a transformation within modernity have left significant traces that still influence contemporary discussions of modernity.[11]

---

6   For a review of these developments within the context of the Catholic Church in England and Wales, see Catholic Bishops Conference of England and Wales 2010. *Meeting God in Friend and Stranger. Fostering Respect and Mutual Dialogue Between Religions*. London: Catholic Truth Society.
7   See Carroll 2009a: 164-69.
8   See Habermas 1985.
9   See Beck 1986.
10   See Giddens 1991 and 1992.
11   See Münch 2002.

In another contemporary sociologist, Zygmunt Bauman, one finds a similar view of modern society to that proposed by Ulrich Beck and Anthony Giddens, in the contention that modernised societies are thoroughly individualised.[12] Yet, Bauman also marked a new departure in conceptualising modernity and its characteristic ethics in terms of its relation to the Holocaust. He argued that the Holocaust emerged out of the inner dynamics of modernity itself which through bureaucratic procedures strove to control and design a world that would be free of ambiguity and impurity.[13] The Holocaust was the outcome of this modern drive and became a bureaucratised mass murder. Such negative diagnoses of modern society have been common in recent social theories.

Robert Bellah's and his co-authors' thesis developed in their *Habits of the Heart: Individualism and Commitment in American Life* of the need to find forms of common cultural orientation which can offset the atomising forces of modern society is a good example of just such a diagnosis of the ills of advanced modernity. Following in the tradition of Alexis de Tocqueville's 1835 *Democracy in America*, Bellah argued that in order for democracy to reproduce itself in a healthy manner it is necessary for a dynamic relation between the public sphere of democratic debate and the private sphere of shared convictions and values to inform one another. When citizens confine themselves to the private sphere of family and community then the necessary animating values of democracy are not fed through to the public sphere and the state alone is left to administer and manage democracy in an emaciated public sphere.

No less significant than Robert Bellah's diagnosis of advanced modernity has been Jürgen Habermas's analysis of the pathological developments of modernity as a colonisation of the lifeworld in the second volume of his monumental *The Theory of Communicative Action*. Here Habermas argued that the systemic imperatives of money and power have pathologically encroached upon the normal reproductive mechanisms of the social lifeworld resulting in a distortion of the communicative action which is required to normatively ground the legitimacy of modern democracies. His later work on the nature of law in advanced modern democracies has sought to theorise just how law may act as a buffer against these systemic encroachments into the lifeworld and so protect the integrity of the normative structures of the communicative reproduction of modern democratic societies upon which the legitimacy of the Western project of modernity ultimately depends.

But not all is considered negative in the characterisation of advanced modern societies. Increasing capacities of communication and transport have all literally made a reality of what earlier writers, such as Marshall McLuhan, spoke of as "a global village" of the planet.[14] The development of such an interconnected world, of a globalised world, has produced varying theoretical analyses

---

12   See Bauman 1997: 204.
13   See Bauman 1989.
14   See McLuhan 2001.

of just what global societies are like.[15] Whilst interpretations may differ as to
the best way to describe globalised advanced modern societies (and globalisa-
tion has brought with it new threats and dangers such as global economic crises,
environmental disasters, and challenges of responsibly managing immigration),
our knowledge of world events, of the different cultures and societies which
make up our planet has never been greater. Advanced modern societies in the
West are knowledge rich societies which have applied the human capacity of
rationality to an ever increasing array of domains. It is this ability to ask questions and explore possible answers, to control the material and fabricate a virtual reality, and to invent social and cultural institutions that organise, administer, and educate citizens that has made the societies of advanced modernity in
the Western world such sought after places to live and to move to. Cities such
as London, Paris, Brussels, Berlin, New York and Chicago all attract huge
numbers of foreign migrants seeking a better life. This attests to the fact that
advanced modern societies are attractive, exciting, and inviting to many seeking
to thrive in a challenging era.[16] The qualities of economic prosperity and political stability alone do not explain this positive outlook. Whilst these are highly
important qualities one has also to consider the open, tolerant, and generous
nature of Western societies to really understand what it is that continues to draw
countless migrants to leave all and risk a new future in a new homeland. This
combination of prosperity and openness, of the chance for a better life and at the
same time the opportunity to live in a free and open society with democratic
accountability, responsibility for poorer countries, and concern for social equality within Western countries makes advanced modern societies with all their
challenges and problems so attractive places for people to live in. As the economic prosperity of countries such as Brazil, Russia, India, China, and South
Africa begins to reshape the global economic landscape the West still provides
the best example of democratic and free societies on offer at this time in the
world's history. The recent conflicts in Tunisia, Egypt, Libya, and Syria all testify to the desire of people's around the world to live in a democratic society.
The ability of the West to integrate, tolerate, and secure a variety of peoples,
religious traditions, and lifestyle choices testifies to the quality of pluralistic
democratic Western societies in the contemporary world. It is this ability to
combine a range of differences in stable and open societies that are relatively
prosperous which characterises what one might call the "democratic genius" of
late modern Western societies. And, it is just such an ability which the program
of Catholic Modernity can learn from. Tending to exclude other positions and
also, to a certain extent, often adopting a degree of tribalism Catholicism has a
history of dealing poorly with difference. It is no wonder that Charles Taylor
admits that the advances of secular modernity over against the former fusion of
the gospel and culture are not to be traded away by a return to the Western pe-

---

15   See Goldblatt, Perraton, Held, McGrew (eds). 1999.
16   See Zakaria 2008:258-59.

riod of Christendom.[17] The ability of Catholic Modernity to appropriately situate itself within advanced modernity whilst avoiding the dual traps of attempting to colonise it or shrinking to a marginalised corner of Western society defines the prospective location of this program for advanced modernity.

Such contemporary secular social scientific analyses of modern society provide a synchronic view of the current problems and opportunities which constitute the modern situation. However, they often fail to provide a diachronic (historical) analysis of how societies came to be like this. In providing a distinctive confessional reading of modernity, the program of a Catholic Modernity distinguishes itself from those analyses which overly homogenise the reading of modernity as simply a secular and non-confessionally structured reality. Classical social theorists, such as Max Weber, viewed the story of the emergence of modernity is intimately bound up with the story of the emergence of Protestantism. Forged in the nineteenth century early German social theory together with its sister disciplines of history and historiography took it for granted that the modern world was forged through a break with feudal Catholic structures and the development of an individualised and free society which thought itself within a Protestant architecture.[18] This is not necessarily to say that it was a believing Protestant vision. Often, its exemplars such as Max Weber were famously "unmusical" in religious matters. Rather, it is to say that even when the religious conviction had died out the structures of thought and patterns of culture still survived in a cultural Protestantism which fitted well with a modern bourgeois belief in progress and German unity.[19] A diachronic analysis of the emergence of these structures of thought and culture reveals theological presuppositions and methodological choices which have structured a modern secular understanding of central categories such as faith and reason, grace, nature and culture, and individual freedom and assent to a teaching Church. It is such now hidden theological presuppositions which have taken on the guise of neutral, secular, objective criteria for thinking the social realm and in the work of thinkers such as Max Weber and those who follow in his footsteps such as Jürgen Habermas, provide, what I have argued elsewhere, a Protestant account of modernity.[20]

In revealing these subterranean confessional tectonic plates of our understanding of modern society as confessionally influenced, the program of a Catholic Modernity situates itself as a different reading of modernity. Rather than following the standard interpretation of moving from a feudal society structured by the thought patterns and culture of Catholicism, to the early modern societies structured by those of Protestantism, and then eventually to those of a confessionally neutral secular society, a Catholic Modernity shows how on

---

17 See Heft, ed. 1999: 16-19.
18 See Carroll 2007: 229-54.
19 See Blackbourn 1997:293.
20 See Carroll 2007.

a number of different levels a change of confessional presuppositions makes real historical and sociological difference to our understanding of modernity. On the level of reading the history of modernity, rather than overlooking the importance of Catholicism to the creation of modern societies a Catholic Modernity recovers it. Thus, not only considering the importance of the Protestant Reformation for the creation of the modern world, a Catholic Modernity also looks at how following the Catholic Reformation, or Counter-Reformation, patterns of modernisation were fostered by Catholicism which had their own distinctive character.[21] For example, in developing a spirituality which affirmed the world, the Catholic apostolic religious order of the Society of Jesus promoted a vast array of initiatives that incarnated a spirituality which saw grace and nature, faith and reason, individual freedom and assent to a teaching Church as fully compatible with each other in a number of action domains that fitted well with the humanism of the early modern period. By the middle of the eighteenth century the Jesuits had founded over eight hundred educational centres throughout the world that had developed their own humanistic curriculum and pedagogy that would inspire many to copy them. Particular art and architectural styles were developed that expressed this new world-affirming spirituality in countless church paintings, drawings, and sculptures of the early modern period. New Christian missionary strategies, new for the Western Latin Church at least,[22] were developed in the the sixteenth and seventeenth centuries that saw the grace of God as already present in foreign and sometimes quite alien cultures. As a consequence, missionaries learnt local languages and used local customs and practices (inculturation) to express the truths of the Christian faith in ways which expressed this new spirituality of affirming the world.[23] Together with new practices of social disciplining, of church law, and of increasing bureaucratisation, all these features provide ample material for charting the Catholic contribution to modernity. In developing such an array of modern techniques and methods an equally new understanding of rationality is developed that is not seen as in opposition to faith but rather as complementary to it. Central to the differences between Protestant and Catholic conceptions of modernity would be the contrasting attitudes to reason that would either place faith in opposition to the worldly powers of humanity (fides aut ratio) or rather as one of the ways in which it could be developed (fides et ratio).

---

21   See Carroll 2009: 80-95.
22   Eastern Christianity has long developed a tradition of dialogue with other cultures through being tied with commercial and trading in the Far East. In contradistinction to Western Christianity which tended to advance through more militaristic alliances, the Church of the East pre-figured later attempts by Western Christian missionaries to inculturate the Christian faith in non-Greco-Roman cultures such as Seventh Century China. See MacCulloch 2009: 267-69.
23   Charles Taylor in his attempt to develop the idea of a Catholic Modernity draws on the missionary work of the Italian Jesuit Matteo Ricci (1552-1610) to illustrate how Catholicism and modernity have shown aspects of complementarity in the past. See Taylor 1999.

It is unfortunate, however, that historians and historical sociologists have insufficiently considered the role of Catholicism in producing the societies of the modern and advanced modern world and this, as I have argued elsewhere, is due to both an anti-Catholic bias in the emerging secular social sciences and also due to a hostile nineteenth century attitude by the Catholic Church to modernity encapsulated in what later came to be known as the "Modernist Crisis".[24] The program of a Catholic Modernity thus seeks to redress this balance and to re-inscribe the story of Catholicism in the narrative of the emergence of modernity and in the range of world affirming action domains that have been inspired by this Catholic Reformation spirituality. Moreover, as Bernard Yack has argued, it seeks to dethrone a certain overly homogenised conception of modernity that has simplified modernisation as an integrated process.[25] If today, within a globalised world we are becoming increasingly aware that European patterns of modernisation are not necessarily the global pattern of modernisation, then also within Western modernity far too much homogenisation has been taken for granted. In portraying Western modernity as primarily a Protestant Modernity, the role of Catholicism has been obscured and has provided an understanding of the Church and world relation as mediated through Protestantism. The program of Catholic Modernity seeks to redress this balance and to recover the historical role of Catholicism in forming the modern world and to highlight the revolutionary turn of the Catholic Church towards the world that took place at the Second Vatican Council and which, despite some countervoices, still structures an affirming attitude by the Catholic Church to the modern world.

Explicating the relevance of confessional influences on our narratives of modernity is also important as it corrects often standard accounts of the origins of the secular state. One only needs a cursory knowledge of modern political theory to understand that the origins of the secular lie in the perception that religion when not controlled leads to social division and conflict. From Thomas Hobbes's *Leviathan* through to John Rawls's *Political Liberalism* and Jürgen Habermas's *An Awareness of What is Missing* the picture is clear. The secular is required to provide a public space in which private religious views are held in check by the state, used as motivational resources for political discourse, and translated into a publically available language that secular citizens can understand. Though accentuating different aspects of the public-private split, what unites these quite different thinkers is the view that, left unchecked, religion provides an irrational counter-voice to the public reason of the secular state, which may threaten at any moment to fundamentally destabilise it. This oppositional model of the secular to the religious sphere clearly has historical origins. The seventeenth century wars of religion in Europe, most especially the Thirty Years War of 1618-1648, left a memory of religious conflict destabilising po-

---

24 See Carroll 2010.
25 See Yack 1997.

litical stability and removing the possibility of coming to rational agreement about matters of fundamental religious conviction.[26] In viewing the secular as in fundamental opposition to the religious one can easily gain the false though nevertheless commonly assumed impression that the origins of the secular lie outside of the religious in a scientific or rationalistic mentality.[27]

The recent work by Charles Taylor, *A Secular Age*, makes an important contribution in this regard. He narrates the origins of our current secular age as starting from the reform movements in both Protestantism and Catholicism in the early modern period leading to Deism and eventually to exclusive humanisms which make no reference whatsoever to God or the transcendental realm. Taylor's genealogy of secular modern societies is interesting because rather than viewing the secularity of modernity as emerging separate from its religious origins, he ties religious developments and secularity very much together. Reminiscent of earlier debates between Hans Blumenberg and Karl Löwith,[28] and the Weberian thesis of Marcel Gauchet,[29] Taylor argues that the modern age emerges out of a long process of secularisation which itself was initiated by internal reforms within Christianity.[30] But rather than Gauchet's claim that Christianity results in the "exit from religion", Taylor concludes that the reality is not so cut and dried. Rather, he argues that our secular age presents a complex epistemic environment in which both religious belief and unbelief are possible although he admits that in the West the default setting has shifted to unbelief. Rather than modern science and rationalism providing the origins of secularity, these developments come much later when Deism has already gained a major foothold and only then does the so-called "subtraction account" of secularity come into being. By "subtraction account", Taylor refers to the view that once religion has been shown up to be nothing more than a superstitious overlay covering the truth about humanity, then science and reason can get on with the real job of discovering the nature of human beings and their place in the cosmos. Religion in this "subtraction account" is thus equivalent to anti-humanism. Whether it be in the forms of Darwinian natural selection, Galilean physics, Feuerbachian alienation of the subject, Freudian psychoanalysis, or the Nietzschian will to power, scientific reason is seen as clearing the way to the truth about human beings after the illusions of an anti-naturalism or transcendentalism which confined humanity to the state of child-like dependence. It is this later "subtraction account" as outlined by Taylor which chiefly gave rise to the current perception of an oppositional understanding of the relation between the secular and the religious.

---

26   See, for example, Rawls 1993.
27   For an recent interesting symbiotic view of religion and secular liberal democracy that avoids both the oppositional secular model and traditionalist religious perspective, see Stout 2005.
28   See Wallace 1981.
29   See Gauchet 1985.
30   See Taylor 2007: Part I, "The Work of Reform".

In providing an alternative genealogy of the secular thinkers such as Charles Taylor have gone some considerable way in articulating the historical origins of modernity in the various religious reforms. In the program of a Catholic Modernity, this oppositional model of the secular is further broken down between the overly Protestant dominated narratives of modernity (and even Taylor's share in this to a degree),[31] and so the account of the genealogy of modernity is corrected from this bias which has dogged it since the nineteenth century.[32] The importance of providing an alternative account of modernity for advanced modernity is twofold. First, it allows advanced modernity to consider alternative pathways to conceiving the relations between faith and reason, grace and nature, authority and freedom, which have been obscured through following only Protestant inspired accounts of these relations which tend towards the oppositional. Protestant accounts of reason have typically opposed the Catholic complementary model of *fides et ratio* and rather followed the *fides aut ratio* pattern,[33] which has meant that religion is viewed as incompatible with science and rationality. The rallying calls of the Protestant Reformation: *Sola Scriptura*, *Sola Fide* and *Sola Gratia* decry human effort and human reason as vehicles of salvation. The unintended consequence of this separation is that secular autonomous human action and reason will be gradually removed from the drama of salvation and emptied of religious significance. This Protestant account of the trajectory of modernity has dominated in the narratives of modernity and has played a major role in producing the oppositional secular model, which structures modern Western societies' approaches to religion today.

A significant moment in this evacuation of religion from the understanding of the secular arises paradoxically in nineteenth century liberal Protestantism, in which Christianity was effectively reduced to morality as sacramental conceptions of grace and nature were replaced by Kantian inspired accounts of free moral action.[34] It would be later Protestant thinkers such as Karl Barth who would denounce this liberal Protestantism for reducing the gospel to a morality serving cultural and political ends. But this so-called 'dialectical theology' would in its turn set apart revelation and cultural mediation of the gospel because of an understandable desire to prevent the gospel being instrumentalised for merely immanent human ends. The legacy of Protestant trajectories of modernity have been to either over-identify the gospel with culture as in liberal Protestantism or to over-distance it from the autonomous realm of action and reason as in Barth's dialectical theology. Shorn of a sacramental imagination, it is little surprise that Protestant Modernity has left as part of its legacy an oppositional secular.

---

31   See Joas 2009.
32   See O'Malley 2000.
33   See Carroll 2007: 167-176.
34   See Carroll 2009: 62-63.

The consequence of the dominance of Protestant accounts of modernity has been that in producing an oppositional secular, religions are viewed with suspicion as being irrational and at best confined to the private sphere. The current emergence of religions into the public sphere is thus a phenomenon that modern secular societies forged in the oppositional tradition are struggling to cope with.[35] Whilst the oppositional model of the secular may suit certain forms of Protestantism which naturally separate public and private, such as Pietism, when it comes to understanding religious traditions like Roman Catholicism and Islam who do not separate religion and daily life in this way, secular modern societies forged in the tradition of an oppositional mentality have found this much more difficult to cope with. It is such stresses and strains on the modern secular mentality that have given rise to attempts to understand the emergence of religion into the public sphere in an ever increasing array of theories of a post-secular reality in the West. The program of a Catholic Modernity should be understood as one contribution to these current debates which attempts to both uncover diachronic trajectories of modernity that have been overlooked and synchronic analyses of the place of religion in contemporary societies.

4. Some gains for advanced modernity from a catholic modernity

In theorising a Catholic Modernity one should raise the question of just what late modernity might have to gain from such a program. I would like to consider this question by focussing on two major areas were such an encounter could be beneficial. First, that of the important lessons which can be learned by advanced modernity from the encounter of world religions within the modern world, which has very much typified the program of Catholic Modernity since the Second Vatican Council. I shall look at just why it is that advanced modernity seems often to lack the ability to relate to this encounter within contemporary societies in a positive and constructive manner. Second, I shall take up Charles Taylor's suggestion of how exclusive humanist positions characterising advanced modernity can better fulfil their own normative projects of solidarity and compassion by opening out to the possibility of a transcendental horizon of human freedom and values.

4.1 Interreligious dialogue and the normative reshaping of the secular

In the period prior to the Second Vatican Council the normative position of the Catholic Church with respect to other religious traditions and to secularity was pretty much one of condemnation. The modernist crisis in the nineteenth and early twentieth centuries highlight this position in a particularly dramatic way. However, the Second Vatican Council represents a rapprochement with secular modernity, democracy, and other religious traditions that has deepened

---

35   See Casanova 1994.

since the Council. The recent teaching document of the Catholic Bishops of England and Wales, *Meeting God in Friend and Stranger. Fostering Respect and Mutual Understanding Between the Religions*, states that "the present-day Catholic Church's promotion of interreligious dialogue has marked a new departure, setting the Church on a new path....We can see how God is thus inviting the Church to reconsider her relationship to those religions hitherto regarded in a negative or very distant way".[36] This turn to dialogue inaugurated by the Second Vatican Council is normative and something that Charles Taylor calls in another context a "ratchet effect". That is to say, it is irreversible. This has implications for our understanding of the very nature of the secular itself if, as I have argued above, we have inherited an oppositional model of the secular then this has received in major part its justification from the fact that Christian confessions, and religious traditions have mutually excluded one another from a relationship of dialogue. Forged in this heritage of confessional and interreligious strife the development of an oppositional secular sphere quite naturally understood the religious domain to be incapable of dialogue. However, with the dialogical shift of Catholicism and other religious traditions in recent years the paradox is that it is often the un-dialogical secularists who seem to be more dogmatic that those of religious conviction.[37] Recent interventions by the so-called "New Atheists" have illustrated their inability to enter into dialogue with religious traditions because their own self-identity is constructed on the basis of opposition to religion. To accept the fundamental conditions of dialogue, namely, mutual respect and tolerance would have the corrosive consequence of denaturing the very oppositional identity which constitutes their position. It is thus unsurprising that their tone tends to be polemical rather than dialogical and this steers them in the direction of a performative contradiction as they are supposedly arguing for democratic freedom and a tolerant society.

In arguing that there has been a dialogical turn in religion I am, of course, not denying that there are also fundamentalist elements in most world religious traditions and that these reject the normative basis of democracy in mutual respect and dialogue. However, as documents such as *Meeting God in Friend and Stranger* make clear these are not the legitimate voice of the Catholic Church and nor are they the legitimate voice of the vast majority of other religious traditions.[38] Consequently, the legitimacy of a fundamentally oppositional secular is undermined by this shift to dialogue in the world religions. This seems a major part of why it is that in contemporary Western societies religious issues are often poorly understood and handled by governments.[39] Shaped by former oppositional narratives which at best have relegated the "problem of religion" to the private sphere, government policies and legal arrangements are bending un-

---

36   *Meeting God in Friend and Stranger*, p. 51.
37   For a review of the New Atheists and their inability to come to terms with this dialogical turn in religion, see McGrath 2011.
38   See Barnes 2002.
39   See Pope Benedict XVI 2010: 52.

der the strain of religious traditions which have taken the dialogical turn and which are not content to remain confined to the private sphere.[40]

It is this dialogical turn in religions that can provide advanced modernity with much needed normative resources for dealing with contemporary issues of religious diversity and multiculturalism. There is, as *Meeting God in Friend and Stranger* puts it a "change in government thinking coming from the welcome realisation that religious communities are an extremely important part of civil society, with a contribution no other group can provide".[41] Such change in government thinking is due to a realisation that the normative resources of modern democratic societies are often scare in terms of fostering solidarity, political engagement, and citizenship. The potential civilising effect of religions on modern societies through various forms of faith-based action such as volunteering, compassionate service of the poor and marginalised, and educational projects is undoubtedly an enrichment that they provide for all Western societies. Yet, even more than these internal aspects of civil society involvement there is another area in which advanced modernity can greatly benefit from the program of a Catholic Modernity, namely, in matters of facing human suffering and death.

The secular horizon of modern societies is often poorly equipped to deal with the tragic aspects of human life such as illness, suffering, and death. Short of resources of existential meaning purely secular programs in advanced modernity often turn to chemical solutions to extinguish the pain and existential angst that face us at such times. These solutions, whilst having an important contribution to make, do not provide adequate support in these moments of human life. In many studies of death and dying it seems that these limit issues of human life are fundamentally concerned with the spiritual problems of human beings and these can only be met by spiritual means.[42] Religious and spiritual traditions in advanced modernity provide often scarcely available resources of existential meaning. These are, of course, not always provided by the traditional institutional religious as the growth in new age spiritualities has demonstrated. However, it is still the case that in hospices and hospitals in the Western world chaplains of all religious traditions provide the vast majority of spiritual care to the sick and dying which is of great value even to those beyond their own official traditions.

The importance in modernity of limit questions at the end of life is something which has not gone unnoticed by social theorists. Max Weber, for exam-

---

40   See, for example, the intervention of the Archbishop of Canterbury on the matter of incorporating aspects of sharia law into UK law, available on his website at http://www. archbishop-ofcanterbury.org/articles.php/1137/archbishops-lecture-civil-and-religious-law-in-england-a-religious-perspective .

41   *Meeting God in Friend and Stranger*, p. 74.

42   See Cobb, Mark. 2001. *The Dying Soul. Spiritual Care at the End of Life*. Open University Press; and Stanworth, Rachel. 2003. *Recognising Spiritual Needs in People Who Are Dying*. Oxford: Oxford University Press.

ple, noted in analysing the world religions according to their attitudes to the theodicy question that as the rationalisation of modern societies increases there is also a growing need to understand the meaning of suffering and death.[43] This can lead some to question the very meaning of life and within a current dominant naturalistic paradigm it is not at all evident how such resources of human meaning can be provided and sustained.[44] It is just such possibilities of meaning and hope in the face of the finitude of human life which religious traditions can provide. As Charles Taylor notes, in recovering the Catholic trajectory of modernity, Western societies can make available resources of meaning which have shaped the normative horizon of modernity especially in its universalistic humanitarian aspirations.[45] This is not at all to suggest that secular citizens should adopt a Catholic religiosity. Rather, the claim being made is that recovering one of the constitutive traditions of Western secular modernity allows resources of existential meaning to be made available in the face of suffering and death (perhaps only in a vicarious manner), to Western modern societies that are not necessarily incompatible with a rational outlook on life. When a complementary relation between faith and reason is given space to be entertained then it can dethrone a monopolistic attitude of the necessary incompatibility of faith and reason which may be sufficient to expand the normative horizon of some in modernity to be better able to face questions of meaning, suffering and death. The legacy of the oppositional nature of the modern secular has perhaps unnecessarily closed off an avenue of existential meaning by so structuring the faith and reason relation that even the vicarious route might seem fantastic and impossible. In holding the faith and reason legacy alive, the program of Catholic Modernity may well have resources of existential meaning that go well beyond those adherents of the Catholic faith.

4.2 Transcendence from within

The second major area that advanced modernity can benefit from in seriously engaging with a Catholic Modernity is that of recovering lost resources of solidarity and compassion that have their origin in a transcendental vision of the world and of the human person. As Charles Taylor has argued, the universalistic impulses of advanced modernity have their origins in the Judeo-Christian tradition of viewing the natural order as made by a creator God and the human person as made in the image and likeness of God. These accounts of the cosmos and of humanity have serious ontological and normative implications which advanced modernity could draw upon to help address its current environmental crisis and the crisis of the compassion and solidarity deficits that are all too apparent in the modern Western world.

---

43   See Carroll 2007: 94-101.
44   See De Caro and Macarthur (eds.) 2010.
45   See Heft (ed.) 1999: 30.

In the case of our current environmental crisis, it has become apparent over many years that the great world religions have fostered attitudes and behaviour of respect for the integrity of creation that purely materialistic accounts of the world struggle to provide. Considering nature as the creation shifts the onto-logical status of matter from being merely the inert given to representing the gift of the creator God who wills that humanity nurture and care for it as a divine inheritance that can only be generously received through wise stewardship. Even more, in religious traditions such as Catholicism, nature itself has been considered to manifest a *vistigium trinitatis* or a trace of the Holy Trinity in its very structure. In this account of the world, matter and all it represents is more than simply a valueless thing, devoid of any intrinsic meaning, but rather it manifests the creative generosity of the giver of life. It becomes a place to en-counter the holy and as such it is to be treated with reverence and care. As a result of such religious attitudes, the Catholic Church together with other Chris-tian denominations and world religions has fostered national and international meetings to promote a sense of "ecological conversion" and "eco-justice". The development of this tradition of reflection in the Catholic Church has ancient roots but has taken a particular step forward in recent years with the writings of popes such as Paul VI, John Paul II, and Benedict XVI. Since the Second Vati-can Council, human activity has been understood as the cultivating process through which nature comes to bear more fruit and human gifts and talents are developed to the full. In the Constitution of the Church in the Modern World, *Gaudium et Spes*, the world is seen as a garden in which we are called on by God to cultivate and shape it so that all may benefit and rejoice in its beauty.[46] Such theological visions of nature provide an alternative ontology to the natu-ralistic materialism which has so devastated the planet and its ecosystems. Vi-sions such as that of the Catholic Church provide advanced modernity with valuable resources with which to shape human imaginations about their use of the environment. Networks such as the Global Forum of Spiritual and Parlia-mentary Leaders promote these values at a global level and throughout the world faiths. Recent meetings in Oxford (1988), Moscow (1990), Rio (1992), and Kyoto (1993) have focussed on the role of religions in tackling the envi-ronmental crisis, and the International Union for Conservation organised the first panel on "Spirituality and Conservation" at the World Conservation Con-gress in Barcelona in 2009.

In his 1990 message on the environment Pope John Paul II called the eco-logical crisis a "moral crisis", a theme which has been developed by Pope Benedict XVI in his call for the need to develop a "human ecology" which de-velops a lifestyle that respects the environment and which treats the covenant created between humanity and nature in the Book of Genesis. This intertwining of human and ecological concerns characterises the teaching of the Catholic Church since the Second Vatican Council and portrays a Catholic vision of

---

46   See *Gaudium et Spes* paragraphs 53-62.

modernity in which humans and nature live in a harmony that is based on the ontological principle that both humans and nature have their common origin in the creative and redemptive power of God. One may even speak here with the beautiful canticle of St. Francis of Assisi in terms of "brother moon and sister sun". Such a vision promotes an ecological solidarity that is much needed by advanced modernity and because global religious traditions such as Catholicism have universal significance they have the potential to provide resources at a global level for problems which transcend national political agency. Transnational political action on issues such as environmental concern requires global visions such as that promoted within a Catholic vision of modernity in order to motivate common and concerted action to preserve our fragile environment.

No less significant is the need for advanced modern societies to find moral resources of universalistic solidarity and compassion with the poor and vulnerable not only within their own societies but between themselves and other societies especially those in the Southern hemisphere who experience extreme challenges of poverty, war, and environmental threat. Again the global spread of Catholicism, especially in the Southern hemisphere, aids a conscientisation of the richer advanced modern societies to the plight of countries in great poverty and in social unrest. One might read the development of modern Catholic Social Teaching since the nineteenth century until today as attempting to articulate the social dimension of a Catholic Modernity in which the principles of universal solidarity, compassion, and justice express the normative resources present within the fundamental vision of the human person as made in the image and likeness of God. Such a normative vision of the human person transcends national political recognition of subjects as citizens and grounds a universalistic conception of "divine citizenship" based on the common "territorial" belonging in the Kingdom of God both on earth and in heaven. This interpenetration of the Kingdom of God within history and society allows for transcendence within the world to be experienced that thinkers from St. Paul and St. Augustine onwards have expressed as our mutual belonging to the City of God whilst also living in the earthly city. The moral consequence of this ontological vision of the human person serves to motivate countless Catholic initiatives of social solidarity between individuals, parish communities, school and university establishments, dioceses, and Catholic non-governmental organisations, such as the San'Egidio community, that are well known throughout the world. They make visible and manifest the moral vision of a Catholic Modernity which transcends national and regional solidarities and reaches out universally to all peoples of the planet regardless of religious or political affiliations. Such an impressive network of global concern witnesses to advanced modern societies that compassion and solidarity are never exhausted when they are grounded in such a transcendental vision. It is this vision which helps to sustain many Catholic networks to engage in the most difficult and arduous social and moral action when other organisations seem exhausted and suffering from "compassion fatigue". In fact, thinkers such as Charles Taylor and Jürgen Habermas both notice the significance of such faith-based action in the secular public sphere of advanced modern societies and Habermas notes that it seems a particular strength of religious communities to have preserved a sensitivity to the poor and marginalised that the secu-lar postmetaphysical societies of advanced modernity are currently struggling to reproduce and to maintain.[47]

5. The gains for a catholic modernity from advanced modernity

How can the program of Catholic Modernity benefit from its encounter with the challenges presented to it by advanced modernity? Answering this question is important if the program of Catholic Modernity is to be presented as truly dialogical and not simply, as often in former times, as the teaching Church educating the learning world. I intend to demonstrate that the program of a Catholic Modernity can enter into mutual learning processes with the wider secular society of advanced modernity that will help Catholic Modernity to develop its own program.

5.1 Catholic modernity in advanced Modern Plural Democracies

In order to consider just how Catholic Modernity can learn from its engagement with advanced modern societies, I would like to focus on the recent history of dealing with child sexual abuse that has caused great scandal for the Catholic Church. Several reports, such as the Ferns Report published in 2005 which was the official Irish Government report on alleged abuses in County Wexford, Ireland, have painted a picture of systematic abuse by Catholic clergy over a considerable period. This report concluded, as have many others, that there was a culture of secrecy in the hierarchy of the Church which was more concerned to protect its own image than to come to terms with the systematic sexual abuse by members of the clergy. Failures to report to the police incidents of sexual abuse known by the local bishop in charge, Bishop Donald J. Herlihy, and his successor Bishop Brendan Comiskey, revealed that rather than face up to these issues priests were regularly moved to other parishes. Rather than being seen as isolated incidents of individual priests and bishops further reports, such as the Murphy Report of 2005 and the Ryan Report on sexual abuse in the archdiocese of Dublin in 2009, drew similar conclusions.

Pope Benedict's pastoral letter to Irish Catholics on 19 March 2010 was unprecedented in that it openly acknowledged the widespread and systematic abuse and apologised to the victims and people of Ireland for the betrayal of trust that had happened. Referring to the many scandals around the world that have come to light in his Christmas address to the Roman Curia of 20 December 2010 he spoke with real openness when he commented, "We must ask ourselves what we can do to repair as much as possible the injustice that has oc-

---

47   See Habermas and Ratzinger 2005: 31.

curred. We must ask ourselves what was wrong in our proclamation, in our whole way of living the Christian life, to allow such a thing to happen". In this anguished appeal by Pope Benedict one can detect a real questioning of the internal difficulties facing Catholicism in the twenty-first century. I suggest that there are a number of ways in which advanced modern societies may be able to help the Church to find better ways of dealing with these issues and so to enable a Catholic Modernity to fully play its role in helping to build stable and democratic societies.[48]

The first area to consider is that of structures of governance. It is clear from the recent experience of sexual abuse within the Catholic Church that what one might call "feudal structures" of governance are still operating in the Church. By "feudal structures", I mean the tendency to keep decision making within the hands of the "feudal overlord", or in this case, the bishop and to prevent proper democratic accountability to ensure and protect that decisions made are not done so in the interest of simply protecting the image of the Church. In preventing proper scrutiny of decisions and of allowing such information to enter the appropriate channels of the public domain the Church has been operating a form of "super injunction" or so called "gagging orders" in the area of dealing with criminals within its midst. Not dissimilar to a number of recent governments' and high profile individuals' attempts to prevent the release of information into the public domain, the Catholic Church has compromised its integrity by colluding with those who have abused their power and privilege in religious ministry, to cover up criminal behaviour for the sake of protecting its corporate image. The lesson to be learnt from the democratic world of advanced modern Western societies is that in order to maintain credibility in advanced modernity nothing less than transparency will do. This does not mean, of course, that appropriate levels of discretion and privacy need to be trumped by fully blown media coverage of each and every Church matter. It does, however, mean that the Church needs to demonstrate in its dealings with abusers, its financial accounting, and structures of power, that it is open to outside and independent scrutiny and in this way demonstrate that it does not consider itself to be above the law. Secrecy clearly has its place but it has been abused in the Church to cover up dysfunctional practices that serve only the interests of corrupt individuals both within and without the Church.

If a program of Catholic Modernity is to take its place in advanced modern societies it will be necessary for church structures to be adapted to meet this transparency criterion and so to regain a trust that has been severely damaged at present. This clearly goes against much in the culture of the Church which has a tendency to see itself more as the body which gives advice to the world rather than as in need of advice from it. However, it is now beyond doubt that the dys-

---

48   See Pope Benedict's address to politicians, diplomats, and business leaders in Westminster Hall, Palace of Westminster. Pope Benedict XVI. 2010. Pp. 48-56 in *Heart Speaks Unto Heart*. London: Darton Longman and Todd.

functional nature of the current hierarchical structures will only lead to the
Catholic Church becoming even more distrusted in advanced modern societies
than it already is. As is clear from Pope Benedict's Christmas address of 2010,
the Catholic Church has teetered on the brink of a meltdown in its very institutional fabric and if it is to seriously address this problem it will require adopting
a humble and learning attitude to those who both from the inside and from the
outside of the Church have experienced its dysfunctionality.

Central, of course, to this dysfunctional mode of operating has been the
structures of power which has maintained an air of charismatic insulation
around the very ministers who have been charged with the service of the faithful. A significant part of this culture of specialness has been generated by the
priestly rule of celibacy being imposed as a sine qua non of ordained ministry.
Separated from the ordinary world of production and reproduction, ministers
have been removed from the lot of lay people and held up behind a sacred aura
of holiness. Despite the common rhetoric of the vocation of the laity, in terms of
the actual power structures of the Church priestly celibacy has been and still is
the essential entry requirement necessary to have the dignity of service within
the governance of the Church. Moreover, only men are able to play a real part in
the governance of the Church and this is without doubt a central fault line between the Catholic Church and the Western world of advanced modernity in the
twenty-first century. This position is supported by theological arguments drawing on a certain unchanging reading of tradition. However, the rational that this
reading of tradition engenders excludes woman from ordained ministry and
from the governmental structures of the Church, and, for advanced modern societies expresses a patriarchy, traditionalism, and irrationality that many consider to be defining of an outdated and oppressive Catholic Church. Why exactly God does not want women to play their part in these roles is never clearly
explained other than by appealing to the traditional precedent of the past or to a
particular gendered understanding of the relation between Christ and the Church
in Hans Urs von Balthasar's dramatic theology. This is, however, one clear area
were the culture of advanced modernity has moved beyond that of the Catholic
Church in its understanding of gender relations and power. It is difficult to
imagine a program of Catholic Modernity that did not address these gender
asymmetries and find ways of both respecting differences between men and
women and ensuring that paternalistic and patriarchal structures that marginal-
ise women are challenged and eliminated from the Church. In addressing these
issues the Catholic Church has a great deal to learn from advanced modern societies and their own struggles, which are by no means finished, to ensure political, economic, and social equality between men and women.

No less significant an area that Catholic Modernity has a great deal to learn
from in dialogue with advanced modern societies is that of the matters of sex
and sexuality. As Charles Taylor comments in his *A Secular Age*, part of the
problem of Christianity today is presenting an excarnated vision of the human

person were sex and sexuality are poorly integrated into the life of holiness.[49] Despite attempts by Pope John Paul II to develop a theology of the body, it is still the culture of the Catholic Church to equate holiness with abstinence from sexuality. This tradition goes back to the early centuries of the Christian era and has cast a long shadow over the history of Christian reflection on the body.[50] It has, moreover, encouraged an image of ordained ministry as the new form of martyrdom in which sexual renunciation takes the place of religious persecution. Such a sublimation of earthly desires into a transcendental longing for the divine clearly has its justification when chosen freely.[51] However, the cultural consequence of linking this sublimation to ministerial service has been to create a certain sacred aura around the ordained ministry that can attract candidates who have been shown to be highly unsuited to such positions of power and responsibility. In attracting such men with pathological affective desires and providing them with a platform to indulge them, the Catholic Church has served neither these men nor the communities that they have been sent to minister to. In its encounter with advanced modernity the program of Catholic Modernity will need to address the structural dynamics which have aggravated these pathological tendencies within the Catholic Church and which no doubt reach much wider than the area of sexual abuse but represent a whole network of power relations.

Not unrelated to the issue of priestly celibacy is that of the Church's attitude to homosexuality. Although, for obvious reasons, clear data is not easy to come by, it is an open secret within the Catholic Church that the ordained ministry and religious life have a much higher proportion of homosexual men than generally found in society. That this is at least in part due to the affirmation that a man receives from the faithful in renouncing his sexuality in ordained ministry is not an unreasonable assumption. As a Catholic, a homosexual man or woman is faced with the prospect of living a celibate life if they are to remain faithful to the teaching of the Church. It is therefore not surprising that the celibate lifestyle provides a place for homosexual Catholics to live in harmony with their faith and their sexuality. But those Catholics who cannot live up to this ideal are clearly faced with a dilemma that has no easy solution. Either one suspends one's belief in the official teaching of the Church and leads an active homosexual life in relative secrecy or one lives a life which is affectively impoverished. Advanced modern societies, although far from free of prejudicial attitudes to homosexuals, are clearly making important steps in law and social acceptance to redress these attitudes and practices of condemning active homosexuality. This is another area in which a Catholic Modernity can learn a great deal from advanced modern societies.

---

49 See Taylor 2007.
50 See Brown 1988.
51 See Sipe 1996.

Fundamentally the issue comes down to real dialogue with people of homosexual orientation rather than simply pronouncing a priori doctrines and policies which do not fit their experience. It is the ability of advanced modern societies to listen to such people and to open out to encounter other ways of life and sexuality that has led them to learn that homosexual people have a right to live in a way which allows them to be truly themselves and not to have to pretend that they are something that they are not. The tendency of the Catholic Church to preach at people rather than to listen to their experience is in part due to a dogmatic structure which forecloses possible experience as already abhorrent. No doubt a certain conception of the non-historical nature of natural law has fostered an understanding of human sexuality which is increasingly out of step with how this is understood in advanced modern societies. Sometimes condemning the views on sexuality of these societies as degenerate and hedonistic, the Catholic Church has been unable to hear the prophetic voices of those within and without the Church who have called for reform on these matters.[52] In developing the program of Catholic Modernity listening to such voices in advanced modernity will help the Catholic Church to develop its vision of the human person as made in the image and likeness of God and for the fullness of life.

A final area of learning from advanced modern societies that I would like to consider is that of the use of the new media. This is an area in which the Church has already begun to make enormous progress in how it communicates the gospel message to the wider world and often to those who are outside its official fold. The success of the British Jesuits in launching a podcast called "Pray-as-you-go" has been extraordinary since it was launched in 2007. In the four years of its existence it has been downloaded five million times! The podcast consists of a guided meditation or prayer of the day which lasts around fifteen minutes and can be played on an MP3 player on the way to work or college or at any time of the day. Such use of new media technologies characteristic of the culture of advanced modernity is something groups within the Church have already adapted for their own uses and purposes and is demonstrably one way in which the Church has learned from the technological developments of advanced modern societies.

The mediatisation of papal visits around the world is clearly another example of just how the Catholic Church and advanced modern societies have entered into symbiotic relations for the mutual benefit of both parties. The recent coverage of the papal visit to the United Kingdom in September 2010 was an extraordinary success with numbers tuning into the BBC coverage of the event exceeding expectations which had been dampened down by significant negative coverage of the Catholic Church prior to the actual papal visit. The use of the new media and television broadcasting by a broad range of religious groups has even caused some sociologists to speak of this new reality as the catalyst in cre-

---

52   See Allision 2001.

ating a post-secular society.[53] Whatever the implication of the explosion of the use of new media by religious groups there is no doubt that these mediations of religious messages are reaching people in ways in which parish structures are unable to compete with. They may well even be new forms of Church in advanced modernity which sociological analyses of traditional parish Church attendance are not registering in surveys. Corresponding to a greater individualisation within advanced modern societies such forms of religious belief and belonging may well already represent ways in which Catholic Modernity has adapted itself to the new networks of advanced modern societies.

The witness to the Catholic Church of late modern democratic societies is clearly that differences can be held together by mutual respect, understanding and an ability to listen without prejudging what is and what is not normal human experience. The modern desire of the Catholic Church expressed at the Second Vatican Council of wanting to enter into dialogue with the world rather than simply to condemn it motivates the program of Catholic Modernity to find ways of taking this courageous step further and to allow people of advanced modern societies to hear a voice which has been far too often obscured by an inability of the Church to face up to its own blindness, faults, and failings.

6. Conclusion

No doubt the picture of Catholic Modernity sketched above could be objected to as representing both a too liberal and benign image of the Catholic Church and as having little chance of evolving in the proposed direction. Furthermore, the development of counter-modern Catholic programs at the present time with much more conservative agendas concerning Church teaching and stances to the advanced modern world is clearly a reality which makes the landscape of Catholic programs on modernity much more varied than that proposed simply by the program of Catholic Modernity sketched above. Clearly, a systematic development of a Catholic Modernity will require a much more complex account of this varied landscape in greater detail than in possible in this context. But on the question of considering the program of a Catholic Modernity to be hopelessly utopian one needs to be careful of conflating the theological sacramental imagination of the Church and world relation as developed at the Second Vatican Council with simply a political strategy of rapprochement with the modern world. This all too common political reading of the Council makes the secularist assumption that what is really going on beneath the theology is the political. Understandable though this assumption may be it essentially trades on a category mistake that description of the reality is only possible in secularist terms. This epistemological assumption presumes that the theological self-understanding of the Church is merely an epiphenomal description of an underling political reality. As such, political descriptions of the Church as either

---

53   See Eder 2002.

"liberal" or "conservative" are seen to unmask the truth of what is really going on in the reality described by the term "Church". This attempted undermining of the legitimacy of theological discourse is itself part of the dogmatic legacy of a certain secularist understanding of the Enlightenment that has in many quarters come in for serious questioning today.[54] But in challenging the hegemony of secularist readings of reality the program of Catholic Modernity does not seek to de-legitimise the perspective of social scientific enquiry but rather to place it into a truly dialogical relation with theological discourse and this needs to be a dialogue of equals if it is to move beyond the often banal power plays of providing the single "master discourse of the totality".

The recovery at the Second Vatican Council of a Christological humanism and an intrinsic conception of grace has fundamentally shifted the theology of the Catholic Church such that outright condemnation of the world is no longer a possibility in Catholic theology as it was prior to these theological shifts. Moreover, it is now clear that such attitudes of condemnation really owe their origins more to political wrangling between the church authorities than deeply worked out theological principles which by all consent should animate the orientations of the Catholic Church. When these theological transformations are taken into account one can more easily understand that the fault lines currently exposed between the Catholic Church and advanced modern societies are often contingent matters of church disciplinary law than deeply worked out theological positions. They stand out precisely because in the general new context of the Catholic Church's affirmative stance to the modern world they seem to contradict or at least deviate from standard agreed norms in advanced modern societies. Take, for example, the issue of women's ordination to the priesthood. In advanced modern societies it is in principle, at least if not always in practice, the case that men and women can freely choose their occupations without fear of discrimination. The principle of being excluded from the possibility of serving in ordained ministry contradicts this principle in the eyes of many. The response of the Catholic Church to this exclusion is to say that this is not a matter of discrimination but rather a matter of divine decree that God only wants men to serve in the ordained ministry of the priesthood and that because of this the Church does not have the power to change this discipline. In order for this argument to be accepted by advanced modern societies who recognise the legitimacy of the theological discourse as a rational discourse it would be necessary for the Catholic Church to explain why it thinks God wants men only to serve in this way. It is clear at the present time that convincing theological arguments are not forthcoming from the Church and that is why simply dogmatic pronouncements of "no further discussion" have been enforced to close debate down. Whilst such shows of strength reassure certain groups that the Church does not simply go along with each new fad of the modern world they are not convincing as rational theological arguments to anyone outside the Church and

---

54   See, for example, Milbank 1990.

in fact to many within the Church either. Given the Catholic Church's commitment to faith and reason it will be necessary for these conflictual areas with advanced modern societies to be resolved by rational argumentation and not simply by dogmatic decree if the Church is to remain faithful to its own tradition.

But one would also misunderstand the program of Catholic Modernity if it were to be seen as simply the Catholic Church accommodating itself to advanced modern societies. As Catholic Modernity is truly a dialogical program committed to rational dialogue it will be necessary for the equally dogmatic and often irrational positions held by advanced modern secular societies towards religion and religious traditions to be put into question. I have considered above the origins of this in the formation of an oppositional model of the secular. Encounter between the program of Catholic Modernity and advanced modern societies will increasingly expose often dominant secularist dogmatic positions that have very little to do with democratic argument and debate and a great deal to do with anti-religious prejudice. The attitude of the French state towards Islam and its recent banning of Islamic dress in the public forum and even the attitude of the French state to the teaching of theology at state universities are just some examples of how unchecked dogmatic and secularist attitudes can be equally un-dialogical and embodied in the policies of modern democracies.

In bringing the program of Catholic Modernity truly into dialogue with advanced modern societies it seems as if the real challenge will be overcoming the often dominant irrational and dogmatic voices within both the Church and secular advanced modern societies, which seek to preserve the status quo of their respective dogmatic positions. However, if both advanced modern societies and the Catholic Church are to overcome their current problems only a truly dialogical engagement between these traditions will provide the means to learn new ways forward. Whilst dogmatic shows of strength sometimes provide short-term reassurance they seldom develop processes of mutual learning or build long-term strategies of survival and development. The logic of development is clearly on the side of rational engagement though one should always recognise that the historical dynamics of development are seldom linear.

References

Allision, James. 2001. *Faith Beyond Resentment: Fragments Catholic and Gay*. London: DLT.

Barnes, Michael. 2002. *Theology and the Dialogue of Religions*. Cambridge: Cambridge University Press.

Bauman, Zygmunt. 1989. *Modernity and the Holocaust*. Cambridge: Polity Press.

Beck, Ulrich. 1992. *Risk Society. Towards a New Modernity*. London: Sage.

Bellah, Robert N. *et al*. 1986. *Habits of the Heart. Individualism and Commitment in American Life*. New York: Harper Perennial.

Benedict XVI. 2010. *Heart Speaks Unto Heart. The Complete Addresses and Homilies*. London: DLT.

Blackbourn, David. 1997. *The Long Nineteenth Century*. London: Fontana Press.

Brown, David. 1988. *The Body and Society. Men, Women and Sexual Renunciation in Early Christianity*. New York: Columbia University Press.

Caro, Mario de & David Macarthur. 2010. *Naturalism and Normativity*. New York: Columbia University Press.

Carroll, Anthony J. & James Hanvey. 2005. *On the Way to Life*. London: CES.

Carroll, Anthony J. 2007. *Protestant Modernity. Weber, Secularisation, and Protestantism*. Scranton and London: University of Scranton Press.

Carroll, Anthony J. 2009a. Church and Culture: Protestant and Catholic Modernities. *New Blackfriars* 90: (1026) 163-177.

Carroll, Anthony J. 2009b. The Importance of Protestantism in Max Weber's Theory of Secularisation. *European Journal of Sociology* 50: (1) 61-95.

Carroll, Anthony J. 2010. The Philosophical Foundations of Catholic Modernism. Pp. 38-55 in Oliver P. Rafferty (ed.). *George Tyrrell and Catholic Modernism*. Dublin: Four Courts Press.

Casanova, José. 1994. *Public Religions in the Modern World*. Chicago: University of Chicago Press.

Catholic Bishops of England and Wales. 2010. *Meeting God in Friend and Stranger. Fostering Respect and Understanding Between the Religions*. London: Catholic Truth Society.

Cobb, Mark. 2001. *The Dying Soul. Spiritual Care at the End of Life*. Oxford: Open University Press.

Eder, Klaus. 2002. Europäische Säkularisierung – Ein Sonderweg in die Postsäkulare Gesellschaft? *Berliner Journal für Soziologie* 3: 331-343.

Gauchet, Marcel. 1985. *Le désenchantment du monde. Une histoire politique de la religion*. Paris: Gallimard.

Giddens, Anthony. 1991. *Modernity and Self-Identity*. Cambridge: Polity Press.

Giddens, Anthony. 1992. *The Transformation of Intimacy: Sexuality, Love, and Eroticism*. Cambridge: Polity Press.

Goldblatt, David *et al.* (eds.). 1999. *Global Transformations: Politics, Economics, Culture*. Cambridge: Cambridge, Polity Press.

Habermas, Jürgen. 1986 and 1989. *The Theory of Communicative Action*, Vol I. and II. translated by Thomas McCarthy. Cambridge: Polity Press.

Habermas, Jürgen. 2008. *Between Naturalism and Religion*. Cambridge: Polity Press.

Habermas, Jürgen. 2010. *An Awareness of What is Missing. Faith and Reason in a Post-Secular Age*. Cambridge: Polity Press.

Habermas Jürgen & Joseph Ratzinger. 2005. *Dialektik der Säkularisierung. Über Vernunft und Religion*. Freiburg im Breisgau: Herder.

Heft, James L. (ed). 1999. *A Catholic Modernity? Charles Taylor's Marianist Award Lecture*. New York and Oxford: Oxford University Press.

Hellemans, Staf. 2001. From 'Catholicism Against Modernity' to the Problematic 'Modernity of Catholicism'. *Ethical Perspectives* 8: (2) 117-127.

Hellemans, Staf. 2010. *Das Zeitalter der Weltreligionen. Religion in agrarischen Zivilisationen und in modernen Gesellschaften*. Würzburg: Ergon.

Joas, Hans. 2009. Die Säkulare Option. Ihr Aufstieg und ihre Folgen. *Deutsche Zeitschrift für Philosophie* 57: 293-300.

MacCulloch, Diarmaid. 2009. *A History of Christianity*. London: Penguin.

McGrath, Alister. 2011. *Why God Won't Go Away: Engaging with the New Atheism.* London: SPCK.

McLuhan, Marshall. 2001. *Understanding Media*, second edition. London: Routledge.

Milbank, John. 1990. *Theology and Social Theory. Beyond Secular Reason.* Oxford: Blackwell.

O'Malley, John. 2000. *Trent and All That. Renaming Catholicism in the Early Modern Era.* Cambridge, Mass.: Harvard University Press.

Münch, Richard. 2002. Die Zweite Moderne: Realität oder Fiktion? Kritische Fragen an die 'Theorie reflexiver Modernisierung'. *Kölner Zeitschrift für Soziologie und Sozialpsychologie* 54: (3) 417-443.

Rawls, John. 1993. *Political Liberalism.* Cambridge, Mass.: Harvard University Press.

Reinhard, Wolgang. 1977. Gegenreformation als Modernisierung? Prologomena zu einer Theorie des konfessionellen Zeitalters. *Archive for Reformation History* 68: 226-252.

Reinhard, Wolfgang. 1995. Was ist katholische Konfessionalisierung? Pp. 419-452 in Wolfgang Reinhard and Heinz Schilling (eds.). *Die katholische Konfessionalisierung: Wissenschaftliches Symposium der Gesellschaft zur Herausgabe des Corpus Catholicorum und des Vereins für Reformgeschichte.* Münster: Gottesloher Verlaghaus.

Sipe, A. W. Richard. 1996. *Celibacy. A Way of Loving, Living, and Serving.* Missouri: Triumph Books.

Stanworth, Rachel. 2003. *Recognising Spiritual Needs in People Who Are Dying.* Oxford: Oxford University Press.

Taylor, Charles. 1999. A Catholic Modernity? Pp. 13-37 in James L. Heft (ed.). *A Catholic Modernity? Charles Taylor's Marianist Award Lecture*, Oxford: Oxford University Press.

Taylor, Charles. 2007. *A Secular Age.* Cambridge, Mass.: Harvard University Press.

Tocqueville, Alexis de. 2003. *Democracy in America.* London: Penguin.

Wallace, Robert M. 1981. Progress, Secularisation and Modernity: The Löwith-Blumenberg Debate. *New German Critique* 21: 63-79.

Yack, Bernard. 1997. *The Fetishism of Modernities. Epochal Self-Consciousness in Contemporary Social and Political Thought.* Notre Dame: Notre Dame University Press.

Zakaria, Fareed. 2008. *The Post-American World.* New York: W.W. Norton and Company.

"A Purifying Force for Reason":
Pope Benedict on the Role of Christianity in Advanced Modernity

Peter Jonkers

1. Introduction

Advanced modernity – the catchword to designate contemporary culture – poses many challenges to Western societies; one of these is intellectual. The central question of this contribution is if and how the Catholic Church responds to this intellectual challenge in the current cultural situation. Given the fact the Catholic Church has become a minority church, implying that its voice has become much weaker than before and that its message is often a priori being reduced to a parochial one, can it still give a meaningful answer to the existential, moral, and political questions of all humanity?[1]

For obvious reasons I have to confine myself to only a small aspect of this encompassing and multi-layered question. I shall discuss, from a philosophical perspective, an example of the Catholic intellectual contribution to the public debate about some burning issues of advanced modernity. In particular, the focus of this article lies on Pope Benedict XVI's position and arguments in his discussions with some prominent intellectuals of our time. My main reasons for this approach are, first, that the incumbent pope is not only an outstanding intellectual with strong opinions about, among many other things, the role of religion in contemporary society, but as the highest authority in the Catholic Church he also defines the Church's official position in this debate. Second, the Pope has defined the reasonable apologia of Christian faith in the face of the modern world as one of the most important priorities of his pontificate. He therefore does not limit himself to preaching to the already converted, but wants to discuss the Church's position on these issues with the world at large in a critical, but nevertheless constructive, way.

Because Pope Benedict's bibliography contains a vast number of books, articles, and speeches, a further limitation of the scope of my text is necessary. Therefore I shall only discuss his recent writings, i.e., from 2004 onwards. My main reason for this is that, ever since the terrorist attacks of September 2001, the nature of the debate about the role of religion in the public sphere has changed dramatically (Habermas 2003*b*, 101f.). In the wake of these acts of religiously-fuelled violence, all religions, including Catholicism, have been forced

---

[1]　See the text of S. Hellemans in this book, in which he analyzes the transition of ultramontane mass Catholicism towards choice Catholicism and discusses the challenges with which the Catholic Church is confronted in this new formation.

in a defensive position. They are challenged to explain their position as to the age-old question of how they can reasonably hold on to their universal truth-claims in a radically plural world based on the principles of democratic political rule and freedom of religion. Obviously this issue has also influenced the discourse of the Pope and his writings wherein the idea of (religious) truth takes such a prominent place. Furthermore, I shall confine myself mostly to his texts and speeches for a secular audience because, in these, he has to defend the Catholic position with the help of natural reason alone rather than by using doctrinal arguments. Concretely, this article contains a discussion of the Pope's view of the Christian ideas of reason and truth as he develops it in a discussion with some leading social and political philosophers of our time.

Having limited the material scope of my paper to manageable proportions, it is necessary to specify a bit further my principal research question. As will shown in more detail below, the Pope focuses on the intellectual contribution of Christian religion to advanced modernity as being "a purifying force for reason" (Ratzinger/Pope Benedict 2008, nr. 11). Strategically, and as regards content, he thereby offers an intriguing example of a Catholic modernity.[2] This focus is quite natural since, given the fundamentally plural character of advanced modernity, the Church has to speak a language which, in principle, can be generally understood, i.e., that of philosophical reason. But upon closer examination, the reasons for the Pope to speak this language are much more fundamental than a superficial 'sales-strategy'. They actually highlight an interesting aspect of what Christianity is all about: as a religion of the *Logos,* it does not consider reason to be a contingent by-product of the development of the world, but is convinced that the world comes from reason, so that reason is the world's criterion and goal (Ratzinger/Pope Benedict 2006a, 49), that Christianity is "a religion in keeping with reason" (Ratzinger/Pope Benedict 2006a, 47).[3] Therefore, the Pope cannot accept a separation of faith and reason, or, phrased positively, he holds that a religiously inspired reason can play an equally important role in the public debate as secular reason. That is why the concepts of reason and truth take such a prominent place in almost all his writings. In fact, he compares his strategy with that of the apostle Paul, almost two millennia ago, when Paul discussed the truth of the Christian message in the multicultural megalopolis of Rome, the Babylon of that age. Paul also tried to convince his audience, who took nothing for granted, and criticized the decadence of Roman culture by

---

2   For a definition of his term, see the contribution of A. Carroll in this book. It has to be noted, however, that Carroll's ideas about the content of Catholic modernity differ considerably from the Pope's.

3   In his contribution to this book, Carroll gives an in-depth analysis of the fact that the general view of the relation between faith and reason in modernity has been dominated by a rather Protestant interpretation of it. This has led to the liberal view of the place of religion in society as limited to the private sphere. Given the need to redefine this role in the light of the current debates, he argues that a Catholic modernity could offer an interesting alternative in this respect.

making use of a 'public reason', which could be understood by all. According to the Pope, "Paul's words are essentially painting the picture, not of some particular historical situation, but of the permanent situation of humanity, of man, vis-à-vis God" (Ratzinger/Pope Benedict 2006a, 97).

In this context, it is interesting to note that the Pope, in his discussion with advanced modernity, applies central elements of the Christian tradition in a completely new cultural context. Just as at the beginning of the 20th century the Church used neo-Thomistic philosophy in order to respond to the rise of atheistic positivism by showing that God was the necessary metaphysical foundation for the natural sciences, the current situation confronts the Church with new questions, in particular, people's need for orientation in a world which has become radically plural and, hence, rather cluttered. This is why the Pope focuses on the fundamental question of how Christianity can succeed in formulating its idea of truth in such a way that it serves as a point of reference for contemporary humans on an existential level. My analysis of the Pope's contribution to the public debate is not only intended to contribute to understanding the transition towards a new church formation in general, but also the specific focus of the Church's intellectual debate with advanced modernity.[4]

In the next section I shall analyze Pope Benedict's interpretation approach of reason and truth in Christian religion against the backdrop of some dominant philosophical trends in advanced modernity. Then, I shall examine if he succeeds in having the Christian contribution to the public debate on these issues accepted as a meaningful one by analyzing his discussions with some prominent contemporary philosophers.

2. Pope Benedict on reason and truth

As indicated in the previous section, the Pope claims to be engaged in a critical yet constructive dialogue with advanced modernity. Although he criticizes various problematic aspects of our times, such as its blind faith in scientific progress and in the redeeming power of technology (Ratzinger/Pope Benedict 2007b, nr. 17) as well as the (social) drawbacks of globalization (Ratzinger/ Pope Benedict 2009a, nr. 33), this "has nothing to do with putting the clock back to the time before the Enlightenment and rejecting the insights of the modern age. The positive aspects of modernity are to be acknowledged unreservedly: we are all grateful for the marvelous possibilities that it has opened up for mankind and for the progress in humanity that has been granted to us". (Ratzinger/Pope Benedict 2006b, nr. 15; see also 2006a, 47). The Pope recognizes that certain values, although originally stemming from the Enlightenment, have universal validity, such as "the insight that religion cannot be imposed by the state, but can be welcomed only in liberty; the respect of the fundamental

---

4   For an elaboration of the concept of religious modernization, see the contribution of S. Hellemans in this book.

rights of man, which are equal for all; the separation of powers and the control of power" (Ratzinger/Pope Benedict 2006*a*, 39). In sum, the Pope's stance towards (advanced) modernity comes down to the thesis that the Church should not reject the Enlightenment and its ramifications in advanced modernity, but follow the exhortation of the *Pastoral Constitution on the Church in the Modern World* of the Second Vatican Council, which reasserted the deep correspondence between Christianity and Enlightenment. Hence, the Church should not reject the Enlightenment, but complement its profound incompleteness (Ratzinger/Pope Benedict 2006*a*, 43). This incompleteness has various aspects: it concerns the failure of the Enlightenment-culture to refer to the intrinsically good and true as objective points of reference in existential issues, its inability to see all people as having an inviolable dignity, and its a-historical character, i.e., its incapacity to acknowledge and value the moral and spiritual roots of Western culture, especially its Christian legacy.

2.1 Reason and truth in advanced modernity

Let me first give more philosophical body to the way in which the incompleteness of the Enlightenment-culture manifests itself in advanced modernity, and show why it not only constitutes an important barrier against a constructive discussion about the relation between religion and secular society, but also, paradoxically, jeopardizes some basic acquirements of the Enlightenment-culture itself.

Following Rorty, one of the main theoreticians of advanced modernity, the growing individualization and pluralization of our life-world correspond, on an philosophical level, to the awareness that all the grand, overarching narratives of modernity, such as Christianity, the great ideals of the French revolution, objective truth, and even Reason's universal capacity to judge impartially religions and secular philosophies of life, have lost their plausibility. All these narratives are seen as but contingent "final vocabularies", whose truth can only be demonstrated by means of circular arguments; hence, truth is a basically parochial matter, i.e., confined to the persons or local communities using or sharing these vocabularies. Unlike modernity, which lived on the belief that all specific final vocabularies were to justify themselves before the tribunal of reason, which served as a kind of impartial meta-vocabulary that judged their pros and cons, advanced modernity has lost this faith. Nowadays, the dominant conviction is that all religious and secular traditions are nothing but contingent social constructions, available only on the local market and, hence, cannot legitimately lay any claim to objective truth. It is therefore no surprise that, on a practical level, we see people taking an attitude of irony with regard to all traditions, including their own: ironists are "never quite able to take themselves seriously because [they are] always aware that the terms in which they describe themselves are subject to change, always aware of the contingency and fragility of their final vocabularies, and thus of their selves" (Rorty 1989, 73f). This means that Nietzsche's prophecy of the death of God has become true in our times: people have lost their faith in the truth of all transcendental ideas, like God, the Absolute, reason, truth, etc.

However, in this situation people run the risk of not belonging to anything anymore, which leads to a complete loss of their identity. The only way they can avoid this is by devoting themselves to the way of life with which they are familiar, which concretely means that they simply declare that there are limits to what they can take seriously (Rorty 1991, 187f). In sum, although all substantial traditions, religious as well as secular ones, are reduced to the level of complete contingency, i.e., of sacred cows, funny habits, and politically correct ideas, people are nevertheless fully entitled to be attached to them, albeit on merely psychological rather than rational grounds. In short, ethnocentrism is the paradoxical but inevitable consequence of the awareness of the contingency of all our substantial traditions. Of course, this partisanship has to remain confined to the private sphere, while in public people are expected to take a completely pragmatic, neutral attitude in order to safeguard their peaceful co-existence in a plural society. This means that the public debate has to be strictly secular, excluding any input of ideas stemming from particular traditions. This explains the striking phenomenon that requires people in the public sphere to display a kind of unlimited openness and tolerance towards people with completely different ideas and practices, at least as long as they do not violate certain basic principles of secular society, while, simultaneously, in the private sphere to confine themselves in their relationships to those people with whom they feel comfortable, in other words to people from their own ethnos or club.

On the face of it, the individualization and pluralization of our (religious) commitments and ideas is quite appealing: we do not have to feel sorry for the lack of common ground when talking about diverging ways of life and our commitment to them, but are fully entitled to embrace the one that best fits our needs. If we are religious enthusiasts, we can even create our strictly personal religious lifestyle, thereby making use of elements from various traditions. Because it liberates us from the need to look for and think about the 'true' meaning of life, as well as from the painstaking task of developing reasonable justifications for it, this attitude gives human existence a certain lightness. We can clear our bookshelves of most philosophical (especially metaphysical) and theological (especially in the field of dogmatics) books and start collecting novels, because they give us an inside view into a wide variety of concrete lifestyles with which we can identify ourselves. The Pope identifies this stance with a kind of relativism (Ratzinger/Benedict 2006a, 45; 2006d; 2009a, nr. 2, 26; 2009b), but, philosophically speaking, it is more appropriate to call it an ethnocentric view, holding "that there is nothing to be said about either truth or rationality apart from descriptions of the familiar procedures of justification which a given society – *ours* – uses in one or another area of inquiry" (Rorty 1991, 23). In any case, this view puts an end to our belief in an overarching rationality and truth.

But perhaps the processes of individualization and pluralization, however influential they are, are only at work on the surface and are, in fact, overruled by another aspect of the fate of reason and truth in advanced modernity, viz., the all-unifying power of an instrumental and reductive rationality. Although this kind of rationality has been on the rise ever since the emergence of modernity, it has stepped up to a qualitatively new phase of its development in advanced modernity, consisting in what is commonly called the naturalization of the human person.

A concrete and quite influential example of this naturalization is Peter Sloterdijk's *Rules For the Human Park*. I will not discuss here the ins and outs of the heated debates about the moral acceptability of the genetic manipulation of human embryos and its eugenic consequences, which his essay provoked in Germany in 1999, but focus, instead, on the way in which he paves the way for the necessary (in his eyes) transition from humanism to post- or trans-humanism. First of all, he lays bare, in the heart of all traditional forms of humanism, an intrinsically elitist "sect- or club-fantasy – the dream of the ill-fated solidarity of those who have been elected to be able to read" (Sloterdijk 1999, 10). Because of this capacity, the cultural elite could impose its view of what it truly means to be humanized upon the rest of humanity; Sloterdijk defines this process as one of taming or domesticating. A concrete example of this was the introduction of the ideal of humanism in the higher forms of secondary education (especially the gymnasiums) of the 19th and 20th century, meant to tame the youth. In this way, Sloterdijk unmasks the egalitarian and universal pretension of the humanism of the Enlightenment as essentially authoritarian and parochial. Due to the rise of modern mass-culture this humanism has come to an end in our times. Thus, the question arises "what still tames man, if humanism as a school of taming humans fails?" (Sloterdijk 1999, 31f).

Besides a taming capacity, humans also have the power to breed. With this, Sloterdijk, being inspired by Nietzsche, wants to open a new horizon for thinking beyond humanism: "With the thesis of man as breeder of man the humanist horizon is shattered, insofar as humanism can and should never think any further than the question of taming and educating" (Sloterdijk 1999, 39). The central question of post- or trans-humanism then is in which direction this breeding of humans will go: "Whether the long-term development will also lead to a genetic reform of the properties of the species; whether a future anthropo-technology will penetrate as far as an explicit planning of these properties; and whether humanity will be able to realize a transformation of the whole species from fatalism of birth to birth-by-choice and prenatal selection – these are questions, in which the evolutionary horizon [of trans-humanism] starts to lighten up in front of us, however vague and uncomfortable" (Sloterdijk 1999, 46f.). In any case, the future belongs to humans as active breeders, who do not accept anymore that a higher power (e.g., God) acts instead of them.

What strikes me in this text is not so much that it opens up the possibility of radically new forms of human biotechnology – which makes this part of his essay belong to the domain of science fiction rather than philosophy – but that Sloterdijk consistently naturalizes human beings and their culture by using terms (not metaphors) stemming from the world of animals, namely, a human park that is managed by taming and breeding. He therewith offers a striking example of the naturalization of the human person in contemporary thinking.

2.2 A broadened idea of reason

Returning to my main research question, I want to examine if Pope Benedict is able to interpret the Christian tradition in such a way that it can serve as a plausible intellectual response to the challenges of advanced modernity, in particular, with regard to its interpretation of reason and truth as analyzed above. Although he does not explicitly refer to the publications of Rorty and Sloterdijk, it will become clear that he has their ideas in mind while criticizing specific aspects of what he calls the hubris of reason in advanced modernity.

First of all, the Pope has to defend himself against the obvious critique that the Christian message is inevitably a parochial one, i.e., only relevant to Christians and hence of no concern for advanced modernity at large. Has he, as the highest authority of the Catholic Church, anything meaningful to say to a secular audience? Of course the Pope has to "care for [his] community" and "keep it united on the way towards God, a way which, according to the Christian faith, has been indicated by Jesus – and not merely indicated: He himself is our way". But because this community also lives in the world, which implies that its circumstances, history, example, and message inevitably influence the entire human community, "the Pope, in his capacity as Shepherd of his community, is also increasingly becoming a voice for the ethical reasoning of humanity" (Ratzinger/Pope Benedict 2008, nr. 3). The crucial question is if he can substantiate this claim, which seems to be in flat contradiction with the universal principle of tolerance and freedom of religion cherished so much by almost all contemporaries. To phrase this objection in his own words: "Surely the Pope does not really base his pronouncements on ethical reasoning, but draws his judgments from faith and hence cannot claim to speak on behalf of those who do not share this faith" (Ratzinger/Pope Benedict 2008, nr. 4). As became clear in the above analysis of Rorty's position, this objection is indeed insurmountable from a postmodern perspective, according to which every vocabulary is inherently perspectivistic, excluding the very possibility of an objective meta-vocabulary and, consequently, of a common ground for discussion.

Paradoxically, however, postmodernism simultaneously allows the Pope to stand by the meaningfulness of his ethical reasoning, but under the condition that he confines its scope to the Christians, to the members of his own 'club'. But he rejects this easy way out as running counter to the truth of faith: "Over and above his ministry as Shepherd of the Church, and on the basis of the intrinsic nature of this pastoral ministry, it is the Pope's task to safeguard sensibility to the truth; to invite reason to set out ever anew in search of what is true and good, in search of God; to urge reason, in the course of this search, to discern the illuminating lights that have emerged during the history of the Christian faith, and thus to recognize Jesus Christ as the Light that illumines history and helps us find the path towards the future" (Ratzinger/Pope Benedict 2008, nr. 13).

So the basic question remains: How can the Church, obviously being a particular voice in the choir of ethical reasoning, *legitimately* claim that its message transcends the particularity of its origin and the fact that it nowadays represents only a minority of people, so that it also has something meaningful to say for the secular majority in advanced modernity? As pointed out in the introduction, a prerequisite condition for the Pope's message to be understood at all in a plural society is that he speaks the language of natural reason. But at the same time he redefines this concept in such a way that some of its meanings, which remain hidden in or are even repressed by advanced modernity, are uncovered. I shall first give a general idea of how the Pope redefines reason in general, and then analyze how he develops it more in detail. First of all, in almost all his (recent) writings, the Pope pleads for a broadening of reason, thereby criticizing the incompleteness of the rationality of advanced modernity, which is characterized by perspectivism, scientific reductionism, and a disregard of history and tradition. The plea for a broadening of reason is obviously intended to include the reasonableness of (religious) traditions, and to have a religious perspective accepted in the public debate. Secondly, this broadened reason is not to be seen as a purely subjective capacity of humans, as is the case in the way of thinking that dominates (advanced) modernity. On the contrary, it is closely connected to the idea of truth, which stands for the reasonableness that is inherently present in the world and which hence serves as a transcendent and objective point of reference for human reason. Thirdly, and in sum, this union of reasonableness and truth, to which Christian religion and all other major (religious) traditions testify, is not purely theoretical or doctrinal, but concerns primarily existential issues, in particular, the origin and destiny of the human person and society, the distinction between right and wrong, etc. Although, from a Christian perspective, reason and truth fundamentally stem from God, this does not mean that they can only be grasped through revelation; on the contrary, these ideas can be understood by all humans because Christianity is a religion of the Logos. Hence, the Christian ideas of reason and truth are not completely different from those in other religious and secular traditions, or from the way in which these notions are used in the public debate, but have in common that they play a pivotal role in human attempts to respond to existential questions.

Bearing this in mind we can start analyzing the Pope's contribution to the current debate. First, he proposes to approach the Christian Salvation-message not so much as a doctrine but rather as an expression of divine 'wisdom', thereby building on a long-standing tradition whose origins date back to the Book of

Wisdom in the Old Testament.[5] He defines wisdom as an existential knowledge, i.e., as a kind of knowledge that answers the question of how we can "attain our destiny and thereby realize our humanity" (Ratzinger/Pope Benedict 2006a, 77). Wisdom takes the concrete cultural situation of humans as its point of departure and relates it to the idea of the good life, which is an exemplification, on an existential level, of truth. Because all forms of wisdom are culturally embedded, they are distinguished from a purely theoretical or scientific knowledge; because of its orientation towards truth and goodness wisdom steers away from the obvious risk of being swayed by the issues of the day. Hence, by defining Christian religion as divine wisdom the Pope specifies a first aspect of what it means to be a purifying force for reason.

As said, wisdom is not the monopoly of Christian faith, but also characterizes many other religious and secular traditions. All of them claim to give a true orientation to human life. Although their heterogeneity makes them look similar to the above-analyzed incommensurability of final vocabularies, all these traditions nevertheless have a fundamental question in common: What does it truly mean to be a human person and how can we actualize the vocation implied in this truth; in other words, what is the destiny of our lives? The idea of wisdom is embedded in all longstanding religious and secular traditions, and hence it can serve as a common ground for all religious and secular traditions. With this, the Pope highlights a second aspect of his conviction that Christianity can serve as a purifying force for reason, thereby particularly referring to the postmodern evaporation of an overarching reason. Concretely, he proposes the idea of "the true development of the whole of the person in every single dimension" (Ratzinger/Pope Benedict 2009a, nr. 11) as a common ground for all the traditions of wisdom.[6]

The Pope's identification of Christian religion with a tradition of wisdom enables him to criticize a third aspect of the incompleteness of modern rationality, viz., an "a-historical form of reason that seeks to establish itself exclusively in terms of a-historical rationality". In comparison with such a reductionism, "humanity's wisdom – the wisdom of the great religious traditions – should be valued as a heritage that cannot be cast with impunity into the dustbin of the history of ideas" (Ratzinger/Pope Benedict 2008, nr. 4). This remark is directed against the tendency, characteristic of the Enlightenment-culture, to identify science with rationality as such and faith with a kind of emotive expressivism; this inevitably leads to the well-known dichotomy between faith and reason as subjective versus objective, emotional versus rational, etc. According to the Pope, the consequence of this reductionism is that science and religion become pathological: a hypertrophy in the field of technical-pragmatic knowledge and a

5   Cfr. Sir. 14:20-27. In his Encyclical Letter *Fides et ratio,* Pope John Paul II develops extensively the theme of wisdom as a unity of faith and reason (John Paul II 1998, nr. 16f).

6   The Pope adopts this idea from Pope Paul VI's Encyclical letter *Populorum progression.* See also Ratzinger/Pope Benedict 2006b, nr. 13.

relapse of religion into superstition and magic practices. "If man cannot use his reason to ask about essential things in life, where he comes from and where he is going, about what he should do and may do, about living and dying, but has to leave these decisive questions to feeling, divorced from reason, then he is not elevating reason but dishonoring it" (Ratzinger/Pope Benedict 2004, 158; see also 2006*a*, 39ff).

In sum, according to the Pope, both the form and the content of the Church's intellectual contribution to the public debate in advanced modernity rest upon its fundamental idea of a broadened, existential rationality and truth, which is commonly defined as wisdom. It is a kind of reason which is not opposed to faith, but congenial with it; this reason is not a-historical, but incorporates the invaluable insights of religious and secular traditions; it is not a social construction, but is inherently present in the world. As such it is a purifying force and a completion of the parochialism and incompleteness, characteristic of advanced modernity's idea of rationality. This idea of wisdom is meant to establish a common ground for discussion between Christian religion and secular society, thus preventing the ethical reasoning of the Church from being downgraded a priori as 'parochial'. The historical character of wisdom does not mean that it is relative, i.e., subordinate to the contingent preferences of humans or dependent on always varying circumstances. On the contrary, the metaphysical and hence objective character of the idea of truth is essential to prevent wisdom from becoming an instrument in the hands of ideologists and partisans, always defending particular interests. Truth is the ultimate criterion reason has to obey by trying to discover essential meanings in the contingencies of history. But one should also avoid interpreting the metaphysical character of truth as if it were a kind of demonstrable evidence, available to humans and in the possession of (the leadership of) the Church. Precisely because of its divine character humans have always to interpret the truth, and similarly the Church does not possess truth, but encourages people to discover the truth (Ratzinger/Pope Benedict 2008, nr 11).

As regards the other aspect of reason in advanced modernity, its instrumentalism and reductionism, leading to the naturalization of the human person, the Pope considers this to be one of the greatest dangers of our times: Humankind "has deciphered the components of the human being, and now he is able, so to speak, to 'construct' man of his own. This means that man enters the world, no longer as a gift of the Creator, but as the product of our activity – and a product that can be selected according to the requirements that we ourselves stipulate. In this way, the splendour of the fact that he is the image of God – the source of his dignity and of his inviolability – no longer shines upon this man; his only splendour is the power of human capabilities" (Ratzinger/Pope Benedict 2006*a*, 26; see also 2006*d*, 75; 2009*a*, nr. 74). Although he does not explicitly quote him, the Pope probably has Sloterdijk's suggestion of an anthropo-technology in mind when he warns against a naturalization of the human person.[7] As a consequence of his general approach, he is not only opposed to this because it runs counter to the doctrine of the Church, but especially because it illustrates the apex of the hubris of reason in advanced modernity (Ratzinger/Pope Benedict 2006c, 78). Humankind's discovery of the unlimited capacities of scientific reason to penetrate the mysteries of the world and our own existence has had a disenchanting effect upon the traditional life-world, as is common knowledge. But, paradoxically, this disenchantment has, especially since the Enlightenment, led to a new kind of enchantment, namely, the enchantment of reason by itself. Hence, scientific reason has come to see itself as absolute, and its products as its autonomous creation; in sum, reason has become completely immanent, thus rejecting every transcendence.[8] This rejection not only concerns the belief in a transcendent God, but also non-religious forms of transcendence, such as the truth embedded in the wisdom of previous generations and secular traditions. A completely immanent reason narrows the idea of truth down to what can be demonstrated scientifically, and hence completely disregards the spiritual dimension of human existence. The consequences of this reductionist idea of reason are devastating, again not only for religion, but far more importantly also for the values of human dignity and the inviolability of the human person as such, being the ultimate foundation of every human civilization. These values then inevitably lose their universal and unconditional character; because scientific reason has no access to them, it often reduces them to nothing but subjective preferences. Hence, the Pope warns: "If technical progress is not matched by corresponding progress in man's ethical formation, in man's inner growth [...], then it is not progress at all, but a threat for man and for the world" (Ratzinger/Pope Benedict 2007b, nr. 22; see also 2006a, 27). In order to stave off this danger he again proposes the idea of a broadened reason and truth, as exemplified by the wisdom of (religious) traditions, thus complementing the reductionist and instrumentalist idea of reason, which dominates anthropo-technology. As a necessary complement to a reason that has become completely immanent he points to the idea of transcendence, which does not necessarily have to be interpreted religiously, but can also be secular, as long as it is able to serve as a pre-political normativity for all vital human issues. So, here again, the Pope uses the idea of wisdom as a force to purify scientific reason from its own enchantment, and as a common ground for discussing bio-ethical issues in a pluralist society.

---

7   In order to substantiate this 'probability', I refer to the fact that the German philosopher Robert Spaemann wrote a very critical response to Sloterdijk's essay in the *Frankfurter Allgemeine Zeitung* of October 7, 1999. Spaemann is a personal friend of Pope Benedict and they regularly meet to discuss all kinds of intellectual issues. Interestingly, the core of Spaemann's response reflects, in many aspects, the position and argument of the Pope.

8   As I pointed out above, Sloterdijk is an excellent illustration of this position (see Sloterdijk 1999, 45).

2.3 Living as if God existed

In his book on *Christianity and the Crisis of Cultures,* the Pope gives an intriguing, but also very controversial, interpretation of this idea of transcendence in a secular society. How can secular people be convinced to accept an idea of transcendence, which stands for a pre-political normativity in all human affairs? For the Pope it goes without saying *that* every society, religious or secular, has to accept such an idea, since excluding it would inevitably lead to the annihilation of humankind, as the postmodern evaporation of an overarching reason and the recent ideas about anthropo-technology have patently exemplified. Therefore, he suggests that a secular person, "who does not succeed in finding the path to accepting the existence of God ought nevertheless try to live and to direct his life *veluti si Deus daretur,* as if God did indeed exist" (Ratzinger/Pope Benedict 2006a, 51). The Pope realizes that he herewith turns one of the most basic axioms of the Enlightenment upside down. According to Grotius, who lived at the time of the religious wars, it is imperative to define the essential moral values in such a way that they would be valid *etsi Deus non daretur*, for only in this way could they be kept free from religious controversies and be undergirded with an evidence independent of the existing religious divisions. In other words, a secular approach of all vital moral principles is essential to secure peaceful coexistence.

Why does the Pope make such a bold suggestion to secular people, asking them, of all things, to reverse one of their most fundamental convictions? He points to a crucial difference between modernity and advanced modernity concerning the acceptability of a common moral ground: in modernity "the great fundamental convictions created by Christianity were largely resistant to attack and seemed undeniable. But this is no longer the case. The search for this kind of reassuring certainty, something that could go unchallenged despite all the disagreements, has not succeeded" (Ratzinger/Pope Benedict 2006a, 50f.). The main reason for the collapse of this idea is the rise of pluralism as a consequence of the processes of individualization and globalization (Jonkers 2009, 276ff.). Hence, the reasonable consensus, on which this common ground has always been based in a democratic society, is nowadays, more often than not, confronted with the undermining question: whose rationality is this? Actually, the Pope wants to point to the fact that the approach of modernity to solve the problem of (religious) pluralism by relying on the model of reasonable consensus is not satisfactory anymore in advanced modernity, mainly due to the 'perspectivization' of reason and the evaporation of the idea of truth. The consequence of this loss of common ground is a dramatic lack of orientation, of points of reference with the help of which people can direct their lives, both on the level of the individual and of society. All traditional forms of orientation or points of reference have lost their plausibility to a great extent and have been reduced to subjective preferences. The inevitable result is that contemporary people are confronted with a feeling of deep uncertainty as regards all existential questions. In this situation, their only secure option seems to be to rely un-conditionally on the objectivity and impartiality of scientific reason in all hu-man affairs, as is exemplified by the success of anthropo-technology and social engineering. But, actually, this means selling oneself to the devil, since scien-tific reason is, because of its reductionist character, unable to give the indispen-sable reasonable support to the respect for human dignity and the inviolability of the human person, the principles on which every human civilization is ulti-mately founded. Instead, scientific reason threatens to annihilate these princi-ples because it has, as *scientific* reason, no access to them.

The Pope's suggestion to secular people to live as if God existed should be seen in this context. According to him, "this does not impose limitations on an-yone's freedom; it gives support to all our human affairs and supplies a criterion of which human life stands sorely in need" (Ratzinger/Pope Benedict 2006*a*, 52). He does not expect secular people to be converted to Christianity, since this would run counter to the very point of departure of his argument. Instead, he wants his suggestion to be understood in line with Kant's postulates of practical reason (Ratzinger/Pope Benedict 2006*a*, 51). For Kant, these postulates refer to a transcendent domain, to which theoretical reason has no access, but whose reality has nevertheless to be accepted by practical reason in order to give orien-tation and meaning to all our moral actions. Hence, living as if God existed has to be interpreted here to mean that God serves as a symbolic representation of the universal principles, mentioned above, which transcend all political consen-sus-building. Living as if God existed means that all people, religious and secu-lar, should be prepared to let their lives be oriented by these principles. But by phrasing God's existence in a conditional way, i.e., as an 'as if', the Pope, again following Kant in this respect, also admits that God's existence cannot be demonstrated by scientific reason and, hence, is not an objective reality in the same sense as the objects of sensory experience. It is exactly the openness of this approach that allows secular people not to believe in the Christian God but, nevertheless, to accept a reasonable faith in some transcendental principles that underlie human existence as such. It also enables them to accept these principles as a common ground of advanced modernity, but also to interpret them in a dif-ferent way than Christian doctrine. In sum, living as if God existed serves as the concretization of wisdom as an existential, orienting kind of knowledge that is a common ground for all people, but also allows plurality. Only if we are pre-pared to live in this way do "we become capable of that genuine dialogue of cultures and religions so urgently needed today" (Ratzinger/Pope Benedict 2006*b*, nr. 16).

3. Christianity as a purifying force for reason?

After having analyzed the Pope's position with regard to some important in-tellectual challenges of advanced modernity, it is time to ask how it relates to the current philosophical discussion on these issues. Interestingly, the Pope discusses his ideas with two leading philosophers, Jürgen Habermas and John Rawls (see Ratzinger/Pope Benedict 2006c; 2008). I shall analyze these two debates, thereby focusing on the Pope's primary concerns as regards advanced modernity: the evaporation of reason and truth, leading to radical pluralism, and the naturalization of human beings. In sum, is his contribution to the discussion with these two philosophers, in particular, his suggestion of a broadened reason, indeed a reasonable one? This approach implies that I shall not give an opinion about who is right or wrong in these debates, since this would largely exceed the purview of this contribution due to the complexity and scope of the ongoing discussions.

3.1 Christian wisdom as a response to the evaporation of reason

First of all, Habermas and Rawls agree *and* disagree with the Pope as regards his critique of the evaporation of reason in advanced modernity and the need for a common ground for discussing the vital questions of our times. According to Habermas, it is essential for a modern democratic society to have a reasonable justification of its normative foundations. This reasonableness, which results from an ongoing learning process, is the common ground that enables us to communicate with each other about these foundations within the framework of a constitutional democratic state. This implies that Habermas rejects the radical skepticism, popular in postmodern philosophy, with regard to reason's overarching capacities to realize consensus (Habermas 2006, 37f). Moreover, against the contentions of some radically secular philosophers, he defines contemporary society as post-secular and, hence, fully accepts Christianity as an equal participant in this justificatory debate, precisely because it has shown itself to be capable of reflecting reasonably on its own position in a pluralistic society. Basically, religious expressions can have a cognitive content and therefore can justify themselves reasonably. This cognitive content, found in sacred scriptures and religious traditions concerns "intuitions about error and redemption, about the salvific exodus from a life that is experienced as empty of salvation; these have been elaborated in a subtle manner over the course of millennia and have been kept alive through a process of interpretation" (Habermas 2006, 43). This is why religion can offer an invaluable contribution to contemporary secular society, and also explains why philosophy should be prepared to learn from religion.

But for Habermas it is also essential that this justification of a constitutional democratic state should be post-metaphysical, i.e., "renounc[ing] the 'strong' cosmological or salvation-historical assumptions of the classical and religious theories of the natural law" (Habermas 2006, 24). This renunciation is crucial, since it is a direct consequence of the equality of the members of the modern state, its religiously neutral character and, consequently, the final safeguard for its (religious) pluralism. Hence, he distances himself from the idea that a transcendent, metaphysical concept of truth could still serve as a pre-political normativity of contemporary, pluralist society, thereby criticizing the Pope's position in this respect (Habermas 2006, 24ff.).

Rawls, too, is looking for a common basis of principles and ideals with which citizens affirming conflicting religious and non-religious convictions can reasonably agree. He formulates the leading question of his *Political Liberalism* as follows: "How is it possible for those affirming a religious doctrine that is based on religious authority, for example, the Church or the Bible, also to hold a reasonable political conception that supports a just democratic regime?" (Rawls 2005*a*, xxxvii; see also 2005*b*, 458). Hence, reasonable pluralism is the normal result of a democratic culture of free institutions. Rawls defines reasonable pluralism as "the fact that a plurality of conflicting reasonable comprehensive doctrines, religious, philosophical, and moral, is the normal result of its culture of free institutions" (Rawls 2005*b*, 441). However, the *reasonable* character of Rawls's idea of pluralism prevents it from lapsing into its simple or gratuitous variant, being an inevitable consequence of the postmodern evaporation of reason. In order to actualize this it is imperative that the constitutive parts of this reasonable pluralism, i.e., the comprehensive doctrines covering the major religious, philosophical, and moral aspects of human life in a more or less consistent and coherent manner, are reasonable themselves. Basically, the reasonableness of a comprehensive doctrine consists in that it organizes and characterizes recognized values so that they are compatible with one another and express an intelligible view of the world. Furthermore, a reasonable comprehensive doctrine "normally belongs to, or draws upon, a tradition of thought and doctrine. [...] It tends to evolve slowly in the light of what, from its point of view, it sees as good and sufficient reasons" (Rawls 2005*a*, 59). It is obvious that Christianity complies with these characteristics of reasonable comprehensive doctrines. Since a public and common basis of justification that applies to all comprehensive doctrines is lacking in the public culture of a democratic society, the best one can reasonably expect is an overlapping consensus resulting from the debates between (the representatives of) these reasonable doctrines. It has to be noted that this consensus is more than a pragmatic *modus vivendi*, since "first, the object of consensus, the political concept of justice, is itself a moral conception. And second, it is affirmed on moral grounds, that is, it includes conceptions of society and of citizens as persons, as well as principles of justice, and an account of the political virtues through which those principles are embodied in human character and expressed in public life" (Rawls 2005*a*, 147).

But, just like Habermas, and on the same grounds, Rawls refuses to 'upgrade' reasonableness to a transcendent idea of truth or pre-political normativity to which everyone has to orient him- or herself, since this would give a preferential treatment to one comprehensive doctrine (the true one) above all others. Instead, Rawls proposes "that in public reason comprehensive doctrines of truth or right be replaced by an idea of the politically reasonable addressed to citizens as citizens" (Rawls 2005*b*, 441; see also *2005a*, 216f.). Again, the principled background of this distinction between reason and truth is that this political conception provides the basis for a public discussion about the justification of its fundamental values while, at the same time, accepting pluralism as its permanent feature. The fact that persons are reasonable beings does not mean that they all affirm the same comprehensive doctrine and share the same ideas about truth and goodness, implying that fundamental political questions cannot be decided by the idea of truth, but only by reasons that might be shared by all citizens as free and equal.

Secondly, Habermas and Rawls criticize, in the same vein as the Pope, the reductionism of instrumental rationality. Habermas, in particular, is very critical of the naturalization of the human person and the effects of anthropo-technology:[9] "Nature as an object of science is no longer part of the social frame of reference of persons who communicate and interact with one another and mutually ascribe intentions and motives" (Habermas 2003b, 106), thus stripping our self-awareness from any social dimension. A naturalization of the human person inevitably blurs the distinctions between is and ought, between description or explanation and justification, which are essential for our moral judgments. It reduces the first-person participatory perspective, from which we lead our daily lives, to third-person descriptions from an observer's perspective. As a consequence, it makes any attempt to justify our acts to concrete others by addressing them as 'you', as well as their reactions to these justifications from a second-person perspective, pointless. In sum, "the scientistic belief in a science which will one day not only supplement, but *replace* the self-understanding of actors by an objectivating self-description is not science, but bad philosophy. No science will relieve common sense, even if scientifically informed, of the task of forming a judgement, for instance, on how we should deal with prepersonal human life under descriptions of molecular biology that make genetic interventions possible" (Habermas 2003b, 108).

Rawls, for his part, criticizes the problematic political consequences of a naturalization of the human person, viz., its failure to recognize reciprocity as a basic value underlying the relations between the members of a society. In order to make his point clear he distinguishes between the reasonable and the rational. "Reasonable persons [...] desire for its own sake a social world in which they, as free and equal, can cooperate with others on terms all can accept. They insist that reciprocity should hold within that world so that each benefits along with others" (Rawls 2005a, 50). Rational people, by contrast, are rational in the sense that they use their powers of judgment and deliberation in seeking ends and interests that are peculiarly their own; their rationality remains restricted to how they adopt and affirm them, as well as to how they give priority to some ends and interests over others. The rational is predominant in the sphere of profitable relations between interested individuals or groups, whereas the reasonable

---

9   It has to be noted that Habermas's position on this issue has been largely influenced by the fierce debates between Sloterdijk and other German intellectuals, including Habermas himself. See: Habermas 2003a, 22.

is essential to realize a kind of cooperation based on fairness and reciprocity. Hence, it does not make sense to oppose the reasonable and the rational radically, since they have to complement each other in order to make society work. Rawls opposes the reduction of the reasonable to the rational, as is clearly implied in the naturalization of the human person: "What rational agents lack is the particular form of moral sensibility that underlies the desire to engage in fair cooperation as such and to do so on terms that others as equals might reasonably be expected to endorse" (Rawls 2005a, 51).

It is against this background that both Habermas and Rawls value the relevance of Christianity in the context of advanced modernity, especially its view on the human person as a counter-voice against the tendencies of naturalistic reductionism. According to Rawls, Christianity has a long-standing tradition of preaching the ideals of fairness and reciprocity and of bringing people up to a reasonable attitude towards others. Hence, it is no wonder that he considers Christianity to "constitute a very great public good, part of society's political capital" (Rawls 2005a, 157). Habermas in particular develops this point at length: religious traditions often express normative truths, in which a secular society can recognize crucial moral intuitions with which it has lost contact in the course of time. A concrete example of this is the biblical story of God's creation of man: "God created man in his own image; in his own image He created him" (Gen. 1:27). According to Habermas, this religious belief expresses the idea that God, as a God of love, created Adam and Eve as free beings, similar to, but at the same time absolutely different from, Him: "God remains a 'God of free people' only as long as we do not level out the absolute difference that exists between the creator and the creature. Only then, the fact that God gives form to human life does not imply a determination interfering with man's self-determination" (Habermas 2003b, 114f.). Habermas takes this religious insight to express, indeed, a fundamental normative truth, highlighting the problematic social and moral effects of gen-technology. This technology destroys freedom and mutual recognition, which are essential characteristics of all humans, irrespective of their being religious or not: "One need not believe in theological premises in order to understand what follows from this, namely that an entirely different kind of dependence, perceived as a causal one, becomes involved if the difference [between God and man] assumed as inherent in the concept of creation were to disappear, and the place of God be taken by a peer – if, that is, a human being would intervene, according to his own preferences and without being justified in assuming, at least counterfactually, a consent of the concerned other, in the random combination of the parents' sets of chromosomes. [...] Would not the first human being to determine, *at his own discretion,* the natural essence of another human being at the same time destroy the equal freedoms that exist among persons of equal birth in order to ensure their difference?" (Habermas 2003b, 115).

It is not my intention here to offer a detailed analysis of the controversy opposing Habermas and some other thinkers (in particular, Sloterdijk) on the issue of the acceptability of gen-technology. The above example only serves as an illustration of the importance of a Christian contribution to the current public debate. Apparently, the Pope has a point in stating that the normative truths of Christian religion not only orient the lives of Christians, but can also have a fundamental significance for secular people. In particular, they can indeed serve as a purifying force for the evaporation and reductionism of reason in advanced modernity. Moreover, because he stands in the Catholic tradition, according to which "religion [is] in keeping with reason" (Ratzinger/Pope Benedict 2006a, 47), he is also able to contribute in a meaningful way to the discussion, fuelled by Habermas, Rawls, and many other prominent religious and secular philosophers, about the question if religious truths have to be translated into the language of public, i.e., secular, reason before they can be taken into account in the public debate.[10] By broadening the idea of reason in such a way that it includes religious (and secular) traditions, the Pope is able to substantiate his claim that these traditions are never solely a particular comprehensive doctrine, but also belong, because of their reasonableness, to the domain of public reason (Ratzinger/Pope Benedict 2008, nr. 11). In sum, advanced modernity is not only post-secular because religion, as a matter of fact, has not disappeared from the public scene, but also because religious traditions are the bearers of important moral intuitions with which society may have lost contact but which, nevertheless, have a universal meaning. For this reason even Habermas admits that "philosophy must be ready to learn from theology, not only for functional reasons, but also [...] for substantial reasons" (Habermas 2006, 44).

3.2 Religious truth and the challenge of pluralism

Whereas the importance of religious traditions as a purifying force for advanced modernity is a major point of agreement between the Pope's position and that of Habermas and Rawls, their ideas about transcendent (religious) truth differ fundamentally. As shown in the previous subsection, both philosophers refuse to upgrade the reasonableness of religious and secular traditions to a claim of their transcendent truth or pre-political normativity. In their eyes religious neutrality belongs to the very essence of the modern state, just as reasonable pluralism is a safeguard for social stability, so that any claim to a metaphysical or transcendent idea of truth as held by (religious) comprehensive doctrines is putting these fundamental democratic values at risk. For Habermas, the critical question of whether the modern state rests on normative presuppositions that it is unable to guarantee not only casts doubt on the question of whether the democratic, constitutional state is able to renew these normative presuppositions

---

10   See, for example, Rawls's famous idea of the proviso: "Reasonable comprehensive doctrines, religious or nonreligious, may be introduced in the public political discussion at any time, provided that in due course proper political reasons – and not reasons given solely by comprehensive doctrines – are presented that are sufficient to support whatever the comprehensive doctrines are said to support" (Rawls 2005b, 462).

of its existence from its own sources, but also suspects that these presuppositions are the result of specific ethical traditions, which, nevertheless, are presented as having a collectively binding character. Therefore, he defends a political liberalism, which "understands itself as a nonreligious and postmetaphysical justification of the normative bases of the democratic, constitutional state" (Habermas 2006, 24). Systems of right are essentially to be legitimized in a self-referential way, purely through legal procedures that have come about democratically and are based on the constitution. From this perspective, a religious tradition cannot by itself claim the universal truth of its moral intuitions, but it can, at best, be a serious candidate for public recognition as a result of democratic decision-making. Rawls, for his part, also defends reasonable pluralism as a basic assumption of modern politics: "Political liberalism assumes that, for political purposes, a plurality of reasonable yet incompatible comprehensive doctrines is the normal result of the exercise of human reason within the framework of the free institutions of a constitutional democratic state" (Rawls 2005a, xvi).

Against this background, the crucial question is whether the Pope can hold on to his idea of religious truth without undermining the plural character of modern society. First of all, it is important to ask for the Pope's reasons as to the truth of Christian religion and his critique of Habermas and Rawls in this respect. Starting with Rawls, the Pope appreciates Rawls's acknowledgment of the reasonableness of comprehensive religious doctrines, which, although the latter does not accept them as belonging to the domain of public reason, nevertheless incorporate a non-public reason that cannot be simply dismissed by those who maintain a rigidly secularized rationality (Ratzinger/Pope Benedict 2008, nr. 4). But, as noted above, Rawls refuses to 'upgrade' their reasonableness to a (universal) truth. At this point the Pope asks a critical question: "What is reasonable? How is reason shown to be true? In any case, on this basis it becomes clear that in the search for a set of laws embodying freedom, in the search for the truth about a just polity, we must listen to claims other than those of parties and interest groups, without in any way wishing to deny the importance of the latter" (Ratzinger/Pope Benedict 2008, nr. 10). As pointed out above, for Rawls, overlapping consensus is the eventual result of a reasonable public debate between persons and groups with conflicting yet reasonable comprehensive doctrines. Although this consensus is by definition fallible, he has enough confidence in the self-regulating powers of reason to prevent the outcome of a reasonable deliberation from leading society astray. In any case, a democratic polity can by no means accept a position that claims to be principally different from all the conflicting interest groups, as the Pope does. The Pope invokes this position because reason has too often proven to be an instrument in the hands of groups that claim their specific interest to be the public interest. In order to counter this danger he suggests that reasonable consensus is subordinate to truth, thereby fundamentally criticizing Rawls's idea that social stability is the result of consensus: "The pursuit of truth makes consensus possible, keeps public debate logical, honest and accountable, and ensures the unity which vague notions of integration simply cannot achieve" (Ratzinger/Pope Benedict 2009*b*).

The Pope's critique of Habermas runs parallel to that of Rawls, focusing also on the fallibility of the democratic processes of consensus-building. According to Habermas, one of the sources for the legitimacy of a constitutional charter lies in the reasonable manner in which political disputes are resolved. This 'reasonable manner' is not a matter of arithmetical majorities, but must have the character of a process of argumentation sensitive to the truth.

But, according to the Pope, the concept of reason runs the risk of being narrowed down to the rationality of a coincidental majority: "Sensibility to the truth is repeatedly subordinated to sensibility to interests" (Ratzinger/Pope Benedict 2008, nr. 9). Whereas this danger perhaps still could be staved off in a small, well-organized community, it has become far bigger and more imminent in today's globalized world. Nowadays, every proposal for consensus is more often than not confronted with the unsettling question: whose consensus is this? (Ratzinger/Pope Benedict 2004, 250f). Habermas considers the declaration of human rights, implied in the constitution that the unified citizens give to themselves, as the final, non-transcendent, post-metaphysical point of reference for the justification of a democratic state. But, for the Pope, such a self-referential justification is too weak. Rather, the idea of human rights itself refers to "self-subsistent values that flow from the essence of what it is to be man, and are therefore inviolable" (Ratzinger/Pope Benedict 2006*c*, 61), thereby pointing to the need of a pre-political normativity.

In sum, for Rawls and Habermas it is not an option to appeal to an idea of truth as a transcendent point of reference to judge crucial political issues, since it is at odds with the plural and democratic character of modern society; rather, they rely on the self-regulating capacities of reason (Rawls) and on the capacity of societies to learn from their errors of judgment (Habermas). The Pope, on the other hand, although consistently stressing the importance of natural reason in all human affairs, is much more pessimistic about reason's self-regulating and learning capacities. He substantiates this attitude by highlighting "the pathologies of reason" (Ratzinger/Pope Benedict 2006*c*, 77), which have become manifest in the wake of the Enlightenment. The kernel of this disagreement concentrates on the following question: Has reason enough self-regulating and learning power to criticize its own short-sightedness, or does it, as a subjective human capacity, need to refer to a transcendent idea of intrinsic truth and goodness, which serves as a normative point of reference for political consensus? He does not plea for a tutelage of reason, but suggests that "perhaps religion and reason [should] restrict each other and remind each other where their limits are, thereby encouraging a positive path" (Ratzinger/Pope Benedict 2006*c*, 66).

This mutual restriction of reason and religion offers an interesting view of the Pope's answer to the problem of a transcendent normativity, and, hence, of his contribution to the debate about these issues in advanced modernity. The restriction of religion by reason means that religious norms cannot be founded on divine authority alone, i.e., on a voluntary God who at his own discretion decrees the truth of moral norms, but have to be recognized by reason as well. The Pope's critique of this kind of 'authoritarian' transcendence is quite explicit: "God does not become more divine when we push him away from us in a sheer, impenetrable voluntarism; rather, the truly divine God is the God who has revealed himself as *logos* and, as *logos*, has acted and continues to act lovingly on our behalf" (Ratzinger/Pope Benedict 2006*b*, nr. 7). Essentially, it is the task of human reason to show the reasonableness of God's will. In this sense, the Pope agrees with Habermas's and Rawls's rejection of a transcendent normativity that lies beyond any rationality, and therewith aims to take the edge off their critique of the transcendent-authoritarian character of religious comprehensive doctrines, especially Christianity.[11] But, on the other hand, religion should also restrict reason. In our personal and political lives we are often confronted with essential truths that cannot be demonstrated unambiguously, e.g., through so-called scientific arguments. The idea of human dignity and the inviolability of the human person are clear examples of this. As noted above, these kinds of truths can be seen as expressions of wisdom, and religious traditions have always been the treasuries of this wisdom, even though they often have not lived up to them in the course of history. Furthermore, precisely because of their traditional character, religions have preserved truths that were out of vogue for some time, but are nevertheless essential. Although Habermas and Rawls appreciate religions as treasuries of wisdom, they nevertheless expect that these truths can be incorporated in the process of the forming of consensus. According to the Pope, however, both authors show here a rather unrealistic trust in the capacities of human reason to overcome its spacio-temporal and cultural limitations. He qualifies this as an expression of the hubris of reason, which can only be countered by strong religious (and secular) traditions of wisdom.

What is at stake here is the crucial question of how to find an effective ethical consensus which is based on a transcendent idea of truth, i.e., the idea of human dignity, and at the same time able to sufficiently motivate and inspire us in order to respond to the enormous challenges of a globalized society. For an adequate response the Pope is convinced that we actually need an even broader rationality than the kind of secular reason proposed by Rawls and Habermas, because the latter is still too much bound by a specific, Western culture and, hence, cannot count for the whole of humanity. In other words, notwithstanding its great merits, political liberalism probably cannot be implemented in societies that are democratic but also far more traditional than Western ones. More generally, the Pope concludes that "the rational or ethical or religious formula that would embrace the whole world and unite all persons does not exist; or, at least,

---

11   Habermas's and Rawls's focus on God's absolutely free will (rather than on his reason) and, hence, on the authoritarian character of his decrees, depends largely on the Protestant rather than Catholic background of their thinking about God's nature.

it is unattainable at the present moment" (Ratzinger/Pope Benedict 2006c, 76). Instead of an abstract formula he proposes the whole tradition of (religious) wisdom as a much broader and more concrete approach to overcome the one-sidedness of Western rationality, and as a way to uphold the essential link between rationality and truth.

But, although the idea of wisdom also leaves room for some degree of plurality, since the former is embedded in the great variety of personal lives, as well as in that of the traditions of all great cultures, the crucial remaining question is how the Pope deals with the issue of pluralism in his discussion with Rawls and Habermas. Although both reject the postmodern or unreasonable form of pluralism, they have also shown that *reasonable* pluralism is not a transient but a fundamental reality of modern societies and thus has to be taken into account in all debates about the role of religions and Churches in our times. Rawls gives a pertinent definition of reasonable pluralism: comprehensive doctrines may fundamentally diverge as to their basic principles while, at the same time, lacking a shared basis of justification that applies to all of them (Rawls 2005a, 60f.). Especially in a globalized society this divergence has become an ever more important issue, both on a theoretical and on a practical level. In his attempt to answer this question, the Pope starts by admitting that accepting the intercultural dimension is a prerequisite for an adequate discussion of the fundamental question of what it means to be human in a globalized world. Moreover, all major cultural spaces (e.g., the Western world, Islam, Hinduism, and Buddhism) are confronted with profound internal tensions, which make an intercultural dialogue about fundamental existential questions even more difficult. As a first step to solving this problem the Pope suggests "[including] the other cultures in the attempt at a polyphonic relatedness, in which they themselves are receptive to the essential complementarity of reason and faith, so that a universal process of purifications (in the plural!) can proceed. Ultimately, the essential values and norms that are in some way known or sensed by all men will take on a new brightness in such a process, so that that which holds the world together can once again become an effective force in mankind" (Ratzinger/Pope Benedict 2006c, 79f.). This means that the Pope fully accepts a certain degree of plurality but, at the same time, is confident that this will only be a transitory phase on the way to the universal splendor of truth and its acceptance by all people.

A serious problem arises in this respect. The Pope's explicit use of the plural form of the term purification as well as the polyphonic character of the relatedness of cultures suggest that he considers these purifications and relations to be reciprocal. As shown above, the Pope has good arguments for his basic thesis that Christianity is a purifying force for reason in advanced modernity. But is he also prepared to accept a purification of the Christian tradition and a polyphony in which his tradition will not be the leading voice? In his discussion with Habermas he leaves open the possibility that Christianity "may perhaps be universal *de jure*" (Ratzinger/Pope Benedict 2006c, 73), and in his discussion with Rawls he opposes Christianity's sensibility to the truth against the sensibility to particular interests (Ratzinger/Pope Benedict 2008, nr. 9). Although one cannot reasonably expect the Pope, as the head of the Catholic Church, to strive for a purification of his own religious tradition, and although it is quite understandable that he hopes that Christianity will indeed turn out to be universal *de jure* as well as *de facto*, he nevertheless downplays with these two remarks even the possibility of a purification of Christianity by other traditions and of the Christian tradition as being just one voice in the polyphonic choir of all traditions of wisdom. But accepting this possibility is precisely the prerequisite condition for the truly intercultural and inter-religious dialogue the Pope claims to be advocating. In sum, if he expects all religious traditions to converge in to Christianity, this comes down to treating Christian comprehensive doctrine as 'the whole truth'. And if he expects secular traditions also to converge in to the Christian one this would turn his advice to secular people to live *as if* God existed, into simply requiring them to believe in God. In any case, this would come down to marginalizing reasonable pluralism as a fundamental reality in a globalized world.

The discussion between the Pope and some prominent contemporary philosophers leaves us with an aporia. Apparently, the predicament of societies in advanced modernity is that they need a normative idea of truth and goodness as a point of reference, but are utterly unable to reach a consensus even as to its minimal content, especially on a global level. The current controversies about the actual universality of the 'universal declaration of human rights' of 1948, which is seen by many countries as infested with Western prejudices, and, on a more fundamental level, about the question of whether there are indeed universal human values, are telling examples in this respect. Apparently, the reasonableness of reasonable pluralism has come increasingly under pressure ever since the process of globalization has taken a firm hold. Consequently, even a minimal definition of what the idea of human dignity as a common ground for all cultures comprises has come under pressure too. Perhaps a broadened idea of reason, as suggested by the Pope, implying that religions and traditional societies are not forced to comply with the rules and standards of secular reason, could be a first step to respond to this aporia. But, as Rawls and Habermas have made clear, one thereby also has to accept that the concretization of this (minimal) idea of human dignity will inevitably differ according to the variety of religious and secular traditions, being not a transient but a permanent characteristic of humans living in a globalized world.

References

Habermas, J. 2003*a* (original 2001). The Debate on the Ethical Self-Understanding of the Species. Pp. 16-100 in Id. *The Future of Human Nature.* Cambridge: Polity Press.

Habermas, J. 2003*b* (original 2001). Faith and Knowledge. Pp. 101-115 in Id. *The Future of Human Nature.* Cambridge: Polity Press.

Habermas, J. 2006 (original 2005). Pre-political Foundations of a Democratic State. Pp. 19-52 in J. Habermas & J. Ratzinger. *The Dialectics of Secularization: On Reason and Religion.* San Francisco: Ignatius.

John Paul II. 1998. *Faith and Reason.* Roma: Libreria Editrice Vaticana.

Jonkers, P. 2009. Religious Truth in a Globalising World. Pp. 177-207 in Ph. Quadrio & C. Besseling (eds.). *Religion and Politics in the New Century: Contemporary Philosophical Perspectives.* Sydney: Sydney University Press.

Ratzinger, J./Benedict XVI. 2004. *Truth and Tolerance. Christian Belief and World Religions.* San Francisco: Ignatius Press.

Ratzinger, J./Benedict XVI. 2006a. *Christianity and the Crisis of Cultures.* San Francisco: Ignatius Press.

Ratzinger, J./Benedict XVI. 2006b. *Faith, Reason and the University. Memories and Reflections.* Roma: Libreria Editrice Vaticana.

Ratzinger, J./Benedict XVI. 2006c (original 2005). That Which Holds the World Together. The Pre-Political Moral Foundations of a Free State. Pp. 53-80 in J. Habermas & J. Ratzinger. *The Dialectics of Secularization: On Reason and Religion.* San Francisco: Ignatius.

Ratzinger, J./Benedict XVI & M. Pera. 2006d. *Without Roots. The West, Relativism, Christianity, Islam.* New York: Basic Books.

Ratzinger, J./Benedikt XVI. 2007a. *Begegnung mit führenden Vertretern des politischen und öffentlichen Lebens sowie dem diplomatischen Korps.* Roma: Libreria Editrice Vaticana.

Ratzinger, J./Benedict XVI. 2007b. *Spe salvi.* Roma: Libreria Editrice Vaticana.

Ratzinger, J./Benedict XVI. 2008. *Lecture by the Holy Father at the University of Rome 'La Sapienza'.* Roma: Libreria Editrice Vaticana.

Ratzinger, J./Benedict XVI. 2009a. *Caritas in veritate.* Roma: Libreria Editrice Vaticana.

Ratzinger, J./Benedict XVI. 2009b. *Meeting With the Civil and Political Authorities and With the embers of the Diplomatic Corps.* Roma: Libreria Editrice Vaticana.

Rawls, J. 2005a (original 1993). *Political Liberalism. Expanded edition.* New York: Columbia University Press.

Rawls, J. 2005b (original 1997). The Idea of Public Reason Revisited. Pp. 440-490 in Id. *Political Liberalism. Expanded edition.* New York: Columbia University Press.

Rorty, R. 1989. *Contingency, Irony, Solidarity.* Cambridge: Cambridge University Press.

Rorty, R. 1991. *Objectivity, Relativism and Truth.* Cambridge: Cambridge University Press.

Sloterdijk, P. 1999. *Regeln für den Menschenpark. Ein Antwortschreiben zu Heideggers Brief über den Humanismus.* Frankfurt: Suhrkamp Verlag.

Reform with Continuity:
Religious Freedom and Canon Law

Ton Meijers

Modern society acknowledges that religious freedom is a human right. Religious freedom is sometimes even referred to as the 'mother' of human rights. Nevertheless, the Catholic Church had to make great efforts to acknowledge religious freedom as a human freedom, which finally occurred at the Second Vatican Council (1962-1965).

With special attention to canon law, this chapter will explain how the Second Vatican Council succeeded in acknowledging religious freedom. I will describe how the development in modern society, which led to the recognition of religious freedom as a human right based on human dignity, urged the Church to examine its own tradition in order to explain how religious freedom is rooted in ecclesiastical tradition and how the Second Vatican Council succeeded in elaborating an ecclesiastical doctrine on religious freedom. In addition, I will examine in which way the recognition of religious freedom has influenced the revision of the ecclesiastical regulations on mixed marriages in order to show that the recognition of religious freedom stands not on its own, but has determined the revision of canon law. The aim of this chapter is to make clear how the Catholic Church has reacted to developments in modern society, a process that can be summarized in what I call reform with continuity.

1. Canon 748

The third book of the Code of Canon Law (*CIC*) of 1983 deals with the ecclesiastical office of safeguarding and proclaiming the divine and catholic doctrine of the Church. This book includes regulations concerning the ecclesiastical Magisterium and the ministry of the Word. The third book opens with some general norms. The first canon relates to the deposit of the Catholic faith and the innate right of the Church to proclaim the gospel to all peoples. The second paragraph of this canon states the right of the Catholic Church to announce moral principles and the right to judge human affairs in so far as this is required by the fundamental rights or the salvation of souls (canon 747, CIC\1983). Therefore, this canon confirms the fundamental right of the Church to proclaim matters of faith and morality as religious truth and truth about human behavior. The following canon reflects the way in which people have to seek and accept the divine truth.

Canon 748 states:

§ 1. All people are bound to seek the truth in those matters, which concern God and his Church and once known they are obliged by virtue of divine law and enjoy the right to embrace and keep it.

§ 2. To no one is it ever permitted to induce people to embrace the catholic faith against their conscience by means of coercion. (*Translation by the author*)

This canon does not reflect only the position of the Christian faithful based on their baptism and membership in the Church, but concerns all human beings. It relates to the human need to seek the truth in religious matters. In regard to this, it expresses the human obligation to scrutinize sincerely by their conscience the religious truth of the Catholic faith. The Catholic faith, however, can only genuinely be accepted and kept by the human conscience when it is free from external coercion. In this way this canon has an anthropological and personalistic foundation, pointed to in the reference to divine law in the first paragraph (Aymans – Mörsdorf 2007, 7-8). But the reference to divine law also refers to the Catholic faith from the viewpoint of the nature of the Catholic truth and affirms its divine and, therefore, binding character.

The fact that canon 748 only mentions the Catholic faith and does not refer to the moral principles as stated in the second paragraph of the previous canon is remarkable. But since faith and morality are considered the domain of the Church, it may be presumed that canon 748 also applies to the moral principles (see, e.g., canones 212, § 3, 749, §§ 1 and 2, 752, CIC\1983).

To scholars in the field of the Second Vatican Council it will be obvious that canon 748 relates to the Declaration on Religious Freedom, *Dignitatis humanae* (DH). A closer examination of the work of the study-group that prepared the drafts of this canon affirms this opinion (Communicationes 1987, 226-227, 251). Therefore, we will investigate DH in relation to canon 748.

2. The declaration on religious freedom

DH signifies a change of attitude of the Catholic Church towards human freedom and, therefore, towards modernity. The negative attitude towards human freedom, which was characteristic of the ecclesiastical teaching of the 19th century, changed into a positive view during the Second Vatican Council.

2.1. Historical background

In the 19th century, the Church in Western Europe was confronted by liberalism, which defended and advocated the freedom of people. Because this movement was also anti-clerical and anti-ecclesiastical, it threatened the position of the Church in society. As a result, the Church reacted defensively and vehemently attacked liberalism. The liberal opinions about human freedom especially in religious matters were qualified as erroneous. The ecclesiastical teaching responded to liberalism by emphasizing the binding character of the divine truth for the salvation of souls and the common good, and by stressing, consequently, the obligation of all humans to obey the divine truth. As a consequence of this rather radical negative attitude towards human freedom, the Church lost sight of its view of human freedom as an esteemed religious value in its own tradition.

As well known, in 1864, Pope Pius IX published the encyclical *Quanta cura* to which a list of eighty erroneous opinions (*Syllabus errorum*) was added (Cottier 2009, 106-107). Both the encyclical and the list comprehend sharp rejections of liberal convictions concerning the freedom of conscience and religion, which are qualified as insane:

> From that whole false idea of social government they do by no means fear to favor that opinion, most destructive to the Catholic Church and for the salvation of the souls by Our Predecessor Gregory XVI called an i n s a n i t y, that namely "the freedom of conscience and worship is a personal right of every man, which by law must be proclaimed and confirmed in every rightly constituted society (...)" (Quanta cura, n. 4). (*Translation by the author*)

This freedom of conscience and religion is characterized as freedom of perdition (*libertas perditionis*). The list of errors comprehends a text that warns of the consequences of the legal recognition of religious freedom in relation to the freedom of speech. Religious freedom will lead to the corruption of morals and create an ambiance of "indifferentism". Due to the use of a double negation (i.e., the formulation of a negative – the error – in a negative sentence), the text is not easy to understand:

> It is of course false, that by the civil freedom of every form of worship and also the full capacity attributed to everyone to express overtly and openly whatever opinions and thoughts will lead to corrupt the morals and souls of the people more easily and increase the pest of indifferentism (Syllabus errorem, n. 79). (*Translation by the author*)

To understand this ecclesiastical policy, one has to take into consideration that the attacked liberal doctrines stand for an almost unconditional and absolute freedom concerning religious matters. They favored and embraced religious indifferentism and relativism, which not only damaged the position of the Church in society, but was (and still is) unacceptable for the Church because of its belief and conviction concerning the truth of the Catholic faith, which, from an ecclesiastical point of view, is not negotiable. The ecclesiastical teaching proclaimed, underlined, and defended – for the benefit of human souls – the truth of the Catholic faith, which is the undeniable mission, task, and right of the Church (Quanta cura, n. 1). By accentuating the truth, and, therefore, the authority of the Catholic faith and its binding character, which demands obedience, there was no room for freedom and dialogue.

To modify the negative attitude towards civil freedom in religious matters, the development of the Catholic Church in the USA is of great importance. Already in 1791, the United States Congress accepted the famous First Amendment to the Constitution, which – among other civil rights – guarantees religious freedom for all citizens. In the 19th century, the Catholic Church in the USA flourished and prospered. US constitutional law guaranteed civil religious freedom, and the Catholic Church enjoyed the freedom and room to develop itself successfully in American society. Thus, the Catholic Church experienced that religious freedom was not disadvantageous for ecclesiastical life *per se*, but could, on the contrary, be beneficial to it. Therefore, it is not surprising that the ecclesiastical reorientation on religious freedom had its roots in the USA. In rethinking the ecclesiastical teaching of the 19th century, the theology of the American Jesuit, John Courtney Murray (1904-1967), was of great importance not only in the period preceding the Second Vatican Council, but also during the Council where he, as an expert (*peritus*), was closely involved in the realization of the Declaration on Religious Freedom (Sebott, 1977).

During the 19th and 20th centuries most of the Western European nations had incorporated in their constitutions religious freedom as a civil right. In 1948, shortly after the Second World War, the freedom of thought, conscience, and religion was affirmed as a human right in the Universal Declaration of Human Rights of the United Nations and, afterwards, in other international treaties. In the same year, the World Council of Churches published its declaration on religious freedom (Declaration on Religious Liberty, 1976). Also in the Catholic Church, some efforts were made to change the negative attitude towards religious freedom into a positive one (Carrillio de Albornoz, 1959). Already before the Council, some Catholic theologians were reflecting on religious freedom as a theological phenomenon.

One of the intentions of the Second Vatican Council was to steer the Catholic Church into modernity. The Church had to give up its negative and defensive attitude towards modern developments and become more open and positive in order to take part in modern society while maintaining its religious identity. The Council intended to take part in ecumenical and inter-religious dialogue and wanted to foster a dialogue with secularism (atheism); thus the Council was urged to deal with religious freedom (Siebenrock 2005, 131). From the start until the end of the Council, several drafts on religious freedom were discussed. The debates went on laboriously because a small group of Council-Fathers were unyielding in their opposition to the doctrine as presented. The main problems focused on the relation between religious freedom and the divine Catholic truth, and the conformity of the developed doctrine with the ecclesiastical teaching of especially the 19th century, which the drafts seemed to oppose. In 1963, and so during the Council, Pope John XXIII published his famous encyclical *Pacem in terris*, which recognized, among other human rights, religious freedom as a human right (Pacem in terris, n. 14, DzH, n. 3961). Naturally, this event had an encouraging influence on the council debates. Additionally, the text of the document was modified in order to meet the wishes of the opposing Council-Fathers. In accordance with Murray's theology, and as is stated in its subtitle, the declaration only deals with religious freedom as a social and civil phenomenon (COD, 1001, 34). In this way, the dogmatic character of the document is more nuanced and its character as a social ecclesiastical teaching is accentuated. The document, however, relates religious freedom also to the human moral obligation to seek the truth. This was needed to avoid possible future interpretations that the Catholic Church seemed to accept indifferentism in religious matters. The Council finally succeeded in agreeing on the declaration, which was published on December 7, 1965 (Pavan 1967, 704-711, Siebenrock, 2005, 152-165). From that time on, the ecclesiastical teaching defends religious freedom as a human right (Couttier 2009, 109-111).

2.2. Religious freedom as a human right

The first paragraph of DH turns its attention to developments in modern society by referring to the value of human dignity and the wish of people to live in responsible freedom, which also concerns religious life. These social developments are taken seriously and the Church is urged to examine its own tradition (DH, 1a). So, modern developments, like the value of human dignity and the human need for freedom, are no longer considered as suspicious, but ask the Church to engage in a critical self-reflection of its tradition.

The opening of the second paragraph of DH states:

This Vatican synod declares that the human person has a right to religious freedom. (DH, 2a, COD, 1002,32-33)

The declaration does not use the concept *docet*, but speaks of *declarat*. The concept *docet* concerns pronouncements of the authentic ecclesiastical Magisterium, which defines matters of belief and morals in an authoritative way. The declaration expresses a new form of ecclesiastical teaching, which can be characterized as pastoral or preaching ecclesiastical teaching (Kolfhaus, 2006, 125-170) as a part of the social teaching of the Church, which regards all people.

From a judicial point of view, it is important to notice that according to the declaration, religious freedom is not granted by positive law determined by civil authority, but is fundamentally rooted in human dignity (DH, 2b). It is, therefore, an innate human right and, thereby, inalienable. The civil authority has to acknowledge this preferably as a fundamental and constitutional civil right (DH, 1a, 2a, 6b, 10, 13c, 15ad).

Religious freedom includes (negatively) the human immunity to external (and internal) coercion in religious matters, so that nobody can be forced to act against her or his conscience and (positively) the right of people to live, within due limits, in accordance with their religious conscience in private as well as in public (DH, 2a). The clause "within due limits" indicates that religious freedom is not an absolute right in the sense that it can be exercised always and everywhere, limitlessly and unconditionally. Religious freedom has to be exercised on the moral basis of personal and social responsibility in view of the common good and may not oppose public order (DH 6a, 7bc).

The judicial doctrine on human rights distinguishes three generations of human rights. First, there are the so-called liberty rights. These rights guarantee civil freedom and forbid governmental intervention (like the freedom of speech and the freedom of association). Second, there are so-called social rights, which require governmental intervention in order to guarantee certain social values (like health and employment). Third, there are the rights of cultural communities. These so-called communitarian rights protect the cultural identity of certain communities in society (like ethnic minorities and spoken languages). In civil law, religious freedom is considered as a human right of the first generation and because of its age, is called the mother of all human rights. Pope John Paul II qualified religious freedom as the matrix and fundament of all freedoms (Gerosa 2006, 81-82) and pleaded for the empowerment of this right (Rico 2002, 124-18). But in which way does DH interpret religious freedom?

As stated above, religious freedom stands for the immunity to external coercion in religious matters. This immunity forbids any intervention by the civil authorities so long as the public order is not disturbed. DH affirms explicitly the equality of all citizens before the law and forbids any form of discrimination of people based on their beliefs (see also NA, 5c, COD, 971,23-25). Furthermore, the national state is not allowed to force citizens to accept or reject any religion or to impede people from entering or leaving a religion. Finally, DH firmly forbids any form of activity by the government that would destroy or repress religion as such (DH, 6de). In this way, DH affirms religious freedom as a liberty right, which forbids the government from intervening in religious matters.

In regard to religious freedom as a social human right, DH emphasizes not only that the civil government has to recognize religious freedom as a civil right in order to guarantee and protect religious freedom from unlawful state-interventions, but also states the governmental duty to foster and promote religious freedom. The civil government has to create the social conditions for citizens to live peacefully in society in accordance with their religious convictions. In some cases, a certain religion may even obtain special recognition by the national state under the strict condition that the religious freedom of all citizens is guaranteed (DH, 3e, 6abc) (Meijers, 2011, 15-16). In this way, DH reflects religious freedom as a social human right.

DH also pays attention to religious freedom as a communitarian right. Because of the social nature of humans and religion, religious life is basically communitarian. Therefore, the individual as well as religious communities enjoy religious freedom in society. DH claims religious freedom not only for the Catholic Church, but also insists on religious freedom for all religious communities (DH, 2a, 3c, 4, 13).

This short analysis clarifies that religious freedom as stated in DH not only recognizes religious freedom as a liberty right, which is the dominant interpretation in civil law, but also emphasizes religious freedom as a human right belonging to all three generations of human rights.

Another point concerns the degree to which civil government may legitimately restrict human rights. The international conventions, which regulate the freedom of thought, conscience, and religion, foresee that the law may restrict these human freedoms in order to ensure certain important public values (like public order, public security, public health, and good morals) (ECHM, art. 9, par. 2; ICCP, art. 18, par. 2). This issue was discussed at the Council. The main problem was determining how to describe the competences of the civil authority so as to prevent them from abusing these competences (Pavan 1967, 727-730). The Council agreed on the following carefully formulated text, which describes the competences of the civil government to restrict the exercise of religious freedom in order to protect the public order, which is ruled by the objective moral order and, therefore, by natural law, which is divine:

> This should be done neither arbitrarily nor with inequitable discrimination, but by legal rules in accord with the objective moral order. Such rules are required for the effective and peaceful harmonising of the rights of all citizens. They are required to make adequate provisions for that general peace and good order in which people live together in true justice. They are required for the due protection of public morality. (...) Nevertheless, that principle of full freedom is to be preserved in society according to which people are given the maximum of liberty, and only restrained when and in so far as is necessary (DH, 7c, COD, 1005,40-1006,4, 1006,6-8).

Human rights do not only regulate relations between the national state and civilians (vertical affect), but also regard mutual relations between all people horizontal effect). In exercising their religious freedom people have to respect the human dignity of all their fellow humans. In DH, this moral responsibility is expressed as follows:

> The moral maxim of personal and social responsibility must be followed in the exercise of all liberties: in the use of their rights individuals and social groups are bound by the moral law to have regard to the rights of others, to their own duties towards others and the common good of all. All should be treated with justice and humanity (DH, 7b, COD, 1005,33-37).

Religious freedom, as described in DH, formulates the doctrine of the Catholic Church in relation to the civil doctrine on religious freedom (DH, 1c, COD, 1002,28-30). By formulating its own position, the Church takes part in the social dialogue on human freedoms and human rights. In this way, the Second Vatican Council succeeded in abandoning its negative and defensive attitude towards human freedoms and adopted, instead, a positive attitude that steered the Church in a positive direction into modernity.

2.3. Religious freedom as a moral obligation

To prevent incorrect interpretations that the Church in DH embraces indifferentism and relativism, DH relates religious freedom to the human moral obligation to seek religious truth. The anthropological presumption is that humans are always in search of religious truth in order to embrace it and live in accordance with it. This truth is found by, and is revealed to, the human conscience. Only by a free and responsible conscientious decision can the truth become a personal and binding conviction, which demands an ambience of freedom and absence from any form of external coercion. Only in this way can the human person find truth (DH, 1c, 2b). Moreover, one can only find truth in a social environment of free and open dialogue. Thus, DH not only affirms the freedom of conscience, but also pleads for an ambiance of free and open dialogue. In doing so, it defends, although implicitly, the freedom of speech:

> Truth, however, is to be sought in a manner befitting the dignity and social nature of the human person, namely by free enquiry assisted by teaching and instruction, and by exchange and discussion in which people explain to each other the truth as they have discovered it or as they see it, so as to assist each other in their search (DH, 3b, COD, 1003,23-27).

In relation to the Christian faithful, however, the declaration emphasizes the importance of the ecclesiastical teaching. By pointing to the sacred and certain doctrine of the Church and to the authentic ecclesiastical teaching, the declaration refers, although indirectly, to the teaching of the ecclesiastical Magisterium, which has to form the conscience of the Christian faithful:

> In forming their consciences the Christian faithful should give careful attention to the sacred and certain teaching of the church. For the catholic church is by the will of Christ the teacher of the truth. Its charge is to announce and authentically teach that truth which is Christ, and at the same time to give authoritative statement and confirmation of the principles of the moral order which derive from human nature itself (DH, 14c, COD, 1010,3-8).

In relation to the truth, DH states succinctly:

> We believe that this one and holy true religion subsist in the catholic and apostolic church (...) (DH, 1b, COD, 1002,18-19).

The concept *credimus* articulates that the Council Fathers, and thereby the Catholic Church, make a faith statement (vertical). This is a religious pronunciation about the revelation of divine truth to the Catholic Church, and therefore, a statement in the field of religion that concerns the transcendence of humans (compare UR, n. 4c, Feiner 1967, 62, GS, n. 76b). The concept *subsistere* indicates the religious conviction that the divine truth can be found in the

Catholic Church (horizontal). This does not, however, exclude that certain elements of divine truth can be found outside the Catholic Church in other Christian churches and Christian communities (LG, n. 8b).

Besides this, DH also pays attention to the moral principles of human behavior and social life. This is called the divine law, which is the truth about human moral behavior, in which all people are divinely enabled to share (DH, 3a, 14b). The sharing in the eternal divine law is called natural law in the social teaching of the Church.

DH connects together divine truth, human conscience, and religious freedom, which comprise the domains of faith and morals. It emphasizes the dialogical character in finding religious truth, the recognition that elements of the Christian faith can be found outside the Catholic Church and the standpoint on human moral behavior. As a result, DH formulates a positive basis for ecumenical and inter-religious dialogue, as well as for a dialogue with secularism. Moreover, it does this, not by denying, but by preserving, the religious nature of the Catholic Church and its conviction about the Catholic truth. In this way, DH leads the Catholic Church into modernity and puts its hopes in human dialogue.

2.4. DH and canon law

DH relates to canon law. Two basic principles of DH are also the subject of canon law: first, the human obligation to search for divine truth; and, second, the freedom of the religious act.

2.4.1. The human obligation to search for divine truth

By referring to divine law, the 1917 Code states the obligation of all humans to acquire duly profound knowledge of the evangelical doctrine and to embrace the only true church of God (canon 1322, § 2, CIC\1917). DH paraphrases this obligation as follows:

> (A)ll people are bound to seek for the truth, especially about God and his church, and when they have found it to embrace and keep it (DH, 1b, COD, 1002,18-20).

Whereas the 1917 Code refers explicitly to divine law and reflects the binding character of divine truth, DH assumes an anthropological approach in view of the human search for the truth. This change of perspective is not a negligible coincidence. DH concerns human nature and human freedom and reflects this from a personalistic point of view. In this way, DH changes the perspective of the ecclesiastical teaching from the traditional approach based on the binding character of the divine truth into an approach based on the truth-seeking nature of the human person in freedom (Pavan 1967, 739-741, Siebenrock 2005, 197).

This principle is adopted in canon 748, § 1 of the *1983 Code* (Communicationes 1987, 227):

All people are bound to seek the truth in those matters, which concern God and his Church and once known the are obliged by virtue of divine law and enjoy the right to embrace and keep it. (*Translation by the author*)

Two additions here are remarkable. First, there is a reference to divine law adopted from the 1917 Code, which indicates the divine origin and binding character of the divine truth. In this way, the canon connects the traditional teaching on the binding character of divine truth with the personalistic teaching of the Second Vatican Council. Second, the canon states the right to embrace and keep the divine truth and, therefore, stresses the right to live in accordance with the divine truth. By referring to the human right of embracing and keeping the divine truth, the first paragraph of this canon is related to the second one, which states:

To no one is it ever permitted to induce people to embrace the catholic faith against their conscience by coercion. (*Translation by the author*)

The human right on divine truth as stated in the canon affirms, therefore, the unlawfulness of external coercion and asserts thereby the religious freedom of humans. In doing so, it refers to the teaching of DH (Communicationes 1996, 237-238).

2.4.2. The freedom of the religious act

The second principle concerns the freedom of the religious act:

The practise of religion of its own very nature consist principally in internal acts that are voluntary and free, in which one relates oneself to God directly; and these can neither be commanded nor prevented by merely human power. The social nature of human beings, however, requires that they should express these interior religious acts externally, share their religion by others, and witness to it communally (DH, 3c, COD, 1003,33-39).

The freedom of the religious act belongs to the traditional ecclesiastical teaching based on divine revelation:

One of the chief catholic teachings, found in the word of God and repeatedly preached by the fathers of the church, is that the response of people to God in faith should be voluntary; so no one must be forced to embrace the faith against her or his will. Indeed, the act of faith is by its very nature voluntary. Human beings, redeemed by Christ their Saviour and called to adoptive sonship through Jesus Christ, can only respond to God as he reveals himself if, with the Father drawing them, they give to God a free and rational allegiance of faith. It is therefore entirely in accord with the nature of faith that every kind of human coercion should be excluded from religion (DH, 10, COD, 1006,36-1007,7).

To confirm this principle as ecclesiastical teaching, DH refers to, among other ecclesiastical sources, canon 1351 of the 1917 Code, which states:

> To embrace the catholic faith nobody can unwillingly be coerced. (*Translation by the author*)

This canon of the missionary law focuses on people who want to assume the Catholic faith. The sources on which this canon is based are papal teachings of the 17th, 18th, and 19th centuries and the Decree of Gratian of the 11th century. In his Decree, Gratian cites Augustine (Conte a Coronata 1931, 275-276). The teaching on religious freedom of the Second Vatican Council is based on, and an elaboration of, this principle of traditional ecclesiastical teaching as stated in canon law. By reconsidering this principle, the negative doctrine based on the absence of coercion has become a positive doctrine on the freedom of the religious act and religious freedom as a human right. In this way, DH succeeds in bringing the traditional ecclesiastical teaching in line with developments in modern society concerning human and religious freedom (see also DH, 9).

Therefore, it is not surprising that canon 748, § 2 of the 1983 Code adopts almost verbatim the prescription of the 1917 Code:

> To no one is it ever permitted to induce people to embrace the catholic faith against their conscience by coercion. (*Translation by the author*)

In accordance with the doctrine of DH some adjustments were made. First, the two separated canons were put together into one canon, the present canon 748. Second, the prescription of the missionary law has become an introductory prescription of the third book of the Code about the teaching office of the Church. Third, an explicit reference is made to the human conscience.

2.5. Reform with continuity

In regard to canon 748 of the present Code there is what I call reform with continuity. On the one hand, there is continuity because canon 748 is based on two canons of the former Code. On the other hand, this continuity is reformed in so far as it is inspired by the doctrine on religious freedom of DH. However, in relation to DH there also exists reform with continuity. By referring to the principle of non-coercion in religious matters of the former Code (continuity), DH succeeds in unfolding the positive ecclesiastical teaching on religious freedom (reform with continuity). Although the doctrine refers to traditional ecclesiastical teaching as stated in canon law, it realizes a radical re-orientation in relation to the dominant ecclesiastical teaching of the 19th century about religious freedom. In ecclesiastical teaching the rejection of religious freedom has changed into the acceptance of religious freedom even as a human right based on human dignity. Thus, the Catholic Church, in a process of reform with continuity, turns towards modernity. In this way, DH realizes *new views always in harmony with the old* (DH, 1a).

3. Mixed marriages and religious freedom

The teaching of DH also touches other canonical regulations. This section will deal with ecclesiastical mixed marriages, which are marriages between Christians of different denominations, because this serves a good example of how, in the light of DH, canonical regulations have been modified (Beal 2000, 1343). Therefore, this section can be considered as a test case concerning the way in which canon law adopts the teaching of DH. Special attention will be given to the situation in the Netherlands. The analysis is confined to marriages between Catholic and Protestant Christians. I will not consider the marriages between Catholic and Orthodox Christians due to the fact that the vast majority of mixed marriages in the Netherlands are between Catholic and Protestant Christians. Also, in marriages between Catholic and Orthodox Christians, some special canonical provisions exist.

3.1. The precautions

The 1917 Code severely forbids mixed marriages. By preaching and pastoral care, priests were required to discourage mixed marriages (canones 1060, 1064, sub 1). This was done for several reasons. Due to the religious difference between the spouses, and possible different opinions about the religious education of their children, the Catholic Church feared that mixed marriages would endanger matrimonial unity and peaceful domestic life (Van Welie 1954, 112). Another argument concerns the different convictions about the sacred nature and the indissolubility of marriages. According to the Catholic doctrine, all marriages between those who have been baptized, which would therefore include also mixed marriages, are sacramental and indissoluble. However the Protestant doctrine considers marriages as non-sacramental and dissoluble. These differences can jeopardize matrimonial life. These considerations were not only hypothetical, but speak to reality, as shown by a study of mixed marriages in the Netherlands in the first half of the 20th century. Compared to homogeneous marriages, mixed marriages led to more divorces and to non-religious education of the children of these marriages (Van Leeuwen 1959, 199-290). Crucial for the canonical regulation were the concern for the fidelity of the Catholic spouse to the Catholic faith and the concern for the Catholic baptism and Catholic education of the children. When these were not guaranteed, mixed marriages were even prohibited by divine law (canon 1060). The regulation was intended to protect the Catholic faith and, in turn, the Catholic truth. For this reason, the Catholic spouse needed a dispensation to enter into a mixed marriage. In order to prevent the violation of divine law, some precautions of a contractual nature had to be made (canon 1061, CIC\1917) (Van Groessen 1958, 562).

Before entering the marriage, the Protestant spouse had to guarantee to exclude any danger of perversion in relation to the Catholic belief of his or her Catholic spouse. Both spouses had to guarantee that the children born from the marriage would be baptized and educated in the Catholic Church. Any parents who willingly permitted their children to be baptized and educated outside the Catholic Church committed an ecclesiastical crime and were suspected of heresy (canon 2319, CIC\1917). The regulation intended to safeguard the interest of the Catholic faith and thereby the Catholic truth.

With the exception of the diocese of Roermond, there existed until 1955 in the Netherlands, the pastoral practice of abstaining from asking for dispensations for mixed marriages (Van Groessen 1947, 581-582). Although there were some differences between the dioceses, requests for dispensations were rare. The effect of this stringent ecclesiastical policy was that people who factually entered into a mixed marriage were, in the eyes of the Catholic Church, not married but lived in an illegitimate relationship. To escape this dilemma, the Protestant spouse could convert to the Catholic faith and enter a Catholic marriage, which happened in practice. The intention of this pastoral policy was to discourage mixed marriages; however, it was not very successful in doing so. The Dutch policy differed from the practice in Germany, were dispensations were routinely granted, as was the case in the diocese of Roermond. From 1955 on, the Dutch dioceses accepted the policy to grant dispensations in accordance with the 1917 Code (Van Leeuwen 1959, 302-356).

In 1970, Pope Paul VI published the motu proprio *Matrimonia mixta*, which intended (among other things) to implement the doctrine of DH in relation to mixed marriages (Archief van de Kerken 1970, 490, 539, 542). The regulation of the present Code is based on this document. In 1993, the Pontifical Council for Promoting Christian Unity published the *Ecumenical Directory* (ED), which contains some guidelines in relation to mixed marriages. These guidelines refer to the conscience and religious freedom of both spouses and, thereby, to the doctrine of DH (ED, n. 146).

Like the former Code the present Code intends to safeguard the Catholic faith of the Catholic spouse and the Catholic baptism and education of the children. In this way, there is continuity between the two Codes. But the most severe prohibition is changed into a simple prohibition and the need for a dispensation is changed into a need for only a license. The priestly obligation to discourage the faithful from entering into mixed marriages has been abrogated. In this way, the present regulation has become milder. Of more importance, however, are some other adjustments.

Unlike in the 1917 Code, the present Code does not require the Protestant spouse to undertake any obligations in relation to the Catholic belief of the Catholic spouse or the Catholic baptism and education of the children. Only the Catholic spouse is required to declare to remove all dangers that may lead to abandoning the Catholic faith. Thus, the Catholic spouse has to maintain the Catholic truth. Besides this, only the Catholic spouse has to promise sincerely to do whatever is possible for the Catholic baptism and education of the children (canon 1125, sub 1, CIC\1983). The contractual obligation of the Protestant spouse as stated in the 1917 Code is substituted in the 1983 Code by a moral obligation of the Catholic spouse. With explicit reference to religious freedom and the conscience of the Protestant spouse, the ED declares that when the Catholic spouse cannot fulfill his or her promise in relation to the Catholic baptism and education of the children, the unity and stability of the marriage prevails, and the Catholic spouse does not commit a canonical crime (see canon 1366, CIC\1983). But the Catholic spouse must still take care as far as possible for the Christian and Catholic spirit in family-life (ED, n. 151). Thus, the possibility that children from mixed marriages are baptized and educated outside the Catholic Church (and receive, for example, a Protestant baptism and Protestant education) is not excluded because both spouses are responsible for the religious education of their children. The new regulation respects the faith and, therefore, the practice of religious freedom of both spouses also in relation to their marriage and family-life, which was not possible according to the former regulation because it intended to protect the interest of the Catholic faith. In this way, the doctrine of DH influenced the reform of the canonical regulation on mixed marriages.

Finally, the Protestant spouse has to be informed about the declaration and the promise made by the Catholic spouse, and both have to be instructed on the Catholic doctrine on marriage (canon 1125, sub 2 and 3, CIC\1983). Therefore, in regard to the nature of sacramental marriage the Catholic doctrine prevails, so long as both spouses intend to enter into a marriage in the Catholic Church.

3.2. The celebration

To discourage mixed marriages, these marriages were, according to the 1917 Code, conducted outside the church building, without celebrating the Eucharist and without any religious ceremony. All sacred rites were prohibited. These marriages normally took place in the sacristy or the rectory (canones 1102, § 2, 1108, § 3, CIC\1917, Van Welie 1954, 119, 286). Only a sober celebration was allowed, in which the spouses entered into their marriage in the presence of the Catholic minister and two witnesses.

The 1983 Code has reformed this regulation in favor of mixed marriages. Like all Catholic marriages, mixed marriages are celebrated in the parish church of the Catholic spouse. However, with license from the ecclesiastical authority, a mixed marriage may occur in another suitable place, for example, the church building of the Protestant spouse (canon 1118, CIC\1983). As in the 1917 Code, the ED states as a rule that the celebration of the Eucharist is habitually not permitted. This is not, however, done to discourage the faithful from entering into mixed marriages, but due to the fact that the Protestant faithful are not permitted to receive the Eucharist (ED, n. 159). Thus, the principle of entering into mixed marriages without celebrating the Eucharist is maintained, but the underlying reason for this has changed. The prohibition no longer exists to discourage mixed marriages, but is maintained because the celebration of mixed marriages has to express the sacramental unity of the marriage, which cannot be symbolized in the celebration of the Eucharist. There are also other sacred rites that are no longer prohibited. For example, the ED allows for the possibility of a Protestant minister to be invited to participate in a marriage celebration if the spouses make such a request and obtain the consent of the Catholic authority. This minister can read from the Scriptures, give a short exhortation, and bless the spouses (ED, n. 158). As a rule, mixed marriages have to be conducted in the canonical form but when serious problems hinder the Catholic celebration of a mixed marriage, the ecclesiastical authority can grant dispensation and permit the marriage to be undertaken in another way while preserving a public form (canon 1127, §§ 1 and 2, CIC\1983). In 1990, the Dutch Conference of Bishops published a decree, which states that dispensation can be granted, for example, if the Protestant spouse has insuperable objections to the Catholic marriage celebration because of his or her religious conviction or if serious difficulties may arise on the part of the Protestant family, or if another sufficient grave reason exists (Analecta Aartsbisdom Utrecht, 63 (1990), 236, Eijsink 1995, 419-420). Therefore, with a dispensation it is possible to celebrate a mixed marriage according to the sacred rites of the Protestant spouse. On invitation of the Protestant minister, and with previous authorization of the Catholic authority, a Catholic minister can take part in the Protestant ceremony and offer additional and appropriate prayers, read from the Scriptures, give a short exhortation, and bless the spouses (ED, n 157). In the Netherlands, most Protestants are Calvinists. Therefore, dispensations allowing for marriages to be performed in Protestant churches are problematic because the Calvinist tradition only intends to bless the marriage rather than regulate the ecclesiastical celebration of entering a marriage.

3.3. The conversion

According to the 1917 Code, the Catholic spouse was obliged to bring about the conversion of the Protestant spouse to Catholicism. This had to happen prudently because the Protestant spouse could not unwillingly be coerced to assume the Catholic faith. It was a duty of love, which had to be fulfilled by prayer and good example (Canones 1062, 1351, CIC\1917, Van Groessen 1958, 564-565, Van Welie 1954, 117). This obligation is abrogated in the present Code. However, *Matrimonia mixta* still affirms that the Catholic spouse has to give witness to the Catholic faith in marriage and in family-life with gentleness, due respect, and conscientiousness (Matrimonia Mixta 1970, n. 14). Although this statement is in line with the 1917 Code, it no longer concerns the conversion of the Protestant spouse, but refers, instead, to the whole marriage and family-life and, thus, respects the religious freedom of both spouses. The fidelity of each spouse to his or her faith does not *per se* undermine the unity of marriage life. Based on their baptism, the spouses are positively challenged to realize Christian moral and spiritual values in their mixed marriage (ED, nn. 144-145). Already in 1981 Pope John Paul II unfolds a positive view on mixed marriages in the apostolic exhortation *Familaris Consortio*. Both spouses are able to realize the unity of the marriage because of their baptism. The text explicitly refers to religious freedom, which both spouses have to respect in their marriage (Familiaris Consortio, n. 78). This reformation can be seen as a fruit of DH, which helped to change the negative view on mixed marriages into a positive and challenging one. The Catechism of the Catholic Church of 1993, however, offers a more reticent view on mixed marriages. It states a difference of religion does not *per se* constitute an insurmountable obstacle for marriage, but warns of the difficulties that can arise in marriage life, due to the different faiths of the spouses (CCC 1993, n. 1634).

3.4. Summary

This analysis shows how DH has led to a reformed canonical regulation on mixed marriages. Based on the 1917 Code, DH has contributed to a new understanding and regulation of mixed marriages. The current regulation respects in a balanced way the religious convictions of both spouses and, therefore, religious freedom, which is the fruit of DH. The severe negative approach of the 1917 Code is changed to a more positive one. This development can be characterized as reform with continuity.

4. Conclusion

How does the Church adapt to modernity? This question is not easy to answer because we all take part in modernity. Perhaps a better question is: How does the Church react to developments in modern society? This reaction can be either defensive or more open. In any case, reactions on the part of the Catholic Church have to be in accordance with its divine mission.

The aim of this chapter was to explain how the Catholic Church reacted to liberalism. Initially, the Catholic Church reacted in a defensive and negative way not only because liberalism threatened the position of the church in society, but also, and more importantly, because liberalism implied indifferentism and relativism, which was (and is) unacceptable for the Church in relation to its divine mission. Therefore, the Catholic Church emphasized and defended in its teaching the importance of the divine truth and its binding character. By doing so, it was not possible for the Catholic Church to estimate in a positive way the liberal-social values of human freedom and the development of human rights. On the contrary, religious freedom was condemned and considered erroneous by the Church.

The Second Vatican Council signifies a change and a reform in the Church's reaction. The Council succeeded in elaborating an ecclesiastical teaching on religious freedom. This did not happen by embracing religious freedom as social phenomena, but by a careful examination of the ecclesiastical tradition, which realizes *new views always in harmony with the old* (DH, 1a). The reflection on the human need for freedom also in religious matters led to a re-estimation of the traditional ecclesiastical teaching about the freedom of the religious act as stated in the former Code. The ecclesiastical doctrine on religious freedom can be considered a more accurate reflection and elaboration of this traditional ecclesiastical teaching in the light of modernity. Thus, the ecclesiastical doctrine on religious freedom was developed estimating the ecclesiastical tradition positively, though in the light of modern developments.

I have typified this hermeneutical process as reform with continuity. As shown, both ecclesiastical teaching and canon law are using this principle in order to accommodate modernity. It implies not a simple adjustment to modernity, but signifies a process of estimating modern developments in the light of the ecclesiastical tradition and, thereby, in the light of the divine mission of the Church, which is not negotiable.

The renewal of the canonical regulations on mixed marriages based on the ecclesiastical teaching on religious freedom came about by using the same hermeneutical principle: reform with continuity. This changed the Church's once negative view on mixed marriages into a more positive one, which is important in the context of ecumenical dialogue.

In this respect, the Catholic Church has successfully made a turn towards modernity. The developments in modern society are taken seriously and valuated in the light of the ecclesiastical tradition and the divine mission of the Church. This process of reflection can be summarized as the hermeneutical process of reform with continuity.

References

Aymans, Winfried & Klaus Mörsdorf. 2007. *Kanonisches Recht. Lehrbuch aufgrund des Codex Iuris Canonici, Band III, Verkündigungsdienst und Heiligungsdienst.* Paderborn u.a.: Ferdinand Schöningh.

Archief van de Kerken. 1970. Motu proprio *Matrimonia Mixta* and Press conference of Cardinal P. Felici and Cardinal J. Willebrands on April 30, 1970.

Beal, J.P. 2000. Mixed Marriages. In J.P. Beal, J.A. Coridan & T.J. Green (eds.), *New Commentary on the Code of Canon Law*. New York N.Y-Mahway, N.J.: Paulist Press.

Conte a Coronata, M. 1931. *Institutiones Iuris Canonici*, Volumen II. Taurini: Marrietti.

Carrillio de Albornoz, A.F. 1959. *Roman Catholicism and Religious Liberty*. Geneva: World Council of Churches.

COD. 1990. Tanner, N.P. (ed.), *Conciliorum Oecumenicorum Decreta, Decrees of the Ecumenical Councils*, Volume Two. Sheed & Ward-Georgetown University Press. *Communicationes*. Pontificia Commissio Codici Iuris Canonici Authentice Interpretando / Pontificium Consilium De Legum Textibus Interpretandis. Roma: Typis Polyglottis Vaticanis.

Cottier, G. 2009. La liberté religieuse dans l'enseignement du Magistrere récent. In R. Latala & J. Rime (eds.). *Liberté religieuse et Eglise Catholique, Héritage et développements récents*. Fribourg: Academic Press Fribourg.

Declaration on Religious Liberty. 1976. (Amsterdam, 1948). In Commission of the Churches on Internationial Affairs (ed.). *Religious Freedom, Main Statements by the World Council of Churches, 1948-1975*. Geneva.

Eijsink, A.H. 1995. *Hartslag van de Kerk: De Parochie vanuit kerkrechtelijk standpunt*, Deel I. Leuven: Peeters.

Gerosa, L. 2006. Religionsfreiheit und vergleichende Rechtswissenschaft. *Archiv für katholisches Kirchenrecht*, 175: 68-90.

Feiner, J. 1967. Decretum de Oecumenismo. In: *LThK², Konzilskommentar*, Teil II. Freiburg u.a.: Herder.

Groessen, H. van & C. van Vlissingen. 1947. *Het kerkelijk recht*. Roermond-Maaseik: J.J. Romen & Zonen.

Groessen, H. van & C. van Vlissingen. 1958. *Het kerkelijk recht*. Roermond-Maaseik; J.J. Romen & Zonen.

Kolfhaus, F. 2006. *Pastorale Lehrverkündigung – Grundmotiv des Zweiten Vatikanischen Konzils. Untersuchungen zu "Unitatis redintegratio", "Dignitatis humanae" und "Nostra aetate"*. Münster: Lit-Verlag.

Leeuwen, B. van. 1959. *Het gemengde huwelijk. Pastoraal-sociografisch onderzoek naar de huwelijken van katholieken met niet-katholieken in Nederland*. Assen: Van Gorcum.

Meijers, A.P.H. 2011. The Independence of the Church from the National State. *Bijdragen. International Journal in Philosophy and Theology Bijdragen* 72: 3-17.

Pavan, P. 1967. Declaratio de libertate religiosa. In: *LThK²-Konzilskommentar*, Teil II. Freiburg u.a: Herder.

Rico, H. 2002. *John Paul II and the Legacy of Dignitatis humanae*. Washington DC: Georgetown University Press.

Sebott, R. 1977. *Religionsfreiheit und Verhältnis von Kirche und Staat. Der Beitrag John Courtney Murrays zu einer mondernen Frage*. Roma: Pontificia Università Gregoriana.

Siebenrock, R.A. 2005. Theologischer Kommentar zur Erklärung über die religiöse Freiheit *Dignitatis humanae*. In P. Hünermann & B.J. Hilberath (eds.). *Herders Theologischer Kommentar zum Zweiten Vatikanischen Konzil*, Band 4. Freiburg u.a.: Herder.

Welie, F.A.M. van. 1954. *Canoniek huwelijksrecht*. Nijmegen: Dekker & Van de Vegt.

"Ecclesia, quid dicis de teipsa?":
Can Ecclesiology Be of Any Help to the Church to Deal with Advanced Modernity?

Henk Witte

1. Introduction

In January 1980, the Particular Synod for the Netherlands – attended also by the Archbishop at the time, Godfried Danneels of Bruxelles-Malines, six prefects of Roman congregations, and the General Secretary of the Bishops' Synod, Msgr. Jozef Tomko – took place in Rome in order to consider the most pressing theological and pastoral problems of the Church in the Netherlands. Pope John Paul II had chosen as the theme and commission of the Synod: "the exercise of the pastoral work of the Church in the Netherlands in the current circumstances, so that the Church manifests itself more as communion" (Brief 1980, 9). In the homily during the Eucharist, which closed the Synod on January 31, John Paul reiterated this commission and referred to the permanent task of bringing Dutch ecclesial experiences back to focusing on an answer to the question posed by the world episcopate at Vatican II: "Ecclesia, quid dicis de teipsa?" or "Church, what do you say about yourself?" (John Paul II 1980, 161). It is remarkable that John Paul perceived the key question of Vatican II as one of ecclesial self-understanding and self-articulation.

John Paul's quote in Latin points to the central subject matter of ecclesiology. Ecclesiology expresses the self-understanding of the Church and her mission in the world from an insider's point of view, not as an outside drafted theory (Kasper 2008, 35). Ecclesiology, therefore, treats questions such as how this self-understanding is put into words and developed during history, how it is founded in the mystery of the triune God, and how it is influenced by the plurality of the historical and societal contexts the Church finds herself situated in.[1]

The scope of our book is the movement towards a new church formation, especially with respect to Catholicism in a late-modern, Western context. The old church formation, which we typify as ultramontane mass Catholicism, taking up Staf Hellemans' characterization, seems to have disappeared slowly but surely since the 1960's (Hellemans 2009).[2] The new formation is still in the

---

1   By their very nature of being contexts, these contexts function as "the historical, cultural and linguistic boundaries of all our experiences and knowledge" (Collins 2008 (1), 136) and additionally challenge the Church to live up to her trans-contextual and trans-cultural dimensions.

2   Cf. his contribution in this book.

making. We do not know yet what shape it will take: that of a major church that appeals to a majority of people; something more like what sociologists call a sect; a leftover of a minority church; or will it almost evaporate into mysticism and "purely fluid and very personally conditioned group building" (Troeltsch 1912, 967)? We do not know if we should hold fast to the preservation of the "solid" system we come from or depart from this and embrace more "fluid" forms of being church. Some church leaders prefer the combination of an open mind to societal developments together with a clear Christian identity. Others stress orthodoxy, especially in moral affairs, and prefer distancing themselves from or even resisting against a society considered to be more or less "sick". In the end, we do not know what the results will be of how the Church deals with late-modern pluralism and individualism.

Can ecclesiology be of any help? At first sight, its contribution seems to be very modest. Societal developments show dynamics of their own. Church formation, as a part of societal formation, changes correspondingly. Ecclesiology is not taking the lead. It is neither a theoretical framework, anterior to its practical application, nor a mere ideological reflection of what is happening in society. The classical substructure-superstructure approach is not of any help in clarifying the contribution of ecclesiology.

Rather, ecclesiology accompanies church life. It articulates the ecclesial self-understanding in "models" (Dulles 1977) or basic or central statements in ecclesiology (Rikhof 1981, 229; Rikhof 1983), which prevail during a certain period. These models have, on the one hand, an explanatory function. They synthesize and deepen the ecclesial self-understanding often given rise to by metaphors used with respect to understanding the Church. They look like short formulas, but veil an entire world of ecclesiological self-understanding. On the other hand, models have a heuristic function. "Ecclesiological models 'catch on' when they account for both doctrinal claims and people's experience, and when they offer an accessible pattern for addressing important questions" (Hahnenberg 2005, 5). But when new questions come up, no matter if their origin is ecclesial or societal, and current models appear to be embarrassed by these questions, the search for new models is opened. Models will accompany church life for as long as they fulfill their explanatory and explorative functions.

In general, we know two forms of this accompanying reflection: a defensive one and a dialoguing one. In the past, even from their late-medieval origins in the anti-conciliaristic writings of James of Viterbo and John of Turrecremata, these accompanying ecclesiological reflections often had an apologetic purpose and, therefore, maintained a one-sided and selective shape. Nowadays, ecclesiological reflection shows a friendlier and more dialoguing and explanatory face, risking, however, being perceived as harmless, innocent, and not clear enough, although sometimes late-modern culture, assessed as being confusing, provokes a new apologetic militancy in certain ecclesial circles.

Can ecclesiology be of any help in discerning in which direction a new church formation will develop or has to be developed? In my opinion, it can be helpful in two ways: by reminding us of the motives, lessons, and pitfalls of the models of the past, and by reflecting on the nature and the mission of the Church in relation to new contextually given questions and assignments. The first way takes shape in analyzing and evaluating, in retrospect, what Max Weber and Ernst Troeltsch call the "elective affinity"[3] between a well-determined church formation and one or more well-determined models of the Church. The second way asks for a more fundamental theological reflection on the Church's place and role in the whole of God's purpose with creation and humankind. However, the degree to which ecclesiology will really influence current and coming church life and church formation largely depends on the plausibility and persuasiveness of its reflections, on the answering capacity, so to say, of the models it prefers, and on its audience's willingness and ability to receive and to incorporate these.

In this contribution, I will first look back on the ins and outs of the most influential models during ultramontane mass Catholicism: the model of the Church as *societas perfecta* and the model of the mystical Body of Christ. I will then consider the prevailing ecclesiological models in the period after the 1960's: the Church as the people of God, as sacrament, and as *communio*. My main questions are: What can we learn from the content, development, use, and pitfalls of the models of the preceding and current church formations in view of the conditions of ecclesial self-understanding in late-modern circumstances? Can these models help the Church to figure out her shape in such a way that it remains faithful to her nature and matches the conditions of advanced modernity? I will address these lessons from the past or for the future in sections following the treatment of the ecclesiological models relevant to the particular church formations.

2. In retrospect: *societas perfecta* and the mystical Body of Christ

During the period of ultramontane mass Catholicism between 1800 and 1960, the model of the Church as *societas perfecta* played a dominating role. In the last quarter of this period, this model was complemented by the model of the mystical Body of Christ. In this section, I will focus on *societas perfecta* at length, as it dominated the "long 19th century" and it contrasts, in terms of point

---

3   The concept of "elective affinity" (*Wahlverwandtschaft*) refers to an inner affinity with a selective character between two different cultural or societal entities (cf. Weber 1988, 26: *innere Verwandtschaft*; 29: *innere Verwandtschaft*; 145: *wahlverwandter*). According to Löwy, the concept originates from medieval alchemy and has likely influenced Weber because of Goethe using it in the title of his novel *Wahlverwandtschaften* (1809), in which he applies the concept to soul-relationships (Löwy 2004). Weber also could have found the concept in Troeltsch's *Die Soziallehren der christlichen Kirchen und Gruppen*, published in 1912. For instance, on p. 967, Troeltsch observes *Wahlverwandtschaft* between mysticism and the autonomy of science and its function as religious asylum for the scientifically educated sections of a population.

of departure of developments in ecclesiology during the last two centuries, most sharply with where ecclesiology has arrived in advanced modernity.

2.1. Church as societas perfecta

At first glance, the expression *societas perfecta* could give the impression of ecclesiastical arrogance in the face of the rest of society. The Church seems to claim to be perfect in comparison with society. "Perfect", however, does not refer to the excellence or holiness of the Church, but to her independence and autonomy in a legal respect. "Perfect" indicates that the Church has all the means necessary at her disposal to reach her goal: the sanctification and redemption of her members. In essence, the issue at stake was the political freedom of the Church in the new 19th-century European nation-states, the defense or even recovery of which had serious impact on the concept of the Church and church formation (Walf 1977; Listl, 1978; Granfield 1982; Lacey 2011).

The concept of *societas perfecta* has medieval roots (Listl 1978, 107-112; Walf 1977, 107; Granfield 1982, 8-9). Philosophically, it is rooted in the Aristotelian-Thomistic philosophy of state, which considers the state as a natural communion (*societas naturalis*) that is not subordinate to a higher communion or authority. Because of this, it is legally perfect (*societas perfecta*) and able to meet the people's needs both legally and actually (*societas completa*). This concept was also applied to the Church. During the Middle Ages, the one *corpus christianorum* or *respublica christiana* was considered to consist of two independent and "perfect" parts: state and church. They each had their own goal, i.e., the terrestrial and the spiritual well-being of human beings, of which the spiritual was considered to be the higher goal. Initially, the concept of two *societates perfectae* was used analogically. It indicated the similarity between the Church and the state with regard to their shape. From the end of the Middle Ages onwards, in particular, during the time of the rise of independent states and peoples in Europe in the 15th and 16th centuries, the change of state formations induced theologians and church lawyers to emphasize the difference between church and state more and more. The adjective *perfecta* gave them the tool to do so (Walf 1977, 107-108).[4]

In the post-Reformation period, two factors forced the Church to clarify her relation to civil authorities. The first concerned the establishment of the system of so-called "state-churches" (*Staatskirchentum*) in Protestantism in which the Church was legally organized and administered as a college within the state (*Kollegialsystem*). The second factor concerned several movements within the Catholic Church during the 17th, 18th, and 19th centuries, which tried to limit Rome's authority over local churches from a nationalist interest and wanted to enlarge the power of civil authorities in church matters. In this respect, Listl

---

4   James of Viterbo (†1308) already saw the Church as state *kat' exochèn* and as the only reality that deserved Cicero's definition of the state truly (Listl 1978, 110).

mentions gallicanism, febronianism, and josefinism (Listl 1978, 54-60); Granfield adds the French Revolution and the *Kulturkampf* in Germany (1871-1890) and its variants elsewhere (Granfield 1982, 9-10).[5] Both factors affirm that the relation between the Church and the state was the horizon of the problems in which the concept of *societas perfecta* gained its meaning.

The full development of the concept was made possible by two factors: the development of public ecclesiastical law (*ius publicum ecclesiasticum*) into an independent subject, and a philosophical underpinning of the Catholic way of looking at the church-state relation, which could serve as an alternative to its Protestant counterpart. After preliminary work by 18th-century church lawyers in Germany[6], it was Cardinal Johannes Soglia (1779-1856) who introduced public church law as an independent subject in the canonical curriculum (Listl 1978, 4-9).[7] It was the Italian Jesuit, Luigi Taparelli d'Azeglio (1793-1862), who established a neo-Scholastic social-political philosophy as the foundation of the concept of *societas perfecta* and the relation between the Church and the state (Listl 1978, 124-133; Behr 2003).[8] In the second half of the 19th century, the use of *societas perfecta* in a context of church-state relations found its acme in utterances from Pope Pius IX (1846-1878) and Pope Leo XIII (1878-1903). The concept continued to have bearing power in this context until Vatican II. At the time, not only was the Social Question becoming more and more pressing,[9] but in Italy, the Roman Question, i.e., the debate over the reforms in the Papal States, the Italian *Risorgimento*, the loss of the Papal States, and the question of what the position and the power of the papacy would continue to be, was also causing concern.[10]

---

5   Gallicanism, the French version of conciliarism, which considered the college of bishops as the highest authority in matters of the Church, implied, among other things, a say by the French king on appointments of ordained ministers and proclamations of papal bulls. Febroniansm, named after Justinus Febronius, a pseudonym of Nikolaus von Hontheim (1701-1790), auxiliary bishop of Trier, was its German relation and the Catholic variation of the Lutheran collegial system. Josefinism implied state control on the Church in the Habsburg Empire.

6   In particular, the Würzburg School and the Heidelberg School (cf. Listl 1978, 13-21).

7   Listl mentions Soglia's *Institutiones Iuris Publici Ecclesiastici*, Laureti 1842 as the kickoff, although it was preceded by the 100 *Theses ex Iure Publico Ecclesiastico* (Rome, 1826), also mainly written by Soglia.

8   In his five-piece *Saggio teoretico di diritto naturale appoggiato sul fatto* (1840-1843). The future Pope Leo XIII was found among his students at the Collegio Romano. Taparelli is considered the main architect of the Catholic social teaching.

9   Behr 2003, 100-101 notes that "the elusiveness in the first half of the nineteenth century of a systematic Catholic approach to the social and political questions of the day had contributed to no small amount of doctrinal and practical confusion among both clergy and lay activist, ever since the human costs of industrialization and urbanization began to become manifest in Catholic areas such as France, Belgium, northern Italy, and the Catholic zones of Germany." The prevailing response (expansion of charitable works and episcopal calls for greater charity and less capitalist greed) did not work any longer and another approach was needed.

10   According to Walf 1977, 109, the papacy could retain, while its visible power was crumbling off, at least what he considers "the illusion of power" in a perception of the Church as a

It was the opposition to the Protestant, in particular, the Lutheran, public church administration that provoked a Catholic alternative in which *societas perfecta* played a key role (Listl 1978, 50-53, 67-82). The Lutheran system implied a concept of church as a *collegium*, a free association of believers as equals (*societas libra et aequalis*) within the framework of a state. The ruler or *Landesherr* administered the external dimension of this church. As a church member, he was equal to other church members (*gregarius miles*) on the one hand, but, as a ruler, he was also responsible for discerning true or false faith and morals in his territory, and, therefore, *primum membrum Ecclesiae* on the other hand (Listl 1978, 72-73). The German lawyer and philosopher Samuel von Pufendorf (1632-1694) underpinned and elaborated the collegial system theoretically and legally. The persecution of the Huguenots as a result of the revocation of the Edict of Nantes by Louis XIV (1685) triggered him to develop his concept.[11]

His concept was partly a continuation of older systems of territorial law (*cuius regio, illius et religio*); mainly, however, it was based upon natural law and the doctrine on social contract in line with Thomas Hobbes (1588-1679), John Locke (1632-1704), and Hugo Grotius (1583-1645). According to this doctrine, association was a free decision of the people. They were supposed to hand over their rights to the state or to the ruler voluntarily, be it explicitly, tacitly, or as achievement of a historical development. According to Pufendorf, the difference between church and state was a question of equality or inequality. The state, after all, was based on and characterized by a voluntary devolution of rights that created an inequality between ruler and subjects. In the Church, however, there is no ruler or subject.[12] Pufendorf's concept fitted in with the enlightened concept of the state, which was perceived to be founded on a free and sovereign decision of the people. It replaced the medieval concept of the state as based on God's order of creation. Pufendorf considered the Catholic Church to be "a kind of state" (*status aliquis*) that ruled over a large part of Europe under the cover of religion (Listl 1978, 61).

In its rejection of the Protestant collegial system, Catholicism emphasized that the Church had to be considered as a state. Listl notes that Cardinal Soglia adopted Pufendorf's definition of a state without any hesitation (Listl 1978, 63). According to this concept, a state is a conjunction of several human beings with a legally independent sovereign authority.[13] Soglia called this conjunction of

---

world power.

11   Principal work *De habitu religionis christianae ad vitam civilem*, Bremen 1687.

12   Here, Pufendorf manifests himself to be an heir of Grotius. Grotius perceived the Church as a *coetus*, made possible and established by divine law and entrusted with natural rights, such as a *regimen constitutivum ex consensu*, according to which a ruler exercised *directio*, but did not have a *regimen constitutivum* at his disposal (Listl 1978, 74-75).

13   Pufendorf, *De habitu religionis christianae ad vitam civilem*, § 11, 33: "Per statum autem intelligimus ejusmodi conjunctionem plurium hominum, quae imperio per homines administrato sibi proprio, et aliunde non dependente continetur." Quotation from Listl 1978,

human beings *societas*, a term preferred by canon lawyers in the 18th and 19th centuries over the older term *coetus*, well known from Robert Bellarmine's comparison between church and state (Listl 1978, 85-93).[14] This understanding of the Church as a state unavoidably implied that the Church was a society of unequal members (*societas inaequalis*). It affirmed her hierarchical organization, passed down through the centuries. Ordained members are equipped with the power to rule and to preside; others are obliged to obey. Two features were added to characterize the Church. First, as a *societas*, she is universal. Secondly, her foundation as a state goes back to Christ. He is the founder (*fundator*) of the Church.[15] The same is the case with the hierarchical organization of the Church. Because Christ was perceived as God incarnated, the divine origin and constitution of the Church as a state was confirmed. Thus, it may be tentatively concluded that the concept of the Church as *societas perfecta* implied that she also was a *societas inaequalis* and was founded by Christ.

As already mentioned, Luigi Taparelli d'Azeglio elaborated the philosophical foundation of the concept of *societas perfecta*. From the mid-1820's onwards, Taparelli promoted Thomas Aquinas and later Scholastics tirelessly, as he was concerned about the metaphysical confusion that resulted from the new philosophies at the time, such as Cartesianism, which was based on doubt instead of certainty (Behr 2003, 100). He also resisted the natural law and social contract approaches of Pufendorf, Thomasius, and Rousseau (Listl 1978, 124-133). Taparelli reproached them for having a perception of human beings that was too abstract and did not take into account the immortal soul and eternal destination of human beings. He took the individual and experience as his point of departure. They disclosed to him the social giftedness and social obligation of humankind. According to Taparelli, a *societas perfecta*, therefore, is an enduring union of several persons who aim together for a common goal and have at their disposal the means to reach it, without requiring the support of a larger entity. Such a *societas* needs a sovereign authority with jurisdiction. Because such a *societas* is based on revelation, it is, therefore, a necessary *societas*. Membership is both voluntary and obliging. It is voluntary in so far as it is based on free choice. It is obliging in so far as a choice essentially is an answer to God's vocation, which makes joining the Church an obligation of conscience. A monarchal-hierarchical organization characterizes the Church. Because of its

---

63, footnote 52.

14   Cf. Robertus Bellarminus, *Controversia IV. De conciliis et ecclesia* III, 2 (Opera omnia 2), Naples 1857, 75: "Ecclesia enim est coetus hominum ita visibilis et palpabilis, ut coetus populi romani, vel regnum Galliae, aut respublica Venetorum." Quoted from Listl 1978, 86, footnote 130.

15   Cf. Soglia's definition in his *Institutiones* II,6: "Primum est: Ecclesiam a Christo fundatam *Statum* esse, sive ut ajunt *Societatem inaequalem*, in qua scilicet alii sunt aliis potestate et ordine inaequales, propterea quod aliquorum est praeesse et imperare, aliorum vero obtemperare et subjectos esse, eamque a civili societate omnio distinctam esse, ab eaque minime dependentem." Quoted by Listl 1978, 61, footnote 46 and 64, footnote 54.

necessity and its divine origin, the exercise of power is independent from the will of the members of the *societas*.[16]

On the level of the teaching authority, the use of *societas perfecta* found its acme during the pontificates of Pope Pius IX and Pope Leo XIII (Walf 1977, 108-112; Listl 1978, 134-172, Lacey 2011). In Pius XI's Apostolic Letter *Cum Catholica Ecclesia* (March 26, 1860) the formula covers, legally and theologically, the freedom of the Church after the annexation of the Romagna by the Kingdom of Sardinia-Piedmont.[17] According to Listl, the most elaborated articulation of *societas perfecta* can be found in Vatican I's draft on Christ's Church. Chapter III characterizes the Church as the mystical Body of Christ and a divinely instituted salvation institution. She is a "true, perfect, spiritual and supernatural society". Christ founded her as a true society, independent from, not to be confused with, and even superior, as much as possible, to other societies (*perfecta*), but comparable to the state equipped with an independently ruling authority, and, because of her foundation and eternal purpose, spiritual and supernatural.[18] Leo XIII vehemently opposed liberalism and popular sovereignty, and promoted neo-Thomism as a safe alternative to liberalism's erroneous philosophical foundations (Lacey 2011, 58, 61-65). He confirmed the teaching on the Church as *societas perfecta* frequently, however, according to Walf, less defensively than his predecessor (Walf 1977, 112). In the first half of the 20th century, the formula became the foundation of the regulation of church-state relationships in concordats, a period that ended with the concordats with Spain (1953), the Dominican Republic (1954), and Bolivia (1957).

---

16   Taparelli's work was very influential. Pope Pius XI still recommended it in his encyclical *Divini illius Magistri* (1929).

17   Cf. its initial words: "Cum Catholica Ecclesia a Christo Domino fundata et instituta, ad sempiternam hominum salutem curandam, perfectae societatis formam vi divinae suae institutionis obtinuerit, ea proinde libertate pollere debet, ut in sacro suo ministerio obeundo nuilli civili potestati subiaceat." Quoted from Listl 1978, 135, footnote 3.

18   "Ecclesiam esse *societatem veram, perfectam, spiritualem et supernaturalem*. Docemus autem et declaramus, Ecclesiae inesse omnes verae societatis qualitates. Neque societas haec indefinite vel informis a Christo relicta est; sed quemadmodum ab ipso suam existentiam habet: ita eiusdem volunte ac lege suam exsistendi formam suamque constitutionem accepit. Neque eadem membrum est sive pars alterius cuiuslibet societatis, nec cum alia quavis confuse aut commiscenda; sed adeo in semetipsa perfecta, ut dum ab omnibus humanis societatibus distinguitur, supra eam tamen quam maxime evehatur. Ab inexhausto enim misericordiae Dei Patris fonte profecta, per incarnate ipsius Verbi ministerium operamque fundata, in Spiritu sancto constituta est, qui in Apostolis primum largissime effuses, abunde etiam iugiter diffunditur in filios adoptionis, ut iidem lumine eius collustrati una mentium fide et Deo adhaereant et inter se cohaereant; ut pignus haereditatis in cordibus suis circumferentes, carnis desideria ab eius, quae in mundo est, concupiscentiae corruptione avellant, et beata una communique spe firmati, consuopiscant promissam aeternam Dei gloriam, atque adeo per bona opera certam suam vocationem et electionem faciant. Quum autem his bonorum divitiis in Ecclesia homines per Spiritum sanctum augeantur, atque his eiusdem sancti Spiritus nexibus in unitate cohaerent: Ecclesia ipsa spiritualis societas est, atque ordinis omnino supernaturalis." Quoted from Listl 1978, 161-162, footnote76.

2.2. Church as the mystical Body of Christ

Usually, the model of the Church as the mystical Body of Christ is considered historically second to the model of *societas perfecta*. Both models, however, belong to the same church formation. At first glance, the model of the mystical Body of Christ appears to be a correction of the preceding one-sided, apologetic, institutional, and juridical approach of the Church. In its final elaboration, however, in particular, as given expression by Pope Pius XII in his encyclical *Mystici Corporis* (1943), this model affirms the basic orientation of *societas perfecta* on the one hand, and complements it with a more theological, i.e., Christological, articulation on the other hand. By doing so, an outwards-oriented view with respect to the Church was complemented with an inwards-oriented view.

The attention to a more inwards-oriented ecclesiology was rooted in Johann Adam Möhler's (1796-1838) introduction of the difference between the Church's institutional manifestation and her invisible essence as an aspect of the mystery of faith, which influenced the Roman School and the preparation of Vatican I (Hahnenberg 2005, 7-9). Following an initial impetus in the preparatory documents of this Council, the concept of the mystical Body of Christ developed into the most discussed model between the First and Second World Wars (Hahnenberg 2005, 9). In this period, the opposition between church and state experienced a more quiet relation. This made retrieval of the Church as an organic community possible (cf. Guardini's famous "the Church is awakening in souls"), which was characteristic of the Interbellum. The Liturgical Movement reinforced this revival of the Church as community. The Church also offered itself as community in view of the social breakdown that was occurring as a result of industrialization, migration, and World War I (Baumgartner 1977, 18-38). The Church was considered the highest expression of an organic community, desired by God, eternal, holy, and mystically united with Christ. As such, she was the counterpart of profane and transitory societal organizations, put together by human beings. According to church historian Peter Nissen (2002, 23-29), this vision, more imagined than really reinvented, of the well-ordered medieval society permitted the Church to maintain the distance she already had towards society and to elaborate her mission in the shape of an independent sub-society.

Accompanying this vision was the model of the mystical Body of Christ. Initially, this model emphasized the vivid and mystical bond of the ecclesial community with Christ and its celebration in the sacraments, in particular, the Eucharist. Mystical body theology took shape "as an affirmation of the Church's mystery dimension, its participation in grace and continuation of Christ's saving presence" (Hahnenberg 2005, 10). The question, however, of how this invisible reality was related to the visible dimensions ended in a harmonization of the image of the Body of Christ and the neo-Scholastic institutional ecclesiology. This was given expression in the encyclical *Mystici Corporis*.

2.3. Lessons from the past

Looking back at developments in the past with our eyes of today could convey the impression of knowing better. The past could not foresee what the conditions of "being church" would be in Western Europe today. Contemporary ecclesiological reflection, however, can learn from the past if it shows a respectful openness to the past's strengths and weaknesses. I will focus on four issues: the costs of an apologetic attitude, the Church's foundation by Christ, the question of equality or inequality amongst church members, and the dilemmatic relation between orthodoxy and catholicity in view of the unity of the Church.

2.3.1. The costs of an apologetic attitude

In the post-Reformation era, ecclesiology took on unmistakably defensive and apologetic features. These would endure up to and including the first half of the 20th century. In view of the Reformation, the main issue at stake was the question of which church was the true church. In view of the new 19th-century liberal nation-states, the main issue concerned the legal autonomy and independence of the Catholic Church. Both questions brought with them an emphasis on the visibility of the Church at the cost of the sensitivity to the theological mystery she also is. She had to struggle in order to safeguard her freedom and what she considered to be her true essence in a mood of being threatened. The mystical body theology did regain, to be sure, the attention to the Church as mystery, but could not alter her restorative attitude towards the world outside.

As a consequence, the significance the world – or, in more dynamic terms, history – has for salvation was judged negatively. Salvation could only be something extrinsic, a supernatural reality added to nature. The world was a sinful and unreliable reality. Outside the Church, mainly pagans, heretics, schismatics, and apostates could be found; there was hardly any divine activity in humankind. This understanding prevented a perception of world and humankind as a place where the Church could find something salutary and valuable, something from which the Church could learn.

Moreover, the defensive attitude of the Church reinforced a closed mindset. The Catholic Church was unable to perceive herself from an outsider's point of view, which implied that she could not develop any positive sense of history and plurality. The concept of *societas perfecta* guarded this mind-set.

Vatican II would bring a change in this respect. The Catholic Church manifested openness to encounter and to learn from other Christian churches and ecclesial communities, other religions, the modern world, and history. She would demonstrate the ability to perceive herself from the point of view of others or as being in relation to others. The subtle "in" in the title of the Pastoral

Constitution on the Church *in* the Modern World bears witness to an attitude that is willing to look at the Church form the point of view of her position in the modern world (Sander 2005, 704-710). If the title had spoken of "the Church *and* the Modern World", the earlier opposition between the Church and the world would have been maintained.[19] This new attitude manifests the Church's ability to take into account that she is in relation to other convictions or communions. This new position manifests a hermeneutical attitude.

Such a more open attitude, however, supposes the fulfillment of an important condition: the Church needs to have at her disposal a positive theological understanding of her essence and mission. Without such a positive understanding, she would revert to a negative symbiosis with external bodies or opinions, articulate her identity as an identity "against", stress her visibility, and forget the differentiation between her theological nature on the one hand, and her visible form on the other. An exclusively apologetic attitude, therefore, ultimately teaches the Church not to forget to reflect upon her theological being.

2.3.2. Foundation by Christ

Both *societas perfecta* theology and mystical body theology show an explicit Christological orientation as far as the theological foundation of the Church is concerned. In the *societas perfecta* approach, the motive of the Church's foundation by Christ was used in order to underpin the difference between the Church and the state and the higher value the Church has as a spiritual communion. Mystical body theology complemented this approach with a view that the source of grace is Christ, who, as the Head of the Church, supplies this grace to the Body that is His Church.

The neo-Scholastic apologetic application of the issue of the foundation of the Church by Christ appealed to a common rationality, shared by believers and non-believers, in order to gain recognition of the Church's claim that she had an exclusive state. Foundation was considered to be a fact in an Aristotelian sense. According to this approach, Christ was seen as the efficient cause (*causa efficiens*) of the Church, while her material cause consisted of the people; her formal cause was the hierarchy and her final cause the sanctification of the faithful (Schüssler Fiorenza 1992, 73-74). Francis Schüssler Fiorenza has demonstrated the failure of this kind of foundationalism because the argument cannot be recognized without faith and, therefore, will not convince non-believers. Therefore, this theologoumenon should not be treated as a subject of apologetics, but as a subject of dogmatics. The Body of Christ theology succeeded in understanding

---

19 A similar subtle indication is the phrase *quamvis credamus*, "though we believe," in the sense of "according to us" and not in the sense of a confessing statement in *Unitatis redintegratio* 22. Cf. also *Dignitatis humanae* 1: ("Hanc unicam veram Religionem subsistere credimus in catholica et apostolica Ecclesia ..."), *Gaudium et spes* 2 ("mundum, quem christifideles credunt ex amore Creatoris conditum et conservatum") and *Gaudium et spes* 10, 11, 38 and 40.

foundation by Christ as a permanent and ever current grace event, as *fundatio continua*. As a result, it expressed the priority of Christ and grace in relation to the Church and affirmed the priority of a theological reflection with regard to the Church.

The question, however, is whether this orientation of Christ as foundation of the Church was solid enough to underpin the Church theologically. What about the role of the Holy Spirit? Was it sufficient to attribute to the Holy Spirit the role of the soul in the Body of Christ?

A second set of questions is connected with the ever more important influence of a historically-thinking mind-set during the 20th century. The concept of an efficient cause was perceived as something a-historical. A historically-thinking mind-set, however, perceives foundation by Christ as a historical fact. As a consequence, this theologoumenon seems to be a mere notification about history with hardly any theological impact or urgency. "Foundation by Christ" not only appeared to be theologically one-sided, but also seemed to lose its theological meaning as an articulation of a divine initiative or gift.

2.3.3. Societas aequalis or inaequalis?

The *societas perfecta* model included a statement on the relation between the members of the Church according to their states of life and duties: a relation of inequality. The model of the mystical Body of Christ affirmed this. The statement concerned both the Church's organization and her sacramental order.

The definition of the state at the time greatly influenced *societas perfecta* theology in order to strengthen the traditional hierarchical differentiation among the faithful. As an argument, the statement was cogent so long as state and authorities were considered as divine institutions and not the result of social events. However, the main point of the statement was the rejection of the Protestant emphasis on the royal priesthood of all the faithful, from which their equality was perceived to be a consequence.

However, is the Protestant position more adequate to deal with late-modern choice behavior in ecclesial affairs? In particular, churches with a Congregationalist type of organization seem to be able to respond better to choice behavior (Volf 1996, 11-18). However, Protestantism was not motivated to emphasize equality between the faithful by market oriented, pick-and-choose behavior; rather, Protestantism aimed to reject a higher, in particular, papal, authority so that: "Nobody will rule over you".

The framework of the Catholic-Protestant controversy in which this issue was dealt with caused one-sidedness in the approach of the internal relations between baptized and ordained members of the Church. Issues of authority and obedience were approached primarily legally, while the theological, in particular, sacramental, basis of this differentiation, which points at symbolic representation in sociality of the primacy of grace (Witte 2010), was neglected.

A related question concerned the approach of church membership. The *societas perfecta* and mystical body theologies emphasized legal and visible dimensions. Being a member of the Church was a question of "yes" or "no", with nothing in between, and membership was for life. Vatican II deliberately renounced any approach that used terms of membership in this sense. It preferred, instead, to speak in terms of "full incorporation" (*plene incorporantur*) with respect to Catholics, "being connected to" (*coniunctam*) with respect to other Christians, or "being related to" (*ordinantur*) with respect to non-Christians (*Lumen gentium* 14-16; Wijlens 2000, 75-208). Vatican II also valued the inner disposition of those who are fully incorporated (*Lumen gentium* 14), thereby offering possibilities of more differentiated ways of being involved in ecclesial life.

2.3.4. Unity by orthodoxy or catholicity?

Walf noted that a striking implication of the concept of *societas perfecta* is the philosophical conviction that perfection implies oneness. Only one can be perfect. Such a claim puts the Catholic Church in confrontation with other religions and other Christian confessions, the existence of which the Catholic leadership of the 19th century was hardly aware (Walf 1977, 115). Vatican I mentions the Catholic unity of the Church among the features that give evidence of the Church's credibility (DH 3013). In the formation of ultramontane mass Catholicism, tensions between orthodoxy and the catholicity of the Church were not really noticeable. Orthodoxy and catholicity functioned together as the pillars of the unity of the Church, which, as a consequence, was conceived as universal uniformity. It was the time of great missionary expansion. Mission was understood as converting indigenous people to the Christian faith and planting the Church in their countries. Corresponding to this missionary paradigm, catholicity was perceived quantitatively in the sense of geographical distribution. Ultramontane mass Catholicism could permit itself a rather closed attitude, in which the Church acted as the sender of the Gospel's message and people were attributed the role of recipients.

In late-modernity, however, the relation between orthodoxy and catholicity seems to be a dilemmatic one. Emphasis on orthodoxy tends to support a small minority church with a clear and uniform profile. Emphasis on catholicity seems to advance a big Church, although one without an easily recognizable faith profile. The concept of catholicity has also been deepened by Vatican II (De Mey, 2002; Witte 2006; De Mey 2009). In *Lumen gentium* 13, the quantitative understanding is enriched with a qualitative meaning, which deliberately recognizes pluriformity within the unity of the Church, and has, as a consequence, a communicative import in two respects. This view invites each individual part of the Church to contribute "through its special gifts to the good of the other parts and of the whole Church" with the conviction that "through the common sharing of gifts and through the common effort to attain fullness in unity, the whole and each of the parts receive increase". The enriched concept of catholicity also has importance with respect to the Church's contact with peoples. In a phrase that testifies to a more receiving missionary attitude, the Council affirms the Church's willingness to foster and take in, "insofar as they are good, the ability, riches and customs in which the genius of each people expresses itself". In this process, the Church "purifies, strengthens, elevates and ennobles them". The future will tell whether this more open and communicative understanding of catholicity will second a less forced, but not concessive, dealing with orthodoxy.

3. Recently developed models: People of God, *sacramentum mundi*, and *communio*

We characterize the period since the 1960's as choice Catholicism. During this period, three models have taken the lead in articulating ecclesial self-understanding. In the build-up to Vatican II, two models came to the fore: the Church as the people of God and the Church as sacrament. Both concepts were considered innovative and firmly confirmed by scriptural and patristic evidence. The Council confirmed their importance. These models would determine the ecclesiological debate during the post-conciliar decades, although the model of the Church as *sacramentum mundi* seems to have been less influential due to its theological complexity. A subsequent development in the use of models in ecclesiology is related to the 1985 Extraordinary Synod of Bishops, which promoted the understanding of the Church as *communio* and downplayed the model of the people of God (Willems 1986; Comblin 2004, 62). Since this time, *communio* has determined the ecclesiological discussion.

In addition, other models of the Church circulate; however, their influence is limited partly because some models belong to a well-determined context, and partly because some images live, so to say, a more sleeping existence. Contextual limitation is evident in the case of "the Church of the poor", frequently mentioned in Latin American liberation theology (Witte 1995, 199-207), and in the case of "*Ekklèsia* of Women". A sleeping existence could be ascribed to, for instance, the Church as a "temple of the Spirit". Its cursory mention in *Lumen gentium* 6 did not raise much attention in the post-Vatican II period. This cannot be imputed to a lack of attention to the Holy Spirit, but, instead, is likely connected with a certain aversion to or uneasiness with the image of a temple, including the associations it evokes with priests, sacrifices, and high liturgy, during a period when attention was fixed on equal participation of all involved.[20]

---

20 Recent attention to a well-balanced presentation of the Trinitarian basis of the Church is inclined to mention the Church as People of God, called by the Father, as Body of Christ, and as Temple of the Holy Spirit next to one another (cf. Kasper 2009, 52-62).

3.1. The Church as the People of God

In the early 1940's, a time when the model of the mystical Body of Christ was almost exclusively dominant, authors such as Lucien Cerfaux and Mannes Dominikus Koster appealed to the idea of a people of God to disclose, in part, the Jewish roots of Saint Paul's understanding of the Church (Cerfaux 1942), to promote, in part, a scientifically more sound ecclesiology, which did not get stuck in mere metaphorical language, and to resist against an individualistic experience of salvation (Koster 1940; Koster 1971; cf. Congar 1965, 14; Witte 2009, 123-124). Their initial impetus invited a large number of reflections (Hahnenberg 2005, 14).

The Second Vatican Council received these reflections in a threefold way. In the first place, the meaning of the people of God helped the Council to elucidate the position and role of the Church in salvific history between the prefiguration in the old covenant with Israel, the fulfillment in Christ as new covenant, and the completion in the Kingdom of God (*Lumen gentium* 9; Witte 2009, 120-121). Secondly, the model of the people of God made it possible to put the relation between clergy and laity into a new perspective of togetherness and co-operation instead of the preceding emphasis on clericalism. Evidence of this new perspective is given by the insertion of a new chapter II on this subject into the final version of *Lumen gentium* prior to the chapters on the hierarchy and the laity, the title of this new chapter ("The People of God", derived from "The People of God and the Laity in Particular", which was the title of chapter III in the preceding 1963 draft), and the elaborate attention given to the participation of the Church as a whole in Christ's threefold mission (*Lumen gentium* 10-12), a participation which supposes "a true equality between all with regard to the dignity and to the activity which is common" to them (*Lumen gentium* 32; Witte 2009, 119-120). A third meaning concerns the historical character of the Church's pilgrimage towards the kingdom of heaven. Being a setting in which the Church is on pilgrimage, history affects the Church positively (cf., e.g., *Gaudium et spes* 44) or negatively (she moves forward "through trial and tribulation" and is confronted with weakness and sin; cf. *Lumen gentium* 9). History challenges the Church to be open to the "authentic signs of God's presence and purpose in the happenings, needs and desires" of our times (*Gaudium et spes* 11), while also renewing herself and her institutions (*Lumen gentium* 9, *Lumen gentium* 48; Witte 2009, 121-122).

The post-conciliar reception of the model of the people of God was ambivalent: it was both appreciated very much and also unappreciated. In a Western context, the motives of declericalization and church renewal were stressed, which triggered the insertion of motives typically belonging to the inheritance of Enlightenment or modernity, e.g., democratization, autonomy, equality, and emancipation, whereas, the salvific historical approach and meaning, in particular, was neglected, except for attention paid to the Church's relation to the people of Israel (Witte 2009, 123-129). Questions arose regarding the understanding of "People" (*laos* or *dèmos*?), its biblical roots (more Old than New Testament?), and the neglection of a preceding receptive female or "Marian" attitude in favor of a more male or organizational one (cf. Koch 2007, 29-33, 231-232). The use of the model in magisterial teaching was all but silenced from the debate on liberation theology and the 1985 Extraordinary Synod of Bishops, although it was and is cherished on lower ecclesial levels. The question concerning the concept of "people" in the "people of God" still remains unresolved: is it spanning humankind as a whole or is its reach restricted to the faithful?

3.2. *The Church as* sacramentum mundi

In the lead up to Vatican II, reflection on the Church in sacramental terms was stimulated by two questions (Van Eijk 1984, 295-300). The first concerned the connection between the seven sacraments. This question was answered by pointing to Christ as basic sacrament (*Grundsakrament*) and to the Church as originating sacrament (*Ursakrament* or *Wurzelsakrament*), thereby indicating a Christological and ecclesiological framework as the connection between the sacraments. Ecclesiologically, this resulted in the insight that the Church is constituted by the sacraments and expresses herself in celebrating them. Theology, however, was well aware that it spoke about the Church as sacrament analogically, as shown by the use of prefixes like *Grund-* and *Ur-* in German.

The second question concerned the possibility of salvation outside the Church or, put differently, the question of the Church's necessity for salvation. How is it possible to understand and reconcile the claim that "God will have all people be saved" (1 Tim 2,4) with the bare fact that people with other religious or philosophical convictions could not all be expected to convert to and enter the Catholic Church during their lifetimes? Karl Rahner, who was involved in this question from the early 1950's onwards, relied on a rather technically conceptual distinction from sacramental theology in order to answer this question. Whereas, as a rule, the sacramental sign and the reality of grace it signifies, conveys, and passes (*res et sacramentum*) are joined, two exceptions are possible: in the case of a grave sinner, grace is lacking while the sign is present (*sacramentum tantum*); and, in the case of a non-Christian, grace can be present while the corresponding sign is lacking (*res tantum*) and will find a quasi-sacramental expression (Rahner 1954, 7-93; cf. Van Eijk 2000, 131-136). In these thoughts, Rahner anticipated his considerations on "anonymous Christians" and worded a reality known by the Catholic Church as the yearning for the Church (*votum Ecclesiae*). More important, perhaps, was that Rahner offered a keynote of a sacramental nature, which made it possible for the Catholic Church to enter into a positive relation with non-Christians and – perhaps even more importantly – to perceive herself from an outsider's point of view.

Vatican II appreciated the sacramental approach of the Church. The model explicates the relation of the Church to humankind and to the world in a positive way. The Church is considered to function "in Christ" as a sign and instrument "both of a very closely knit union with God and of the unity of the whole human race" (*Lumen gentium* 1). She is "the universal sacrament of salvation" (*Lumen gentium* 48), in short, *sacramentum mundi*. The Council was well aware that the mediating role of the Church between the mystery of the triune God and the human race is articulated in this formula. The concept of sacramentality also elucidates the deep structure of the Church. In essence, she has to be considered, analogically to the incarnation of the Word of God, as "one complex reality which coalesces from a divine and a human element" (*Lumen gentium* 8). The Council emphasized the oneness of this complex reality with a warning to avoid a dichotomy that is inclined to consider the divine and the human elements of the Church as two different and separate realities.

In the period after Vatican II, the model of *sacramentum mundi* was lively received in theology. It appeared more scantily, however, in everyday faith communication, due likely to its rather technically theological vocabulary. In ecumenical conversations, the model appeared to be quite unusual for Protestants, in contrast to the models of the people of God and the mystical Body of Christ. Also, a climate of ecclesial atheism or ecclesial deism that is inclined to separate the divine and human dimensions of the Church evokes, as a counterbalance, a new interest in the sacramentality of the Church (Witte 2008).[21]

One of the more crucial questions concerns the understanding of the genitive *mundi* in *sacramentum mundi*. The question draws attention to a certain ambivalence of this ecclesiological model. A *genitivus objectivus* would imply an emphasis on the teaching and evangelizing role of the Church in relation to the world: it is her mission to show ("sign") God's love to the world and to effectuate ("instrument") it in the world. This position can bring about a preference for the certainty the faithful have about truth and salvation and for efforts to convert people. A *genitivus subjectivus* would imply attention to a more receiving and learning attitude of the Church in relation to the world in so far as God's grace is already present in world and history. In this case, it is the mission of the Church to articulate God's grace and celebrate it gratefully. This ambivalence comes to a head in the question of whether the Church, in her relation to the world outside, is a sender or a recipient in the first place.

3.3. The Church as communio

The attention to the Church as *communio* is rooted in the biblical and patristic *ressourcement* in the period preceding Vatican II (Hahnenberg 2005, 16-20),

---

21 Ecclesial atheism or, more precisely, ecclesial deism may be considered, as the ecclesial version of deism, as an attitude towards the mystery of God. Like deism, it restricts God's activity with respect to the Church to the beginning (foundation by Christ) and, if desired, to the end of history (Reign of God). God's activity, however, is not perceived as a current event. Ecclesial deism implies that responsibility for the Church's mission and organization is considered to be human business almost exclusively. By doing so, it appears to be a kind of "belonging without believing."

in which this model was promoted as a counterweight to the over-accentuation of the Church as an institution. This model required attention to themes such as the mutual exchange between local churches, common decision-making, and episcopal collegiality. It did not strongly come to the fore in the documents of Vatican II, but was promoted as a leitmotiv of Vatican II's ecclesiology, synthesizing the main insights of the "people of God" and *sacramentum mundi*, from the 1985 Extraordinary Synod onwards, after Hans Urs von Balthasar's programmatic contribution on *communio* in the very first issue of the periodical of the same name (Von Balthasar 1976).

The elaboration of the model, in particular, in documents by the teaching authority, shows a twofold dimension. First, the model reminds us of the Church's grounding and participation in the life of the triune God. The aspect of grounding brings about awareness of the Church as a pre-existent mystery in the interiority of the mystery of God prior to each visible realization. The Church's participation in the life of the triune God is mediated through Word and sacrament, and makes the Eucharist the source and summit of the Church as *communio*. In addition to the elaboration of this divine dimension, the current magisterial elaboration of the *communio* model focuses on the structure of the Church. This is evident in an issue such as the mutually perichoretic relation between the universal Church, which, according to *Communionis notio* 9, is "*ontologically and temporally* prior to every *individual* particular Church", and local churches. It is also evident, through catchwords like *communio fidelium* and *communio hierarchica*, in an issue such as the relation between baptized and ordained members of the Church. Comparable attention is paid to the implied ecumenical consequences in questions about the adequate ecclesial designation of other churches (sister churches, ecclesial communities) and the degree of ecclesial communion (full communion, imperfect communion) they share with the Catholic Church. More exceptionally, however, *communio* theology induced considerations on (late-)modern phenomena such as social isolation, pluralism, and individualism in relation to the communion the Church is and offers (e.g., Kasper 2008, 405-408). Here, some ambivalence can also be noticed in so far as world and society could be perceived as sources of problems and the ecclesial communion as their solution. In this case, the Church seems to forget that she also owes much to the outside.

4. By way of conclusion: lessons for the future

Revisiting the prevalent ecclesiological models of ultramontane mass Catholicism and assessing the models after the 1960's, two main developments can be noticed. First, there is a progressive consciousness of and putting into words the Church's relation to the divine mystery in which it is grounded. This awakening started as Christological (foundation by Christ, Christ as the Head of the Body that is His Church) and developed more and more to become Trinitarian, although the pneumatological dimension still remains rather underdeveloped. Possibly, an approach of the Church as the "icon of the Trinity" can develop into being a new model. A condition, however, is that not only the immanent Trinity, i.e., the perichoretic relation between the divine persons, is brought into relation to the Church, helpful as it is to understand and to realize inner ecclesial dynamics such as those between unity and diversity and between universality and locality, but the economic Trinity, i.e., the missions of the divine persons, must also be brought into relation. An important ecclesiological task, therefore, consists in articulating ecclesial self-understanding in the light of these divine missions in the cosmos and humankind.

A second important development took place in the relation between the Church and world or society. A perception of being threatened and an attitude of distance, which brought with it a strongly opposing disposition, also expressed in a pro-active missionary form, slowly changed into an attitude of openness, a disposition of being a recipient of "the ability, riches and customs in which the genius of each people expresses itself" (*Lumen gentium* 13), and a self-perception from an outsider's point of view. It cannot be said, however, that this development is already finished. Reflection on models such as *sacramentum mundi* and *communio* continues to show ambivalences between an emphasis on orthodoxy and identity and an open, receiving, and dialoguing catholicity. Breaking through this dilemma requires bringing into relation the way the Church perceives the world on the one hand, and her understanding of the divine mystery on the other.

4.1. The mission of the divine persons as point of departure

The point of departure for further development of ecclesiological models is reflection on the mystery of God in relation to humankind and the cosmos. According to Johann Baptist Metz's reflections on Karl Rahner's theological heritage, God is a universal theme, a theme of humankind, and not the private property of the Church (Metz 2006, 108-116). According to Gerard Mannion and Kenneth Wilson, it is in the framework of such a "theo-logical ecclesiology" that the Church will find again its position and function (Mannion & Wilson 2008, 1-4). They admit that the Church's search for survival strategies instinctively brings about documents that strive to maintain current positions. They value, however, such documents as self-regarding and "to be as much concerned with social anthropology and the resolution of cultural issues as they were with theology", ecclesiology in particular (Mannion & Wilson 2008, 1). According to them, the Church must focus her attention on God,

> whose work is world focused not church-contained. The church's task is to witness to God and to God's presence. It is God, we therefore believe, who should be and must be the focus of the church's worship, teaching and life. Since God is the redemptive Creator of all that is, and since God has given Godself in Christ to making a success of that creating, we cannot conceive of a time when God will abandon this world to its own devices. (Mannion & Wilson 2008, 2)

The structure of *Lumen gentium* confirms this approach in so far as it starts in the sections on the Father and the Son (*Lumen gentium* 2 and 3) with speaking about the cosmos and humankind before saying anything about the Church.

The opening sentences of *Lumen gentium* are permeated with a conscience of mission. It places its reflections on the Church in the framework of her task "to bring the light of Christ to all men" by "proclaiming the Gospel to every creature" (*Lumen gentium* 1). Mission, however, has not to be understood as recruitment for the Church primarily, but in its original reference to the divine persons of the Trinity. It refers to *missio Dei*, God's continuous self-giving in the creation of the cosmos and humankind, in the redemptive re-creation in Jesus Christ, and in the completion of the cosmos and humankind by the Holy Spirit (Collins & Powell 2008, 188-197). It is with this sense of mission that the Church invites us to look beyond her institutional borders and inner ecclesial tensions and conflicts, to discern whether and where God's creative and redemptive Spirit is at work in the cosmos, history, and humankind, and to make a connection with it. What does this orientation imply in view of the mission and the shape of the Church?

4.2. The mission of the Church

The epilogue of *Gaudium et spes* articulates a fundamental orientation: "By virtue of her mission to shed on the whole world the radiance of the Gospel message, and to unify under one Spirit all men of whatever nation, race or culture, the Church stands forth as a sign of that brotherhood which allows honest dialogue and gives it vigor". The Council is aware of the homework this mission implies in the midst of the Church herself. It "requires in the first place that we foster within the Church herself mutual esteem, reverence and harmony" through recognition of diversity and mutual dialogue (*Gaudium et spes* 92). A condition of this is to be a sign and an instrument of the unity of humankind in relation to the mystery of God. The realization of this condition, however, requires a constant openness to the world and humankind while giving attention to the ever-greater mystery of God in himself, to the *mayor Gloria de Dios*, as Saint Ignatius would say.

It is in this perspective that the Church as a worshipping community gratefully celebrates the presence of God on behalf of all people and all creation (Wilson 2008 (2), 37-42). Moreover, she "offers to the human community an experience and example of the sociality and fellowship (*koinonia*) to which all people, as God's creatures, are called and destined" (Collins 2008 (2) 174). The experience of worship, after all, is not something to be possessed, but rather something to be shared with all creation. Nicholas Lash expresses a similar orientation when he calls the Church 'people called together for some task'. This people, however, is not, as we would possibly expect, the community of the faithful, which we would usually call "church", but the human race. It is the human race that is "called, out of nothing, into common life, communion, in

God". Lash is well aware that this does not make all human beings into Christians. It gives him the opportunity to describe what we usually call "church" as "that *particular* people which thus announces, symbolizes, dramatizes the fact and possibility and promise of the common peoplehood, exceptionless communion, of the whole mankind" (Lash 2004, 27).

This view on the mission of the Church implies open and grave attention to the world and humankind equal to the attention given to the mystery of God. The task of "[giving] attention to God" is "a task that has to be learned by every member of the community of faith. It is a task, too, for which the community of faith has regularly to be rescued from error, complacency and indifference" (Wilson 2008 (1), 9). According to Lash, this task concerns discerning "gods" and God, for "we treat as sacred, a vast diversity of ideas and institutions, people, places, stories, customs, which are, at worst, destructive of ourselves and of the world in which we live and, at best, ambivalent imitations of where true holiness, beyond all our construction and imagination, might be found" (Lash 2004, 39; cf. Murray 2007). This task implies an emphasis on the learning attitude of the Church. Like all great religious traditions, the Church can be considered to be a "school", a gathering in which "people learn that there is no feature of the world (...) that is, quite simply, sacred" and "that we are called *beyond* the worship of the creature" (Lash 2004, 40).

The Dutch theologian and spiritual author André Zegveld broadens this approach in a mystagogical sense. According to him, it is the task of the Church to lead people into the mystery they are themselves by showing God's indwelling in them and the shape it has in Jesus' way of life. Daily life, and all its business, is a place where God works. It can become a ladder, like in Jacob's case, to climb into God's mystery. The particular role of the Church in this respect concerns the interpretation of daily life in the light of the faith in the resurrection, and showing what it means to rise from the dead. This interpretation takes place in all things believers do, say, tackle, omit, in the way they present themselves, spend their money, exert authority, trust people, make them great, or belittle them (Zegveld 2009, 75-76).

4.3. Church formation

According to Cardinal Walter Kasper, when the Church wants to reflect something of God's glory, she needs to free herself from a false ecclesiocentrism, and from fixation on the parish as her main institutional shape. "We are too much concerned with ourselves and think this is what particularly interests people. If they are religiously interested, they do not ask for the Church but for God; they ask for the Church only in so far as she radiates something of God's reality" (Kasper 2008, 63-64). In view of church formation, Kasper, therefore, recommends that we stop approaching the shape of the Church from a notion of deficiency (shortage of priests, shortage of communities) and that we stop attempting to spread things evenly all over the Church, which results in her presence becoming ever more thin and shabby. Instead, he argues that we need to create strong pastorally and spiritually competent centers with radiance, surrounded by a network of small communities with specific tasks. The current reorganization of the Catholic Church in Western societies affirms the urgency for this form of concentration.

Does this imply that the Church in the future will include a majority or a minority of the people? The organization of the Church cannot answer this question. Organization is just a matter of facilitating. The openness of the faithful to people outside their communities is decisive, and probably will imply a lack of clarity and certainty about who exactly is in or out. Advanced modernity challenges the Church to deal with such lack of clarity and certainty.

4.4. What about the models of the Church?

As already mentioned, models of the Church are historical phenomena that help the Church to articulate her self-understanding in a well-determined period of time. The question of whether the current models will continue to accompany reflection on a new emerging church formation depends on their capacity to explain and explore the questions with which the Church is confronted. The models of *Sacramentum mundi, communio,* and even the people of God demonstrate the potential to do so. However, regardless of whether these models, or others, have a future, the question, "Ecclesia, quid dicis de teipsa?" cannot be silenced.

References

Balthasar, Hans Urs von. 1976. Communio. Een programma. *Communio* 1: 1-8.

Baumgartner, A. 1977. *Sehnsucht nach Gemeinschaft. Ideen und Strömungen im Sozialkatholizismus der Weimarer Republik*. Beiträge zur Katholizismusforschung Reihe B. München-Paderborn-Wien: Schöningh.

Behr, C. 2003. Luigi Taparelli d'Azeglio, S.J. (1793-1862) and the Development of Scholastic Natural-Law Thought as a Science of Society and Politics. *Journal of Markets and Morality* 6: 99-115.

Brief van paus Johannes Paulus II aan de kerk in Nederland. 1980. Pp. 9-11 in *Bijzondere Synode van de Bisschoppen van Nederland Rome 14-31 januari 1980. Documenten*. Utrecht: Secretariaat van de R.K. Kerkprovincie in Nederland.

Cerfaux, Lucien. 1942. *La théologie de l'Église suivant saint Paul*. Unam sanctam 10. Paris: Cerf.

Collins, Paul M. 2008 (1). Ecclesiology. Context and Community. Pp. 135-156 in Paul M. Collins *et al. Christian Community Now. Ecclesiological Investigations*. Ecclesiological Investigations vol. 2. London: T&T Clark.

Collins, Paul M. 2008 (2). Ecclesiology: Worship and Community. Pp. 157-178 in Paul M. Collins *et al. Christian Community Now. Ecclesiological Investigations*. Ecclesiological Investigations vol. 2. London: T&T Clark.

Collins, Paul M. & Gareth Powell. 2008. Afterword. The Gift of Mission. Pp. 188-197 in Paul M. Collins *et al. Christian Community Now. Ecclesiological Investigations*. Ecclesiological Investigations vol. 2. London: T&T Clark.

Comblin, José. 2004. *People of God*. Edited and Translated by Ph. Berryman. New York: Maryknoll.

Congar, Yves. 1965. De kerk als volk van God. *Concilium* 1: (1) 11-34.

Dulles, Avery. 1977[2]. *Models of the Church*. Dublin: Gill and Macmillan.

Eijk, A.H.C. van. 1984. De kerk als sakrament en het heil van de wereld. *Bijdragen* 45: 295-330.

Eijk, Ton van. 2000. *Teken van aanwezigheid. Een katholieke ecclesiologie in oecumenisch perspectief.* Zoetermeer: Meinema.

Granfield, Patrick. 1982. Het verschijnen en verdwijnen van de societas perfecta. *Concilium* 18: (7) 8-14.

Hahnenberg, Edward P. 2005. The Mystical Body of Christ and Communion Ecclesiology. Historical Parallels. *Irish Theological Quarterly* 70: 3-30.

Hellemans, Staf. 2009. A Critical Transition. From Ultramontane Mass Catholicism to Choice Catholicism. Pp. 32-54 in P.C. Beentjes (ed.), *The Catholic Church and Modernity in Europe*. Tilburg Theological Studies vol. 3. Münster: LIT-Verlag.

John Paul II. 1980. Homiliae exeunte synodo particulari episcoporum Nederlandiae. *Acta Apostoliae Sedis* 72: 160-169.

Kasper, Walter. 2008. *Die Kirche Jesu Christi. Schriften zur Ekklesiologie* I. Gesammelte Schriften Bd. 11. Freiburg-Basle-Wien: Herder.

Kasper, Cardinal Walter. 2009. *Harvesting the Fruits. Basic Aspects of Christian Faith in Ecumenical Dialogue*. London-New York: Continuum.

Koch, Bishof Kurt. 2007. *Die Kirche Gottes. Gemeinschaft im Geheimnis des Glaubens*. Augsburg: Sankt Ulrich Verlag.

Koster, Mannes Dominikus. 1940. *Ekklesiologie im Werden*. Paderborn: Bonifatius.

Koster, Mannes Dominikus. 1971. Zum Leitbild von der Kirche auf dem II. Vatikanischen Konzil. Pp. 172-193 in Mannes Dominikus Koster. *Volk Gottes im Werden. Gesammelte Studien*. Hrsg. v. H.D. Langer & O.H. Pesch. Mainz: Matthias Grünewald.

Lacey, Michael J. 2011. Leo's Church and Our Own. Pp. 57-92 in Michael J. Lacey & Francis Oakley (eds.). *The Crisis of Authority in Catholic Modernity*. Oxford-New York: Oxford University Press.

Lash, Nicholas. 2004. *Holiness, Speech and Silence. Reflections on the Question of God*. Aldershot: Ashgate.

Listl, Joseph. 1978. *Kirche und Staat in der neueren katholischen Kirchenrechtswissenschaft*. Staatskirchenrechtliche Abhandlungen Bd. 7. Berlin: Duncker & Humblot.

Löwy, Michael. 2004. Le concept d'affinité élective chez Max Weber. *Archives de sciences sociales des religions* 49: 93-104.

Mannion, Gerard & Kenneth Wilson. 2008. Introduction. Pp. 1-8 in Paul M. Collins *et al. Christian Community Now. Ecclesiological Investigations*. Ecclesiological Investigations vol. 2. London: T&T Clark.

Metz, Johann Baptist. 2006. *Memoria passionis. Ein provozierendes Gedächtnis in pluralistischer Gesellschaft.* In Zusammenarbeit mit Johann Reikerstorfer. Freiburg-Basle-Vienna: Herder.

Mey, Peter de. 2002. Is the Connection of 'Catholicity' and 'Globalization' Fruitful? An Assessment of Recent Reflections on the Notion of Catholicity. *Bulletin ET* 13: 169-181.

Mey, Peter de. 2009. Eenheid in verscheidenheid. Het katholiciteitsbegrip van Vaticanum II. Pp. 31-46 in Peter De Mey & Pieter De Witte (red.). *De K van Kerk. De pluriformiteit van katholiciteit.* LOGOS 4. Antwerpen: Halewijn.

Murray, Paul D. 2007. Theology 'Under the Lash'. Theology as Idolatry Critique in the Work of Nicholas Lash. Pp. 4-24 in Stephen C. Barton (ed.). *Idolatry. False Worship in the Bible, Early Judaism and Christianity.* London: Continuum.

Nissen, Peter. 2002. Samenhang in de samenleving. Een katholieke droom? Pp. 17-45 in Henri Geerts & Johan van Woerkom (red.). *Samenleving in samenhang. Doet geloven ertoe?* Nijmegen: Valkhof Pers.

Rahner, Karl. 1954. Die Gliedschaft der Kirche nach der Lehre der Encyclika Pius' XII. "Mystici Corporis Christi". Pp. 7-93 in Id. *Schriften zur Theologie.* Bd. II. Einsiedeln-Zürich-Köln: Benziger.

Rikhof, Herwi. 1981. *The Concept of Church. A Methodological Inquiry into the Use of Metaphors in Ecclesiology.* London-Shepherdstown: Sheed & Ward-Patmos.

Rikhof, Herwi. 1983. De kerk als "communio". Een zinnige uitspraak? *Tijdschrift voor Theologie* 23: 39-59.

Sander, Hans-Joachim. 2005. Theologischer Kommentar zur Pastoralkonstitution über die Kirche in der Welt von heute. Pp. 581-886 in Peter Hünermann & Bernd Jochen Hilberath (Hg.). *Herders Theologischer Kommentar zum Zweiten Vatikanischen Konzil.* Bd. 4. Freiburg-Basle-Vienna: Herder.

Schüssler Fiorenza, Francis. 1992. *Foundational Theology. Jesus and the Church.* New York: Crossroad.

Troeltsch, Ernst. 1912. *Die Soziallehren der christlichen Kirchen und Gruppen.* Gesammelte Schriften Bd. 1. Tübingen: Mohr.

Volf, Miroslav. 1996. *Trinität und Gemeinschaft. Eine ökumenische Ekklesiologie.* Mainz: Matthias Grünewald.

Walf, Knut. 1977. Die katholische Kirche – eine »societas perfecta«? *Theologische Quartalschrift* 157: 107-118.

Weber, Max. 1988 (orig. 1920). *Gesammelte Aufsätze zur Religionssoziologie* I. Uni-Taschenbücher 1488. Tübingen: J.C.B. Mohr (Paul Siebeck).

Willems, Ad. 1986. Het mysterie als ideologie. De bisschoppensynode over het kerkbegrip. *Tijdschrift voor Theologie* 26: 157-171.

Wilson, Kenneth. 2008 (1). Giving Attention to God. Pp. 9-20 in Paul M. Collins *et al. Christian Community Now. Ecclesiological Investigations.* Ecclesiological Investigations vol. 2. London: T&T Clark.

Wilson, Kenneth. 2008 (2). The World as Creation. The God-given Context of God's Glory. Pp. 21-42 in Paul M. Collins *et al. Christian Community Now. Ecclesiological Investigations.* Ecclesiological Investigations vol. 2. London: T&T Clark.

Witte, Henk. 1995. Das Erneuerungspotential von Metaphern von Kirche. Zur innerkatholischen Rezeption von 'Volk Gottes' und 'Kirche der Armen'. *Bijdragen* 56: 187-211.

Witte, Henk. 2006. Orthodoxie en katholiciteit. Pp. 25-49 in F.A. Maas, H.P.J. Witte & P.A. Nissen. *Orthodoxie en belevend geloven. Symposium ter gelegenheid van het gouden priesterjubileum van Ton Baeten o.praem., emeritus-abt van de Norbertijner Abdij te Heeswijk-Dinther.* Tilburg: Theologische Faculteit Tilburg.

Witte, Henk. 2008. Sacramentaliteit als kwaliteit vieren en kerk zijn. Pp. 6-20 in J. Staps (red.). *God in ons midden. Over sacramentaliteit. Verslag van een liturgische studiedag.* Liturgische handreikingen 32. Breda: Bisdom van Breda.

Witte, Henk. 2009. The People of God. An Admired and Depreciated Concept. Pp. 117-132 in P.C. Beentjes (ed.). *The Catholic Church and Modernity in Europe*. Tilburg Theological Studies vol. 3. Münster: LIT-Verlag.

Witte, Henk. 2010. Der Diözesanbischof und die Kooperation der Laien in der Seelsorge. Amtstheologische Reflexionen. Pp. 77-92 in Benedikt Kranemann & Myriam Wijlens (Hgg.). *Gesendet in den Weinberg des Herrn. Laien in der katholischen Kirche heute und morgen*. Erfurter theologische Schriften Bd. 35. Würzburg: Echter Verlag.

Wijlens, Myriam. 2000. *Sharing the Eucharist. A Theological Evaluation of the Post Conciliar Legislation*, Lanham-New York-Oxford: University Press of America.

Zegveld, André. 2009. *Worden wat God is. Mensen op het spoor van God brengen*, Tielt: Lannoo.

Catholicism in Britain:
A Church in Search of its Way

James Sweeney

1. Introduction

There are many sources to draw on for the story of the contemporary Catholic Church in Britain, but a comprehensive modern history has not yet been written. Here we deal with but one aspect - the process of change triggered by the *aggiornamento* that Pope John XXIII sought when he summoned the Second Vatican Council (1962-65). Some significant changes would certainly have occurred quite apart from the Council since the conditions forcing them were already present, but from the mid-1960s the line of development of the Church in Britain took a new direction. This entailed a break with the operational model of church – the so-called 'fortress church' – in force in the early and middle modern period. Beginning with the situation before the Council, this chapter will trace the multiple ways and initiatives taken in search of a new way of grounding the Catholic Church. It will deal with initiatives for renewal in a number of specific fields in their different historical contexts and end with some brief reflections on the trajectory of change and how it might develop in the future.

Following on from the pre-Council and Council years 1958-1965 (John XXIII to Paul VI), the post-conciliar era can be divided into three main periods:

- The first post-conciliar period – 1965-1980 (Paul VI to John Paul II)
- The second post-conciliar period – 1980-2000 (John Paul II)
- Beyond the Council? – 2000 onwards (John Paul II to Benedict XVI)

Some headline events that mark these periods in Britain are:

- 1980 - the National Pastoral Congress in England & Wales
- 1982 - the first Papal Visit of John Paul II
- 2010 - the second Papal Visit of Benedict XVI

2. The 'Fortress Church'

2.1 Historical background

The Catholic Church in the United Kingdom of Great Britain and Northern Ireland is rather unique in that its organization within the one political state falls under no less than three episcopal conferences, that of England & Wales being separate from Scotland while the dioceses of Northern Ireland are part of the Irish conference. This unusual structure reflects the long political and religious history of the country. As elsewhere in Europe, Catholicism was for four hundred years in a deeply conflicted relationship with the churches of the Reformation. Ireland has always been predominantly Catholic, except for the north eastern part of the island where there is a majority of Protestants, Scottish and English in origin. This is what accounts for the partition of Ireland at independence in 1922, resulting in a two thirds/one third split between Protestants and Catholics in the Northern counties which remained within the UK. Scotland before the Reformation cherished its independence both from the English state and the metropolitan authority of the English church; after the Reformation the country became predominantly Calvinist and today's state established Church of Scotland, the 'Kirk' as it is known, is Presbyterian. The English Reformation took its own path, giving birth to Anglicanism, and the established Church of England is episcopal with the monarch as its 'Supreme Governor' under the title 'Defender of the Faith'. In what follows I will deal only with the Church in Britain and not with the very different situation of Ireland.

For centuries British Catholics were a persecuted and tiny minority locked in opposition to the state established churches and the 'Free Churches' (Baptists, Methodists, etc.) which existed alongside them in an avowedly Protestant state. Catholicism retained a slender foothold; some English aristocratic families (the 'recusants') remained Catholic throughout, including the most senior figure in the aristocracy, the Duke of Norfolk; while in Scotland a few isolated communities in the remote Highlands and the Hebrides cherished the old faith. This all began to change with large-scale immigration of Irish Catholics after the great potato famine in the 1840s.

Since the French Revolution there had been an influx of new Catholic resources from continental Europe. The English College at Douai, established in exile in 1561, was repatriated in 1793, becoming St Edmund's College in Ware (and now Allen Hall seminary in London) and Ushaw College in Durham (closed in 2011). So too, houses of formation of religious orders, such as the Jesuit college at Liege (founded in Louvain in 1614; now Heythrop College in London, 1970) established themselves on home territory. Some French orders of sisters also sought refuge in the erstwhile hostile territory of England. From mid-nineteenth century a major Church expansion took off, and the missionary structure of vicariates apostolic gave way to formal dioceses and the hierarchy was re-established in 1850 in England & Wales and in Scotland in 1878.

In common with the rest of Europe, major church institutions were established or re-constituted. Parishes, churches and schools, monasteries and convents were founded. As well as the influx of religious orders from abroad some new local orders emerged. It was all a project on a grand scale, carried out in the ultramontane spirit which was consolidating the directive power of the papacy. This was not always so well received; the Catholic Church in England had survived largely under lay control – or better, aristocratic patronage – and it had a distinctive form of piety, but this was now supplanted by more Italianate styles. This was despite the still strong influence of a more English approach, exemplified in prominent converts of the time such as John Henry Newman (1801-90).

The new ways, however, flourished and the growth trajectory of British Catholicism continued right up until the 1960s. One of its distinctive characteristics was the retention, in contrast to some other European countries, of the working class. Catholics were predominantly poor and culturally 'other' and the Church was a focus of communal identity; it provided a network of educational and social services that enabled them to survive in material terms and ultimately to prosper; the operational model was the 'Fortress Church'. Whereas other churches experienced a gradual decline in membership and participation beginning with the First World War, the indices of Catholic institutional life (baptisms, marriages, conversions, ordinations, church attendance) all showed consistent upward movement through the first two thirds of the 20th century.

2.2. The Church in Britain at Vatican II (1958-65)

The Church in mid-20th century Britain was established in four ecclesiastical provinces in England, one in Wales and two in Scotland. Currently, there are nineteen dioceses in England, three in Wales and eight in Scotland. Although the picture has now changed dramatically, a great network of institutions had been built up – seminaries (five in England, two in Scotland, five abroad), many teacher training colleges, some medical facilities, retreat houses, monasteries and convents. This was in addition to an extensive network of Catholic primary and secondary schools. There were also the many associations of the laity – St Vincent de Paul Society, the Legion of Mary, Catholic Women's League, Knights of St Columba, etc. In the 1950s eighty such organizations were listed in the *Catholic Directory*.

The Church in these countries, however, neither expected nor was geared up for major change as the 1960s dawned. This was not because of any lack of creativity or dynamism. On the contrary, as the historian Adrian Hasting notes, 'the sheer vitality and range of committed ability, lay and clerical, present in the Church at that time and just waiting for a new lead' (Hastings 1991, 4). The liturgical movement was making an early impact especially in some of the laity associations in England. The Newman Association, founded in 1942, provided a forum for lay intellectual engagement; in the 1950s the Newman Demographic Survey, undertaken at the instigation of the hierarchy, was a model of professionalism - even for the Church today.[1] A new lay agency, the Sword of the Spirit (later re-named the Catholic Institute for International Relations [CIIR] and now Progressio) was founded in 1940 and, despite coolness from the Vatican, worked at the interface with other churches and secular society. An increasing number of Catholics were coming through the universities, benefiting from the post-War reforms inaugurated by the 1944 Education Act. The Welfare State was transforming the social order; full employment policies, the National Health Service, National Insurance providing unemployment benefit and pensions in old age and new municipal authority housing all began to roll back the grinding poverty that been the lot of whole communities, where Catholics were disproportionately represented. A Catholic middle class was emerging. The imperative to defend the 'fortress' was becoming less urgent (Hornsby-Smith 1987, 1991).

When, with the election of Pope John XXIII in 1958, a new era dawned in the Church at large, the Church in Britain was pastorally very vigorous; but it took its theological bearings rather exclusively from Rome. Theology was the preserve of the seminaries and was taught Roman manual style. In the major religious orders such as the Benedictines, Dominicans and Jesuits there was perhaps greater creativity, but theology was still an exclusively clerical pursuit and at this point there was no university level Catholic theology in Britain. The flood of new ideas which resulted from the Council, stimulating exploration of the *nouvelle theologie*, was to transform the scene.

The leaders of the episcopate charged with charting the way ahead in the following decades were:

- 1965-1980 – Card. Heenan to Card. Hume & Archb. Worlock (England & Wales)
  – Card. Gray and Archbishop (later Card.) Winning (Scotland)
- 1980-2000 – Card. Hume & Archb. Worlock (England & Wales)
  – Card. Winning (Scotland)
- 2000 on – Card. Murphy-O'Connor to Archb. Nichols (England & Wales)
  – Card. O'Brien (Scotland)

3. The first post-conciliar period (1965-1980)

The Council's program of *aggiornamento* or renewal was variously received across the Church. Some European countries were better prepared than others, religious orders were generally more prepared than the diocesan clergy,

---

1   See *A Use of Gift: The Newman Association 1942-1992*. The aims of the Newman Demographic Survey are still pursued by the Pastoral Research Trust and its founder Anthony Spencer who originally founded the Survey and worked on its staff.

the articulate laity were more receptive than the more devotionally inspired ordinary person in the pew, Scotland was more conservative in inclination than England. In Britain the first impact of the Council was more as change than renewal, something of a tsunami of change in fact. The introduction of the vernacular liturgy was immediately felt, but it was brought in so quickly that the liturgical and sacramental formation on which it depended was totally inadequate, perhaps inevitably given the low level of theological preparedness.

The immediate result of the Council was twofold. On the one hand, there was a ferment of creative exploration. Retreat houses, pastoral centers and colleges put on biblical and theological courses to introduce the new thinking of the Council, often drawing on the great theologians who had had a hand in drafting the documents. Public lectures by these newly famous figures were organized to debate the new ways of being Church. Retreats took on new forms of dialogue in place of silence. Youth and school retreats became joyous events of celebration. New groups and movements such as the Movement for a Better World, Focolari, Cursillo and Marriage Encounter came on the scene and opened up new perspectives of spirituality and participation. Social action in the cause of justice became a new path of discipleship.

At the same time, there is no denying the destabilizing of established structures. This was heightened by the cultural revolution of the 1960s. The 'aftershocks' of the Council were felt at several levels. Pressures for change mounted in the seminaries and colleges, the religious orders and the parishes. Educational and pastoral centers were in the vanguard of experimentation, but not surprisingly the parish, the focus of everyday Church life, was slower to adapt. The great disturbance was when priests and religious left to marry, something that had previously happened very rarely and was seen as a kind of aberration. The departure in 1967 of Fr. Charles Davis, perhaps the most prominent English theologian of the time, and his abandonment of the Church was a particular shock. The publication of *Humanae Vitae* in 1968 and the public dissent by many prominent priests and theologians further deepened the sense of crisis and polarization.

3.1 Education and theology (1965-1980)

The material resources of the Catholic community in Britain were dedicated primarily to education. The Catholic school system was developed from the 19th century as a communal defense against absorption in the dominant culture of Protestantism. The preference at that time was, if necessary, to build schools incorporating a church rather than a freestanding church; and even today bishops would make a parish school the priority. The financial burden was greatly lessened once the state took over responsibility for church schools, providing all running costs and 85% of capital costs in England and Wales and 100% in Scotland.

In the post-conciliar Church there was, and is, an urgent need for adult education; first of all, to keep knowledge of the faith abreast of higher levels of general education and fit for the challenges of a skeptical culture; secondly, for popular understanding of contemporary theological thought; and thirdly, to bring people beyond the limits, and even compensate for the failures, of their early years religious education.

The transformation that catechesis underwent at this time – going beyond the catechism, redefining it as religious education (RE) rather than religious instruction (RI) – was part of a more general change in educational philosophy and practice with a pupil-centered emphasis. New catechetical materials had to be prepared; teachers had to adapt to new ways of presenting the faith; the Catholic colleges of education had to train a new generation of teachers. The process was uneven; the new experimental texts, more exploratory than definitive, could not transmit the same certainty as the old catechism; established teachers often felt ill equipped to present Catholic faith in a fresh light; and the colleges now had to deal more in the terms of theology than of apologetics.

In addition, the Church educational institutions were in a period of change as the old teacher training colleges were rationalized and re-shaped; amalgamations and closures saw the number of establishments drastically reduced and those that survived took on a broader role as university colleges or departments within larger universities. A major initiative of the late 1960s – the establishment of a national catechetical institute, Corpus Christi College in London – unfortunately failed to flourish. Coming on the scene as the polarized theological debates of the post-conciliar years raged and then the crisis over *Humanae vitae*, it was caught up in controversy from the start and faced mounting criticism from bishops and others. Despite the undoubted charisma of its founding staff, such as Hubert Richards and Peter de Rosa, it did not succeed in establishing itself and closed in 1975.

At the same time, a significant Catholic presence began to emerge in the theology and religious studies departments of the British universities which up to this point had been the preserve of the established churches. From now on it became routine for Catholic theologians to occupy major chairs in divinity in prestigious universities such as Edinburgh, Cambridge, London and Durham (eg, James Mackey, Nicholas Lash, Eamon Duffy, Jack Mahoney, Oliver Davies, Lewis Ayers). Catholics have been prominent in other disciplines as well (eg, Mary Douglas in anthropology, the historian Peter Hennessy, the German scholar Nicholas Boyle, the philosopher John Haldane). On the institutional level, the entry in 1970 into the University of London as an autonomous college and school of philosophy and theology of Heythrop College, the seminary of the British Jesuit province which had become a Pontifical Athenaeum open to others in 1965, was a major achievement. In contrast to Corpus Christi, Heythrop had the advantage of its own long tradition of scholarship; although it too was buffeted by theological controversy its eventual secure establishment in one of the major universities has been a major success story for the Catholic Church in England and Wales.

The 'rebirth' of theology under the impetus of German and French scholarship and the widespread interest in it throughout the Catholic community in Britain was a marked feature of these years. There were vigorous debates, spurred by contemporary events both within the Church and in the secular arena. One forum was the Slant Group, named after the journal they founded, which met at the Dominican Spode House and brought together a loose alliance of Catholic intellectuals - clerical, religious and lay - to engage critically with political and social reality. The writing which emerged from authors such as Terry Eagleton, Herbert McCabe and Rosemary Haughton inspired a generation of radical clergy and lay activists. Another forum was the Downside Symposiums sponsored by the Benedictines which developed theological reflection on topics such as work, worship, priesthood, inter-communion and theology in the University.

3.2 Religious orders and movements (1965-1980)

The traditional religious orders reached the high point of their membership in Britain in the 1960s, but since then, as in almost all Western countries, have suffered a huge decline. They have also been negotiating a major – but not always clear - change in their role within the Church. The established structure before the Council allotted them a clearly defined place. They took care of church schools, university chaplaincies, retreat houses, ministries of preaching and spirituality, hospitals and specialized social services. The diocesan clergy on the other hand ran the parishes and some allied diocesan works including the diocesan seminaries. There was some overlap but the division of labor was by and large clear. The bishop presided over all, but his effective jurisdiction was limited to the parishes and the diocesan clergy. With the Council, however, the bishop's role was enhanced; as church structures moved beyond the previous settled ordering of roles, and as the 'workforce' expanded to include more and more lay persons in a variety of ministries, the diocese became more of a strategic unit with the bishop taking on a more directive role.

The impetus of the Council found a particular resonance in countries in the developing world. Missionaries returning to Britain exercised a 'reverse mission', opening up new ways of synthesizing theological reflection and pastoral experience in the mode of liberation theology. Groundbreaking pastoral initiatives were undertaken in the inner cities by women and men religious and their associates. The new form of religious living as 'communities of insertion' emerged from the early 1970s onwards, with for example, the Passionist Inner City Missions in Liverpool and London (Smith 1983, 1990), and later at Pollok in Glasgow (Sweeney 1994); the Hope Community of the Sisters of the Infant Jesus in Heath Town Wolverhampton; the Franciscan friars in Newcastle; the Emmaus community in Sunderland of Jesuits, Sisters of the Good Shepherd,

Daughters of Charity and Sisters of St Joseph of Peace; the Religious of the Assumption and de la Salle Brothers in Walker Newcastle (Sweeney et al. 2001).

The orders were also at the forefront in promoting new ways of prayer and spirituality. Lay community groups formed around monasteries, such as at Worth Abbey in Sussex; volunteers on placement at home and abroad are sponsored by many orders (the Jesuits, Vincentians, Sisters of the Assumption); houses of prayer were opened (the Carmelites); the renewed Ignatian tradition of spiritual direction contributed to lay, religious and priestly spiritual formation and led to fresh ways of integrating prayer and daily life, contemplation and action (Simmonds, forthcoming).

Alongside the traditional orders are the 'new movements'. These are a prominent feature of the post-conciliar Church; they have been compared with the historic orders, and their apparent dynamism is often contrasted with the difficulties the orders have encountered. They began to emerge very soon after the Council, but they have roots in the secular institutes of the early and mid-20th century and movements such as Opus Dei and Focolari which was born out of the chaos at the end of the War as experienced by Chiara Lubich.

Many such movements – often with origins in the Catholic heartlands of Europe, the birthplace of the historic orders (Italy, Spain, France) – became established in Britain after the Council; for example, the Movement for a Better World founded by Fr Ricardo Lombardi SJ, a confidante of Pope Pius XII; the Fraternities of Charles de Foucauld (sisters and brothers of Jesus); the Cursillos. Prominent among the new movements of the 1970s was Charismatic Renewal; its major impact was in permeating other movements and church life at large. At a later stage other new groups from abroad established themselves - Emmanuel, Communion and Liberation, the Community of St Jean, ATD Fourth World, the Neo-catechumenate, the Franciscan Friars of the Renewal. Some homegrown examples are also to be found: Youth 2000, the Sisters of the Gospel of Life, the Community of Our Lady of Walsingham.

3.3 Ecumenism and inter-faith relations (1965-1980)

It is astounding today to recall that there was no meeting between an Archbishop of Canterbury and a Pope for over 400 years from the time of the Reformation until 1960 when Geoffrey Fisher met John XXIII, and his visit to the Vatican was kept intensely private. The fact is that the national identity of the English, and also the Scots and the Welsh, has been molded historically in strong opposition to Catholicism. There remains at the heart of the British state a deep resistance to any claim of sovereignty by a foreign power (as in popular skepticism about the European Union).

However, inter-church relations have been transformed over the last half century. Vatican II's embrace of the ecumenical movement, and even more its landmark theological and ecclesiological achievements, did much to soften inherited Protestant attitudes. Catholicism had been seen, even in moderate cir-

cles, in the most prejudicial way – a sentiment that was, of course, cordially re-
ciprocated by Catholics! But now visits from Canterbury to Rome have become
routine; Popes have, for the first time, prayed in the most sacred spots in the
Church of England - Canterbury Cathedral and Westminster Abbey - and been
received by moderators of the General Assembly of the Church of Scotland.

The ARCIC (Anglican Roman Catholic International Commission) studies
inaugurated by Pope Paul VI and Archbishop Ramsey in 1966 generated optimism that full visible unity could be established within a short period of time.
That this was unrealistic soon became evident, not only because of the Vatican's reticence about the ARCIC reports, but since the Anglicans were not even
able to agree a unity scheme with the Methodists in 1972. Nevertheless, ecumenism at parish level flourished. The tide of goodwill was somewhat checked
by the years of inter-communal and Catholic-Protestant strife in Northern Ireland which at times spilled over into Britain. In Scotland, while it did not suffer
the same terrorist activity as some of the English cities, deep-seated sectarian
attitudes which were slowly dying out may have revived to some extent.

3.4 Renewal processes (1965-1980)

The liturgical changes got under way even before the Council ended with
the first introduction of the vernacular in the Mass early in 1965; new Eucharistic prayers came on stream in 1968 followed by the *novus ordo* in 1970. The
changes were received with general enthusiasm, but there were pockets of reluc-
tance, primarily in England rather than Scotland. In 1971 Cardinal Heenan
sought and obtained a concession from Paul VI to allow those deeply attached
to the old form of the Mass to retain its use in strictly limited circumstances.

Structured renewal processes emerged first among the religious orders. In
its decree on the renewal of religious life, *Perfectae caritatis* (1965), the Council mandated a twofold process of return to the sources and adaptation to the
new needs of the times in which all the members of religious institutes were to
be actively involved. The participative structures of general and provincial
chapters lent themselves to this and participation could be widened to include
all the members, at least at province level. A period of experimentation with
new forms, suspending existing constitutions, was brought in by Paul VI. The
post-conciliar chapters took up their new mandate with some enthusiasm, drafting interim constitutions. By the mid-1970s, however, it had become apparent
that actually implementing new ways required more than chapter decrees, and
the planning of change became the order of the day. Expert consultants and
chapter facilitators were brought in to help, and they quickly came to be seen as
a necessity. A new specialism of facilitation was born; the Movement for a Better World was among the first to provide such assistance from the early 1970s
and worked with many orders in Britain.

The appointment of Cardinal Basil Hume to Westminster and Archbishop
Derek Worlock to Liverpool in 1976 inaugurated a new phase of renewal in

England & Wales. It was Worlock who masterminded the first great coordinated institutional renewal effort centered on a National Pastoral Congress
(Longley 2000). This was held in 1980 after an extensive consultation across
the dioceses, parishes and other Church agencies. Not formally a synod, this
was nevertheless a synodical Church in operation. The event and its follow-up
by the bishops in *The Easter People* was an inspiration to many and it galvanized new energies (Catholic Bishops' Conference of England & Wales, 1980).
However, it was received coldly in the Vatican.

It was predictable enough that some of the Congress's calls – for a re-think
about artificial contraception, for example – would run into the sand. An institutional effort by the bishops to lower expectations and instill more 'realism'
could have succeeded, but it would have required evidence that the main lines
of the path of renewal as mapped out were still being followed and that the process of participation would continue. Such nurturing of impulses 'from below'
was swamped, however, by the new strategy of top-down inspiration of the
masses which the new papacy of John Paul II (1978-2005) represented.

There was no equivalent of the National Pastoral Congress in Scotland, but
the Church remained buoyant throughout the 1970s. There were, of course, controversies and conflicts. The Catholic community was conservatively inclined,
and the new ways produced friction between older and younger clergy, between
bishops and forward looking groups such as gathered around retreat houses and
the university chaplaincies. But overall there was a robust and ordinary quality
to Scottish Catholicism.

3.5 Church and society (1965-1980)

By 1980 there was a new consensus across Britain that Catholicism no
longer represented a 'foreign religion'. This was in large measure due to the
extraordinary influence of the monk-bishop Cardinal Hume. From his appointment to Westminster (1976-99) he was highly esteemed for his spirituality,
warmth and simple humanness. He became a 'national treasure', and was widely regarded as the pre-eminent English churchman of his times – even by Anglicans. It came down to a quality of Englishness, although as he sometimes said
of himself: 'My father was Scottish, my mother French, and they call me English. What they mean is that I'm not Irish!' In Scotland too, Cardinal Gordon
Gray of Edinburgh (1951-85), the first Scottish cardinal since the Reformation,
was archetypically Scottish, while in Glasgow Archbishop Donald Scanlon
(1964-74) was highly influential in civic circles; he was then followed by the
dynamic Archbishop (and later Cardinal) Thomas Winning (1974-2001).

Significant work in developing the Church's contribution to secular affairs
was carried on by the Catholic Institute for International Relations (CIIR) and
the Catholic Fund (later Agency) for Overseas Development (CAFOD) in England and Wales (founded in 1962) and the Scottish Catholic International Aid
Fund (SCIAF) (1965). These bodies attracted strong support from the outset and

became highly valued as expressions of the solidarity of the Catholic community with poorer nations as well as for their professional analysis of public policy issues.

3.6 Conclusion 1965-1980

The immediate post-conciliar period came to an end with the arrival of Pope John Paul II in 1978. His instincts were not the same as his predecessor. Paul VI's last years were troubled ones as change seemed to be on an unpredictable course. The time since the Council had been a liminal period with the ecclesial experience alternating between communitas and deep anxiety. Could the project of renewal be directed anew? How should the Vatican respond to the fast changing situation across the Catholic world?

The realization was also dawning - the fruit of disappointment and many dashed hopes - that something more than structural change was needed for Vatican II inspired renewal to succeed. It was easier to destabilize existing structures than to build new ones; ingrained attitudes did not give way easily, much effort was required to establish new practices, and resistance to them was not easily overcome.

Paul VI was prepared to put reliance on the local churches. In *Octogesimo adveniens* (1971) he admitted in relation to social teaching that it was not realistic for him to formulate fully universal approaches, and the analysis and impulse had to come from below. The principle of inculturation of the Church's mission in local situations also applied and was underlined in Paul VI's landmark apostolic constitution *Evangelii nuntiandi* (1975) which developed Vatican II's *Ad Gentes* (1965). A participative model of church was in vogue, as with the National Pastoral Congress and in other countries such as the Netherlands.

There was, however, a growing air of pessimism. The heady days of the 1960s were in the past. Paul VI even spoke in 1975 of his of alarm that

> ... through some fissure the smoke of Satan has entered the Temple of God ... something preternatural has come into the world to disturb, to suffocate the fruits of the Ecumenical Council, and to prevent the Church from breaking into a hymn of joy at having renewed in fullness its awareness of itself.[2]

In the Church in Britain, however, this would have seemed alarmist. The pre-conciliar Fortress Church had been left behind. The new bishops who took charge from the mid-1970s in both Scotland and England and Wales were open to change. There were, of course, many challenges to be faced, but on balance the renewal of the Church in the direction mapped out by Vatican II was on course.

---

2   See website of the Holy See for Italian text (see Lash, 2008, p. 259).

4. The second post-conciliar period (1980-2000)

The Church in Britain weathered the storms of the post-conciliar period rather well. More pragmatic in orientation than ideological and with an accumulated capital of loyalty in the face of external hostility, Catholic community solidarity was sustained even under considerable stress. Cordial relations between bishops and the new generation of theologians now entering the universities were deliberately fostered. When the Catholic Theological Association of Great Britain (ctagb@org.uk) was founded in 1984 many of the bishops were among its members. Even though there were some strongly divergent views across the Church, especially in England, this did not lead to a splintering into 'parties', in contrast to some other countries.

The landmark event at the start of this period was the first Papal visit to Britain in 1982. It was an outstanding success and carefully judged in the very difficult circumstances of the ongoing Falklands War, which had threatened its cancellation. There was an extensive program of spiritual preparation beforehand. The event itself, with the huge crowds who attended and the ecumenical breakthrough service in Canterbury Cathedral and the meeting with the Moderator of the General Assembly of the Church of Scotland under the statue of John Knox, set the seal on ecumenism and the Church's new status in British society. What was not so much in evidence, however, was any real dialogue - even a critical dialogue - with how the local church was thinking as brought out in the National Pastoral Congress. But that was hardly noticed in all the enthusiasm.

The pastoral theme that now became prominent was the New Evangelization. The final decade of the second millennium was declared the Decade of Evangelization; this was joined by the other churches in Britain (as the Decade of Evangelism). Established groups and new ones took up the call with enthusiasm and high hopes of turning the tide of secularization. At the end, however, there was disappointment; there was no great influx into the churches. The charismatic wing had been galvanized, but Catholics in general shared the British 'reserve' and were wary of seeming to impose their religious views on others. Evangelization smacked too much of 'in your face' religion; and a more sophisticated theology of evangelization, as in *Evangelii nuntiandi*, had not become common currency.

What in reality marked these decades was secularization. Its progress can be traced in terms of José Casanova's three dimensions of the secularization thesis (1994):

Decline in religious practice: in Britain the statistical indicators plunged, and this now took hold in the Catholic community for the first time.

Privatization: a new culture became dominant in Britain, even more virulent than the cultural revolution of the 1960s and fuelled by the economics of consumerism. This was the era of Margaret Thatcher (1979-1990) and the Conservative government of John Major (1990-1997) – more individualistic and self-interested than community oriented. In Thatcher's defining phrase: 'There's no such thing as society'.

Institutional differentiation: Relations between the state and religious bodies came under strain. This affected the established churches even more than Catholicism – which was now coming in from the cold – as evidenced in the Thatcher government's reaction to the Church of England report *Faith in the City* (1985) as a 'marxist document'.

Paradoxically, the churches in Britain, including the Catholic Church, actually became more highly visible on issues of public policy – poverty, war and peace, the environment, education, etc. – even while being stripped of much of their previous societal role. Negotiating this baffling shift in social positioning was the challenge of the late 20th century.

4.1 Renewal processes and programs (1980-2000)

Renewal in this period became more clearly a 'process'. It also came more firmly under institutional control. The spontaneous currents that had coursed through the Church in the wake of the Council were brought within the purview of the hierarchy. These currents - ranging from liturgical experimentation to new forms of community living and leadership, from life-centered catechesis and experiential forms of spirituality to the Charismatic Renewal, from social action for international justice and peace to solidarity with the poor – were co-opted by the institution. They no longer ranged free as in their first bloom.

The idea of a 'pastoral plan', an articulated program for the development of the Church and its activities, was already understood in some quarters before Vatican II, but it only came to prominence in Britain after the Council, and rather late on in the post-conciliar period.[3] After the first irruptions of change died down it dawned that if change was to become renewal a process had to be envisaged. The religious orders, drawing on their greater international experience, were the first to take this path, and it later became common in the dioceses.

Planning also arose in the context of new forms of 'assembly' – the need to gather together the whole community, whether the members of a religious province, the parish, the diocesan presbyterium, or the whole diocesan family. The chapters of religious orders were extended to include more of the membership. The new structure of the Council of Priests in the diocese, mandated by the Council, usually functioned along with an annual assembly of the clergy. The Pastoral Council of the parish and of the diocese (which were often slow to be established) involved lay parishioners and members of religious orders and special movements, and again learned to operate in conjunction with a wider assembling of the whole people. The sense that 'We are the Church' took hold.

---

3   Pastoral planning was under way in Brazil from the 1950s. MBW was one of the first agencies to promote this.

These structures are relatively easy to establish, but making them effective is a greater challenge, so the need for a coordinated plan became apparent. Dioceses as well as religious orders began the process of strategic planning, sometimes falling under the spell of management consultants and organizational development studies. There were two paths to follow: develop one's own strategy on the basis of an assessment of needs and resources, or 'buy in' a program already developed elsewhere.

A popular form of the latter was the Renew program formulated by the Archdiocese of Newark in the United States. Many of the dioceses of England and Wales and Scotland took over Renew and were helped by the training provided at Newark, which was highly entrepreneurial in marketing its 'product' across the English speaking world. Renew is a well coordinated program which runs over a three year period; the basic activity is the small group meeting in the parish for faith sharing on specific themes. Groups meet a set number of times in three 'terms' each year. The discussion materials are provided by the Renew organization but they can be re-written by the diocese. The setting up and control of the process is tightly coordinated. The long-term aim is that the model of small group experience should take hold and be self-sustaining after the three-year period. This may be judged one of the program's limitations; it does not envisage a longer-term strategy, nor does it tackle the institutional issues that follow from the 'basic ecclesial community' model of church that is implied.

One of the dioceses to adopt Renew in the 1990s was Glasgow. Here, however, it was inserted within a longer-term strategy which the diocese was already following from the late 1980s. This was facilitated by the Movement for a Better World (MBW) which had pioneered the approach in Latin America and then brought it to Italy. This was the outgrowth of the 'communitarian spirituality' that the founder, Ricardo Lombardi, developed under the inspiration of the call by Pope Pius XII in 1952 for action for a 'better world' (ie better than the post-War and Cold War world). Lombardi developed a new form of spiritual exercises, re-shaping the Ignatian exercises in a social direction; after the Council this took on a Kingdom theology focus. The MBW pastoral planning program foresaw the re-orienting of the local church in terms of its mission in and to the world of today and in the form of basic ecclesial communities. The time scale was in the order of fifteen years; and while a strict framework was laid down detailed local analysis and planning was required. A multi-level process of transformation - of diocese, parish and church organizations – was envisaged.

While Renew lacked a long-term perspective and was mainly an 'off the shelf' product, the MBW project was dependent on continuity over an extended period and required ongoing and rigorous strategic planning. The risk in the first case is that the process may end up going nowhere, while the second is subject to disruption due to changes of personnel. In addition, the basic ecclesial community model is less easy to apply in the modern urban and privatized societies of the West; the theological vision it presupposes is especially challenging, to individuals in terms of personal commitment and to the Church institution and its patterns of authority.

There is an underlying issue about personal and structural change and their inter-dependence. It is superficial to think that changing structures will bring about renewal; but an emphasis simply on personal conversion is also insufficient. Effective renewal requires both personal commitment and real decision-making, bringing together individual availability and institutional power. Renew took parishes so far but lacked a long-term perspective; the Glasgow project became wearisome to many and did not long survive a change of archbishop. In addition, these attempts at church renewal were affected by secularization, as the Church became less securely embedded in the local community. These are some of the limitations parish and diocesan renewal programs struggle with.

4.2 Movements and religious orders (1980-2000)

The decline in religious vocations, both diocesan and to the orders, began to bite ever more deeply in these years. The first result was that a new emphasis began to be put on lay and collaborative ministry. The new movements were pioneers here, and many of them, such as Focolari, are structured on a lay-religious-clerical basis. The call for collaboration extended into the parishes, but here of course it depended on the parish priest being in sympathy, which could not be presumed. The religious orders, finding themselves unable to staff all their works, either had to close apostolates down or depend more on lay resources. Schools now began to be handed over to lay headship, as were retreat houses, chaplaincies and other works. Even the new projects undertaken in deprived areas ('communities of insertion') could be re-modeled as lay projects; the Heath Town project in Wolverhampton started by the Sisters of the Infant Jesus was taken over by lay associates at the end of the 1090s; and in Walker in Newcastle the Kid's Kabin is a lay run initiative which emerged out of the religious community that was deeply involved in the local community. Orders also began to explore how lay people might share their charism and spirituality in new ways, reinventing the notion of third orders and confraternities.

The New Evangelization theme promoted by John Paul II in these years started to re-orient the Church to its mission and to look outwards. Despite the enthusiasm of some groups, particularly the new movements, and a general acceptance that secularization was eroding church affiliation, particularly among the young, there was puzzlement as to how evangelization could be made effective. Once again, renewal met intractable problems, this time not located only within the Church but in the growing imperviousness of the culture to the Gospel message. Commitment and enthusiasm were necessary but not sufficient for carrying through a new missionary effort in advanced industrial society.

4.3 Education and theology (1980-2000)

The presence of Catholic theology in the universities already alluded to expand enormously in these years; this was the driving force for the establishment of the British Catholic Theological Association in 1984, which took its place alongside the longer established Catholic Biblical Association (1940) and the Association of Teachers of Catholic Moral Theology of Britain and Ireland.

In view of the critical issues facing the Church there was a clear need for better theological and pastoral formation and for the kind of higher education and research institutes that could inform research based practice. The other churches with greater resources had a head start and led the way (e.g., the Centre for Theology and Public Issues (CTPI) at New College, Edinburgh). The Catholic Institute for International Relations (CIIR) developed as a highly professional source of social and policy analysis and was highly valued by the bishops; as lay led it could articulate a Catholic voice independently of the hierarchy, so without implying a finally established ecclesial position. The Von Hugel Institute at St Edmund's College, Cambridge was established in 1987 and focused mainly on social and pastoral issues. The Centre for Research and Development in Catholic Education was established in 1997 in the Institution of Education in London, the first such research center in Europe.

Three Catholic higher education institutions, the last of the old teacher training colleges, - St Mary's Twickenham, Trinity and All Saints Leeds and Newman College Birmingham – developed as more broadly based university colleges, alongside Heythrop College as the specialist philosophy and theology college of the University of London. Liverpool Hope University brought together three church colleges of education in an ecumenical partnership; in London Roehampton University brought together four such colleges. In Scotland, the remaining teacher training college (formerly Notre Dame, then St Andrew's College) was incorporated in the Department of Religious Education in the Faculty of Education in the University of Glasgow.

Plater College in Oxford (1922-2005) was a pioneer over many years in promoting understanding of Catholic social thought – as well as providing an introduction to third level education for working class Catholics. In 1993, the Margaret Beaufort Institute of Theology was founded as a Catholic house in the Cambridge Theological Federation for the theological education and formation of lay Catholics, and specifically women, for Christian discipleship and ministry. The Maryvale Institute in Birmingham was established as a distance learning college for catechesis, theology, philosophy and religious education. In Scotland several dioceses used the distance learning Limex course run by Loyola University in New Orleans leading to qualifications in ministry.

4.4 Ecumenism and inter-faith relations (1980-2000)

During his 1982 Visit Pope John Paul II made a call – a plea even – for all Christians 'to walk hand in hand'. Five years later, the Swanwick agreement between all the mainline churches launched 'Churches Together'. Catholics for the first time took part as full members of the new ecumenical instruments. The churches committed themselves to an ongoing process of collaboration and structured partnership. At the local level, parishes and deaneries entered into Local Ecumenical Projects and partnerships. In some places shared churches were established as well as a number of ecumenical faith schools. On at least one occasion, a Catholic bishop and a Church of England bishop confirmed their churches' candidates at a joint service. Catholic cardinals took an active part in the service of installation of Church of England primates, and they were present and offered prayers on state occasions. High hopes for church unity were held at the beginning of this period, too high as subsequent events were to show, but in terms of the renewal of the Church community a great deal was achieved. A greater affective unity if not a fully effective one was achieved.

4.5 Church and society (1980-2000)

British politics in these years were dominated by Margaret Thatcher with, at the same time, a deficit of political opposition owing to the weakness of the Labour Party. This thrust the churches – and particularly the Church of England - into the forefront as agents of critique of the harsh economic doctrines of Thatcherism. This was expressed in 1985 in the landmark report *Church in the City*, and in the coolness of the churches to Thatcher's triumphalism in the Falklands war. There was a move across the churches to greater political (in the broad sense) engagement and a readiness to comment on social issues. The new ecumenical body Churches Together in Britain and Ireland (CTBI) published *Unemployment and the Future of Work* in 1997 in the context of the general election of that year. The Catholic Church was, as always, closely identified with moral and life issues (abortion, euthanasia, etc) but now with economic issues as well. The Catholic Bishops' pre-1997 General Election statement, *The Common Good* (1996), based on Catholic Social Teaching was very widely welcomed and showcased this tradition of socio-theological reflection as a powerful resource.

The Justice and Peace groups and diocesan coordinating networks, as well as CAFOD and SCIAF, promoted conscientization on justice and practices such as Lenten family fast days. The English and Welsh bishops set up a coordinating body, the Catholic Agency for Social Concern (CASC – later Caritas Social Action Network), for the many dispersed Church agencies involved across the spectrum of social issues. A focus on justice and a pro-active stance in relation to society and politics was emergent in the Catholic community at this time –

although this did not always converge with the focus on spirituality which was even more strongly espoused.

4.6 Conclusion 1980-2000

In this second post-conciliar period, the project of renewal became something of a puzzle. The reforms of the Vatican Council seemed to have been sidelined in Rome where the preoccupation was to shore up the unity of the Catholic world – and indeed its uniformity. While some impulses from the grass roots – the new movements – were embraced by the Vatican, others were strongly discouraged. Greater control was in evidence; in order to be nurtured by ecclesiastical authority, movements had to be in tune with Vatican policies. Pastoral and ecclesial directions were determined centrally.

The practice of listening to voices from across the Church in preparing statements was discouraged as encroaching on the determinative role of the *magisterium*. At the same time some such a process is followed in preparing the meetings of the Synod of Bishops – but carefully! The preliminary *Lineamenta* or 'green paper' is widely distributed for comment; it leads to the 'white paper' discussed by the Synod itself, which then issues recommendations, and these are incorporated in the Pope's post-Synod Apostolic Exhortation. Such a consultative model is little in evidence, however, in the local churches. It was the approach used by the American Bishops in the lead up to their pastoral letters on War and Peace (1983) and Economic Justice (1986) and even into the 1990s by the Austrian and German Bishops; but the only comparable instance in Britain was the 1980 National Pastoral Congress. The neglect of such a procedure comes at a price; a gulf may open up between ecclesiastical pronouncement and the perceptions of ordinary believers. Moreover, as Michael Fogarty has pointed out, in the absence of an adequate consultative procedure the Church fails to galvanize the kind of popular support needed for leverage over public policy in favor of the kind of cultural and social agenda it would wish to see pursued.[4]

5. Beyond Vatican II? (2000 onwards)

As the millennium came to a close it might have seemed that Catholicism had survived the challenges of the late 20th century and the fissiparous effects of its own renewal Council reasonably well. Indeed, with the demise of European Communism, due in large measure to the stance taken by Pope John Paul II, it could be said to have made a remarkable advance. And yet, something new was beginning to come to light in the character of society in Britain. Cardinal Murphy-O'Connor gave voice to it in a lecture in 2009 marking his retirement:

---

[4]   Fogarty, Michael P. 1999. Catholics and Public Policy. Pp. 122-138 in M. Hornsby-Smith (ed). *English Catholics 1950-2000*. London: Cassell.

Fifty years ago I think most of the values that the Church wanted to uphold were also those that society itself would have agreed with. I am in no doubt that many still recognise and admire the Church's social and charitable work. But for others the Church and indeed Christian life seems to be out of step with 'the spirit of the times'. There has been a subtle but deep change in the way the Catholic Church has been perceived by contemporary culture. It is not that it meets with indifference or even hostility – although that is certainly noticeable – rather it is heard with a certain incomprehension. Incomprehension not only makes it difficult for the Church, and indeed, individual Christians, to make their voice heard, it also means that there is the risk of distortion and caricature.

Similar concerns about the encroachment of a secular society and the loss of Britain's Christian character were voiced by Cardinal Keith O'Brien of Edinburgh. The incomprehension Cardinal Murphy-O'Connor noted suggests some uncoupling of Western society from its historical religious roots. Christianity has, of course, been seriously contested for centuries, with the forces of modernity and religion pitted against each other in passionate debate; and this has erupted anew in fierce critique from today's 'new atheists' led by Richard Dawkins and Christopher Hitchens.[5] While the current attack does not reach the highest intellectual standard[6] it surfs a wave of deepening public skepticism and aversion to religion. Moreover, religion can now be identified, with some plausibility, as fundamentalist, fanatical and dangerous. There is also a growing discordance between traditional Christian moral principles and the standards and values of the social agenda promoted by governments (life issues, gay marriage, etc). All this empowers the secularist campaign against faith communities and their right to contribute to public policy. In these controversies the Catholic Church, no doubt because of the stances it takes on personal morality, becomes the main target – although Islam too is in the firing line.

What now compounds the problem and puts the Church severely to the test are the revelations of clerical sex abuse. The damage this has done to confidence marks the contemporary period, and in a way it questions the whole trajectory of ecclesial renewal. What has this dark secret revealed about who we are, how we are doing, where we are going? The uncovering of abuse has been an international phenomenon, beginning in the United States and Ireland, then Britain and moving on to the countries of continental Europe – and who knows where else. Successive waves of disclosure in each country have caught Church authorities unawares, especially as their own actions and the inadequacy of their handling of the issue has come more and more into the frame. The scandal of the abuse itself was compounded by the way it was dealt with by the institution.

5   Dawkins , Richard. 2006. *The God Delusion*. London: Bantam Press; Hitchens, Christopher. 2007. *God is not Great: the Case Against Religion*. London: Atlantic Books.

6   In the wry words of one commentator: 'we should see Richard Dawkins and Christopher Hitchens as ventriloquists' dummies speaking the words of serious eighteenth- and nineteenth-century thinkers in the demotic accents of the twentieth'. (Plant, Stephen. 23 April 2011. *The Tablet*, 31).

This went right to the top, to the Vatican, even provoking questions about past administrative actions of the Pope. High ecclesiastics were implicated in both abuse and failures of oversight and some were forced to resign their positions.

The debate continues about the real depth of the problem, its causes and where responsibility lies for such a stunning failure in witness and pastoral responsibility. It would be naïve to think it has been fully dealt with. In Britain there have been the same disclosures as elsewhere; cases continue to end up in the criminal courts; the administrative actions of prominent bishops, including the previous Archbishop of Westminster, were called in question. However, the procedures for dealing with it that have been put in place in Britain are reckoned to be among the most robust in the world; but vigilance is still needed about their implementation.

The abuse scandal deepened the sense of crisis that was already growing in the Church as the number of practicing Catholics and vocations to the priesthood and religious life continued to fall and more and more parishes were left without priests. How should the Church renew itself faced with these deep structural transformations?

5.1 Renewal and evangelization (from 2000)

Despite the scandals, the resilience of faith was also in evidence. If you were to ask Catholics about evangelization in Britain at this time, most would have said 'what evangelization?' But in fact some 'green shoots' were beginning to appear. The focus was shifting, even if imperceptibly, to mission and the requirement to proclaim the Gospel in society. This was in response to the ravages of secularization, the drift away from practice and the increasing difficulty of transmitting the faith across the generations.[7]

Dioceses faced the new mission challenge even as their internal circumstances were changing dramatically, especially in terms of the availability of clergy and religious. One way of responding was the permanent diaconate; some bishops had previously been lukewarm about this, but formation and training programs were now firmly in place. University theology degrees became increasingly popular among lay people, including new workplace-linked 'foundation degrees' in parish ministry, chaplaincy, etc.

There was a need for greater attention to pastoral strategy and dioceses developed structured programs of pastoral renewal. For example, the Diocese of Portsmouth's pastoral plan *Go Out and Bear Fruit,* which was developed by a diocesan team rather than taken 'off the shelf', revolved round the centrality of the Eucharist and the creation of larger pastoral areas intended to give the diocese a greater mission focus. Launched after wide consultation at a diocesan gathering in 2005 the plan cascaded through the parishes at a series of launch

---

[7]   Knights, Philip & Andrea Murray.2002. *Evangelisation in England and Wales: A Report to the Catholic Bishops.* London: Catholic Bishops' Conference of England and Wales.

evenings. Communion and Mission were the foundational theological notes.[8] A particular pathway of Stewardship emerged – a 'disciple's response' of conversion to Jesus Christ which involves the responsible and generous disposal of 'our time, our treasure our talents'[9] – and here the diocese adapted materials from a programme developed in the United States.

Another strategy was the Archdiocese of Westminster's *At Your Word Lord* program – an adaptation of RENEW – which the diocese followed from 2002 to 2005.[10] Small groups met in the parishes using specially developed materials for faith-sharing. A subsequent pastoral planning process established pastoral priorities[11] and an Agency for Evangelisation was set up responsible for promoting adult faith formation as well as general catechetics, small communities and youth ministry. The Agency worked with the parishes and provided resources and speakers for deanery level adult education talks. Alongside this, the small groups from *At Your Word Lord* were encouraged to continue meeting.

As mission-oriented renewal came more and more to the fore an issue for Church based institutions – schools and colleges, development organizations and social action groups – was how to maintain their faith character at the institutional level. The question was one of institutional identity. There are many reasons why even religious people may keep their faith under cover - embarrassment, or uncertainty about how to speak of it, or the need to attract funding from a secular source for a social project. Ironically, and although the point has to be hedged around with all sorts of qualifications, in Britain under both Labour and Conservative governments there has been a new openness to faith communities and the contribution they can make to social provision. The slogan of the Cameron government has been the 'Big Society' – the importance of civil society sector groups. At the same time, the cultural pressures on Church institutions can lead them to play down their religious character. The challenge to faith based organizations has been how to be *more* than simply agents of public policy? How as religious groups to 'present' themselves in today's social and cultural climate?

5.2 Groups and movements (from 2000)

Paul VI's *Evangelii nuntiandi* portrayed evangelization as a wide category which took in the many dimensions of the Church's mission including work for social transformation, but a fault line has remained between those committed to 'spirituality' and the enthusiasts for 'social action'. To address these issues

8   Hollis, Bishop Crispian. 2004. *Growing Together in Christ*, Diocese of Portsmouth.
9   Diocese of Portsmouth. 2005. *Go Out and Bear Fruit: a Pastoral Plan for the Diocese of Portsmouth.*
10   The Arundel & Brighton project is thought to be the anonymised subject of the analysis done by Michael Hornsby-Smith, Michael, John Fulton & Margaret Norris. 1995. *Politics of Spirituality: a Study of a Renewal Process in an English Diocese*. Oxford: Clarendon Press.
11   Archdiocese of Westminster. 2006. *Graced by the Spirit* ( ) and *Communion and Mission*.

CAFOD and Caritas Social Action established theological commissions and they had theologians working with them on secondment. London Citizens, a community organizing body, although not itself a religious agency, drew much support from faith groups and had its own theologian in residence in 2011-12. The disjunction of social action and spirituality needed to be overcome for a truly deep renewal in the life of faith, but it remained elusive.

The abiding preoccupation in mission and evangelization was to find effective ways of proclaiming the Gospel in today's society. The intellectual and practical challenges that this presented were clear. The Catholic Education Service commissioned the Heythrop Institute for Religion, Ethics and Public Life to do a study of the contemporary cultural and theological bases for catechesis. The report, *On the Way to Life* (2005) provided an important resource for many groups in search of the foundations for their renewed pastoral action. A crop of new Catholic research and study centers began to emerge – the Centre for Catholic Studies at Durham University; the Digby Stuart Research Centre for Catholic Studies at Roehampton University; the Las Casas Institute at Blackfriars Oxford; the Theotokos Institute for Catholic Studies in Cardiff; and the Centre for Christianity and Inter-religious Dialogue, the Centre for Eastern Christianity and the Religious Life Institute at Heythrop.

At the practitioner level the vision of a 'new evangelization' energized groups and agencies on the Church's spirituality/charismatic wing. A multiplicity of groups was now in evidence, some long established some new. Although this is typical of Catholicism it could also be recipe for confusion. Groups ranged across the whole spectrum of pastoral concerns and theological perceptions – from CAFOD to the Latin Mass Society, from the Movement for the Ordination of Married Men to the traditionalist Priestly Fraternity of St Peter (not to mention groups promoting the ordination of women or the Lefebvrist Society of St Pius X). The upshot was that for the first time a real splintering into parties began to occur within the Catholic community. Debate – if it could be called that - took on a more bitter tone.

A special Catholic Agency for the Service of Evangelization (CASE) had a brief life with a remit to support mission-active groups and communities; starting in 2004 it was replaced in 2009 by a cut-down Home Mission Desk in the Bishops' Conference office. CASE produced a very useful Evangelization Directory. This was a fully comprehensive listing of groups and agencies engaged in mission under the following headings: dioceses; parish and area missions, parish-focused resources and forms of small Christian communities; youth programs and school missions; welcoming back returning Catholics; training/formation centers and courses; prayer groups; initiatives, groups and communities with particular ministries; web resources; printed resources.[12]

---

12   Evangelisation Directory: An Annotated List of Evangelisation Resources for the Catholic
      Communities of England and Wales. London: CASE, 2006.

However, research on a selection of these groups concluded that they:

> ... were mostly concerned with renewal and catechesis rather than evangelisation (even though at times they professed to be concerned with evangelisation). Mission *ad intra* is privileged over *ad extra*.[13]

Nevertheless, 'mission' still lives! Much of the energy and enthusiasm came from the laity. The best known new evangelization (or evangelism) initiative in Britain is Anglican – the *Alpha* course, founded at Holy Trinity Brompton in central London in the 1970s.[14] Energetically promoted and marketed in many countries it has become a phenomenon in its own right. It comes out of the evangelical tradition in the Church of England and its characteristic appeal in London has been to young professionals. Congregations across the country have adopted the course as a basic introduction to Christianity. Catholic groups also adopted Alpha – the appeal being that 'it works'! Even Latin American Catholic bishops came to London for Alpha's annual international convention. The Alpha organizers are keen to widen its appeal and to incorporate Catholic perspectives (sacramental, social justice) into their approach.

A Catholic response to Alpha – not so much a competitor as a companion – was developed by Catholic Evangelization Services. *CaFE (Catholic Faith Exploration)* was set up in 1996 to address perceived imbalances in Alpha. An informal 'café-style' setting at the sessions encourages faith development through group discussion and reflection. The process is aimed at core Catholics. The overall aim is parish renewal and evangelization leading to an outward looking parish. CaFE makes use of media resources and it produced its own video and DVD resources for Catholics of all ages for use in on-going formation, sacramental preparation and small parish groups.

Among the new groups and movements dedicated to evangelization and outreach a few can be mentioned. *St. Patrick's School of Evangelisation* (SPES) which started in the early 2000s in St Patrick's parish Soho in central London, flows from a parish life centered on Eucharistic adoration. The parish runs a fertility center, a homeless project and a telephone prayer helpline. The School itself was inspired by the Emmanuel Community. It provides theological formation for discipleship and attracts young people, in quite small groups, from many different countries. Part of its pastoral activity is street evangelization in and around the Soho area, notable for its colorful night life and the sex industry.

The *Sion Community for Evangelism and National Training* was founded in 1984 from a charismatic background, and is made up of full time and part time members, the majority of them lay but with religious and clergy as well. Their charism is 'evangelization' and the community conducts parish and school mis-

---

13   Sweeney, J. *et al.* 2006. *Going Forth.*
14   http://uk.alpha.org/

sions and youth and family ministry as well as running a nine month training course in evangelization.

Youth 2000 is a Catholic youth initiative, which began in the UK in 1991 but is now international. It seeks to help young adults (aged 16 to 30) to discover Christ and connect with the Church, working through weekend retreats and local prayer groups. The focus is on the centrality of the Mass and adoration of the Blessed Sacrament; devotion to the Virgin Mary; personal conversion and confession; a clear and attractive presentation of the Scriptures and authentic Catholic teaching; personal prayer; and meeting other young Catholics. Youth reaches out especially to lapsed Catholics and non-Catholics. The retreats are run by young Catholics, supported by priests and religious.

A somewhat different kind of group is *London Jesuit Volunteers* which started in the mid-2000s. It adapted an American model which provides opportunities for mainly early retired people to become active in Church mission. In fact the London volunteers 'range in age from 25 to 75+ years old and represent a wide diversity of cultural and international backgrounds. Many of them are young professionals from abroad on work placement in London/[15] The group has a strong foundation in Ignatian spirituality. The combination of active involvement in a variety of settings – with immigrants, in prisons, hospitals, etc. – and shared prayerful reflection on the experience makes a particularly powerful impression. It opens up the dimensions of Christian living both in terms of volunteers' personal lives and the Church community's service of others.

These are just a few examples of the 'new groups and movements' alive in the Church in Britain at this time. A comprehensive study of them has yet to be done.[16] It would be an exaggeration to say that they represent a new 'ferment' in Catholicism or the churches more generally, but they are evidence of initiative and creativity. There are, of course, many other agencies that Catholics, individually and collectively in parishes, support in pursuit of a renewed Church mission – CAFOD and SCIAF, the Society for the Protection of the Unborn Child (SPUC), LIFE, Christian Aid, Church Action on Poverty, etc. Despite the secularism of society, many of the most dynamic agencies in the socio-political sphere have strong church connections. Amnesty International is one (it fell into conflict with many Catholics when it gave support for abortion) and the Samaritans (support for the suicidal) is another.

On housing issues there has been deep involvement by the Catholic community from the 1960s with the Catholic Housing Aid Society. This merged in 2003 with the Churches' National Housing Coalition (CNHC) and later with UNLEASH (Church Action on Homelessness in London) to form *Housing Justice*. This is a national charity giving voice to Christian concerns and action. Its

---

15   http://www.msjc.org.uk/ljv.php
16   The ARCS project (Action Research: Church & Society) at Heythrop College in collaboration with Ripon College Cuddesdon (an Anglican seminary) has researched a range of such groups around London and south of England.

work includes: campaigning and lobbying for more affordable housing and better homelessness services; promoting Poverty and Homelessness Action Week and Homelessness Sunday; a Faith in Affordable Housing project, a guide for churches and denominations in the use of redundant buildings; supporting church run night-shelters such as the CARIS project of seven churches in Islington in London which provide accommodation for homeless people from January to March each year.

5.3 Ecumenism and inter-faith relations (from 2000)

Church ecumenism broadened out progressively in the new millennium to take in the dimension of inter-faith relations, all the more crucial after the September 11th terrorist attacks in the United States and those of 7th July 2005 in London.

Although the earlier high hopes of Catholic-Anglicans unity crumbled with the Church of England's moves to ordain women priests and bishops, the churches did not abandon the process. A new phase of the ARCIC process (Anglican-Roman Catholic International Commission) was inaugurated in 2010. Influential in this field was the 'receptive ecumenism' project promoted by the Catholic Studies Centre at Durham where two major international conferences were held in 2006 and 2009. Another forum was the ecumenical Ecclesiology and Ethnography network.

Ecumenical relations were thrown into some disarray in 2009 when Pope Benedict established the new structure of the Ordinariate for converting Anglicans. For many years former Anglican clergy had been ordained as Catholic priests even if married and they were serving in various capacities in the Church in England and Wales. Now it became possible for whole communities – priests and parishioners – to enter the Church together and establish their own ecclesial grouping and retaining their 'Anglican heritage'. This initiative came directly from Rome with no consultation with the bishops in England and Wales, nor any liaison with the Anglican hierarchy. It naturally provoked questioning about the future of ecumenical relations, as well as the celibacy rule. It did not however derail the good relations between the two sets of British bishops, who had established a regular pattern of meeting together both in Scotland and in England and Wales. The Personal Ordinariate of our Lady of Walsingham, headed by a former Anglican bishop, now a Catholic (mitre-wearing, married) monsignor, was established in 2011 with three former Anglican bishops and about sixty priests receiving Catholic ordination, but fewer than a thousand converting lay people.

5.4 Church and society (from 2000)

The visit to Britain in 2010 of Pope Benedict XVI, the second papal visit, was very different from the first, but equally successful. It was feared that it would be marred by protests about clerical abuse and how that would be used by the 'new atheist' lobby; even some in the Catholic community were skeptical beforehand. In the event the protestors overplayed their hand. In comparison with the mild manner and obvious reasonableness of the Pope it was they who were made to look the fanatics. And anyway, Catholic solidarity re-asserted itself in the face of external hostility!

The feature of the visit that may turn out to have the most long-lasting effect was the fact that it was a formal state visit, with a grand reception by the Queen at the Palace of Holyroodhouse in Edinburgh. This, in principle, closed the long historical chapter of distance between Britain and the Papacy. The extraordinarily warm reception the Pope received next day in the mediaeval Westminster Hall – a mark of respect accorded to only the most significant foreign personalities; the last had been Nelson Mandela – and the deeply thoughtful and irenic speech Benedict XVI gave there to Parliament and representatives of civil society - about faith and reason, religion and society – might come to be seen as a turning pointing in Church-State relations. The implications of the event, and the generous farewell speech by the Prime Minster David Cameron at Birmingham airport, go beyond Catholicism and its place in British society. What was publicly demonstrated was that, even if Britain is a deeply secular society and even though strong popular currents of hostility to religion are abroad, religious faith is still in evidence in the public sphere; and it is accorded in Britain a well-recognized place. The proposal that religion be treated as a purely private matter is just that – a proposal, and a cultural bias - the *political fact* is that religion is much more.

6.   A Future of hope?

Predicting future change is hazardous, just as it would have been hazardous to predict the fall of Communism in 1978 when Pope John Paul II – Blessed John Paul – was elected. But John Paul is now remembered as someone who changed (literally, in some measure) the world. The fact is that there are always factors that can transform social situations. In Europe Christianity and Catholicism seem set on decline, at least numerically. However, one can never be sure how the statistical indicators will eventually turn out. Two things in Britain today that buck the trend are religion in the globalized city and the attitudes of second generation Muslims.

In the global city of London church congregations are larger than in the rest of the country, which suggests that, contrary to the usually secularizing effect of urbanization, religion can actually grow stronger in advanced globalizing urban situations. The statistics make London's different religious profile clear. London accounts for 15% of England's population but 20% of its churchgoers; 53% of English Pentecostal churchgoers are in London; London's population of adherents of world faiths other than Christianity is nearly 3 times the English average; 39% of the London population lives in inner London but 43% of London churchgoers go to church in inner London; 60% of London churchgoers in their 20s go to church in inner London.[17] Many factors contribute to these trends, but what seems clear is that globalization can disrupt established patterns of secularization – and what long-term consequences will be has still to be established.

In similar fashion, it is notable that many second generation British Muslims are more religiously observant than their parents – and therefore more politically radicalized. That immigrants are likely to assimilate to the host society and underplay their ethnic and religious identity is a well-recognized pattern, but here it seems to have been put in reverse; and the pattern of a younger generation being less religious than its elders is also in reverse. None of this is sufficient to predict the future, but these might be straws in the wind. It is not over-fanciful to think that in current circumstances religion's tectonic plates are shifting in unpredictable ways.

For the Catholic Church, however, the current period is marked by the abuse scandal whose long-term effects remain imponderable. Enthusiasm for ecclesial renewal may well have lessened, but nevertheless initiatives and effort continue. What has changed is the background context. The Catholic community has been demoralized, priests and religious in particular. Trust has been badly damaged – between the Church and society, priests and people, priests and bishops, religious and their superiors. The new freedoms and individualism of the first post-conciliar period have been called sharply in question. Did this set dangerous forces loose? But then, the re-assertion of control from the top has also been put in question; for in relation to the abuse it is the institution itself that has been exposed as self-regarding, intent on preserving its own position.

One emerging feature is a greater polarization between different groups. A bitter tone has crept into British Catholic life, with strident criticism coming from some quarters (amplified in the blogosphere) of the liturgical changes, catechetics, pastoral policy, etc. A splintering into parties, more typical of Anglicanism, has begun to infect the Catholic community. Solidarity has come newly under strain.

The current period is also marked by the personality of the new Pope. While he is a very different kind of figure from his predecessor, Benedict XVI stands comparison due to his high intellectual qualities, and he is clearly at pains to unify world-wide Catholicism, to re-balance the Church and recover aspects of the tradition that have fallen into disuse. He positions his magisterium, certainly in continuity with that of his predecessors and Vatican II, but even more in continuity with the long historical tradition of the Church. Some of his initiatives, however, might be seen to be in some tension with tradition.

The re-establishment of the previous form of the liturgy of the Roman Rite, albeit as the 'Extraordinary Form', and its potentially universal availability, implicitly questions the liturgical reforms of Vatican II. Was the liturgy in need of renewal, as the Council evidently thought, or not? Does that requirement of re-

---

17   Ashworth and Farthing 2007; Brierley 2006.

newal apply to what has been newly named the 'Extraordinary Form'? If not –
and reinstatement is simply a return to 1962 – how does that square with the
Council's liturgical constitution? It is also surprising how the motu proprio
Sumorum Pontificum empowered individual priests, so that bishops' jurisdiction
over the liturgy in their dioceses was weakened. This is something of an ecclesiological puzzle. Similarly, the new structure of the Ordinariate for ex-
Anglicans is a novel ecclesiology, all the more so since it was established without consulting the diocesan bishops most closely affected; and implementation
is being directed exclusively from Rome. The impression could be given that
the current papacy, for all that it reasserts tradition and upholds a 'hermeneutic
of continuity', may in fact be taking the Church into uncharted territory.

Renewal – or just change?

Having surveyed fifty years and more of British Catholic life and noted the
trajectory of change, there is no tidy conclusion to be drawn. The Catholic
Church in these countries, which was for so long rather different, has now become much more like the neighboring continental European churches. The effort to face modernity in a new way (*aggiornamento*) gave a powerful stimulus
to change at the beginning of this period. That impetus gradually faded as new
challenges made themselves felt, but it was still a fundamental reference point
for the post-conciliar era up to the end of the century. From about the turn of the
millennium, however, ecclesial change – insofar as we can talk about change
rather than stasis - has been paradoxical. Renewal initiatives in a wide array
continue to be launched but they are no longer in any close conjunction with the
aims and perspective of Vatican II – however much appeal may be made to its
texts – nor a way of responding to the challenges of modernity. In fact it is now
the peculiar challenges of post-modernity – the loss of a 'grand narrative' (e.g.,
'fortress church'; renewal/aggiornamento) and the fracturing into single issue
groupings - that tend to drive change. It might even be said that the Church itself has become 'post-modern'. As a new aesthetics permeates aspects of liturgy
and a neo-traditionalist life style gains ground, it seems clear that a new era is
already upon us. The 'post-conciliar era', when the effort was to realign the
Church with modernity, has closed and now it is the post-modern challenge that
has to be faced.

References

Archbishop of Canterbury's Commission on Urban Priority Areas: 1985. *Faith in the
City: a Call to Action by Church and Nation*. London: Church House Publishing.
Archer, A. 1986. *The Two Catholic Churches: a study in oppression*. London: SCM
Press.
Ashworth, J. & I. Farthing. 2007. *Churchgoing in the UK: A research report from
Tearfund on church attendance in the UK*. Teddington, Middlesex: Tearfund: 48.

Boyle, R. & P. Lynch (eds.). *Out of the Ghetto? The Catholic Community in Modern Scotland.* Edinbugh: John Donald.

Brierley, P. 2006. *Pulling Out of the Nose Dive: A Contemporary Picture of Churchgoing: What the 2005 English Church Census Reveals.* London: Christian Research.

Casanova, J. 1994. *Public Religions in the Modern World.* Chicago: University of Chicago Press.

Catholic Bishops' Conference of England and Wales. 1980. *The Easter People: a Message from the Roman Catholic Bishops of England and Wales in Light of the National Pastoral Congress, Liverpool, 1980.* Slough: St. Paul Publications.

Catholic Bishops' Conference of England and Wales. 1986. *The Common Good and the Catholic Church's Social Teaching.* London: Catholic Bishops' Conference.

Grace, G. & R. Valenti. 2009. Preface and Introduction. In *International Studies in Catholic Education* (ISCE).

Hanvey, J. & A. Carroll. 2005. *On the Way to Life: contemporary culture and theological development as a framework for Catholic education, catechesis and formation.* London: Heythrop Institute for Religion, Ethics and Public Life.

Hastings, A. 1986. *A History of English Christianity 1920-1985.* London: Collins.

Hastings, A. (ed.) 1991. *Modern Catholicism: Vatican II and after.* London: SPCK; Oxford-New York: Oxford University Press.

Hornsby-Smith, M. 1987. *Roman Catholics in England: Studies in Social Structure.* Cambridge: Cambridge University Press.

Hornsby-Smith, M. 1989. *The Changing Parish: a study of parishes, priests and parishioners after Vatican II.* London: Routledge.

Hornsby-Smith, M. 1991. *Roman Catholic Beliefs in England: Customary Catholicism and Transformations of Religious Authority.* Cambridge: Cambridge University Press.

Hornsby-Smith, M. (ed.) 1999. *English Catholics 1950-2000: Historical and Sociological Perspectives.* London: Cassell.

McClelland, V.A. 1999. *From without the Flaminian Gate: 150 years of Roman Catholicism in England and Wales 1850-2000.* London: Darton Longman & Todd.

Lash, N. 2008. *Theology for Pilgrims.* London: Darton Longman & Todd.

Longley, C. 2000. *The Worlock Archive.* London: Geoffrey Chapman.

Newman Association, 1991. *A Use of Gift: The Newman Association 1942-1992.*

O'Shea, J. *et al.* 1992. *The Parish Project: a Resource Book for Parishes to Review their Mission.* London: Harper Collins.

Simmonds, G. (ed). Forthcoming 2012. *A Future Full of Hope?* Dublin: Columba Press.

Smith, A. 1983. *Passion for the Inner City.* London: Sheed & Ward.

Smith, A. 1990. *Journeying with God: Paradigms of Power and Powerlessness.* London: Sheed & Ward.

Sullivan, J. 2001. *Catholic Education: Distinctive and Inclusive.* Dordrecht: Kluwer Academic Publishers.

Sweeney, J. 1994. *The New Religious Order: A Study of the Passionists in Britain and Ireland, 1945-1990 and the Option for the Poor.* London: Bellew.

Sweeney, J. *et al.* 2001. *From Story to Policy: Social Exclusion, Empowerment and the Churches – A Research Report.* Cambridge: Von Hugel Institute, St Edmund's College.

Sweeney, J. *et al.* 2006. *Going Forth: An Enquiry into Evangelisation & Renewal in the Roman Catholic Church in England & Wales.* Cambridge: Von Hugel Institute, St Edmund's College.

Sweeney, J. forthcoming 2012. Religious Life Looks to its Future. In G. Simmonds (ed.). *A Future Full of Hope?* Dublin: Columba Press.

Part II

Ministering the New Church

Individual Pastoral Care in Late Modernity: An Essential Matter for the Church

Stefan Gärtner

Pastoral care is not a peripheral matter for the Church. On the contrary, the Church realizes her essence in a fundamental pastoral orientation. In its Pastoral Constitution *Gaudium et spes,* the Second Vatican Council set out a change from a purely self-referential description of the Church to a description that attempts to take responsibility for the world outside and for all humankind. This is not merely a theoretical responsibility, but should become, above all, practical in the ministry of the Church. Finally, the Church, herself, has an altogether pastoral character.

The Council marked the beginning of a fundamental shift in perspective and place. According to *Gaudium et spes* (GS), the Church's obedience of revelation does not result in an alleviation of the problems that people encounter. As a result, *Gaudium et spes* makes the call for the Church to sharpen her view for the signs of the time and leads to the question of what pastoral responses the historical circumstances demand of the Church. Therefore, the "pastoral path is walked twice in Gaudium et spes, firstly in the attention to what is significant for humanity or inhumanity of people, and secondly in the attention to how the Gospel might be important for this" (Sander 2005, 610).

Concrete circumstances become the place where the Church must ever prove the truth of her message anew. Her pastoral being is realized in service to the world. The Church wants to show the world the light of the Gospel. In doing so, she offers "those saving resources which the Church herself, under the guidance of the Holy Spirit, receives from her Founder. For the human person deserves to be preserved; human society deserves to be renewed" (GS 3). In this sense, the main goal of the Church and her ministry is eventually "man himself, whole and entire, body and soul, heart and conscience, mind and will" (GS 3).

Given the historical distance between today and the time of the Council, a new verification of the social context of the Church and her ministry is required. The optimism with which the Council Fathers spoke about their time and the possibilities of change has given way to disillusionment. Their analysis of the signs of the time carried typical modern characteristics. Half a century later, we have entered the phase of late modernity.[1] In the first section, we will describe the new social conditions for the Church, first in a general sketch (1.1) and then

---

1   By preferring this term I follow A. Giddens. It is similar to the term 'advanced modernity' that S. Hellemans uses in this volume.

from the perspective of the individual (1.2). In the second section, we can ask which basic structure of ministry is appropriate to this time. With this two-step approach, we follow the road that *Gaudium et spes* initiated.

1. Late modernity as a context of pastoral care

1.1 A bird's eye view of late modernity

The term late or advanced modernity refers to the processes of modernization, which have become more radical since the 1960's (Hellemans 2007, 38-41). Late modernity, therefore, does not mark the end of modernity. The term refers, in the first place, to an increased awareness of a sense of crisis that is felt in the modern age. Much empirical evidence suggests that the promises of modernity are empty. There is concern surrounding many experiences – such as the economizing of many areas of life, the historical disasters of the recent past, the injustices of the global economy and their consequences, the destruction of the environment, the inequality of the sexes, the perforation of traditional social contracts, the hermetically working pluralism of aesthetic codes, the failures of technical-industrial progress, the dissolving of reality into virtuality in the media – which all trigger a subliminal sense of crisis and an inadequacy of solutions.

In accordance with the position of a majority of scientists who assume that late modernity does not imply the end of modernity, I thus start out from the idea that late modernity does not implicate a fundamental change but rather a radicalization and a new awareness of modernity, especially an awareness about its own limitations and conditions (Hellemans 2007, 145-149). However, this awareness arises from the very characteristics of modernity itself as a new line of development. Late modernity is about "a specific and today necessary option of modernity. It is nevertheless a qualitative step. (...) The diversity of modernity is no longer seen from the perspective of unity or from the perspective of emancipatory action. The devastating consequences of the totality of modern demands are confronted with the heterogeneity of the multiple" (Widl 2000, 122).

The principles of modernity face a qualitative increase in late modernity and, at the same time, they undergo devaluation. They can no longer be assembled in unity drafts in whatever way – every attempt at such a summary is met with skepticism. This counts for pastoral care as well. Large-scale pastoral projects and comprehensive theories seem to fit less and less (Gärtner 2009, 79-84). In late modern times, the modern age reaches a point at which it intensifies itself. Its own conditions and limitations become obvious, since all supposed normality has become questionable. Therefore, people continually have to justify themselves and their actions (Arens 1999).

Late modernity signals a phase of modernity in which the naturalness of old principles and beliefs has evaporated into a pluralism of options and opinions.

However, in the social segmentation that corresponds with this pluralism, not every reference is lost. There are still, at different levels, forms of social togetherness, agreements of solidarity, common orientations, etc. After all, it is these that make the Church possible in late modernity. On the other hand, social bindings are often proved less mandatory and less robust than in the past. They become liquid (Bauman 2007).

Today, even within the Church, different concepts of ministry exist quite naturally side-by-side. The same goes for society as a whole, both within and between the social and personal systems (Luhmann 1997). The world has become plural. There is, accordingly, insight into the relativity of every practice, which results in processes of self-referentiality, both within and outside pastoral care. As a consequence, this leads to the coexistence of different opinions, rationalities, actions, logics, and aesthetics. The concept of late modernity, therefore, also reflects the social consciousness of difference. It refers to the experience of a "radicalized pluralism, that at present state in the western societies one can meet as the decisive mentality" (Hoff 2001, 355).

However, difference does not disintegrate into pure coincidence and pluralism does not increase automatically, as the concept of post modernity sometimes suggests. Instead, connections and crossings arise in the midst of all differences and actual diversity, even if they appear no longer quasi by themselves but individuals and institutions have to create them (Petzold 2005). Accordingly profound is the duty of individuals and institutions to give reasons for the decisions they make. This is also the case for the Church and her pastoral actions. Nothing is simply unquestioningly plausible for parishioners anymore.

Late modern society is, at all levels, subject to reflexive modernization (Beck 1986). There is a sober, permanent, and critical eye on oneself, on the other, and on the social world, for many once self-evident facts now lie behind us. Things that once seemed to be clearly proved can now be questioned. The intrinsic ambivalences of the modern age lead to a skeptical attitude towards many things (Bauman 1993). If, therefore, the concept of late modernity is "indeed a meaningful name, then [it is] most likely for a new level of self-reflexivity in modernity, reached in the 20th Century" (Körtner 2006, 37).

Moreover, we regard this attitude of skepticism and criticism as legitimate, and one that applies to almost everything and everyone, including the Church, who must still, however, get used to it. Given that nothing is normal anymore, things can always be otherwise. Thus, another characteristic of late modernity is the necessity to choose and to decide under social circumstances that give no solid foundation for either. This characteristic manifests itself again in the current conditions of church ministry. The normative Christian tradition, for example, turns out to be traditions in plurality. This is the same for the way these traditions are dealt with and the resulting actions in pastoral care.

Indeed, late modernity finds expression in a radicalization of modernity, namely, in both a radicalization of its problems as well as the ways to tackle them (Lyotard 1988). There is a continual necessity of self-reflection and decision-making because there are always numerous options. In addition to a sub-liminal feeling of crisis, there is also doubt as to whether the current solutions still fit. In particular, a pure, functional rationality seems insufficient. People make use of non-discursive procedures, for example, pictures, experiences, or egocentristic self-presentations. In other words, reflection manifests itself not only as public or private discourse, but it uses different logics, which, in each case, are inclined towards self-reference.[2]

1.2 Individualization in late modernity

The experiences with the ambivalences of the modern age have left their marks on individuals in late modernity as well (Bauman 2001). When searching for identity, these individuals are confronted with radicalized social circum-stances. The consequences of dealing with these circumstances can be summa-rized in the individualization theorem, the aspects of which I present and dis-cuss below (Schroer 2001). In addition, the process of individualization is by no means exclusively a late modern phenomenon. One can describe the history of the west as a process wherein the individual has experienced ever-increasing autonomy. Christianity, itself, has also contributed essentially to this increase in autonomy, for example, by emphasizing the individual in its practices of prayer, marriage and reconciliation, or in its personalization of the testimony of faith: *I believe* (Junge 2002, 29-42; Beck 2008, 123-152).

Nevertheless, we should notice that the dynamic of individualization is augmented under the conditions of late modernity. Social developments of late modernity such as pluralization, de-traditionalizing, or globalization increasing-ly have consequences for individuals. Indeed, we are focusing here on individu-als that belong to societies of the so-called First World. Only in these societies are the external circumstances, which provide the conditions for the recent push towards individualization, present, such as higher life expectancy, rising pros-perity, growing educational opportunities, resolutions of old residential forms, the social security of the welfare system, and the functional differentiation of society (Beck 1986, 121-130).

In late modernity it is quite normal to regard the individual as a central point of reference. The individual is seen as the producer of the social world and not vice versa. The individual becomes "the life-worldly motor of the social reproduction" (Beck 1986, 209). He or she is entitled to play an ever-bigger role in the process of socialization. Now everyone seems to be the architect of his or her own fortune.

For individuals, individualization is both a freedom as well as a burden. On the one hand, the decreasing stability of social and religious affiliation, the tran-

---

2   The way towards the idea of a broadened reason thus goes further than P. Jonkers takes it in
    this volume with Pope Benedict XVI. From his perspective, non-discursive procedures must
    be seen as unreasonable.

sition to more flexible work, the pluralization of family and partnership models, cultural diversity, the rapid change in values, or the increase in horizontal and vertical mobility all grant a freedom to a variety of options and create more possibilities. Old securities, social bonds, predetermined patterns of life, and self-contained worlds are cancelled out. In addition, traditional symbol-systems and the great meaningful meta-narratives disappear (Lyotard 1984). On the other hand, the individual is obliged to choose and to take responsibility for his or her choices. The problem, however, is that the individual is less and less able to assess the consequences of those choices because they must be made in a "multi-dimensional reality" (Pohl-Patalong 1996, 68). In turn, increasing individualization leads to a segmentation of the social world and to a pluralization of life patterns.

Importantly, the individual in late modernity is not only the producer of the social world, but always remains its product. The individual is subject to new experiences of standardization and normalization, such as those of general consumption, systems of education or vacation, the subliminal norms of age (e.g., there is still a 'right' time for some 'biographical' transitions), the economy, or the role models promoted by mass media. Paradoxically, in late modernity, "standardizing and de-standardizing processes take place at the same time" (Junge 2002, 69). As a result, under the present social circumstances, individualization is a highly ambivalent phenomenon.

Life becomes a confusing mishmash. There is both a choice and, at the same time, an obvious standard with respect to the biography of the individual, for "biographies are subject to, paradoxically, more institutionalization and more individualization at the same time" (Karle 1996, 120). Individuals experience in their lives a combination of dependence and autonomy, standardization and creativity, exclusion and inclusion, strangeness and togetherness, ambiguity and clarity, emotion and rationality, and reality and virtual reality. What seems to be typical in late modernity is that the dividing lines between these polarities become blurred for the individual.

Furthermore, we live in a multi-optional society (Gross 1994). The individual encounters a constant surplus of opportunities while at the same time being increasingly excluded from action. One can do much more today than in the past and, yet, all of these available options are more and more exclusive. In late modern reality many individuals and whole groups remain effectively excluded from making their own decisions due to reasons such as illness, disability, age, gender, and/or social status. As a result, individuals are a priori subject to certain behavioral patterns.

Nevertheless, individuals want to and can come to their own decisions about their lives more than ever before, and individuals are also responsible, at least implicitly, for these decisions. Ultimately, one is responsible for oneself. However, this kind of decision-making and responsibility becomes even more precarious since one can no longer orientate oneself towards traditional unifying concepts, generally accepted beliefs, or the self-evident routine of a community.

Instead, personal identity in late modernity is realized by (self-) "reflexivity" (Giddens 1991, 52).

The conduct of life in late modernity thus remains ambivalent. In view of the continual increase of options, the new standardizations, and the experience of exclusion – while society postulates general inclusion at the same time[3] – life faces constant changes and, in particular, a random and growing complexity. In the end, individuals themselves must accept responsibility for their own lives (Sennett 2003). In this situation, personal identity can only be defined as a temporary unity of a heterogeneous set of pieces. In actuality, the individual is a *dividual*. Life demands different things from the individual in different areas. In the midst of all this, one must still, somehow, create a consistent biography (Gergen 2000).

2. Pastoral care as guiding identity within a Christian framework

The late modern mixture of new freedoms for, and excessive demands on, the individual has, of course, an impact on the Church and her ministry as well (Pohl-Patalong 1996, 55-91). Church ministry is now carried out in an increasingly complex and liquid social reality, which is subject to constant changes and multiple breaks. Therefore, the Church can no longer assume the homogeneity of her members as she once did. Within mass Catholicism this concerned even the experience of discontinuity: transitions such as death, marriage, or adulthood could be addressed in ministry with a relative uniform standard-model of verbal and ritual communication.

In late modernity the social preconditions for this standard-model have radically changed. We saw that the process of building an identity has become fragile. The experience of discontinuity now affects the individual's own life at all stages and aspects. Hence, another priority must be set within ministry; a special focus on the individual and on pastoral care is necessary today, which not only helps to connect the various fragments of one's life to a coherent life story, at least provisionally (Giddens 1991, 75-80), but also demonstrates the role that the Gospel can play in this process.

We have seen the real risks and new pressures that accompany the process of identity formation. Religious identity has also become an interminable project. It is something that is subject to permanent change. In addition, individuals are responsible for who they are religiously. How does this appear in the Church and her ministry (2.1) and what conclusion can we draw from it (2.2)? Our discussion leads, in the end, to a plea for the special significance of pastoral care in late modernity (2.3).

---

3   In a democratic society everyone should have, as a matter of principle, access to any social role.

2.1 Religious individualization in the Church and in ministry

The various pushes towards individualization also appear in the religious sector. However, the religious field remains underexposed, especially in Anglo-American social-scientific discourse (Beckford 2002). Nevertheless, we can use the individualization theorem to analyze the late modern shifts and modifications of both institutional and individual Christian religion (Beck 2008). This theorem is "essential" (Ladenhauf 1995, 41) for our analysis, since it concerns a "key finding about the present religious situation" (Bucher 2001, 19).

Today, Christian faith is performed individually and based on personal responsibility. A guiding principle for a growing majority within the religious field is: 'I decide what God is'. This attitude can easily lead not only to an overload for the religious-productive abilities of the individual, but also to tensions with the doctrines of the Church, her ecclesiastical organization, and her pastoral structures, particularly when these structures are not compatible with the individualized search for religious identity in late modern society. Conversely, this identity might turn out to be incompatible with any form of community, even those with a low binding nature.

The process of individualization results in a reinforced necessity of self-justification. This is also the case in the Church. The question of why one is still a member of the Church must now be answered, even by Pope Benedict XVI, who addressed this question prior to becoming pope (Von Balthasar & Ratzinger 1971, 55-75). Self-justification is necessary because one no longer belongs to a certain religious group or community by birth, destiny, or social control but, rather, by choice. Individual affiliation, selective participation, or withdrawal are increasingly a matter of individual choice, or stand, at the very least, under the imperative that a decision must be made in their regard (Berger 1980). The same counts for the design of one's own belief and religious ideas.

With this development, the individual becomes an important point of reference for ministry in late modernity. "Since the 60s religion makes a turn to the autonomous person ('subjective turn')" (Hellemans 2007, 30), and, vice versa, the individual search for religious identity itself is interpreted religiously, and the result is: "self-awareness by self-reflection as a new form of religion" (Kaufmann 1989, 169). This can be expressed, for example, in a longing for the regulatory function of the Church, given the chaotic social reality experienced by the individual. One seeks to avoid the continual reflexivity of late modernity in a regressive retreat to one specific religious framework. Another example is the narcissistic use of Christian language and ritual, employed only for the affirmation of the self.

There are also other pushes towards individualization that appear in the Church and her ministry, which are linked with the above-described social developments in late modernity. These radicalize the normal hermeneutical process in which an individual becomes familiar with the faith of the Church. The consequences appear particularly in catechesis. Unconventional and new interpretations of Christian heritage arise. Elements from other religions and cultures become combined with the Christian faith. Syncretism and heresy often form a normal state of religious socialization (Hellemans 2007, 177-185). The religious identity of people becomes multi-dimensional and complex as well.

This again shakes the cohesion of the religious communities. Accordingly, they differentiate and become less stable. The Church is undergoing corresponding changes. On the inside, she develops more and more towards a network of heterogeneous persons, groups, movements, and communities, while on the outside, more and more towards a liquid church with soft borders (Ward 2002; Bauer 2009).

The counter-reactions that undoubtedly exist within the Church to these two developments – the internal pluralism and the external loss of contour – become subliminally anachronistic. Even in the religious field, there is a reciprocal dynamic of individual and social segmentation and fragmentation. This remains true even if between both levels of the religious sector there is less simultaneity than in other areas of society.

2.2 The individual as the starting point for ministry

Our above observations are sufficient to make clear that religious identity has also become individualized in late modernity. With this individualization comes again the ambiguity of freedom and new social constraints that the individual has to face in all areas of life. What conclusions can we draw from both developments for the Church and her ministry?

Without being able to give an exhaustive answer here, one point seems to be clear: the individual must be a priority for the Church and her ministry. This applies, in principle, to all pastoral activities. Ministry is indeed about "man himself, whole and entire, body and soul, heart and conscience, mind and will" (GS 3). What differs from the past is that the Church, today, is confronted with various individualized lifestyles and religious biographies, which sometimes remain incompatible with each other. This results directly from the freedom to choose, which itself is a central element of late modern religious identity.[4]

In no case can ministry lag behind the individualization claims of late modernity. The Council has directed the Church from an inward to an outward orientation. The Church should be more than a self-contained religious enclave resistant to actual modernization, even if some believers long for this option. Ministry must aim to face the challenges people have to deal with in their attempts to lead successful (religious) lives for which they take responsibility. The Church must make this aim one of her special points of reference.

Hence, the individual, each with his or her unique biography, becomes the starting point for ministry. Unlike the past, ministry can no longer start out from more or less homogeneous groups and communities. The episcopate, for exam-

---

4   Cf. S. Hellemans in this volume (5.1).

ple, can no longer naturally count on unanimous approval. In late modernity, the authority of the Church as an institution is based on the willingness of individuals to accept the leaders of the Church and to agree with their teachings (Gärtner 2009, 198-205). The same is true for the authority of every single pastor.

This necessary orientation towards the individual includes those pastoral activities in which the community aspect is clearly the center of attention, as in the liturgy or in parish building processes. Even in these, one must take into account the actual pushes towards individualization, for example, by differentiating the meanings of communication. In the end, the goal is about individuals who celebrate their faith together or who form a Christian community. In an individualized society, there is a longing for durable and reliable relationships. However, suitable forms of *koinonia* in the Church must offer to individuals not only enough room for partial participation but also the possibility to withdraw or remove themselves from participation.

The same orientation towards the individual must dominate in other pastoral activities as well. The one who preaches, for example, should realize that under the conditions of late modernity the audience is no longer automatically at one with the meaning of his sermon. Instead, the listeners actively create the meaning that the sermon has for them (Garhammer & Schöttler 1998). Pastoral activities such as this are about an individual application process and no longer about the understanding of a homogenous group of parishioners. From one sermon originates, so to speak, many sermons. A pastor needs to take this into account when preaching and, perhaps, use open phrases, images, parables, and metaphors that stimulate the creative process of application on the part of his audience.

Another aspect of the importance of the individual paradigm in ministry concerns catechesis. Ministry still seems to take insufficient notice of the individualized life patterns of the catechumens. The late modern pluralism of partner and family relationships, for example, is not taken into account in catechetical textbooks (Schomaker 2002). Instead, a harmonious and homogeneous family ideal dominates here, and in other ecclesial texts as well (Dillen 2009). Another example is the necessity to differentiate between the cultural backgrounds of the catechumens or between age groups, since more and more adults are asking for initiation into the Church.

All these examples point to the importance of the individual as the starting point for ministry in late modernity. "In a culture of individualization the Church must leave space for free conversation and for experiment, both on the level of reflection as well on the level of designing life projects."[5] The Church and her ministry need to focus especially on this particular aspect, and reorganize tasks with regard to the heterogeneity of individuals.

This attention to the individual in and for all forms of ministry is already widespread, at least as a postulate. At this point, there is "an extensive agree-

---

5   J. Wissink in this volume. (p. 272)

ment between pastors, theologians and even bishops on the importance of care for the individual as an autonomous person" (Ladenhauf 1995, 36). This consensus appears in academic discourse as well, both in Catholic and Protestant practical theology (Boschki 2005, 62). Nevertheless, the question remains as to whether this attention exists only due to an impassioned demand (Bucher 2005, 188).

Against the backdrop of the Gospel, choosing the individual as the starting point for ministry can only end up favoring those most severely affected by the late modern condition. Those who are ill affected by modernization are hampered by their social situation in developing their identity and their ways of life on the free market. Ministry that takes the Gospel seriously is not concerned with "care for bourgeois-Christian private Me" (Poensgen 1997, 161). Ministry is not primarily aimed at the established middleclass, even if this group actually forms the majority in the churches of the Western world. Instead, ministry deals primarily with finding those who are excluded from possibilities to shape their lives within the complex and incoherent world of late modernity.

2.3 A plea for pastoral care in late modernity

Notwithstanding the increased importance of the individual (especially the marginalized individual) in *all* pastoral fields, pastoral care, which is mainly individual counseling, should become a special priority of the Church in late modernity (Reader 2008, 35-51). This follows quite directly from the radicalized social conditions that influence individuals, even in their religious development.

This preferential option for pastoral care should not, of course, duplicate on a religious level the current trends towards a privatization of religion, a depoliticizing of public discourse (Sennett 2002), and the creation of narcissistic personalities. From the perspective of the Gospel, pastoral care will always remain critical of such trends. Pastoral care connects the orientation towards the individual with an orientation towards his or her social context. Becoming an autonomous person in community, in social responsibility, and in the eyes of God is, accordingly, a major concern in pastoral care (Fürst 2006, 197-201; Mette 2005, 62-99).

Such an option for the individual or for an individual approach in pastoral care is a particular necessity in view of the social demands and the potential for overload in late modernity. "However, this starting point for pastoral care does not mean neglecting the social conditions of individual life" (Gärtner 2003, 128). We have seen that the individualization of life is in many respects a reaction to the current social changes.

The case is similar for the issue of religious identity. It "does not develop solipsistically 'from the inside out' exclusively, but 'in a complicated social process' as 'a dialectical interaction between the person and the society'" (Pohl-Patalong 1996, 131). Our discussion of the circumstances for individual life in late modernity has made it clear that this interaction has become precarious in many respects today. The Church must always enquire prophetically and critically into the concrete causes for this: e.g., loss of the workplace, health damage as a result of malnutrition, medial stereotyping of gender roles, loss of private agendas because of the things forced upon us by social regulations, exclusion from mobile society due to disability, marginalization as a result of illegal status, etc.

Pastoral care that focuses on the individual should therefore be critical of society. It should not be easily satisfied with the expectations of the other social systems in late modernity that mean to limit its function to social hygiene and stabilization. It should cushion therapeutically the undesirable effects of these systems – especially the economy. The Church can only meet these demands if she has first tended to the prophetic-critical 'thorn in the flesh' of the Gospel (Gärtner 2011).

Therefore, biographical orientation and guiding identity processes must be central to late modern pastoral care, which must meet two conditions: it must connect rather than detach the individual from his or her social, cultural, and life-worldly relationships, even if one chooses an individualistic approach (Schwab 2002, 166-169); and, in addition, pastoral care cannot be separated from other pastoral fields but must stand closely connected to them. We have argued that all pastoral activities should focus on the individual as well. We must avoid the creation of feigned opposites.

Under these two conditions, it is a priority for pastoral care to support individuals in the interminable and risky process of forming an identity in difficult late modern circumstances. Pastoral care must be about being helpful in the exploration and transformation of the self. In pastoral care this arises from the critical and affirmative examination of one's own identity in the light of the message of the Gospel (Van Knippenberg 2002).

The background to this is a concept of narrative identity, which the individual constantly creates and changes. For this process, one permanently refers to social patterns. One's personal life story is thus woven with collective stories. At this point, the Gospel, regarded as one specific tradition amongst others, can acquire meaning and significance. It can become beneficial for people, especially when their identity is disturbed by the described late modern demands.

Therefore, pastoral care develops from a comparison of the situation of individuals with the promises of the Christian traditions. Based on these promises, a pastor helps individuals find their way in realizing a personal identity. In their lives nothing appears to be normal or natural any more – not only because their social reality has become polyphonic, but especially because God promises different. If one trusts God, one can gain strength and orientation with regard to one's own identity.

Pastoral care starts out from the concrete living conditions of the individual in late modern society. However, his world with its plausibility and rules is now alienated by the confrontation with the saving will of God. This creates a new view of reality. Change suddenly appears to be possible and meaningful. The individual can take life into her own hands again. And whenever this fails, the transcendent perspective makes identity acceptable to the individual, even if it remains fragmentary and of a provisional nature (Luther 1992, 62-182).

More specifically, pastoral care uses for this alienation and confrontation the images, symbols, stories, rituals, and metaphors of the Christian traditions. "The central purpose of ministry practice is best fulfilled in assisting individuals, families, and communities in the transformation of life by means of the transformation and reinterpretation of their core stories. Such transformations, if they are to be seen as taking place within the ongoing Christian community and its tradition, should rightly by grounded in dialogical interaction with the primary images and themes of the biblical and Christian story" (Gerkin 1991, 59).

The Christian faith itself becomes an orientation for successfully developing people's identity. It offers an alternative and a critique of the late modern living conditions, for God opens up a different perspective on the usual and the normal. It is the task of pastoral care to reveal this promise to the individual life stories of people in late modern society, even if the person sitting opposite does not share this perspective initially. This perspective is, for example, about mercy versus the dominance of performance, about accepting one's own body versus trying to attain idealized and sexualized body images, about openness for transcendence versus pure instrumental reasoning, about respect for the disabled life versus genetic visions of viability, about sensitivity for guilt versus human hubris, about eschatological expectation versus the omnipresence of luck and fun, about reliable binding versus late modern nomadism.

To ensure the credibility of such an approach, pastoral care has to rely on a symbolic anticipation of the conquest of the aporias of late modern society within the Church. This does not mean that the Church herself is a perfect community. Quite often, the mere form of her communication testifies to the opposite. The community of the faithful may have been promised the presence of the Holy Ghost, but as a community of sinful people, it only realizes this promise in a very fragmented way. Nevertheless, the Church has to show in its pastoral practices the same potential for hope that should be found in the personal life story of the individual. The individual must be able to find this hope in the Church as a personal experience.[6]

Because she knows her possibilities are reduced by human limitations, the Church escapes the danger of uncritically following the commandment of perfection, which, in spite of real, experienced fragmentation, is a secret norm of late modern society. This commandment of perfection also applies to the identity of the individual. Yet, at the same time, it is becoming less clear what exactly is natural or normal. After all, any design for life is determined by the segmentation of social reality and the pluralization of possibilities.

---

6   Cf. S. Hellemans in this volume: 5.4.

Pastoral care has to "develop a culture of imperfection, which frees people from the inordinate and therefore unhealthy demand for perfection and the necessity to perform" (Scherer-Rath 2001, 33). The awareness that humans are sinners and that no human community can ever live up to its own pretensions ensures that the real failure of human efforts for identity is not pushed aside for hasty answers. Instead, pastoral care is also about training people to use their talents in a controlled and humble way. One can always trust in God's possibilities, which will always be bigger than one's own. The Church knows about these possibilities. She trusts in God's promises and tries to realize them in late modern society. Her pastoral care is offering support from this perspective (Wittrahm 2001, 230-330).

In conclusion, pastoral care is based on the contrast between the message of the Gospel with the promised future in the kingdom of God and the concrete situation of the individual, which is subjected to individual and/or social sin (Schüßler 2004, 40-44). A pastor tries to draw implications for a changed and changing behavior and thinking from this contrast. With such a profile, pastoral care can contribute to religious identity. Its purpose is to guide individual identity within a Christian framework. Pastoral care makes a substantive offer, by which people might find help within the Church with regard to the reflective standards of their life stories and with regard to the many social constraints and contingencies in late modern society.

References

Arens, E. 1999. Was heißt in der entfalteten Moderne an Gott glauben? *Bulletin ET* 10: 15-24.
Balthasar, H.U. von & J. Ratzinger. 1971. *Zwei Plädoyers. Warum ich noch ein Christ bin. Warum ich noch in der Kirche bin*. München: Kösel.
Bauer, Ch. 2009. Von der Pfarrei zum Netzwerk? Eine pastoralsoziologische Probebohrung. *Diakonia* 40: 119-126.
Bauman, Z. 1993. *Modernity and ambivalence*. Cambridge *et. al.*: Polity.
    Id. 2001. *The individualized society*. Cambridge *et al.*: Polity.
    Id. 2007. *Liquid times. Living in an age of uncertainty*. Cambridge *et al.*: Polity.
Beck, U. 1986. *Risikogesellschaft. Auf dem Weg in eine andere Moderne*. Frankfurt/M.: Suhrkamp.
    Id. 2008. *Der eigene Gott. Von der Friedensfähigkeit und dem Gewaltpotential der Religionen*. Frankfurt/M.-Leipzig: Verlag der Weltreligionen im Insel Verlag.
Beckford, J.A. 2002. Postmodernity, high modernity and new modernity: three concepts in search of religion. Pp. 282-297 in P. Beilharz (ed.). *Zygmunt Bauman III*. London *et al.*: Sage.
Berger, P.L. 1980. *The heretical imperative. Contemporary possibilities of religious affirmation*. Garden City: Anchor Press/Doubleday.

Boschki, R. 2005. Von welchem Subjekt reden wir eigentlich? Für eine beziehungso-
rientierte Subjektkonstruktion in Pastoraltheologie und Religionspädagogik. Pp. 58-
64 in D. Nauer u.a. (Hgg.). *Praktische Theologie. Bestandsaufnahme und Zukunfts-
perspektiven*. Stuttgart: Kohlhammer.

Bucher, R. 2001. Die Theologie im Volk Gottes. Die Pastoral theologischen Handelns
in postmodernen Zeiten. Pp. 13-39 in Id. (Hg.). *Theologie in den Kontrasten der
Zukunft. Perspektiven des theologischen Diskurses*. Graz u. a.: Styria.

Id. 2005. Neue Machttechniken in der alten Gnadenanstalt? Organisationsentwicklung in der Kirche. Pp. 183-199 in Id. & R. Krockauer (Hgg.). *Macht und Gnade.
Untersuchungen zu einem konstitutiven Spannungsfeld der Pastoral*. Münster: Lit.

Dillen, A. 2009. *Het gezin: à-Dieu? Een contextuele benadering van gezinnen in
ethisch, pedagogisch en pastoraaltheologisch perspectief*. Brussel: KVAB.

Fürst, W. 2006. Pastoraltheologie als Seelsorgewissenschaft. Pp. 197-201 in U. Feeser-
Lichterfeld & R. Feiter (Hgg.). *Dem Glauben Gestalt geben. Festschrift für Walter
Fürst*. Berlin-Münster: Lit.

Gärtner, St. 2003. Pastoral care and boundaries. Pp.119-132 in B. Roebben & L. van der
Tuin (eds.). *Practical theology and the interpretation of crossing boundaries*.
Münster u. a.: Lit.

Id. 2009. *Zeit, Macht und Sprache. Pastoraltheologische Studien zu Grunddimensionen der Seelsorge*. Freiburg/Br. u. a.: Herder.

Id. 2011. Prophetic pastoral care. Resistance potential in late modernity? Pp. 23-29
in A. Dillen & A. Vandenhoeck (eds.). *Prophetic witness in world Christianities.
Rethinking pastoral care and counseling*. Berlin-Wien: Lit.

Garhammer, E. & H.-G. Schöttler (Hgg.). 1998. *Predigt als offenes Kunstwerk. Homile-
tik und Rezeptionsästhetik*. München: Don Bosco.

Gergen, K.J. 2000. *The saturated self. Dilemmas of identity in contemporary life*. New
York: Basic Books.

Gerkin, Ch.V. 1991. *Prophetic pastoral practice. A Christian vision of life together*.
Nashville: Abingdon Press.

Giddens, A. 1991. *Modernity and self-identity. Self and society in the late modern age*.
Cambridge: Polity.

Gross, P. 1994. *Die Multioptionsgesellschaft*. Frankfurt/M.: Suhrkamp.

Harvey, D. 1989. *The condition of postmodernity. An enquiry into the origins of cultural
change*. Oxford: Blackwell.

Hellemans, St. 2007. *Het tijdperk van de wereldreligies. Religie in agrarische civilisaties en in moderne samenlevingen*. Zoetermeer-Kapellen: Meinema/Pelckmans.

Hoff, G.M. 2001. *Die prekäre Identität des Christlichen. Die Herausforderung postmodernen Differenzdenkens für eine theologische Hermeneutik*. Paderborn u.a.:
Schöningh.

Junge, M. 2002. *Individualisierung*. Frankfurt/M.-New York: Campus.

Karle, I. 1996. *Seelsorge in der Moderne. Eine Kritik der psychoanalytisch orientierten
Seelsorgelehre*. Neukirchen-Vluyn: Neukirchener Verlag.

Kaufmann, F.X. 1989. *Religion und Modernität. Sozialwissenschaftliche Perspektiven*.
Tübingen: Mohr.

Knippenberg, T. van. 2002. *Towards religious identity. An exercise in spiritual guidance*. Assen: Royal Van Gorcum.

Körtner, U.H.J. 2006. *Einführung in die theologische Hermeneutik*. Darmstadt: Wissenschaftliche Buchgesellschaft.

Ladenhauf, K.H. 1995. Ihr werdet Aufatmen finden für euer Leben (Mt 11,29). Subjektfördernde und kontextbezogene Seelsorge als gesellschaftliche und pastoraltheologische Herausforderung. Pp. 35-58 in H. Windisch (Hg.). *Seelsorge neu gestalten. Fragen und Impulse*. Graz u. a.: Styria.

Luhmann, N. 1997. *Die Gesellschaft der Gesellschaft*. Frankfurt/M.: Suhrkamp.

Luther, H. 1992. *Religion und Alltag. Bausteine zu einer Praktischen Theologie des Subjekts*. Stuttgart: Radius.

Lyotard, J.-F. 1984. *The postmodern condition. A report on knowledge*. Minneapolis: University of Minnesota Press.

Id. 1988. Die Moderne redigieren. Pp. 204-214 in W. Welsch (Hg.). *Wege aus der Moderne. Schlüsseltexte zur Postmoderne-Diskussion*. Weinheim: VCH.

Mette, N. 2005. *Einführung in die katholische Praktische Theologie*. Darmstadt: Wissenschaftliche Buchgesellschaft.

Petzold, H.G. 2005. Unterwegs zu einem "erweiterten Seelsorgekonzept" für eine "transversale Moderne". Pp. 213-237 in K. Henke & A. Marzinzik-Boness (Hgg.). *"Aus dem etwas machen, wozu ich gemacht worden bin". Gestaltseelsorge und Integrative Pastoralarbeit*. Stuttgart: Kohlhammer.

Poensgen, H. 1997. Alles ist Fragment. Kritische Anfragen zu Konzepten heilender Seelsorge in der Pastoral. *Theologisch-praktische Quartalschrift* 145: 155-167.

Pohl-Patalong, U. 1996. *Seelsorge zwischen Individuum und Gesellschaft. Elemente zu einer Neukonzeption der Seelsorgetheorie*. Stuttgart u.a.: Kohlhammer.

Reader, J. 2008. *Reconstructing practical theology. The impact of globalization*. Aldershot-Burlington: Ashgate.

Sander, H.-J. 2005. Theologischer Kommentar zur Pastoralkonstitution über die Kirche in der Welt von heute. Gaudium et spes. Pp. 581-886 in P. Hünermann & B.J. Hilberath (Hgg.). *Herders theologischer Kommentar zum Zweiten Vatikanischen Konzil IV*. Freiburg/Br. u.a.: Herder.

Scherer-Rath, M. 2001. *Lebenssackgassen. Herausforderung für die pastorale Beratung und Begleitung von Menschen in Lebenskrisen*. Münster u.a.: Lit.

Schomaker, M.F. 2002. *Die Bedeutung der Familie in katechetischen Lernprozessen von Kindern. Eine inhaltsanalytische Untersuchung von Konzepten zur Hinführung der Kinder zu den Sakramenten der Beichte und der Eucharistie*. Münster u.a.: Lit.

Schroer, M. 2001. *Das Individuum der Gesellschaft. Synchrone und diachrone Theorieperspektiven*. Frankfurt/M.: Suhrkamp.

Schüßler, M. 2004. Prophetie, Protest, Institution - Praktisch-theologische Beobachtungen zwischen Befreiungstheologie und Systemtheorie. Pp. 38-50 in R. Bucher & R. Krockauer (Hgg.). *Prophetie in einer etablierten Kirche? Aktuelle Reflexionen über ein Prinzip kirchlicher Identität*. Münster: Lit.

Schwab, U. 2002. Wahrnehmen und Handeln. Praktische Theologie als subjektorientierte Theorie. Pp. 161-175 in E. Hauschildt & Id. (Hgg.). *Praktische Theologie für das 21. Jahrhundert*. Stuttgart: Kohlhammer.

Sennett, R. 2002. *The fall of public man*. London: Penguin.

Id. 2003. *The corrosion of character. The personal consequences of work in the new capitalism*. New York et al.: Norton.

Ward, P. 2002. *Liquid Church. A bold vision of how to be God's people in worship and mission - a flexible, fluid way of being Church*. Carlisle-Peabody: Paternoster Press/Hendrickson.

Widl, M. 2000. *Pastorale Weltentheologie - transversal entwickelt im Diskurs mit der Sozialpastoral*. Stuttgart u. a.: Kohlhammer.

Wittrahm, A. 2001. *Seelsorge, Pastoralpsychologie und Postmoderne. Eine pastoralpsychologische Grundlegung lebensfördernder Begegnungen angesichts radikaler postmoderner Pluralität*. Stuttgart u. a.: Kohlhammer.

How the Roman Catholic Church Maneuvers through Liquid Modernity

Kees de Groot

What is the actual position of the Roman Catholic Church in late modernity? At first sight, it seems that the issue is whether or not the Church should modernize. In either case, the Church is considered to be in tension with modernity. Despite the apparent difference in the evaluation of church policies, there seems to be remarkable agreement among theologians on the modernity of the Church. Theological discourse on recent church history in the Netherlands, its success and its failure, is dominated by two scenarios. One scenario holds restorative ecclesial policy after the Second Vatican Council responsible. Church leaders alienated ordinary Catholics by resisting church renewal. Another scenario claims that this very church renewal has alienated the flock. Therefore, the Roman Catholic Church in the Netherlands rightly joins again the traditional course of the global Church (De Groot, 2010c). Apparently, both scenarios agree on the position of the Roman Catholic Church towards the world of today: it is not up to date. According to the first scenario, the Church is not modern enough; according to the second scenario, it is not and should not be modern. Both agree that the Church is not a very modern institution.

An alternative, reactionary view is that the Church is already too modern, and it should wipe out the blots of modernity. I agree with the empirical part of this judgment, that is, that the Church has incorporated organization forms and, moreover, thought patterns of modernity. This is not surprising since the Church has always, more or less critically, accommodated itself to the societal context. The problem is that sometimes these organization structures are considered closed for discussion. This becomes apparent in our currently prevailing type of modernity, or what can be referred to as advanced or '*liquid*' modernity. The Church is also present in liquid modernity in various kinds of ways (think, for example, of the World Youth Days or various Roman Catholic websites), but is equipped with organization styles and modes of thinking that are inherited from what can be called '*solid*' modernity.

An example of this is the assumption that believers should be active participants in the parish to which they belong. This presupposition is reflected in the critical attitude towards the perception of the Church as a service institution for marriages and funerals. Beneath all the ecclesiological arguments for this judgment, there is a modern basic assumption that members should invest in the organization they belong to, preferably at the local level. This modern attitude differs not only from a contemporary approach, but also from an earlier, premodern attitude. The parish started its life as a church polity concept signifying the district of a priest, so that it was clear who was responsible for the administration of the sacraments, and who was entitled to receive the corresponding rewards (Eijsink, 1995, 23).

This very example makes clear that it does not make sense to plead for a return to the tradition conceived as the way it was. Neither, however, does the awareness of the changing of the times lead to the command to go along with the changes. The question is how to deal with the changing context, both among us and in us. This is a question concerning strategy, which requires knowledge of the Church and its context, and an interpretation both of the mission of the Church and of God's presence, or absence, in the world. A practical-theological approach should integrate an empirical, a hermeneutic, and a strategic perspective (Heitink, 1999). It should acknowledge the opportunities and restraints of contemporary culture, understand the theological issues at stake, and suggest directions for adequate actions.

In the first (conceptual) section, I will explain my use of the concepts 'solid' and 'liquid' modernity and introduce my organizational perspective. The second (empirical) section will present case studies of how the Church deals with liquid modernity. The third (hermeneutic) section makes explicit the theological issues that are at stake. In the fourth (strategic) section, I will suggest how professionals in the Church can work on church development, taking theology and liquid modernity seriously or, in more robust terms, 'anchored to the Rock and geared to the tides'.[1]

1. Religion and the Church in solid and liquid modernity

1.1 Religion in solid and liquid modernity

In this volume, we consider the shape of the Catholic Church in the West under the conditions of advanced modernity. In order to specify this stage in the process of modernization, I use a popular distinction between two types of modernity, which I schematize in *Table 1* below (Bauman, 2000). In reality, of course, these types can be recognized in different contexts at the same time and combinations of solid and liquid modern features are also possible. I will characterize these types in a few statements.

In industrial, or solid, modernity, social positions are defined by the production process. This type of modernity defines whether one is a boss, a worker, a housewife, etc. One is either an owner, a laborer, or excluded from this structure. The modern organization thrives: the factory, the union, the party – these are specialized social formations that bring together the masses in a hierarchical

---

1　This was the historic motto of Youth for Christ, originally an American evangelical movement. In the Netherlands it is now a Christian Movement that supports youth ministry in various churches, including the Roman Catholic Church, and provides youth workers in secular contexts as well.

structure. Identity is, to a large extent, ascribed. When one is a worker, one is a member of the working class and this, together with one's ancestry, defines one's identity. Modern life is governed and disciplined, as depicted visually, for example, in Charlie Chaplin's *Modern Times* (1936). In this movie, which is inspired by and commenting on industrial enterprises such as the Ford factories, the worker becomes one with the assembly line on which he or she is working.

Solid modernity stands in contrast with liquid modernity. In post-industrial, or liquid, modernity, consumer life styles have a more decisive impact on identity. Life style is more important than class. The modern *have-nots* are now low budget consumers with a one-sided pattern of spending, buying on credit. People are not only members of a few organizations, but participate in various networks, facilitated by the enormous growth in means of transport and communication. A network is a configuration of social units and their relations. There is more than one center; social units act in relative autonomy (Hochschild, 2003). Life-long participation becomes an exception; sometimes the involvement concerns only a specific interest. A plural identity is always under development and reflection. Since identity is no longer self-assumed, it may become a serious problem for late modern individuals. Life in liquid modernity requires flexibility and the ability to make choices in swiftly changing and differing circumstances. To evoke an image, life in liquid modernity is more like paddling in a canoe than following instructions for operating a machine.

Table 1. Solid and liquid modernity

Solid modernity	Liquid modernity
Production	Consumption
Hierarchical mass organization	Network
Ascribed identity	Reflexive identity

These characteristics correspond with the transformation of religion during the process of modernization. Religion in solid modernity accentuates the distinction between clergy and lay people based on their (lack of) control over religious capital, turning the latter into active members (Hellemans, 2007).[2] Since the industrial revolution, church organization has expanded. In the early seventeenth century, distanced church involvement was common. Since the nineteenth century, we have grown accustomed to churches as institutions that bring believers together every week, in one place, to perform the same actions under supervision. Religion primarily refers to the denomination (Dutch: *gezindte)* to which one belongs.

In our liquid modern times, religion itself appears to be liquid. Those who prefer to do so may choose from a vast array of options in religion, spirituality,

---

2   This tendency was already present in the pre-modern era, during the confessionalization of Europe. In the modern era, members are not only expected to participate in collective rituals, but also to participate in the church organization as volunteers.

and rituals. We are interconnected with others through a web of networks. Religion is experienced and distributed through books, music, movies, TV, informal groups, events, internet-communities, and fairs. 'Believing', or 'spirituality', has become a matter of individual preference and taste, which nevertheless tend to correspond with social milieus. Moreover, people tend to follow or anticipate fashion trends. Paradoxically, the newly found faith itself may promise to emancipate the converted from the agonies of choice (Bauman 1997, 197).

Table 2. Religion in liquid modernity

Modernity	Solid		Liquid	
	Society	Religion	Society	Religion
Dimension				
Social Determinant	Production	Membership	Consumption	Choice
Social formation	Hierarchical mass organization	Institution	Network	Connected communities
Identity	Ascribed	Denomination	Reflexive	Spirituality

The Catholic world takes part in the liquid, late modern preference for personal choice, the importance of networks, and the accent on the religious experience. At the same time, the Church is attached to a solid modern outfit, despite all its verbal resistance to modernity and modernism.

1.2 The Church as a hybrid organization

It is in this context of solid modernity becoming liquid that the Roman Catholic Church operates. In addition, though not unrelated, to dogmatic understandings, it is useful to acknowledge the Church as a human enterprise, vices and virtues included. The Church may be considered an organization with an explicit purpose (to spread the Word and to provide the sacraments through its ministry), structures of authority (the hierarchy), and a relation to the environment (its mission) (Van der Ven, 1996). To a certain extent, this is an organization that unites the masses in a hierarchical system. Yet, both actual practice and theological reasoning show that this is only part of the story. The 'board' is not in control of everything the Church does. It has been noted that the Church is rather like a multinational concern, consisting of dioceses led by bishops who have the authority to manage affairs in their own domain, within canonical boundaries (Fleck and Dyma, 2002). This concern has a dual structure: there is a secular clergy alongside a religious clergy. Religious orders have their own hierarchical structure within the universal Church. Moreover, the faithful are active within the Church, supporting the clergy, or organizing ecclesial activities in a relatively autonomous way. Others are connected at a distance, depending on their life phase and their personal interests. With its dual structure, and the complex interaction of formal and informal, more or less stable social units, the Church as a whole may also be considered a hybrid organization, showing both traits of a linear organization and of a network organization (Gusfield, 1981).

In order to put this notion of a 'hybrid organization' in a workable analytical category, I use the typology Charles Handy constructed for voluntary, or non-profit, organizations (Handy, 1992). Organization science makes a distinction between mutual support groups, service delivery agencies, and campaigning bodies. Support groups unite people with a common problem or enthusiasm, such as alcoholics or fans of certain music. Providing services to those in need is the core business of organizations such as those that help out drivers on the road having trouble with their cars. Campaigning organizations are created to fight for a cause or to act as a pressure group for a particular interest, such as the protection of the environment or against abortion. Handy explains that these three types of organizations each have their own primary target groups, which imply specific styles of management and sets of assumptions. Most organizations, however, end up as a sort of amalgam of all three categories. The Church is one of these organizations (Davidson and Koch, 1998).

The Church has three target groups: those who gather in the Church because of their common engagement (the *members* of the organization, such as engaged parishioners), those who ask for the services that the Church provides (the *clients* of the organization, such as incidental visitors), and those who should be reached with the message of the organization (the *world*).

Table 3. Types of Voluntary Organizations

Target group	Category
Members	Mutual support
Clients	Service delivery
World	Campaigning

The characteristics of these three types of organization can be recognized in the different faces of the Church: the faith community, the service church, and the missionary organization.

As a mutual support group, the Church may appear as a community with frequent informal contacts, characterized by feelings of belonging, and a distinction between those who belong and those who do not (yet/anymore) belong. Management is not popular; interaction is popular, which tends to be a cause for numerous and long meetings. Officials are supposed to support the community.

In a service delivery organization, it is important to have transparency. Those who come to church to pray, to celebrate, to learn, to help, or be helped need to know whom to address and when. Professionals and volunteers require certain qualifications for the work they do.

The mission in the world is central to the Church as a campaigning organization. This mission is the motivating answer to the dissatisfaction with the world as it is. Campaigning organizations are led rather than managed. Membership cards are not considered important; what counts is faith and commitment. In this case, the *Church-as-an-organization* acts as an organization within the larger social movement that is inspired by Jesus Christ and his Gospel.

The combination of congregational life, openness to parishioners at a distance, and taking part in the worldwide Christian mission is what makes the Church vital. Wise church leaders, however, make careful distinctions between the three tasks, since each have their own merits and challenges. They should be joined, but not be mixed.

Many tensions within the Church can be explained by this organizational variety. The accomplishments and desires of the existing community may conflict with the ministry to provide service to those who contact the Church incidentally, e.g., for a ceremony, and both tasks may clash with the mission to spread the gospel.

To this threefold typology, I add another way in which the presence of the Church may take shape, namely, using the Church beyond its sphere of influence. According to sociologist James Beckford, it is to be expected that religion be used as a cultural resource in advanced industrial societies (Beckford, 1989). By selecting, copying, and reconstructing elements of the religious tradition that were exclusively under the safeguard of the Church, other organizations present the Church in society.

In the following, I will investigate how these faces of the Church interrelate. Four cases show the complex ways in which the Church deals with the world of today: the parish, chaplaincy/spiritual care, New Movements, and the use of Christian liturgy in secular theatre.

2.   A hybrid organization dealing with liquid modernity

The Church is present in Western late modern society as a mutual support group providing services, as a service delivery organization founded on a membership-principle, as a campaigning organization that does not succeed in addressing the world, and as a cultural resource for others to draw upon.

2.1 The parish: members and clients

The main building block of the Church as a mutual support group is, or perhaps has been, the parish. Although, since 1848, the parish has been quite successfully modernized, at the present time the modern model of massive active participation and identification is failing. 27% of Dutch Catholics do not consider themselves to belong to a church (Becker 2003, 14). Another 25% attend church regularly (Bernts et al., 2007, 18). In between, there is a category of Catholics who attend church incidentally, for example, to participate in *rites de passages*. Canonically, all Catholics in a certain territory belong to the parish, which is guided by a priest who acts as a *pastor proprius*. In fact, providing ceremonies (especially funeral services) and pastoral care for those Catholics growing up, getting married, having children, and (especially) passing away form the core-business of the Church. The parish has to deal both with Catholics who consider themselves members, and with Catholics who, instead, consider themselves clients. A survey held in 2003 among pastoral councils show that these councils do not make a sharp distinction between the parish as a mutual benefit organization and the parish as a service organization. An (self-reported) attitude of offering support for all those seeking spirituality prevails, only partly combined with a sense of mission and certain expectations of the participants (De Groot et al., 2005).

Both the Catholic tradition of varying degrees of participation and the European tendency to regard the Church as a useful institution seem to generate a 'service church imperative' (De Groot, 2006a). Diocesan policies and attitudes, however, seem recently to move towards the promotion of a congregational model. Bishops tend to condemn the 'religious shopping', which was explicitly facilitated in earlier experiments.[3] The congregational, or even sectarian, strategy seems to surpass the service church strategy.

Both strategies react differently to a context in which there is an ongoing interest in spirituality, and a diminishing appreciation for the Catholic Church as an institution. The service church approach tends to accompany people on their way. In this case, people can continue to make their own choices and develop their spirituality in a reflexive way.

In the survey results, the other strategy – urging people to make a firm choice for the Christian tradition – was hardly present outside the dominant attitude of trying to be accessible. This might have changed in the foregoing years. A strategy that excludes so-called free riders, promotes strictness, and increases the efforts and (supernatural) rewards of being a Catholic may result in a higher commitment of a smaller group of members (church-to-sect scenario). In this approach, the Church provides an alternative for a liquid culture by requiring the choice to make the final decision for the solid rock (De Groot, 2008).

The recent propagation of a missionary zeal[4] may supposedly transcend the opposition between these two strategies. Focusing on God's love for the world might help to redirect the potentially self-centered mutual support strategy, and to inspire the potentially unfocussed service strategy. A missionary initiative from the Protestant Church of Amsterdam ('Amen to the Word of the Layman' (Dutch: *De Preek van de Leek*)) constitutes an interesting example. The 'urban minister' organized a series of church services in which 'contemporary preachers' (artists, journalists, comedians, and politicians) delivered the sermon (Van der Goot, 2010). Here, the gospel is preached to the world and to a church at the

---

3   In 2001, the ministry department of the Archdiocese of Utrecht [Dienst Pastorale Dienstverlening] presented four 'visionary varieties' of a parish that is fit for the future. One of these was the 'Sense shop' [Zinwinkel], an open space that offers attention, rituals, information, and devotional objects from a Roman Catholic background.

4   See J. Wissink in this volume.

same time in the style of liquid modernity. The church joins in with crossing boundaries, playfulness, and flexibility.

The term mission may, however, also conceal the opposition between two different perceptions of what the Church is for. One is that people, estranged from God and the Church, should return to the Church, participate in the local community, and receive the sacraments so that they can live in full communion (*extra ecclesiam nulla salus*). The other is that the Church embodies a tradition of searching for God's presence in the world. In that case, believers are not so much required to invest in their church as loyal members, but, most of all, to open their hearts and their minds to God's grace, and to care for their neighbors and the world at large (*extra mundum nulla salus)* (Borgman, 2010, 138).[5] The combination of missionary initiatives with the goal of membership recruitment radiates a message that differs from the combination with an approach that seeks to respond to the needs and the desires of people, without focusing on their denomination. Often, the motive to strengthen the declining Church prevails.

2.2 Spiritual care: the world embraces a service from the Church

Service delivery is the central focus of the various chaplaincies to which the Church attends. Traditionally, the Church has regarded the care of souls for those in hospital, prison, or in the army as part of its core business: a service for members. In the modern era, pastors (priests, pastoral workers, ministers, rabbis) have specialized themselves in becoming chaplains for a specific domain, taking into account that pastoral care is different in each domain. More recently, in the West (especially in the Netherlands), we see the rise of 'spiritual care' as a new profession. Since 1970, several indicators point in this direction.

Following American examples, Dutch psychologists and theologians started interdenominational psychological and pastoral training (Clinical Pastoral Training) for pastors working in institutional settings. Ecumenical departments for spiritual care were established, firstly in hospitals, and later in other institutions for care as well, e.g., homes for the elderly, mental health care, and care for the mentally handicapped. These pastors started to operate on an interconfessional basis, and were salaried by the institutions themselves. They united in a professional association (Association for Spiritual Counselors in Care Institutions). In 1977, Humanistic spiritual counselors entered the field and, in 1993, Islamic spiritual counselors joined. Since 1985, counselors without an (religious) affiliation have started to manifest themselves. For the time being, they

---

5   Consider the expression *substitit in,* and its various interpretations, in one of the introductory paragraphs of *Lumen gentium:* 'This Church constituted and organized in the world as a society, subsists in the Catholic Church, which is governed by the successor of Peter and by the Bishops in communion with him, although many elements of sanctification and of truth are found outside of its visible structure.' (Ch. 1.8). See also the corresponding document of the Congregation for the Doctrine of the Faith (2007).

have not succeeded in organizing themselves in a separate section within the professional association. This association has formulated a professional standard, recognizes diplomas, and has set up a system of registration (VGVZ, 2002). In a word, it promotes the professionalization of 'spiritual care'.

At the same time, this new profession leans heavily on organized religion. The legal basis for spiritual care is and has been that the state does not interfere with religion, nor does it hinder the exercise of religion. Therefore, the state facilitates spiritual care when people are under a regime that is regulated by state governance: in the army, a prison, or, indirectly, when they are in a hospital or institution. Originally, spiritual care was the continuation of the usual support for members of a particular denomination. In practice, however, confessional identity of chaplains is downplayed by the chaplains themselves and often considered irrelevant by the public (Smeets, 2006). The chaplains tend to perceive themselves as 'spiritual counselors', irrespective of their religious affiliation.

In a context of secularization and increasing religious diversity, recent developments display different trends in the context of care versus the context of state institutions (De Groot, 2010b). Since the nineteen eighties, health care institutions have become less strict in their policy to require only professionals with an official delegation. They have started to employ unaffiliated spiritual counselors as well. These counselors have formed their own association (called 'Albert Camus'). The general professional association is discussing its exclusion of non-affiliated workers. It also tries to fortify its position in the care process. The association has, for example, succeeded in participating in the new Health Insurance System, namely, as a profession that helps outpatients to 'cope' with their handicap or illness.

In the army and prison, the system of Delegating Authorities has been expanded. Next to Catholic, Protestant, Jewish, and Humanistic sections, we now have Muslim, Hindu, and Buddhist sections within the Department for Spiritual Care, which resides under the Minister of Justice. Within these sections, pleas for both a confessional and professional orientation are heard.

The case of spiritual care in the Netherlands shows the following pattern. A new profession starts to establish itself, only partly linked with organized religion. It claims a service expertise in existential issues, and modestly succeeds in being recognized as such. It is successful in the context of care and in the context of the army and prison. The organizational basis in the context of care is firstly (juridical-political) organized religion. Yet, the profession also tries to claim its place in the process of care itself, next to, but different from, social work and psychological help (keyword here: accountability). Thus, it is linked with organized religion, which is still large but declining. It is against this background that this new profession has developed and seeks a new basis of legitimacy. It has its own professional characteristics embedded in theological, religious, and humanistic studies. It also uses psychological categories (e.g., 'coping') in the struggle for public recognition.

The organizational basis in the context of state institutions exists strongly in organized religion. In this way, the government can indirectly exclude unaffiliated or 'sectarian' spiritual counselors, whereas the established 'chaplains' do not have to prove their effectiveness (keyword here: security). Secular soldiers and prisoners receive spiritual care (as an umbrella term), provided by counselors who are affiliated with a church, Humanism, Judaism, Islam, Hinduism, or Buddhism.

During the course of professionalization, a membership-oriented activity becomes a service delivery-oriented activity. In the nineteen seventies, religious diversity was the impetus for the rise of a new profession of secular-religious specialists. Their professional-academic orientation and institutional setting was secular; their expertise was in the religious domain, namely, the provision of meaning in matters of life and death. Increased secularization and pluralization has been answered by two strategies, which can be formally distinguished as follows: first, the extension of the confessional model (*organized religious pluralism*) and second, the definition of a common ground for all professionals in spiritual care, within the context of public accountability (*generalized pluralism*). The first strategy dominates in the context of state institutions, but is not absent in care institutions. Islamic counselors, for example, tend to operate exclusively for Islamic patients, alongside the Christian and Humanistic counselors who take care of all other patients. The second strategy dominates in care institutions, although spiritual counselors in prisons and the army reach people of other faiths as well, and try to prove their usefulness with scientific reports.

This case suggests that liquid modernity leads to 'care of souls' being conceptualized as spiritual care. In liquid modernity, the historical Christian care of souls tends to transform into spiritual care as a new professional service, close to, but distinct from, the services provided by the psychological profession. From the perspective of politics, this new profession is legitimized by the general need for pastoral and spiritual care in society. In the specific context of prisons and the army, their institutional dynamics are ruled by a logic of security, in the context of care by a logic of accountability.

From a campaigning perspective, this process of professionalization and deconfessionalization may be appreciated as a secularizing persistence of an originally ecclesial service. Spiritual care, then, is an example of how the Christian tradition is disseminated in worldly domains; it is a successful example of evangelization. As a result, spiritual care is now integrated in the care for the sick, the elderly, and the handicapped. However, this development may also be considered an alienation of pastoral counseling from its theological origins. From the perspective of the Church as a mutual support group, the Church is responsible for the care of souls for its members. The care for others may be added to this, as a moral duty for the members (*diakonia*). This link is lost when spiritual care is monopolized by a separate profession.

2.3. New Movements: missionary structures for the inner circle

Campaigning seems to be the goal of the so-called New Movements in the Church. A small (0.2%) but significant part of Dutch Catholics (no more than 10,000) is involved in specific communities and organizations (De Groot, 2006b). These groups are often active in the preparation of and participation in events, such as the National and World Youth Days. Some are linked with one or more religious orders (Youth and Mission; Movement for Mercy). Others (half of them) are the Dutch branches of the so-called New Movements. These include international organizations often recognized by the Pontifical Council for the Laity, such as the Catholic Charismatic Renewal, the Emmanuel Community, Communion and Liberation, and the Work of Mary or the Focolare Movement.

Focolare can be considered an *ecclesiola in ecclesia*. It has its own religious discourse ('Jesus in our midst', 'Jesus the Forsaken', 'self-emptying love'). Like the Modern Devotion of Thomas à Kempis, the movement distinguishes different degrees of involvement. The *focolarini* form the core of the move-ment: men and women living in separate communes or in families. *Volunteers* commit themselves to the movement with a vow and contribute financially. *Ex-ternals* are those interested in becoming members; they are sympathizers and incidental or regular visitors of meetings where people contemplate the words of founder Chiara Lubich (the monthly Word of Life). Thus, small communities are at the heart of a differentiated network organization.

The charter of Focolare contains a quotation from the Gospel of St. John: 'That all may be one' (Joh. 17, 21) Letting go of the ego and the devotion to Christ, following the example of Mary, are central in the spirituality of Focolare. Conservative Catholicism goes together with the attention for the per-sonal faith of the individual and abundant use of modern media. This combina-tion corresponds with evangelical styles of operating.

The worldview prevailing in Focolare contains an analysis and a critique of late modern society. In the distanced participation in wider society, supported by the plausibility structure that is provided by its global network, movements such as these are as liquid modern as they are Christian. The submission to what is considered the will of God, which is taught by the Church, may be considered as an answer to the pressures of late modernity (De Groot, 2009). Gilles Kepel, therefore, calls religious movements like these 'true children of our time', un-wanted as they may be (Kepel, 1994).

An analysis of the significance and impact of these movements shows the following pattern. Numerous small groups (sometimes also called Small Chris-tian Communities – a much broader term) are active within the Roman Catholic Church. Often these mutual support groups belong to an international organiza-tion that is part of a broader movement, for example, the charismatic movement. The New Movements are characterized by an attitude of evangelism and a retic-ulate organization (Gerlach and Hine, 1968). Networking takes place predominantly among Catholics. And, although this does not result in an influx of new Catholics, this effect may be considered as quite an accomplishment already, considering the failing socialization of Catholic youth in general. One may expect affinity with these organizations among large proportions of the new generation of priests and seminarians. The formation of groups focusing on personal piety may be understood as a phenomenon of liquid modernity, since the propagation of submission may be interpreted as a reaction to a culture that celebrates experience. The strong international orientation and the use of modern media suggest that these organizations are, in certain aspects, at home in contemporary culture.

Although these organizations have limited followings, they will probably transform the appearance of the Roman Catholic Church to a great extent. The service the Church delivers will undergo the influence of the movements' spirituality, diverse as this may be. In this way, a minority will change the general image of the Church. The Church will become less popular Catholic, and more Catholic with a distinct profile. It remains to be seen whether this transformation will be appealing or appalling to those addressing the Church as a service delivery organization.

The institutional Church facilitates and supports these movements, and appreciates their inspiration which it sometimes seeks to moderate. At the same time, the institutional Church is strongly influenced by their spirituality. From a campaigning perspective, these movements – or rather, these evangelistic networks of mutual support groups – are appreciated for carrying a missionary zeal. In this campaigning, however, a negative image of the world may prevail, forgetting the presence of God outside the movement and outside the Church. Delivering services to those outside the original scope of the movements might lead to a more nuanced view on the spiritual status of modern people, Catholic or not, who hold the Church at a distance, or who are held at a distance.

2.4 The Church as a cultural resource

While the case of spiritual care already showed a considerable influence of secular institutions on the way the Church is present in late modern society, the following case illustrates how the Church is present beyond its own sphere of influence. Christian, even ecclesial, language, symbols, and rituals are used both within and outside the religious field. Examples are to be found in politics (where non-Christian politicians appeal to 'the Judeo-Christian tradition'), in business (where the management spirituality of St. Benedict is praised), in journalism and the marketing industry (where religious imagery is considered sexy), and in culture, e.g., where theatre plays present themselves as church services.

In contemporary theatre, several examples of this phenomenon can be found, including an alternative Midnight Mass that has been organized every year since 2009 in the Urban Theatre of Amsterdam. No churches participate in this event. The show resuscitates a ceremony that is considered something of the past, which now can only be understood in secular terms. Another interesting case is the show 'Donkey God and the Bonus Sacrament' by two female performers called 'The Flourishing Virgins', assisted by a gospel choir singing to the accompaniment of an organ. The show was originally performed at a festival in a neo-gothic church building that was no longer in use for church services. The show contained an introit, a confessional rite, a lecture, a sermon, a responsorial, an offertory, the sharing of wine, a blessing, an interactive act of absolution, and was closed by a vision of encompassing love called 'a revelation'. Various songs and three so-called passion plays were also part of the performance. The show also required active participation of the audience, who were asked to reflect on their experiences. At the heart of the show was the question: 'How to deal with evil?' The explicit purpose of all acts was to eliminate shame, to admit wrongdoings, and to express negative emotions in order to let love flow freely.

Apparently, the format of the church service invites people outside the church – the artists do not have a religious affiliation – to arrange events at the boundaries of church and theatre. Interesting in this case is the contrast with official church services. In this playful service, provocative elements of the Christian tradition, such as confession, penitential psalms, and the uncensored input of mass intentions are used, whereas modern church services tend to leave these elements aside, or transform them into something more 'civilized' (De Groot, 2010a).

Here, Christian liturgy is used freely as a cultural resource. Elements are derived from the Christian tradition in a process that is beyond the control of any churches. From a campaigning perspective, theology may appreciate such developments as a dissemination of the gospel so long as it is, indeed, the Good News that is preached here, regardless of the status of the ones who preach it. Sure enough, the Netherlands Interdenominational Broadcasting Company (IKON) invited the performers to record a series of videos. A few local Reformed political parties and Pentecostal churches, however, protested loudly. Those using sacred symbols outside their original context run the risk of being accused of blasphemy by those who watch over the proper use of sacred discourse – in this case not church leaders, but local politicians. The fluidity of the boundaries between social fields is characteristic for liquid modernity as such. This raises the intriguing question: To what extent are protests like these actually a defense of solid modernity? It does seem to be the case, at the very least, that these protests stem from the mutual support model: non-members are not allowed to 'pretend' that they are members.

3.   Practical-theological questions

The preceding section has provided some evidence of how the Church is transforming under the conditions of liquid modernity. The parish has come to function as a service institution – a tendency opposed by the Church in its re-

cent policy. Chaplaincy has given rise to spiritual care, conceptualized and organized differently in the various domains. New Movements have come to the
fore, showing an evangelistic pathos, but, in fact, uniting religious virtuosos in
specific networks with their own style of religious experience. Outside the
Church, religious traditions form an attractive resource. On one hand, the
Church immerses itself, and gets immersed, in liquid modernity; on the other
hand, it tends to continue the thought patterns of solid modernity, taking mass
Catholicism as the norm.

Late modern social and religious reality evokes questions. Should parishes
facilitate pick-and-choose behavior? Should Catholic hospital chaplains focus
only on Catholic patients? How should we appreciate ecclesial initiatives more
or less outside the parish structure, such as the New Movements? How do we
evaluate theologically the fact that people use Christian symbols and rituals in
other domains? My suggestion is to postpone any particular judgment and to
analyze the issue that is at stake. We will then come to the fundamental question
that lies beneath. In what follows, I will explicate the implicit theological choices that have been made in the various ways in which the Church is present in
modern society becoming liquid, and confront these with alternatives.[6]

3.1 How is the Church dealing with this world?

The question of whether this context deserves acceptance or, instead,
evokes resistance appears as a central issue. The World Youth Days are a striking example of the ambivalent way the Church participates in liquid modernity.
The Church speaks the language of the 'experience society' ('Erlebnisgesellschaft'), while the Pope takes on the role of 'star' in a global event
(Schulze, 1993; Forschungsgruppe WJT, 2007). At the same time, there is a
negative attitude towards the atmosphere of this event, or at least with respect to
Benedict XVI's performance. In his concluding homily in Cologne, Pope Benedict spoke very critically of religious seeking and of turning religion into a
commodity. He also warned the New Movements to preserve communion with
the Pope and with the Bishops, so that they would not get lost on 'private paths'
(Benedict XVI, 2005)

Indeed, there is reason to be vigilant about the dominating role of experience in late modern religion (Bauman, 1997, 180). On the other hand, there is
also reason to be critical about the existing infrastructure. The territorial parish
structure tends to hinder diversity. It is dominated by older generations with a
traditional, bourgeois lifestyle. The behavior of seekers, clients, and members,
and the corresponding structures, should all be considered critically from a
theological point of view. Movements, events, and informal initiatives should

---

6   The subsections correspond with the four frames that are used in congregational studies:
     context, identity, structure, and power (Brouwer e.a., 2007; cf. Ammerman *et al.*, 1997).

not be depreciated because they do not meet the standards that are implied by an unrealistic, idealized image of the parish as an open and supportive community.

The question of whether the present context deserves acceptance or resistance is already answered on a fundamental level, for God loves this world (John 3, 16). 'This world' means: the younger generations with their *Facebook* accounts, their cell phones and MP3 players, flashy businessmen with their bonuses and their BMW's, as well as the residents of deprived areas, struggling with nuisance, garbage, and isolation. When the *world-as-it-is-today* is embraced, the challenge for the Church is to develop an infrastructure that engages critically with this environment. The aim of the Church should be to attain a similar impact and message on society as the early Church did in its context (in accordance with the structure of adequate proportionality) (Schillebeeckx, 1989, 59-61). Often, however, the *world-as-it-was* is embraced instead. The value of the parish structure is considered self-evident; newer forms, such as youth and student ministry and Urban Mission, are scrutinized very critically. The essential question is: How are we supposed to be a church in this world?

3.2 Where is church happening?

It is often the case that festivals, prayer groups, choirs, bands, Christian youth clubs, associations of seniors, etc. are considered by their participants to be manifestations of church more so than the services of their parish church. Formally, these activities can count only as para-ecclesial at most. Although sound ecclesiological reasons may account for this, there may also be a solid modern perspective at work in this categorization (Ward, 2002). Rather than going into the question, 'Is it (really) church?', I would suggest an alternative approach that asks: Where can one detect new emergences or manifestations of being church? Where is the communion of God and people expressed?

This question invites us to look for networks of Christian faith-in-action, of whatever variety of Christian spirituality. This 'appreciative enquiry' may be accompanied by various ecclesiological approaches. For example, an ecclesiology from a Congregationalist background will focus on the confession of Christ in local, interconnected communities (Volf, 1998). An ecclesiology that attributes a central role to ordained ministry will perceive manifestations of church where members of the clergy, as religious virtuosos, promote the networking of interested laypersons (Hochschild, 2003).

Since our ecclesiological understanding tends to reflect the church formation of the past, it is necessary to keep our theological outlook open for new forms. The Anglican Church calls attention to 'fresh expressions': Where in this flexible, fluid culture are God's people in worship? Where is the gospel communicated? Where is God served? Where are people on a mission for God?

They may be in bars, schools, and shops, on the internet, in theatres and festivals, factories, and sporting clubs.[7]

As long as the comparison with the territorial parish structure is not omnipresent, a concept such as *communio*, perceived especially as Walter Kasper did as 'the participation of individuals in the life of the triune God', may become disentangled from the partly fictitious parish *community* (Van Eijk, 2000, 158-165).[8] Then, the ecclesial qualities of the phenomena described above might come to the fore without necessarily identifying them fully with *the* Church.

3.3 How is space created?

Sometimes the structures of new ecclesial and religious movements are considered too restrictive. The network structure of the New Movements ('come in') presents a challenge and a pitfall in this respect. Communication lines are numerous, which facilitates access, be it predominantly to Catholics. The pitfall is that those who favor a particular type of spirituality are attracted. When the intensity of the participation in the network increases, a negative attitude to the outside world, including other Christians, may be enhanced. Especially when children are socialized primarily within a particular environment, such as that of the Emmanuel Community, the whole of the Church may fall out of the picture.

On the other end of the spectrum, when the Church sets up structures to participate in the world ('go out'), the reproach is heard that the boundaries of the Church are drawn too wide or have become too vague. The same is true for the initiatives described above, where the ecclesial tradition is used as a cultural resource. What are the criteria for a theological evaluation? One should be careful not to let the preference for a small community or the participation in the world at large be the judge. A more confronting question for ecclesiological reflection would be: How open are we for the dynamics of mission? Do the religious virtuosos have their own structures for learning, experiencing, testifying, and practicing their faith? Is the Church open for connections with the secular world as a source of precious testimonies of faith? Matthew's account of how Jesus was laboriously converted by the Syrophoenician woman to heal her sick daughter (Mt 15, 21-31; cf. Mc 7,25-30) may remind the Church of its incidental or frequent stubbornness. Witty outsiders may convince its representatives that the Church is not going to the dogs, only because existing structures are changed.

3.4 How can the exercise of authority be sanctifying?

In late modern social formations, it is often difficult to tell who is in charge. Authority has a human face in a hierarchical mass organization at every level.

---

7   www.freshexpressions.org.uk [accessed 6/16/2011].
8   See the contribution of H. Witte in this volume.

This does not imply that these people actually run the organization, but it is the situation that is defined as real. In a network of interconnected communities the locus of power is more difficult to detect. It is no longer the hierarchical structure that warrants the integration of members in the whole of the organization, but the use and internalization of a program, an approach, or a mentality. Power is exercised in tacit tactics, silently present in personal choices and private experiences. Rather than in authority – the legitimized chance of having others follow one's directives – power is exercised in the cultivation of (embodied) styles of experience. The dimension of power is never absent, but can endanger personal freedom when group culture becomes too strict. This danger may be high when a certain style of spiritual experience blends with the demand to be loyal to ecclesial doctrine. At particular moments, some New Movements seem to be suffering from this peril (Kepel, 1994; Boudewijnse, 1995).

In the cases of confined religious communities, abuse of power appears as manipulation. When the Church is involved in projects with other parties, its influence may become too small. When representatives of the Church cooperate with directors of museums, theatres, festivals, or institutions for care, the same activities will be appreciated from the perspective of the Church and from the perspective of culture, education, or care (Schilderman, 2006; Van der Ploeg and De Groot, 2006). The goals of the Church may coincide with the goals of other domains, such as social cohesion, amusement, and effective care, but it can also happen that the goals of the Church are not realized precisely because of the interests of these other parties.

When the ecclesial hierarchy is regarded as the historical successor of Christ's authority, the proper exercise of power can be warranted by safeguarding a link with ecclesial authorities.[9] Since, however, this is no longer a convincing argument (Fiorenza, 1984, 73-74), it could be wise to explore an underlying question: How can the exercise of power represent servant leadership (Borgman, 2006, 246-265)? With respect to power inside, outside, and on the boundaries of the Church, the question can be asked: How is the Name sanctified? Then, the legitimacy of power becomes a matter of faithful discernment.

4. Networking

The enhancement of contemporary forms of being church presupposes awareness. It is both necessary and difficult not to let solid modernity be our guide. Youngsters, for example, are often primarily seen as the category that is absent in church. From our perspective, one could start with the basic acknowledgement that young people, too, have hope for this world, despite all that threatens what is good; that they are looking for beauty, and have love for the truth, against all self-interested claims for truth. An appreciative enquiry might make those who work in the Church aware that they are often hindering new

---

9   See the contribution of H. Witte in this volume.

initiatives because of their attachment to particular organization structures. At times, these structures are useful, but they can be harmful as well. Long-term planning, bureaucratic procedures, and an overdose of meetings might hamper the openness for new initiatives, for example, for youngsters. In this case, the *Church-as-an-institution* acts as the disciples who rebuked the children for wanting to come to Jesus (Mark 10,14)

The enhancement of being church in liquid modernity does not require master plans. Often, new forms emerge from outside the existing organization structures. The institutional Church might come to terms with liquid modernity by getting into the act of networking, which implies three ways of doing: to facilitate, to moderate, and to connect. The following explains this threefold advice.

In liquid modernity, the dependency on church officials is relatively low. The availability of means of transport and communication promotes private initiative, for example, organizing faith groups or events. Certain formats may appear useful in this respect, such as the local formula *FaithNow* (Dutch: *GelovenNu*) that has been adapted by the Archdiocese of Utrecht. Another example is the format of *Youth Churches*, which has inspired several small communities of young (evangelical) Protestants to organize attractive church services for a young audience. Churches have buildings, art, traditions, and all kinds of unforeseen treasures at their disposal that are capable of producing new things. The keyword here is *facilitate*.

Concrete activities, for example, involving prayer, gospel music, or art, might benefit from the participation of a pastor, a theologian, or youth worker in the process of finding new sources of inspiration, or of mitigating exalted religious zeal. The classic function of the moderator, now a common phenomenon on internet forums, is available again.

The third aspect of networking is to make connections between existing networks. Both physical and virtual communities tend to attract those who are like-minded. On websites, hyperlinks refer visitors to other addresses. Pastors, who are called to transcend particular scenes and to represent Christ, might promote openness by drawing connections between various groups. The pious prayer group might get into contact with the center for the homeless; the scouting club might visit the nursing home; the youth choir might perform in prison. Allies can be found in unexpected places. Church development in liquid modernity means doing 'plumber's work': to connect and repair pipes in order to open up lines of communication (Morrisy, 2004).

5. Summary and conclusion

Our starting question asked for the way the Roman Catholic Church deals, and should deal, with liquid modernity. It appears that, alongside an actual involvement in liquid modernity, a solid modern orientation often prevails. An ongoing focus on mass membership might explain some of the controversies described here. In the preceding sections I have suggested ways to get beyond the solid-liquid opposition.

Ecclesiological views on the position of the Church in the world of today often contain theological translated preferences for types of organization and types of modernity. This chapter has specified these types in order to promote an analytical distinction between sociological preferences and matters of faith. (Of course, in practice, they cannot be separated completely). The Roman Catholic Church is a mixed organization, i.e., an organization that combines three types of activities: mutual support, service delivery, and campaigning. Each type raises its own theological issues. In the West, this organization is moving from a solid to a liquid modern context, i.e., from a context that defines religion in terms of institution, registered membership, and denomination to a context that defines religion in terms of (the experience of) community, choice, and spirituality. This transition is accompanied by a decrease in religious participation. As a result, there is a dispute about the evaluation of the service to non-practicing Catholics, about the appreciation of religious seeking, the impact of New Movements, and the use of the ecclesial tradition outside the Church.

My thesis is that the Roman Catholic Church is, in fact, present in liquid modernity in various ways, just like it was in solid modernity, despite anti-modern statements. However, ecclesiology should not be guided by preferences for a solid or liquid type of modernity. Ecclesiological reasoning should recognize the characteristics of the *Church-as-it-is* and the *world-as-it-is*, and then distinguish the spirits on the basis of Bible and Tradition.

The analysis of the normative questions that are often raised uncovered underlying theological questions: How do we appreciate and deal with this world? Where do we locate manifestations of being church? How open are we to the dynamics of mission (undermining our conceptions of inside/outside)? Where does leadership sanctify the Name?

From a strategic perspective, church development in liquid modernity means networking, that is, the task of the institutional Church is to facilitate, to moderate, and to connect existing and emerging networks. Its focus is to keep the networks open for communication.

Liquid modernity provides various opportunities for communicating with others and with the Other. The Church is already active in this changing context. Following the successful adaptation of the solid modern approach in the parish system, a late modern approach presents itself in the promotion of small communities, events, and liturgical and pastoral services for the public-at-a-distance. The Church is also used as the archetypical representative of religion, once dominant, now adhered to by a minority.

Amongst such a fast breakdown of institutions that have flourished in solid modernity, it is tempting to want to preserve them. It is vital to make theological sound distinctions. Familiar structures may be more or less valuable for the young generations and the generations to come. What is needed is the faith that

God is also present in the land of liquid modernity. This faith opens up the Christian tradition and frees it from solid modern constraints.

As the Reformed theologian Peter Cruchley-Jones writes in his plea for missiology:

> Christian tradition holds the belief that God is not at our disposal. He is present, not only in the church, but in the world as well.
> Western culture and plurality provides a ferment of views and values that can be destructive and impoverishing, but also can be liberating and enriching, and provides for us significant arenas beyond the church for practicing the alternative perspectives on life faith can bring. As churches seek to tackle what is unjust and celebrate what is good, they find partners in unlikely places. This tells us people will engage with us on things that count. However, our narcissistic ecclesiological obsessions and our fear of decline are always in danger of distorting the value we give to what and who counts (Cruchley-Jones, 2008, 128-129).

Although the Church in the West cannot refrain from being surrounded by liquid modernity, its leaders could continue to think and act according to the schemes inherited from solid modernity. People living in contemporary network society, under the regime of consumerism and reflexive individualism, however, are probably better off with a Church that embarks on this course with trust, discerning with its oars not just the rocks and the hard places, but the flow as well, and goes with Grace.

References

Aartsbisdom Utrecht - Pastorale Dienstverlening. 2001. *De boodschapcentrale parochie. Tussentijds verslag van een tweejarig bezinningsproces*. Zeist: Diocesane Pastorale Dienstverlening.

Ammerman, N. *et al*. 1997. *Congregation and Community*. New Brunswick NJ: Rutgers University Press.

Bauman, Z. 1997. *Postmodernity and its discontents*. Cambridge: Polity Press.

Bauman, Z. 2000. *Liquid Modernity*. Cambridge: Polity Press.

Beckford, J.A. 1989. *Religion and advanced industrial society*. London *et al*.: Unwin Hyman.

Benedict XVI 2005. *Homily of His Holiness Pope Bededict XVI. Cologne*. http://www.vatican.va/holy_father/benedict_xvi/homilies/2005/documents/hf_ben-xvi_hom_20050821_20th-world-youth-day_en.html

Bernts, T., G. Dekker & J. de Hart. 2007. *God in Nederland 1996-2006*. Kampen: Ten Have/RKK.

Beroepsstandaard voor de Geestelijk Verzorger in Zorginstellingen. 2002. Amsterdam: Vereniging van Geestelijk Verzorgers in Zorginstellingen (VGVZ).

Borgman, E. 2006. *Metamorfosen. Over religie en moderne cultuur*. Kampen-Kapellen: Clement/Pelckmans.

Borgman, E. 2010. ...als het ware een sacrament. Naar een theologische visie op de reëel bestaande kerk. *Tijdschrift voor Theologie 50:* (1) 123-143.

Boudewijnse, H.B. 1995. De katholieke charismatische vernieuwing. Een overzicht. *Religieuze bewegingen in Nederland 30*, 63-89.

Brouwer, R. e.a. 2007. *Levend lichaam. Dynamiek van christelijke geloofsgemeenschappen in Nederland*. Kampen: Kok.

Congregation for the Doctrine of the Faith. 2007. *Responses to some questions regarding certain aspects of the doctrine of the church* http://www.vatican.va/roman_curia/congregations/cfaith/documents/rc_con_cfaith_doc_20070629_responsa -quaestiones_en.html

Cruchley-Jones, P. 2008. Findings. One foot in the grave? Pp. 117-129 in Id (ed.), *God at ground level. Reappraising church decline in the UK through the experience of grass roots communities and situations*. Frankfurt am Main: Peter Lang.

Davidson, J.D. & J.R. Koch. 1998. Beyond Mutual and Public Benefits: The inward and outward orientations of non-profit organizations. Pp. 293-306 in N.J. Demerath III *et al.* (eds.). *Sacred Companies: Organizational Aspects of Religion and Religious Aspects of Organizations*. New York-Oxford: Oxford University Press.

Eijk, T. van. 2000. *Teken van aanwezigheid. Een katholieke ecclesiologie in oecumenisch perspectief.* Zoetermeer: Meinema.

Eijsink, A.H. 1995. *Hartslag van de kerk. De parochie vanuit kerkrechtelijk standpunt.* Leuven: Peeters.

Fleck, M. & O. Dyma. 2002. Bischöfe als mittleres Magament des Weltkonzerns Kirche. Pp. 165-176 in B. J. Hilberath and B. Nitsche (eds.). *Ist Kirche planbar? Organisationsentwicklung und Theologie in Interaktion*. Mainz: Grünewald.

Gerlach, L.P. & V.H.H. Hine. 1968. Five factors crucial to the growth and spread of a modern religious movement. *Journal for the Scientific Study of Religion* 7: (1) 23-40.

Goot, Y. van der. 2010. Mag iedereen aan het Woord komen? *Theologisch Debat* 7: (1) 45-48.

Groot, K. de, J. Kregting & E. Borgman. 2005. The Positioning of the Parish in a Context of Individualization. *Social Compass* 52: (2) 211-223.

Groot, K. de. 2006a. At your service. A Congregational Study in Dutch Catholicism. *International Journal of Practical Theology* 10: (2) 217-237.

Groot, K. de. 2006b. Orthodoxie en beleving. Bewegingen in de Rooms-Katholieke Kerk in Nederland. *Religie & Samenleving* 1: (3) 151-173.

Groot, K. de. 2008. Three types of liquid religion. *Implicit Religion* 11: (3) 277-296.

Groot, K. de. 2009. Christelijke jongeren: ongewenste kinderen van de laatmoderniteit. *Theologisch Debat* 6: (2) 6-17.

Groot, K. de. 2010a. Theater als wij-water: gemeenschap en liturgie bij de Bloeiende Maagden. Pp. 63-80 in J. Bekkenkamp & J. Verheijen (red.). *Als ik W!J word. Nieuwe vormen van verbondenheid*. Almere: Parthenon.

Groot, K. de. 2010b. The institutional dynamics of spiritual care. *Revista de estudos da Religião - Rever* 10: (1) 21-28.

Groot, K. de. 2010c. Two scenarios of alienation. *Explaining the distance between Catholics and Roman Catholic Church in the Netherlands*. Paper presented at the International Society of Empirical Research in Theology, Rome. To appear in F.-V. Anthony & H.-G. Ziebertz (eds.). *Religious Identity and National Heritage, Empirical Studies in Theology*. Leiden: Brill.

Gusfield, J.R. 1981. Social movements and social change: perspective of linearity and fluidity. Pp. 317-339 in L. Kriesberg (ed.). *Research in social movements, conflicts and change*. Greenwich.

Handy, C. 1992. Types of Voluntary Organisations. Pp. 13-17 in J. Batsleer, Cornforth C., Patton, R. (eds.). *Issues in Voluntary and Non-profit Management*. Workingham: Addison-Wesley Publishing Company/Open University.

Heitink, G. 1999. *Practical theology. History, theory, action, domains. Manual for practical theology*. Grand Rapids, MI: Eerdmans.

Hellemans, S. 2007. *Het tijdperk van de wereldreligies. Religie in agrarische civilisaties en in moderne samenlevingen*. Zoetermeer-Kapellen: Meinema/Pelckmans.

Hochschild, M. 2003. Networking. *Diakonia* 34: (1/2) 5-20.

Kepel, G. 1994. *The Revenge of God. The resurgence of Islam, Christianity, and Judaism in the modern World*. Pennstate: Pennstate University Press.

Morrisy, A. 2004. *Journeying out*. London: Moorhouse.

Ploeg, J. van der & K. de Groot. 2006. Towards a city museum as a centre of civic dialogue. Pp. 90-96 in R. Kistemaker (ed.). *City museums as centres for civic dialogue?* Amsterdam: Amsterdam Historical Museum.

Schilderman, H. 2006. Religie en zorg in het publieke domein. Pp. 395-416 in W.B.H. J. Van de Donk e.a. (eds.), *Geloven in het publieke domein. Verkenningen van een dubbele transformatie*. Den Haag-Amsterdam: WRR/Amsterdam University Press.

Schillebeeckx, E. 1989. *Mensen als verhaal van God*. Baarn: Nelissen.

Schulze, G. 1993. *Die Erlebnisgesellschaft. Kultursoziologie der Gegenwart,* Frankfurt/New York: Campus Verlag.

Schüssler Fiorenza, F. 1984. *Foundational theology. Jesus and the church*. New York: Crossroad.

Smeets, W. 2006. *Spiritual Care in a Hospital Setting: an empirical-theological exploration*. Nijmegen: Proefschrift Radboud Universiteit.

Ven, J. A. van der. 1996. *Ecclesiology in context*. Grand Rapids, MI: Eerdmans.

Volf, M. 1998. *After our likeness. The church as the image of the trinity*. Grand Rapids, MI: Eerdmans.

Ward, P. 2002. *Liquid Church*. Peabody, MA-Carlisle: Hendrickson/Pater Noster.

WJT Forschungsgruppe. 2007. *Megaparty Glaubensfest. Weltjugendtag: Erlebnis - Medien - Organisation*. Wiesbaden: VS Verlag für Sozialwissenschaften.

Liturgy of Real Presence: From Books to Communication

Willem Marie Speelman

1. Introduction

Liturgy is the celebration of the presence of the Lord. The liturgy of the Roman Catholic Church is a rich practice celebrating the Lord's presence in the Eucharist, the service of the Word, the sacraments and blessings, and in the Liturgy of the Hours. In the liturgy, words and rituals play an important role in remembering that the Lord is with His Church, here and now. But the role of the words and rituals has undergone a change, whereby the centrality of the liturgical books is shifting towards liturgical communication as a practice.

Since the Late Middle Ages, the liturgy has had a clear center, which was the Roman liturgy as it was gathered and written down in books, and then read by the priest and interpreted by the hierarchy. For centuries, this practice of liturgical books and reading hardly changed. Thus, the Roman liturgy suited the period of Modernity in which the printed book was the standard (Ong 2002:115-133). Since the twentieth century, during which electronic media became the nervous system of the advanced modern society, culture has been undergoing a thorough transformation (McLuhan 1964) in which the book and reading practices no longer carry the same weight they once did.

Responding to this tendency, the Second Vatican Council set out to center the liturgy in the community of faithful, though not without books. Instead, the liturgical books were to be reformed in order to make possible a fully conscious and active participation of the faithful (SC 14). Thus, the intention of the liturgical reform was to shift the center of the liturgy from books to practice, with practice understood as the communicative relation between the liturgical book and the celebrating community. Recently, two leading Dutch liturgical scholars argued that the liturgy has lost its center, and that the periphery has become a plurality of centers (Barnard, Post 2008). How is this observation related to the Second Vatican Council's intention to center the liturgy in the communicative relation between the liturgical books and the celebrating community? What really is the center today, and what are the chances for the Church and her liturgy?

The communicative approach advocated here is inspired by the spiritual method of Kees Waaijman, who approaches spirituality as a transforming relation between God and humans. The relational process changes God and changes the human, so that they are being shaped in and towards each other's presence (Waaijman 2002: 426ff). I believe that every communicative practice will cause the agents of that practice to adapt to each other. The communication itself, as a process, determines this mutual transformation. The Church, who has been formed in relation with Christ, is sent to communicate the Gospel to the world and its people. In the continuing encounter with the world and the people, she will change and realize herself time and again. A communicating Church is, in principle, *semper reformans*, or perhaps we should say, always new. The Church is not restricted to the hierarchical institute or the books or the faithful people, but the Church is the communicative relation and transforming process between them. In this contribution, the Church is approached as the community reflected in the liturgy and the liturgy recognized by the community. Thus, the Church is realized time and again in her celebrating presence.

In what follows, I will describe the intention of the liturgical reform of Vatican II and how it was elaborated in the liturgy and the community in the Roman Catholic Church in the Netherlands. I will place this overview in relation to ritualizing practices in our pluralistic and individualized society. I do not ask the question of whether the liturgy has improved or deteriorated; rather, I will try to describe the tendencies and tensions of today's liturgical situation, the risks and chances. My diagnosis is that there is no real communication in the advanced modern society because people are not open to transformation. I believe that an open and balanced communicative relation will give the opportunity for the development of the individual person and the Church as a community. In this relation, the Church has to offer God by offering herself as a non-possessive share of the relation and as a sensitive human body. The only reason for the Church to exist is that she is present, and her presence reflects the presence of the Lord.

2. The liturgical reform

2.1 The shift of the center: From book to practice

A great centralizing force in the liturgy has been its codification in books, especially since the twelfth and thirteenth centuries. By that time, the *actio liturgica*, in which the celebrant, ministers, singers, and faithful collaborated and had distinctive and cooperative roles to play, was replaced by a celebration in which the priest became the sole actor, and was henceforth provided with a liturgical book in which the whole liturgy is gathered (Vogel 1986:105). The *missale plenum*, the *breviarium*, the *pontificale romanum*, and the *rituale romanum* were written. In and by these books the Church was identified with the Roman Curia (Palazzo 1998:208). Thus, one centralized Roman liturgy was established in liturgical books, which were copied and distributed to the parishes in the towns and villages.

As a medium, the book is a closed and static tradition. The living practice is written down and thus fixed in a static thing, only to be re-lived through its reading. The liturgy came to be identified with its written form read by the priest-celebrant. Praying and even singing became a matter of reading. Eventually, the priest "was under obligation to recite, at least in a low voice, the sung parts of the Mass, even though they were executed by the choir, and the various readings, even though they were proclaimed by the deacon and subdeacon" (Palazzo 1998:107).

According to current interpretations, the motor behind this development is the clericalization of the liturgy, started by the Gregorian Reform of the eleventh and twelfth centuries (Vogel 1986:105; Wegman 1991:195; Palazzo 1998:107). The centrality of the cultic priesthood caused a need for one liturgical book, in which the priest-celebrant could read the whole celebration. Although there probably was no intention to take the liturgy away from the faithful (Wegman 1991:238), the clericalization of the liturgy had this effect. Liturgy became a matter of the clergy, and was very often celebrated in so-called private masses and private offices.

It seems to me that the medium, i.e., the book, plays a more decisive role in this process than the quoted authors admit, if only by offering opportunities to history. The liturgy came into a process of unification into which Roman, Frankish, and German influences were synthesized. This unifying process offered the opportunity to bring the diverse liturgies together in one book for the mass, one for the office, one for the rituals performed by the priest, and one for the rituals performed by the bishops. The book offered the opportunity for the celebrant to celebrate the mass and the office privately. Furthermore, the books offered the opportunity to spread one integral Roman liturgy over the whole world. We should not underestimate the centralizing force of the medium itself, i.e., the liturgical book. The celebrant was first and foremost a reader of the books and a performer of the prescribed rituals and offices.

The liturgical books were in Latin, which was already a strange language to the people at the time when the books were written. What was said in the liturgy was therefore not communicated to the faithful. When Francis of Assisi heard the Gospel in which Jesus sent his disciples to spread the Word, he understood little of it; after the celebration he had to ask the priest what the words of the Gospel meant (1Cel 22). This situation lasted until the Second Vatican Council, when the *aggiornamento* started to counteract the centralizing force of the books.

2.2 The secularizing tendency of the aggiornamento

The *aggiornamento* shifted the liturgical center. It directed the Church towards the changing world, the diversity of cultures, and the individualizing people. The closed and static tradition of the book was opened up in a communicative relation to the secular. This communicative relation transformed the Church and the liturgy. Its language was translated into a plurality of languages. The rituals were adapted to local use and circumstances. Thematic services were celebrated in which the liturgy related to secular questions like the environment, peace, and communication. Celebrations for special groups within the community, e.g., children and the diseased, directed the liturgy towards the individuality of the faithful. Instead of only a performed scenario of salvation, the liturgy itself became a countenance in which the faithful could recognize themselves. Consequently, the faithful would be given the opportunity to find and form their identity vis-à-vis the Church.

The Constitution on the Sacred Liturgy of 1963 stresses that the nature and purposes of the liturgy are clear to the people, and that they participate actively and consciously in the celebration. Apparently, it was felt that the congregation did *not* participate in the liturgy, and that the people did *not* understand its meaning. The churches were full, but most of the faithful were not really there. Apparently, it was also felt that the liturgical tradition should not be a static image dividing the Church from the world. The *aggiornamento* changes the vision on tradition (SC 23). In short, the allegiance to the Scriptures and the apostolic tradition (DV 7-10) demands the "incarnation" of the Word in the world of today (GS 53-56). When tradition "incarnates" it enters into a communicative relation with the world and changes. Tradition becomes a dynamic. It is being realized again and again, whereby the Church reflects herself in the living people and the changing world. In fact, this reflection revealed to the Church that her tradition has always been dynamic and pluralistic. And, in the light of the *aggiornamento,* it should not be otherwise.

2.3 Reform of the liturgical books

The reform of the liturgical books took several years. The Missal appeared in 1970, the Ritual between 1969 and 1991, the Pontifical between 1968 and 1990, and the Liturgy of the Hours in 1971-72. Characteristics of the reformed liturgical books are the importance of the following:

- the *active participation* of the faithful, so that there are always parts to be fulfilled by them;
- *understanding the meaning* of the ritual, so that every celebration begins with introduction and nearly every celebration contains a homily;
- the Scriptures, so that every celebration has a *service of the Word*;
- the adaptation to the specific situation, so that there is always a *choice* between alternative prayers and readings.

First of all, the books were to be translated into the vernacular. In the Netherlands, the liturgical books have been translated since 1975. The project is still ongoing because the Missal has already had a third typical edition. The translation falls under the responsibility of the National Bishops' Conference. This has been and still is a project in which at least two main tendencies come to the surface, one stressing the sacral nature of the book and the other the secular nature of the living people. Ko Joosse gives a lively description of the tensions that this project has produced (Joosse 1991:63-107).

During the process of realizing the Dutch liturgical books, the clergy was already bringing the liturgy to the people (Lamberigts 2006:293-297). In the preparation of their liturgical celebration, the clergy made their own translations or used translations from other pastors. With the most active participants, the pastors shared the responsibility for the parish life and liturgy. Participants contributed their specific liturgical tastes and helped the liturgy to become personal. The result is that, next to the liturgical books, self-made leaflets are used in the celebrations, which, of course, give the opportunity to a further adaptation of the liturgy to the local situation. The liturgical leaflets, songs, and prayers may be gathered and published. Thus started the rise of liturgical centers and a vast repertoire of (unofficial) liturgical books.

The reform of the liturgical books was received well by a number of faithful. This selected number accepted the invitation to participate actively in the celebration of the liturgy. As a result, there has been a growing understanding of what the liturgy and the Church are about. Through the participation of the faithful, the liturgy and its rituals have been recharged with meaning. And, where Roman Catholics used to be known for their lack of biblical knowledge, today many have learned and are still learning to read the Bible. Although the masses left the Church, more people are present now, for the measure of their presence has grown. I will argue that this growth in presence is a key characteristic of the Church of the near future, and that it is important to have faith in these present people.

2.4 The quest for an adequate liturgical language

The translation of the Roman liturgy into the languages of the people involves more than a mere translation of Latin texts into the vernacular. Translating an old language into the languages of the present time and culture implies the adaptation of a classic manner of speaking to the sensitiveness and taste of the people. Questions come up about the adequate language for liturgy, but there are also questions about the addressor and the addressee. Who is communicating with whom in the liturgical celebration? And how can the participation of all the faithful be facilitated? After the liturgical books have been translated, these questions remain, for the liturgy will continuously search for adequate melodies, words, and gestures to celebrate the presence of the Lord with the people in today's world. Because of this quest, the liturgy is transforming vis-à-vis the faithful, and the traditional is becoming personal.

The translation of the Roman liturgy into the language of the people is only one aspect of a bigger process called "inculturation". Inculturation is a theological term referring to the interaction between the cult, i.e., the liturgy, and the culture. It is related to, but also distinguished from, the sociological term "acculturation", which refers to the interaction between different cultures (for a discussion, see Lukken 2004:169ff). As a theological term, inculturation is considered in the light of "the incarnation of the Gospel in the native cultures and the introduction of these cultures into the life of the Church" (*Slavorum Apostoli* 1985: nr. 21), and is thus an integral part of the tradition. The process of inculturation involves a transformation of the cult, for the communicative relation with the culture transforms both the liturgy and the culture. An example of inculturation is the introduction of a folk song into the liturgy: the liturgy changes because of the incorporation of folk elements and because the whole congregation participates in the singing, and the song changes because it may get another text, rhythm, and way of singing. The consequence of inculturation is, for example, that a Dutch Roman Catholic liturgy is different from an American one. As long as the community recognizes itself in these different inculturations, the diversity is felt as richness. The diversity of the community's presence may also be an important characteristic of the Church in the near future.

2.5 Participation as a form of appropriation

The Church's intention to reach the faithful personally has been responded to by an appropriation of the liturgy by the people. The term "appropriation" refers to Michel de Certeau's distinction between the strategy of the dominant culture and the tactics of the practitioners, who participate in this culture (Certeau 1990: XLIV-XLVIII). In this case, the strategy is to offer the practicing faithful the opportunity to participate in the celebration as written in the liturgical books. The Church offers the liturgical 'grammar', so to speak, to the people, and the people respond to that offer by their participation in the liturgical communication. But, inevitably, the use of this 'grammar' will change it. Therefore, although appropriation of the liturgy may be the proper response to the offer of the Church, it may also lead to tensions, e.g., between the prescribed liturgy and people's ritualizing tendencies. People tend to find their own forms.

The Vatican tries to guide the developments by releasing instructions, of which *Liturgiam authenticam* (2001) is the most recent one.[1] The instructions criticize a translation of the liturgical texts that is too free, and demand that "the original text, insofar as possible, must be translated integrally and in the most exact manner, without omissions or additions in terms of their content, and without paraphrases or glosses. Any adaptation to the characteristics or the nature of the various vernacular languages is to be sober and discrete" (LA 20). The instruction can be seen as an attempt to stress the weight of the book in the liturgical center without hindering the faithful to take part in this center.

Shifting the center from book to practice and from the traditional to the personal is a quest in which the Church is still trying to find the balance. In this respect it is important to note that the appropriation of the liturgy by the faithful is not an expropriation of it from the Church, which I described here as 'the

---

[1]   The other instructions are *Inter Oecumenici* (1964), *Tres abhinc annos* (1967), *Liturgicae instaurationes* (1970), *Varietates legitimae* (1994).

community reflected in the liturgical books and the liturgical books recognized by the community'. The communicative practice itself will guide the process so that appropriation is not a matter of possession but of familiarity, to make oneself familiar with the liturgy. In a communicative appropriation the liturgy becomes personal, thus offering the community the opportunity to recognize itself in its plural shapes. According to the French liturgist and pastor Louis-Marie Chauvet, the properly appropriated and thus personal celebration is the authentic one giving way to Christ Himself to celebrate the liturgy (Chauvet 2002:59).

3. The diversification of liturgical practice and community

3.1 A diversified liturgical practice

The desire of the Second Vatican Council to bring about an active participation of the faithful has given the opportunity to concentrate on the place and role of the faithful in the Church and in the liturgy. The Church became more sensitive to their languages, their cultures, and their worlds. The liturgy could become responsive to the sensitivities and tastes of the faithful, and become personal. The development of a more personal liturgy has led to a diversity of Roman Catholic liturgical practices. Several local churches and groups have developed their own spiritual language and their own liturgical taste. One only needs to look around on a Sunday morning in a small town, where one may chose to participate in a liturgy of a student church, in a hospital, for families with small children, or in a Latin, Byzantine, or monastic liturgy. Every liturgical practice produces its own books or ring binders or leaflets. To get some grip on the diversified situation within the Roman Catholic Church, I distinguish five fields of liturgical practices. These five practices do not exclude each other, but interfere with one another, often within one parish: family liturgy, pastoral liturgy, identity based liturgy, confession based liturgy, and parish liturgy. The diversified practice reveals the multi-faced countenance of the Roman Catholic community. But there are also tensions, namely, when the balance is lost and appropriation tends to become a matter of possession.

Family liturgy

An important part of parish life is the religious service to what can be called the 'marginal faithful' from the neighborhood. With the term 'marginal faithful' I indicate the people who only momentarily engage themselves with the parish or the Church, i.e., when they wish to celebrate their marriage, their child's baptism and First Holy Communion, or the funeral of their relatives. They are the faithful that do not participate actively in the liturgy. To them, the liturgy is as much a celebration of the Church as it is a celebration of family and friends (Speelman 1997). A significant aspect of such a family centered celebration is that it is continued at home or in a party room. The Church considers this family liturgy as an important field of pastoral care.

There are tensions, especially with the most active participants or 'volunteers', for they may feel used for a kind of ritual service. After the celebration, only very few will respond to invitations for continuing contact or further pastoral care. As if a ritual consumer, the marginal faithful is willing to pay for the 'service' offered, whereby he or she has some special wishes concerning the liturgy. This development has given the opportunity for a ritual market, which, for the Church, is an uneasy field of conduct. We will come back to this matter. But, in spite of the uneasiness, it is important that the Church is there when she is needed, and that she speaks the words of Christ: "What do you want Me to do for you?" (Mt 20:32).

Pastoral liturgies

The intention to bring the liturgy closer to the people in their world has led to a kind of pastoral liturgy. As an integral part of the pastoral care, this liturgy aims at a specific category of faithful: children, diseased, imprisoned, military, etc. In category based celebrations, the faithful are addressed as sharing a personal quality: they are faithful *as* child or *as* diseased. This shared personal quality has been the ground for the development of liturgical forms – texts, music, and gestures – proper to this quality. There is much creativity in pastoral liturgies, and much freedom is taken, for the services are relevant to the extent that they reach their target group. To this field of liturgy, I also reckon the liturgical celebrations in the electronic media. They are considered as a form of pastoral care for those who cannot go to a church (Speelman 2004:17-21). The pastoral liturgies sometimes cause tensions, e.g., between the book and the practice, between the pastor and the diocese, or between the specific group and the parochial community. But in a creative process tensions are needed to keep the movement going. Eventually, the Church will find a balanced relation.

Identity based liturgies

Closely connected to the preceding, a third liturgical field can be distinguished. This liturgical field is not so much a form of pastoral care as it is an appropriation by the category involved on the basis of a certain aspect of their identity. Some youth liturgies, feminist liturgies, and the "Pink Sunday" celebration by homosexuals are forms of liturgy in which the different categories of the Church community express their presence in the Church. Their celebration, sometimes critically called "the celebration of themselves", is, in itself, a question of how the Church can give room to their presence. For, as I said earlier, their presence may well be the key characteristic of the Church in the near future.

Related to this is a variant based on a shared taste or *sound*. Martin Hoondert describes a Gregorian chant liturgy, a Taizé liturgy, and a liturgy of the youth choir as "ritual-musical movements in the margin of the parish" (Hoondert 2006). Sound based liturgies allow people – not always faithful – to identify themselves with people of the same taste. The shared sound makes them feel at home in the Church.

Although the monastic liturgy is a practice on its own, in parish life it may have an identifying function also. Many parishes are led by religious orders and thus embedded in the liturgical atmosphere of that order. But there are also many faithful who choose to attend the liturgical celebrations in monasteries or religious communities. They feel at home in this spiritual style (Majoor, Sonnberger 1999).

To a certain extent, the Church's intention to reach the individual faithful may be fulfilled in these pastoral or identity based practices. When people attend celebrations of their category or style on a regular basis, they will meet other people like them, get to know them, and may feel something in common with them. Martin Gertler even found a form of community building among the faithful who shared watching television services (Gertler 1998). The quality of this community will likely be more personal and more communal than the congregation of their (territorial) parish. Of course, if a community is nothing more than a feeling, it is as fragile and momentary as a feeling is. But if the Church succeeds in becoming a home with many rooms (Joh 14:2) in which a diversity of people can be present, with these people she may realize the presence of the Lord in the world.

Confession based liturgy

As this contribution focuses on the Roman Catholic liturgy, I should leave out the obvious distinction of the field of confession based liturgies. But I have decided to mention it because within the Roman Catholic liturgy practices resound from other churches. Songs and prayers from Protestant traditions have found their way into Catholic celebrations (and *vice versa*), icons have found a place in Catholic churches. In ecumenical churches it is sometimes difficult to decipher who is a Catholic and who is a Protestant. And, when the differences between the Churches are being discussed, one will often only hear anecdotal differences, for most faithful do not know or understand the dogmatic questions. There are tensions when the differences suddenly become important, for example, when intercommunion has become a normal practice in a parish and then a new priest explicitly invites only Roman Catholic faithful to communion. People from other confessions feel that they are part of the community, and then someone tells them that they are not. Would it not be better to approach these fellow Christians at another time, in another situation, and in a more inviting manner than to drop a bomb on them during a liturgical service?

Parish liturgy

The basis of liturgical practice is still the parish, where people from the same neighborhood gather together. As each of the four fields mentioned have an effect on the parish liturgy, the liturgy in the parish is not a homogeneous field. In fact, the heterogeneity is an integral part of the parochial practice. One

Sunday, when there is a priest, a Eucharist following the Missal is celebrated. Another Sunday, when the youth choir sings, members of the choir may have prepared the liturgy, including the prayers and the sermon. And on a third Sunday, when no priest is available, the parish celebrates its own liturgy of the word, with or without communion. In some Dutch cities were several parishes have been merged, the large parish offers liturgical celebrations of different "tastes" every Sunday morning in the different churches. There is church for a liturgy in the monastic style, a church for the families, and a church for a 'traditional' Eucharist. People can freely choose in what kind of service they would like to participate. Thus, the parish meets the personal needs and tastes of the faithful.

Ultimately, the active participants in the parish can easily change between the different fields. In fact, the active participants take part in all fields of the liturgical practice. The less engaged faithful will possibly only show up when *their* liturgy is celebrated. But, generally speaking, a living community is open to the differences and celebrates its diversity. Being a community means that people become familiar with each other's needs and tastes also.

The different fields of the liturgical practice show that the Council succeeded in its aim to a conscious and active participation of the faithful in the liturgy. But the community has become diversified. This is only logical when we realize that a communicative practice inevitably transforms the agents of that practice, i.e., the books and the community, or the liturgical practice and the different categories of faithful. The communication itself will be looking for a balanced relation. If there is no communicative relation the community will be scattered in fragments. But if there is a sense of community, the diversification can be experienced as richness, as a countenance with different faces, or as a body with different senses. After having described that liturgical situation, I will proceed with a description of the problems and the chances offered by the diversification of the community.

3.2 The tensions of a diversified community

Opposed tendencies in community building

The Constitution *Sacrosanctum Concilium* is aiming at the community of faithful (SC 26). In the view of the Church the community is prior to the individual believer. The individual is considered as a member of the community, also in the bodily sense of the word (1Cor 12,12-27). The secularizing tendency of the *aggiornamento* is thus moving from the community to the individual. But this tendency interferes with an opposing one. In advanced modernity, the community is not a 'family' into which one is born and receives one's faith and personal identity. On the contrary, the tendency is that one leaves one's family and religion in order to find one's own friends and one's own way of life. We can recognize this in the field of identity based liturgies, which has developed because the faithful of the same category and style found each other while they were searching for religious meaning and identity. Instead of being given, the community is considered to be the result of its own choices and it is the community's responsibility to realize itself. The community then is a gathering of individuals who find each other in their shared experiences, shared tastes, and shared choices (cf. Schulze 2005:75). The individuals want to feel *communitas* in which the differences have lost their teeth (Turner 1969: 94-130), but this *communitas* is fragile in the sense that anyone can leave at any moment (Taylor 2007:303-304). The advanced modern tendency is that individuals go to church, not because they *are* a community, but because they are searching for a moment of *communitas*. The question, of course, is how the secularizing movement from the community to the individual can elicit a Christianizing movement from the individual to the one body of Christ? Individual people feel welcome in a sharing community, where they meet presence and can be present, where the differences may be there, and where people have faith in each other and in each other's otherness.

Community based on the measure of participation

Traditionally, the liturgical community is considered as a hierarchy of functions and roles, installed by rituals of initiation and ordination: baptized, acolyte, lector, deacon, priest, and bishop. The liturgical action of this community – with reminiscences to the medieval *actio liturgica* – is that every member of the community performs an office doing "all of, but only, those parts which pertain to his office by the nature of the rite and the principles of liturgy" (SC 28). It is a corporate cooperation, an office performed by a "body".

In the parochial practice, however, the liturgical community is also ordered by the measure of participation in the parish. It is a circle of participants. The center of this circle is the pastor. The choir, the members of the liturgical teams, and frequent practitioners belong to the inner circle. Together they represent the parochial and liturgical community. Then there are the less frequent participants, e.g., the families who only visit the church when there is a celebration for a relative or friend. They form the outer circle of the community. An advantage of this model is that people from other confessions or even not baptized participants may also belong to the inner circle of the parish. A disadvantage is that the liturgical circle may feel some tension when a priest not belonging to the circle celebrates the Eucharist in the church.

The situation becomes more complex when we consider different churches within one town, in today's practice often merged into one larger parish. The liturgical circles of participation in different churches are different: active participants in one church do not automatically belong to the inner circle of another church. As a result, one larger parish may have different liturgical circles. Actually, the different fields of liturgical practice all have their own liturgical circle: the youth choir, the children's choir, etc. And, as the liturgical circles defend their own celebrating practice, these circles tend to act as closed communities. 'Guests' or newcomers, even active participants, cannot easily join the circle. In the processes of merging parishes, it seems almost impossible to reform these different liturgical circles into one community.

Ultimately, and in harmony with the advanced modern individual searching for a moment of *communitas*, everybody is his or her own liturgical center. The outspoken tendency is that one does not need to engage in the church, which is just another circle, to be able to communicate with God. It is enough to form one's own circle by gathering some close friends and relatives, choosing some tasteful practices, giving one's own interpretations, and there you have a cele-bration. Sometimes a ritual professional or commercial ritual office is hired to help with the ritual procedures. Needless to say, this leads to tensions within the Church, for the Church considers herself the owner of the rituals. Indeed, the Church does not actually own the rituals – in the sense that she does not possess them – and, furthermore, the appropriation of rituals by individuals is not neces-sarily an expropriation from the Church; however, I also see how difficult it is for closed circles to really enter into the communicative relation of the Church. Perhaps the tactile presence of the hierarchy and the books may bring some bal-ance and open up the circles.

The managing pastor

In parochial practice the pastor inevitably feels the tension between "the church" and the individual faithful. In this context, "the church" is any religious institution confronting the individual: sometimes the hierarchy, other times the liturgical books, but also the local liturgical circle. And the pastor is approached as a mediator. Instead of being called to keep his flock together and lead it to green pastures, the mediating pastor has to negotiate in order to keep the peace. In the context of the tensions described, he has to manage the relation between the individual and the community, the different liturgical circles, the diocese and the parish, etc. All the while he has to manage his own time and energy in order to be … a pastor.

Louis-Marie Chauvet points at another tension. It was once the case that the pastor joined in the charisma of the office, and his *officium* was to "read" the Mass and the prayers. Now, the pastor is considered to have a personal charis-ma, and he is approached as an '*animateur liturgique*' (Chauvet 2002:49). His liturgical services are evaluated in terms of their success in eliciting a personal, impressive, and festive atmosphere. As a result, the pastor devotes much of his time to the preparation of the liturgy, especially the sermon and the prayers. These texts have to respond to the faithful in their personal situations. It is only logical that in this practice some pastors are better than others. The most suc-cessful obtain a circle of followers, of which they form the center. Theological-ly, this is not a problem, for the pastor has a sacramental function of presiding *in persona Christi* and *in persona ecclesiae*. His personal presence communi-cates the presence of Christ and the presence of the Church. But when it comes down to his individual personality alone, his personal charisma, he will carry a heavy task. It is often felt that when a charismatic pastor retires, his circle has no future.

Some pastors have discovered a ritual market responding to the liturgical quest of their faithful and of others. They start ritual offices offering services to people who want to develop and perform personal rites of passage outside the Church. Pastors and other ritual guides write texts and songs on request, they lead the ritual services, and may offer some sort of pastoral care. Books appear helping people to ritually shape important moments of passage in their lives: birth, marriage, death, but also "divorce, emigration, reconciliation, and euthanasia" (Berkvens-Stevelinck 2007). The world religions tend to be approached as ritual repertoires from which one freely may choose and use. The tendency is to free the ritual from its traditional background and meaning, so that it is easier to meet the personal needs of their clients. But the more personal the ritual gets, the heavier the personal responsibility for its effectiveness (cf. Chauvet 2002:63).

Suddenly, the Church finds herself as a player in a ritual market. Questions come up about ownership and responsibility, money and salvation. The question of money and salvation has had an answer in Acts 8:18-24, where Simon Magus is reprimanded. But the questions of ownership and responsibility are a little more complicated. To a certain extent, a community 'owns' its rituals because the community has put its identity and tradition in them. The rituals belong to that community in a kind of spiritual ownership. But this does not mean that the community *possesses* them. There is no copyright on rituals. On the other hand, the right to appropriate a ritual and offer ritual services to the market carries an obligation. The ritual guide bears a responsibility to pastoral guidance. It is true that rituals are like body languages conveying meanings that cannot always be translated into verbal cognitive meanings (Torevell 2000:48 vv). But spiritual guides have always accompanied the rituals by providing the gestures with stories and meanings, so that people can take them up in their personal life story. Books about ritual design are and should be different from books about flower arrangement, for example. When a ritual guide disposes the rituals of a tradition, it cannot offer its clients more than personal care and help to find the gestures that suit their personal feelings. Can the individual person of any ritual guide be strong and vast and open enough to bear this responsibility all by oneself? Is it not healthier to use tradition as an extension, as it were, of the individual person, so that the ritual guide can sometimes admit that it does not understand and that it does not know, and that the tradition may "help my unbelief" (Mc 9:24)?

The faithful as pilgrims
Active participants are willing to form a community even if it does not always feel comfortable, and they work together in the development of their own and each other's life and religion. But there are also faithful who seem more interested in religious feelings than in their redemption. Or, "the carrying out of

the work of our redemption" (Roman Missal, Preamble) should at least *feel* like redemption. This is more than a desire; it is an imperative: a celebration *has to be* an experience (Schulze 2005:58-60). After a celebration there is coffee and tea, and people discuss, among other things, the quality of the 'performance'. This may, of course, encourage the pastor and the choir to improve their performance. But the discussion also shows that the faithful feel a responsibility for the liturgy. They, too, have an obligation to make the celebration an impressive experience. This feeling of responsibility makes the liturgy a very touchy field. If the Church does not allow the faithful to develop their own liturgy, even more than not being taken seriously, they feel frustrated in their assignment to create a meaningful and personal liturgy. If the service is not good enough, *they* have failed also. The feelings that go together with the imperative of the experience – insecurity and disappointment (Schulze 2005:60-67) – may even threaten a free and uninhibited celebration. Just as living in a community is not the same as feeling *communitas*, the "carrying out of the work of our redemption" is not the same thing as having sacral feelings.

The conscious and active participation has led people to a critical evaluation of the faith of the Church. Some of the faithful enter into a real communication with the dogmata and the commandments, and thus renew their personal faith *and* the faith of the Church. Other faithful choose to use the Christian faith as a repertoire for constructing their own religion. Apart from this repertoire, other non-Christian repertoires are also used. For example, I have heard among active members of the Church several variants on the dogma of the resurrection of the body, from re-incarnation to mere remembrance. The faithful of today are all *searching* for religious meaning and identity. This is also true for the liturgy, which, as I said earlier, has become a quest. The faithful are not only members of the Church, but they also take part in a ritualizing culture outside the Church. And, they take their experiences and expectations back, asking what the Church has to offer. Chauvet notices that the role of the faithful has changed from practitioners (who practice their faith) to "pilgrims" who search for a personal experience of the holy (Chauvet 2002:52). If their need for the holy is not met in the parish, then they will go to another liturgical center where they can find *their* ritual landscape and soundscape. Pilgrims tend to consider the community as a traveling companionship of people meeting each other along the way and feeling *communitas*. Some of them will look for this in the Church; some of them will also look for this elsewhere.

If the pilgrim faithful enter into communication with the faith of the Church, it may be expected that their conversation with faith will lead to conversions in both directions, for in this conversation the faithful renew their faith and the faith itself is renewed at the same time. To communicate with the tradition is not the same as to identify thoughtlessly with it. On the contrary, communication (including critical communication) will turn faith into a shared responsibility. When responsibility is shared, its weight is shared also. Just as the pastor tends to overload his personal identity when he shuns presiding *in perso-*

na Christi, the faithful will put too much responsibility on their shoulders when they shun being part of a tradition.

4. Ritual developments in today's world

As we may expect, in a communicative relation, the countenance of today's Church as described above has been formed in the engagement of the Church in today's world. But to measure the opportunities of the Church in the near future, we need a more thorough description of the advanced modern tendencies concerning the individual, the culture, and the media. The analyses, which I often borrow from other authors, may seem sharp because they tend to discuss models and tend to put more stress on the models than on real people and real institutions. On the other hand, the analyses give a clear view of the tensions and tendencies with which we all have to cope. Martin Hoondert criticizes the validity of the model of inculturation in the light of the radically pluralistic culture; Paul Post analyzes the late modern rituals as *ritualizations*, in which rituals have become empty vessels and instruments of coping; and Jean Martín-Barbero describes the appropriation of the media in terms of *mediations*, whereby communication is reduced to networking and people compose their own religion in terms of "being connected". The center of everything is the modern self, which Charles Taylor describes as a "buffered self", disengaged from any outside reality. The most important value of this buffered self is autonomy; there seems to be no room for transcendence other than the extensions of the self. My conclusion in this section will be that the self-centeredness of the advanced modern society leads to empty rituals and empty media, and that this emptiness may hinder real transformative communication.

Inculturation?

A keyword in the development of the liturgy is inculturation, which is the communication between the cult and the culture transforming both. Inculturation presupposes that there is a dominant and fairly stable culture. However, in the last century, culture has changed from an identifiable pattern of behavior of a certain people, e.g., the Dutch culture, into a "global village" containing various patterns of behavior freely interacting with one another (Speelman 2001b:183-184). We cannot make clear distinctions between the cult and the culture, or between the one and the other culture (Hoondert 2006: 87-117). For example, where the entering of a popular song into the liturgy used to lead to an adaptation of the song to the qualities of the liturgy, nowadays the popular song may be performed *as is* in the liturgy, often with the help of electronic media. Both the song and the liturgy are changed, but not by adapting to each other. They just become each other's background and are not transformed by their communication. As a matter of fact, the same is true for the exchange between different cultures. When we eat pizza, for example, an element of the Italian culture enters *as is* into our Dutch culture. There is no adaptation, only addition. Every individual is at any moment free (and obliged!) to compose his or her own 'culture' from diverse elements from various cultures. For example, I know Dutch people who eat Italian food, dress in Italian clothes, and decorate in Italian style, but do not speak Italian. This poses no problems, for there is no need for communication or understanding.

As the concept of culture has become an interaction between patterns, has not the cult, c.q. the liturgy, become just another pattern, like eating pizza? It would certainly explain why there are young and modern people with a very traditional conception of liturgy: they do not believe in God, but they believe in Gregorian chant, in a so-called 'authentic' monastic performance. After the performance, having experienced a moment of monastic silence, there is no reason why they should not go dancing. In this dynamic, it is perfectly understandable that an individual may enter into the liturgical celebration every now and then, without really engaging to it. The individual may be moved, but will not be transformed. It is just another feeling. Inculturation, then, has become interference between patterns of behavior, reflecting one another and being each other's background, but not transforming one another (cf. Post 2001:56-61). The tradition and the meaning are gone, and everything comes down to the choice and the taste of the individual person.

From ritual to 'ritualizing'

Somehow connected to the personal appropriation of cult and culture is the development in the realm of ritual. Over the last decades there has been a growing interest in ritualizing practices inside and outside the Church (Post 1998, 2000, 2001, 2003; Lukken 2004). People, including those who have left the Church, rediscover ritual practices such as singing Gregorian chant or painting icons. Outside the Church as well it seems that people have rediscovered rituals. However, they do not perform rituals in the traditional way and setting. Instead, they reconstruct and reinvent rituals in their own way; in other words, they 'ritualize' or engage in 'ritualizations' of the rituals. Especially in situations of crisis – that is, when their identity is in danger – people tend to organize and participate in newly formed rituals, for example, a silent procession after an incident of senseless violence or a service of remembrance after a disaster. Paul Post describes this ritual revival as a recharging of old devotional practices with a new personal meaning, disengaging it from its embeddedness in the Church. The traditional ritual is played out in a "vessel-ritual" offering the user the format and opportunity for his or her own individual religious feelings (Post 2000:109-110). The question is not what the original meaning of the ritual would be, but whether or not the 'ritualizer' recognizes him- or herself in it.

The reinvented ritual is an instrument for coping with our fears and disasters, for affirming our identities, and for giving us a feeling of orientation. But the research of ritualizing practices remains rather vague about questions concerning their meaning. What *is* mentioned is the feeling the ritualizations elicit: carnival is about an oceanic feeling (Wijers 1995), and long distance walks elicit religious feelings (Albers 2007). Perhaps the focus on the feelings is due to a special characteristic of ritual, which is an utterance in which the body and our *bodiliness* is involved. The advanced modern self, in his or her bodiliness, is the center of the ritual circle. To this individual the ritual is an instrument for eliciting feelings and establishing an identity, for I am what I feel (Schulz 2005:46).

If we combine the notion of reinventing, which is a form of reproduction, and the notion of disposing the ritual of its tradition, we may be reminded of a famous essay from the philosopher Walter Benjamin on the work of art in the age of mechanical reproduction (Benjamin 1982). The point Benjamin makes is that the reproduction of an artwork disposes the work from its authenticity, its "aura" or uniqueness. The authentic setting of the work is its tradition, in which and because of which the work has a cult value. When this tradition is lost or when a work is disposed of its tradition, its cult value is replaced by an exhibition value. Think, for example, of religious objects in a museum. The reproduction of rituals today may be interpreted in terms of exhibition because, often, the rituals, especially the great public events, have a strong show character. But for the discussion here it is more important to notice that the reproduction of rituals goes together with a loss: the loss of tradition, of values, and of meaning.

To be honest, Benjamin's analysis did not see that the reproduction techniques of film and photography would lead to new works of art, with their own aura and their own tradition, and that this tradition would be perfectly in line with the greater history of art. In serious art, reproduction appeared to become just another technique in the hands of creative artists. It remains to be seen whether the new ritualizations will be more than emptied vehicles for individual feelings, or if they will become the rituals of a new religious formation (cf. Hellemans 2007).

From media to 'mediations'
The emptying of the traditional in the cults and rituals can also be recognized in the media of advanced modernity. We started this contribution with the remark that the book, which had so much influence on the liturgy, has lost its central position. This may be due to the development of the electronic media, which has become the nervous system of advanced modernity. As a nervous system, the electronic media themselves must be as empty as possible. They are used as mere instruments of transmission. On the other hand, the electronic media have their own characteristics, and these characteristics will influence communication. Especially in the most recent forms, the electronic media reach out for every individual. Electronic media make connections – this is what they do. They work in the closed circuit of the network. As the various forms of electronic media condition communication, they create the opportunity for people to appropriate the media individually and to become connected, to become networking networks. Communicating with the electronic media comes down mainly to individually making connections.

The real center in advanced modernity is the individual self as one who must be reached, who must be brought into connection. The appropriation of the media by the advanced modern selves has led Jean Martín-Barbero to talk about mediations instead of media (cf. 'ritualizations' instead of rituals). People make their own news, their own programs, and their own comments. In the communication through the electronic media, therefore, not the content but the connection is essential. What is important is that people feel connected, not that they have something to say. Every individual is virtually connected to almost everything at every level of intimacy.

Martín-Barbero and others have described how people reconstruct or reinvent religion and ritual in the media. The virtual realm might even be called the cathedral of advanced modernity, in which people find a space for new connections (Martin-Barbero 1997; Schilson 1995). The media form a "time-out culture" in which stars create an atmosphere of sacredness, a liminal space in which the audiences can find their "real selves" in the mirror of the stars (White 1997). Apparently, in media events like the funeral of Princess Diana, people feel utterly connected. This particular event has even had a healing effect on the recipients allowing them to reflect their own emotions and thoughts in a distant mirror (Speelman 2001a). After the terms 'mediation' and 'ritualizing', we may try to find an active form of reproducing religion in the media. Given that the etymology of the word 'religion' points at the Latin *religare* (to reconnect), this new term might be 'religation'. The most important role for this reproduced religion, this 'religating', is indeed the establishing of the self through making connections. One can often hear people say: "I have my own connection with Him up there. I don't need a church for that".

But the media do not connect us with a transcendent reality that comes to us and is received by us, transforming us. On the contrary, reproduced "transcendence" is a reconstruction of the self in all kinds of extensions. For example, the ghosts in the shows of Derek Ogilvie are always deceased relatives who have no other message than that they are in connection with and protecting the one who is missing them. There is never an angel with a warning or an assignment. And God in movies like "Bruce Almighty" and "Oh God" is an actor who does nothing but respond to the needs of the hero. Charles Taylor calls these new 'religating' media events "feasts of self-assurance" (Taylor 2007:51). The question is not what a transcendent reality – God or any other otherness – might want to say to us, but the question is only whether or not I recognize myself in this event.

'Buffered selves'

It is clear that the center of the tendencies described in the last paragraphs is the self, the individual and autonomous subject who has appropriated the cult, the ritual, and the media. Who is this advanced modern center of the universe? What are we?

The philosopher Charles Taylor describes the development of the present secular age as a project of disengaged reason by the "buffered self" (Taylor 2007:37-44). The buffered self is the identity that does not allow influences from outside to get to it. This self believes that the fullness of life comes from within. The buffered self believes itself to be invulnerable. But the invulnerable is inevitably closed and insensitive. The buffered self stresses the transcendence of God, thus driving Him out of the world, as it were, and considers the (immanent) world as a closed reality. In a way, the buffered self is also "transcendent", for by being disengaged the reasonable subject actually has left the world and creates a world of its own. In this self-made world, everything has become an option, a matter of choice. The tragic result of this modern faith is a disenchanted, empty, and meaningless world. Taylor writes: "Our disenchanted world lacks meaning; in this world, the youth in particular suffer from a lack of strong purposes in their lives (...). This malaise is specific to a buffered identity, whose very invulnerability opens it to the danger that not just evil spirits, cosmic forces, or gods will not 'get to it', but that nothing significant at all will stand out for it" (Taylor 2007:303).

Although the reader may not recognize him- or herself completely in this model, the tendency can be recognized easily in ourselves and in our society. Moreover, Taylor's analysis fits in with the descriptions of ritualizations and mediations in the previous paragraphs. People reproduce their own culture to feel at home, they reinvent their own rituals to reach their "real selves", and they use the media to form a closed circuit of networks so that they may live in their own virtual reality ... until everything falls to pieces.

In advanced modernity there seems to be no community but only clouds of individuals, no liturgy but only repertoires of ritualizations. The effect of the appropriation of the media in 'mediations' is that communication has little content. The medium has become the message, and communication is what the media do: to connect and to build networks. But networking does not lead to transformation, and is thus not *real* communication. How can the Church communicate the Lord's message in this environment? How can the liturgy be a shared celebration of the divine presence? Following the intentions of the Second Vatican Council, I chose to consider the liturgical situation in the Church of today in terms of a communicative relation. If communication in advanced modernity is mainly to be connected, the one and only chance for the Church and the liturgy today is to be present when things go wrong. This chance is to stay present as she is: "in the world but not of the world", and to be there with and for the selves that happen to lose their buffers.

5. Real presence is what the Church has to offer

How can we be present in a world in which the user is the center, and where this user is a buffered, disengaged self? We can write books in which we stress that the self needs otherness in order to become a self, and that the individual needs a communicative relation with others in order to form a community. But books will not convince people, especially when people are used to appropriating their meaning in such a way that it does not get to them. What will convince them? When Walter Benjamin described the disappearance of the aura of the work of art in the age of mechanical reproduction, his last hope was the human countenance emanating an aura even from photographic reproductions (he was thinking of portraits, but we may also think of other forms of presence). The countenance is the appearance of a living presence, albeit in a reproduced utterance. The Church has kept faith in the divine countenance radiating through the living presence of the Church and the faithful. The chance, then, for the Church to be there for the buffered and disengaged self is to be present when she is needed. Her presence with the people will be a convincing testimony of the presence of the Lord, and His presence will be a call for the people to be really present.

Real presence: An offer and a response

Presence is what the Church has to offer, in the sense that this is the mission of the Church. Presence is a gift from God. God has offered and is still offering His presence to His people (Ex 3,14). As a gift the presence is also a mission, for the gift calls for a response, and the proper response to the gift of presence is to be present. In the liturgy, too and especially, the proper response to the real presence of the Lord is not to question the logic of it, but to be really present when He offers Himself (Speelman 2006). Presence is always experienced as a gift: to be here and now, in communion with the One (Speelman, Van Veghel 1999).

Real presence is what the Church has to offer, also in the sense that it responds to the needs of the people. Here, too, the countenance of God as He appeared to the Church gives direction. God appeared in the flesh; He approached people in the way they are, so that they are able to receive Him. We should never forget that the human condition is thoroughly determined by being flesh. Sometime, someway, every buffered self will recall that, in fact, it *is* engaged in this world, that, in fact, it *is* as vulnerable as human flesh is. At the moment when the self is being confronted with its true condition, it needs someone to turn to. Another buffered self cannot be that someone, for it is used to keeping out threatening signals. What is more threatening than the message that it may not be as autonomous and as invulnerable as it believed itself to be? The Church can offer her real presence by receiving these people and their shared vulnerability. Thus, her countenance radiates the presence of the Lord who revealed Himself as near to us as our own flesh is (Joh 1,14). To be present in the flesh means to be real, sensible, and sensitive. Thus, the Church may be the "porous self", as Taylor calls it: the open, vulnerable other to the buffered self.

Real presence is a communicative relation in which the participants do not stay unmoved. It is important that when the moment of breaking through the buffers happens, the Church searches for a communicative approach in a balanced relation. A communicative relation is the proper answer to the self that has become vulnerable. It is an open and respectful relation, which gives room to blessing and gratitude. By offering blessing and grace, the Church remembers the blessing and grace offered by God. A blessing is the affirmation that the gift of creation is good (cf. Gen 1,31), and gratitude is the affirmation that the gift is well-received. In the communicative relation the center is not the Church, or the book, or the individual self; rather, the center is that which happens between the one and the other. This communicative relation offers the opportunity for the development of the human person as a real presence and the Church as a community.

In a balanced communicative relation, the Church and the individual faithful will both have to have control over the media and the messages. They should not be governed by the media, but only by the communication. Appropriation of the media makes one responsible. A responsible 'mediator' does not want to know or say everything, but rather watches over what he or she mediates: "The bad words that come out of your mouth are what make you unclean" (Mt 15,11). The control is a shared responsibility. Appropriation is thus not possession, for the media, as well as the symbols, traditions, and the meanings, are shared. From the revelation of God as a *communio* we can learn that the sharing is the proper way of communication (*Communionis notio*, nr. 3). Thus, everything the Church has to offer is and remains a gift, a shared gift.

Real presence: A transformative relation

In a balanced communicative relation, the participants are in transformation: God, the Church, the liturgy, and the individual faithful all adapt to each other and are thus present to each other. Transformation, then, is a sort of verification of communication. There has been communication if you have been transformed, or better: renewed.

One of the questions that might come up in using the communicative approach is: To what degree is God transformed by communicating with us? Kees Waaijman, who developed the spiritual method that inspired this communicative approach, answered this question by asking: "To what degree do you believe that God became flesh?" God communicates with humans in the most humble human manner. This gift of incarnation calls for a response. I have already suggested that the first response to the incarnation is that the Church becomes human, and returns to her bodiliness. Communication with the incarnated God turns the Church into flesh, a body in the most humble sense of the word (Henry 2000:23). As a body, the Church is able to communicate in a real, sensible, and sensitive way. To be flesh means to be vulnerable and sensitive, transient and secular; but to be flesh means also to be real.

The Thomist principle that everything that is received, is received in the manner of the receiver (*quidquid recipitur ad modum recipientis recipitur*) could lead us to think that a communicative relation with the world would inevitably transform the Church into a buffered self, disengaged from the world and creating her own "sacred" but virtual reality. Indeed, we should always be aware of this tendency! But this would hinder the communication itself. It is better that the Church adapts to the buffers of the world by not attacking but by waiting. Using Certeau's words, I would say that the Church does not need a strategy, for approaching the buffered world with a strategy would elicit only defense mechanisms. By taking the position of the weak (*le faible*) the Church needs a tactic. The "tactic of the practitioner" is to wait for the moment and to be sensitive (the word tactic has to do with tactility), and reach out for the individual in a sensitive, bodily, tangible way.

The communicative relation with God will also transform the Church to the way God is. Communicating with God renews the Church by sharing her in the *communio* of the Father, the Son, and the Holy Ghost (LG 4). God's being is a sharing, and He has shared His sharing with humans. An example of this sharing is the way God sees. As I have suggested above, the Church may share in the way God looks at His creation: that it is very good (Gen 1,31). Spiritual seeing is a form of blessing, *bene dicere*, saying that it is good, that this individual creature is good. The value of the Church in the advanced modern world is that she is capable of blessing with her eyes and with her words. Moreover, to transform vis-à-vis the sharing God will lead to the Church becoming a true communion. This communion will also be communicated to the individual people who turn to the Church. The communicative relation between the hierarchy and the faithful, then, is one of sharing. Consequently, as we have said several times, appropriation is not a question of possession but of sharing.

The Church as a communicative practice is always new, always in transformation. Therefore, her tradition is dynamic and polyphonous. This dynamic is a constant renewing realization of the presence of the Lord with the world and with the people. Actually, the Church has no future; she is only now, mediating the presence of God.

References

Albers, I. 2007. *Heilige kracht wordt door beweging losgemaakt. Over pelgrimage, lopen en genezing*. Groningen: Liturgisch Instituut.

Barnard, M. & P. Post. 2008. Nogmaals: de Liturgische Beweging voorbij. Pp. 7-22 in *Jaarboek voor Liturgie-onderzoek* 24.

Benjamin, W. 1982. *Das Kunstwerk im Zeitalter seiner technischen Reproduzierbarkeit*. Frankfurt a.M.: Suhrkamp.

Berkvens-Stevelinck, C. 2007. *Vrije rituelen. vormgeven aan het leven*. Zoetermeer: Meinema.

Certeau, M. de. 1990. *L'invention du quotidien. 1. arts de faire*. Paris: Gallimard.

Chauvet, L.-M. 2002. La présidence liturgique dans la modernité. Les chances possibles d'une crise. In J. Lamberts (red.). *'Ars celebrandi'. The art to celebrate the liturgy*. Leuven: Peeters, pp. 49-64.

Communionis notio – Letter to the Bishops of the Catholic Church on some aspects of the Church understood as Communion, May 28, 1992, nr. 3.

Gertler, M. 1998. *Unterwegs zu einer Fernsehgemeinde. Erfahrung von Kirche durch Gottesdienstübertragungen.* Köln.

Hellemans, S. 2007. *Het tijdperk van de wereldreligies. Religie in agrarische civilisaties en in moderne samenlevingen.* Zoetermeer: Meinema.

Henry, M. 2000. *Incarnation. Une philosophie de la chair.* Paris: Seuil.

Hoondert, M. 2006. *Om de parochie. Ritueel-muzikale bewegingen in de marge van de parochie.* Heeswijk: Abdij van Berne.

Horsfield, P.G. 1997. Changes in Religion in Periods of Media Convergence. Pp. 167-183 in S.M. Hoover & K. Lundby (eds.). *Rethinking media, religion, and culture.* London: Sage.

Joosse, K. 1991. *Eucharistische gebeden in Nederland.* Tilburg: Tilburg University Press.

Lamberigts, M. 2006. Entwicklungen nach dem II. Vatikanum in den Niederlanden. Die liturgische Entwicklung als Fallstudie. Pp. 283-312 in P. Hünermann (Hg). *Das Zweite vatikanische Konzil und die Zeichen der Zeit heute.* Freiburg-Basel-Wien: Herder.

Lukken, G.M. 2004. *Rituals in Abundance. Critical Reflections on the Place, Form and Identity of Christian Ritual in our Culture.* Leuven: Peeters.

Majoor, I. & K. Sonnberger (red.). 1999. *Kerken in de abdij. De inspiratie van een monastieke beweging voor het parochieleven van vandaag en morgen.* Kampen: Kok.

Martín-Barbero, J. 1993. *Communication, culture and hegemony: From the media to mediations.* London.

Martín-Barbero, J. 1993. Mass Media as a Site of Resacralization of Contemporary Cultures. Pp. 102-116 in S.M. Hoover & K. Lundy (eds.). *Rethinking media, religion, and culture.* London: Sage.

McLuhan, M. 1962. *The Gutenberg Galaxy.* University of Toronto.

McLuhan, M. 1964. *Understanding Media. The extensions of man.* New York: Routledge.

Palazzo, E. 1998. *A History of Liturgical Books from the Beginning to the Thirteenth Century.* Minnesota: Liturgical Press.

Ong, W. 2002. *Orality and Literacy. The Technologizing of the Word.* New York: Routledge.

Post, P. *et al.* (eds.). 1998. *The Modern Pilgrim. Multidisciplinary Explorations of Christian Pilgrimage.* Leuven: Peeters.

Post, P. 2000. *Het wonder van Dokkum. Verkenningen van populair religieus ritueel.* Nijmegen: Valkhof Pers.

Post, P. 2001. Feast as a Key Concept in a Liturgical Studies Research Design. Pp. 47-77 in P. Post *et al.* (eds.). *Christian Feast and Festival. The Dynamics of Western Liturgy and Culture.* Leuven: Peeters.

Post. P. *et al.* (eds.). 2003. *Disaster Ritual.* Leuven: Peeters.

Schilson, A. 1995. Das neue Religiöse und der Gottesdienst. Pp. 94-109 in *Liturgisches Jahrbuch* 45.

Schulze, G. 2005[2]. *Die Erlebnisgesellschaft. Kultursoziologie der Gegenwart.* Frankfurt: Campus.

Speelman, W.M. 1997. Hedendaagse huwelijksrituelen. Pp. 55-60 in P. Post & W.M. Speelman (eds). *De Madonna van de Bijenkorf. Bewegingen op de rituele markt.* Baarn: Gooi & Sticht.

Speelman, W.M. 2001a. The 'Feast' of Diana's Death. Pp. 775-801 in P. Post *et al.* (eds.). *Christian Feast and Festival. The Dynamics of Western Liturgy and Culture.* Peeters: Leuven.

Speelman, W.M. 2001b. Over liturgie en muzische taal. *Tijdschrift voor Liturgie* 85: 175-187.

Speelman, W.M. 2004. *Liturgie in beeld. Over de identiteit van de rooms-katholieke liturgie in de elektronische media.* Groningen-Tilburg: Instituut voor Liturgiewetenschap/Liturgisch Instituut (=Netherlands Studies in Ritual and Liturgy 3).

Speelman, W.M. 2006. De spiritualiteit van het lichaam volgens Franciscus. *Tijdschrift voor Theologie* 46: 120-142.

Speelman, W.M. 2008. The celebration of the body. Pp. 166-176 in L. Leijssen (ed). *Initiation chrétienne et la liturgie / Christian initiation and the liturgy.* Leuven: Peeters.

Speelman, W.M. & H. van Veghel. 1999. Over de betekenis van de eucharistie. Pp. 213-234 in *Jaarboek voor Liturgie-onderzoek* 15.

Taylor, Ch. 2007. *A Secular Age.* Cambridge: Harvard University Press.

Torevell, D. 2000. *Losing the sacred: Ritual, modernity and liturgical reform.* Edinburg: T&T Clark.

Turner, V. 1969. *The Ritual Process: Structure and Anti-Structure.* Ithaca (NY): Cornell University Press.

Vogel, C. 1986. *Medieval Liturgy. An Introduction to the Sources.* Portland: Pastoral Press.

Waaijman, K. 2002. *Spirituality. Forms, Foundations, Methods.* Leuven: Peeters. (= Studies in Spirituality, Supplement 18)

Wegman, H.A.J. 1991. *Riten en Mythen. Liturgie in de geschiedenis van het Christendom.* Kampen: Kok.

Wijers, C. 1995. *Prinsen en clowns in het Limburgse narrenrijk: Het carnaval in Simpelveld en Roermond 1945-1992.* Amsterdam: Meertens Instituut.

Abbreviations

1Cel   Thomas de Celano, 1995. *Vita Prima S. Francisci Assisiensis*, Pp. 275-424 in *Fontes Franciscani.* Assisi: Porziuncola.

Reaching out beyond the Fortissimo's?
Youth, Church, and Religion

Monique van Dijk-Groeneboer

The main aim of this chapter is to look at the relationship between youth and religion in the Netherlands. More specifically, this chapter looks at youth, namely, the generation comprised of individuals between the ages of 15 and 25, and their search for religion and belief, and whether it is possible for the main religions in the Netherlands to play any role in their search. We will focus on describing the characteristics of this generation together with their religion and religious activities. We will then describe, specifically, the position of the Catholic Church in the Netherlands concerning youth and what challenges the Church must meet.

In my first section, I start by showing some main research outcomes from a variety of scientific sources. In the second section, I focus on what these results tell us about youth in the Netherlands. Here, I introduce four different 'types' of young people (*Fortissimo's, Tranquillio's, Legato's, Spirituoso's*), grouped according to their religious behavior and the extent to which it forms their identity. Section three shows what objectives the hierarchic Catholic Church has for youth, while section four looks at the strategy of the worldwide Catholic Church and, in particular, what the local and dioceses workers in the Catholic Church in the Netherlands have to offer to youth. Finally, in section 5, I further concretize the theory about the challenges these results give to the Church of today. I point at the four described different types of young people and what offers could be made by the Church to reach out to them all, and not just to the *Fortissimo's* alone.

1. Research on youth and religion

The place of youth in the Dutch society of 2011 is not really very different from the rest of Western Europe. As a result, I will use some recent publications[1] to characterize 'today's youth', a generation that is sometimes called Generation Y, Generation Einstein, or the Boundless Generation (I come to these terms later on).

---

1   Spangenberg, F. and M. Lampert, 2009. *De grenzeloze generatie*; Boschma, J. and I. Groen, 2006. *Generatie Einstein: slimmer, sneller en socialer. Communiceren met jongeren van de 21e eeuw*; Collins-Mayo, S. *et al.* 2010. *The Faith of Generation Y*; Dijk-Groeneboer, M. van (ed.). 2010. *Handboek Jongeren en Religie?!*

Today's 'generation' or 'cohort' of young people is, in most cases, defined as people between 15 and 25 years of age. During these years, young people develop and undergo big changes. For example, they move from school life to further education at a high school, academy, or university, or they start a job. They transition from living at home with their parents to moving out into the world and becoming autonomous. The search for relationships is very important in these years, and spending time with peers is the main way of dealing with the many changes and challenges experienced. There are so many choices to be made, and as a result of globalization and the internet, the entire world is now available to choose from.

1.1. In the research conducted by Motivaction (Spangenberg and Lampert 2009), we find some main topics specific to the youth in the Netherlands nowadays. Since 1984, Motivaction has interviewed over 10,000 youth and parents (i.e., 1250 Dutch citizens a year). Over the years, the authors discovered a thorough change in the so-called social sensitivity of people, something which is commonly seen in all of Western Europe. They found that in every new generation, a larger part of the respondents is *pragmatic*. They are also what the authors call an *outsider*. These two groups oppose those who are either *responsible* or *dutiful*. Those who are pragmatic are assertive, like to travel, are well educated, and believe in their own abilities. They are self-assured. They also seem to accept a high (and increasing) level of violence and they value hierarchy. They ask for respect without being respectful themselves, and they call for a strong man in a democratic world. The survival of the fittest becomes more familiar here, while empathy disappears. This is the group that has gained the name of 'the Boundless Generation': the sky is the limit for them. The second largest group is the outsiders. These individuals are not respectful to higher positions, are impulsive in their buying behavior, and need structure, order, and discipline. For example, they dream of a happy family life in which the father is the boss. These two large groups are increasing and the differences between them are growing. The other two groups, the responsible and the dutiful, are decreasing, which, according to the authors, is dangerous for a society. People need to choose not only for their own good but also for the good of other people and society as a whole.

This development of the four different groups emphasizes the fact that more young people every year become less socially interested in or committed to society, and are more and more focused on themselves and their individual experience. They care less about others and are – due to the liberal, *boundless* upbringing they received from their parents – used to living without boundaries or limitations. These are more reasons why the authors have used the name 'the Boundless Generation' to refer to them. This is a new moniker that replaces the previous one of 'Generation Einstein'. The Einstein generation was more socially involved and, as a result, stronger in their interactions with other people and better at dealing with the problems of growing up. They could make it in the world on their own.[2]

In contrast, in 2010, the new generation of boundless young people is described as more hedonistic, materialistic, and individualistic. This group of youth has higher expectations of life and society even though the future might not be as secure as they would hope due to the financial state of society and the world as a whole. This generation is "focused on networks, outward appearances, and kicks, and not so much on their own well-being, society, or environment" (Spangenberg and Lampert 2009, p. 80).

1.2. Every five years since 1997, van Dijk and Maas have conducted a survey among Dutch pupils at Catholic secondary schools regarding their religion, beliefs, and values in life.[3] In 2008, they reached 2050 pupils in 13 Catholic secondary schools. The age of the participants varied from 15 to 18 years old. 51% of the pupils were boys and 49% were girls. 40% called themselves Catholic, 12% Protestant, and 3% Muslim. 43% claimed no membership of any church or religion.

A part of the 2008 questionnaire directly asked pupils whether they had anything to do with religion, faith, and God. 69% did *not* call themselves religious; only 14% claimed do be religious; the remaining 17% did not answer the question. Only 10% said they *wanted* to believe but could not do so. 46% claimed to know exactly what they believed in, whereas God was only important for 14%. The most important values (out of a list of 23) were "to be free and independent", "have a happy relationship", and "be a good human being". All the values connected to faith or belief scored low, e.g., "having faith", "trust in God", and "having a life guided by God".

Pupils were asked to describe in their own words what was important for them in the fields of religion, faith, and the meaning of life. Important threads in these answers were that faith has its limits ('One can believe as long as it does not hurt other people') and faith has also to deal with other things such as 'finding worldly matters important' and 'trying to keep the balance between believing and living'. Many responses stressed the importance of a balanced whole, i.e., 'everyone can believe what he or she wants, as long as this belief is not foisted on anyone else'. Also, the tolerance of everyone's faith was mentioned a great deal as well as the importance of being aware of the excesses faith can cause, as seen, for example, in recent wars and in the murders of Pim Fortuyn

---

2   cf. J. Wissink in this volume: social people are looking for communities although the forms of these communities have changed, for example, small whole families of the past are now often broken or blended families due to divorce.

3   Earlier published in this regard: Searching during a lifetime *(Op zoektocht; levenslang)* (2001) and Faith? Let's see *(Geloof? ff checke!)* (2005), in which data is used from respectively 1997 and 2002. In the last report, Religion? Important! *(Godsdienst? Lekker belangrijk!)* data is used from research conducted five years later: 2007/2008.

and Theo van Gogh in the Netherlands (which happened recently prior to the time the 2008 survey was conducted).

1.3. In the book *The Faith of Generation Y* (2010), Collins-Mayo *et al.* report a study in England of over 300 young people between age 18 and 23. Two main conclusions tell us more about the religion of youth today. Young people have not inherited the rebellious hostility to religion and church as seen in their parents' generation; instead, for many youth, religion is simply irrelevant for day-to-day living.

The findings from the study suggest that for most young people faith is located primarily in family, friends, and themselves as individuals, which is defined as "immanent faith". "For the majority, religion and spirituality was irrelevant for day-to-day living; our young people were not looking for answers to ultimate questions and showed little sign of 'pick and mix' spirituality." Collins-Mayo goes on to say:

> "On the rare occasions when a religious perspective was required (for example, coping with family illnesses or bereavements) they often 'made do' with a very faded, inherited cultural memory of Christianity in the absence of anything else. In this respect they would sometimes pray in their bedrooms." (Collins-Mayo *et al.* 2010, p. 32)
> "What is salutary for the Church is that generally young people seemed quite content with this situation, happy to get by with what little they knew about the Christian faith." (Collins-Mayo *et al.* 2010, p. 108)

This research shows that religion seems to have a coping function for young people, however, they do not miss having knowledge of faith or going to church.

1.4. These three examples of research conducted concerning young people and their religion show us this is a difficult topic. Central features common among today's youth are, for example, that parents and children treat each other as equals (Ziebertz *et al.* 2009), and they live in small families, one third of which are 'broken or blended'. Main important values for youth are independence, good education, a humane world, and future family life (Ziebertz *et al.* 2009). Young people want to be free and independent above all else. They do not want anyone imposing anything upon them, and they especially do not want anyone prescribing them a way to live.

Of the many choices they are faced with in growing up, religion is not really a main one. "Many are not looking for answers to ultimate questions at all." (Collins-Mayo *et al.* 2010, p. 31). It is on this point that I disagree with and will diverge from Collins-Mayo. Instead, I argue that the youth of today are indeed searching for answers to the big questions; they just go about it in less traditional ways. I suggest that researchers are looking at young people and their religious questions in an old fashioned way. For example, researchers are going to churches and searching for young people, or they are asking scholars what young people think of religion, i.e., are young people going to church and reading the bible? These old ways no longer fit when studying the beliefs of young people today. The way young people form their identities and find answers to the big questions in their lives is very different than in the past, and requires a new approach of scientific examination.

We saw in the research of Motivaction that there is a part of today's young generation that has difficulties dealing with all the choices that can be made in our global world. This is a group of youth for which life can be difficult. They will easily drop out of the ordinary ways of finding meaning in their lives. For this group, for instance, a religion that has a clear framework can become attractive to answer the difficult questions in life. The 'society of experience' also tries to provide meaning for this materialistic, hedonistic, non-religious group of people by offering special 'experiences'. The solution society offers is, however, very flimsy and fleeting: these experiences provide commercials and festivals that offer instant experience but nevertheless do not offer any transcendence, connection, or lasting meaning for life.

2. Types of religious youth

I present now a typology of religious youth. These concepts are principally developed out of my own research, complemented by other quantitative studies, as those described above from Motivaction, Ziebertz *et al.*, and Collins-Mayo *et al.*, but also complemented by qualitative research, among which cultural anthropological and theological studies are taken into account. Catholic, Protestant, and Muslim youth are all part of the studies used to create these youth-types.

Analyzing these data, one can see a division into four groups.[4] I divide the groups along two dimensions: the connection or commitment to a religious institute on the one hand, and the place of religion in forming identity on the other. The first dimension is to be seen as the way one commits oneself to a religious institute such as a church or a mosque. Does one attend the institute regularly (e.g., church on Sundays or mosque on Fridays), is one active in groups attached to this institute, and so on. The second dimension regards the way in which religion plays a role in life choices, such as in coping with problems, finding friends, making big decisions, behaving in everyday life, choosing life purposes, and so on. I simplify the reality behind this two-dimensional thinking to create a yes/no scale in each dimension; either one is committed to a religious institute or not, and one either gives religion a place in forming one's

---

4   This division of four groups is developed and illustrated in Dijk-Groeneboer, M. van (ed.).
     2010. *Handboek Jongeren en Religie?!*, as well as in the conducted research I used to come
     to this.

identity or does not. In doing so, a four-group division of young people and their religion can be pointed out:

	Active, concerned with religion in forming their identity	Not-active, not concerned with religion in forming their identity
Committed to a religious institute	Fortissimo's	Legato's
Not committed to a religious institute	Spirituoso's	Tranquillio's

These are, of course, ideal types of people, but this line of thinking helps us to describe the different types of youth we see in many different research outcomes. I also try to give an indication of the percentage of youth that belong in each group, but this is tenuous given that it is very hard to conduct quantitative research that can specifically divide everyone into these groups.

The first group comprises very engaged and committed young people who, for the most part, have grown up in a religious family, have been acquainted with religion from their early years, and are themselves highly connected to a religious institute such as a church or mosque. This group is very active in their own religion and also in trying to convert other people. They try to fulfill all the demands their religion asks of them, and they adopt the entire identity of their religion as their own. We also find in this group individuals such as neo-Catholics, or young people who have recently converted to a religion. Most people in this group are orthodox in their religion and the way they treat the hierarchic organization of some churches. They are obedient and non-critical, a bit close-minded but rather solid. In research, they are called the 'Tough Core', and make up about 10-15% of youth. For my purposes, I call them the *Fortissimo's*. In my research among pupils, I categorized them as such because they answered 'yes' to all questions like: "Do you go to church or mosque?" "Are you religious?" and "Do you belong to a religion or church?" They also find life purposes such as 'a life guided by God' and 'putting your faith in God' very important. Quotes from two pupils illustrate this:

> "I find it very important to believe in God. He gives me strength in difficult situations (even if I did not ask for it). The church is for me a place to express my faith with others (…)."
> "I perform many activities as a volunteer in the church, it is good to help people and focus on God on the same time."

The second group – the largest in my research group as well as in society (I estimate this group makes up 40% of young people) – is comprised of all the youth who have nothing to do with religion. They are sometimes very aggressive against religion, and sometimes they just do not care. All of them are neither active in a church or mosque nor connected to religious institutes in any way. They are not concerned with any form of spiritual or religious questions. I call this group of young people the *Tranquillo's*. In my research, these pupils answered 'no' to all the same questions the Fortissimo's answered yes to. Again, quotes from two people from this group are illustrative:

> "I am an atheist, I don't believe in anything higher. I see God as a fiction of humanity to explain certain phenomena and to pretend you can become a better person by taking certain actions."
> "I find it important to feel a connectedness with one's friends, family, or other people close to oneself. And that your life and that of those among you has a meaning. Faith or church has not to be a part in this."

The third group is well known to religious organizations such as churches or mosques. The young people of this group sometimes attend religious gatherings, mostly on festive days. They know religion from their family life, although mainly from a distance, from the 'olden days' of their grandparents and so on. These young people are connected to religious organizations when it is relevant to them, for example, when they want to get married in a church. They are not, however, actively committed to the religious institute, and religion or spirituality does not have a large influence on their entire life. I call these young people the *Legato's*, and they make up 20-25% of youth. These pupils answered 'yes' to questions such as "Do you belong to a church or religion?" and "Do you go to church or mosque on festive days?" but answered 'no' to "Are you religious?" Quotes from two people from this group follow:

> "I am not religious. I hardly go to church, so religion plays hardly any part in my everyday life."
> "I do not believe, but I do think there is something higher. I do not usually think about it, but when I am in a church I think of my grandma who was very religious."

Finally, the fourth group is recognizable in all the material in my research and in the results of research conducted by others. This group also makes up 20-25% of all youth. The youth of this group are not attached to one main religion. Instead, they invent a 'religion' for themselves in which parts from several religions and spiritual movements are combined. For instance, they like to go to church to light a candle when they need strength, they retreat to Taizé to take a break and reload their energy, they like to walk in nature and make this a real spiritual experience, and so on. This is the group that 'shops around' for all kinds of religious and spiritual offers, and picks and chooses pieces from here and there in order to combine them into a religion that is self-suiting. However, they do this with much emphasis in their lives. I call the youth of this group the *Spirituoso's*. The pupils that fall into this group are those that call themselves religious or engage in religious activities such as going to church and praying, attending religious events and/or watching religious TV-programs. They do not, however, find it important that God guide their lives. They also do not think that church and religion have anything to do with each other. Again, two quotes:

> "Everyone has to have his own idea about faith and others have to respect that. I don't like 'church-believers' very much. I believe there is something but I am not certain about anything. Every man should be able to be happy."
> "I do not believe in God, but I do believe there is something that determines your destiny. I believe in reincarnation and I don't believe we are the only life in the universe."

3. The aim of the Catholic Church towards youth

The Catholic Church – seen not as a community but as an institution in this sociological view – has a clear view regarding the importance of reaching the youth in order to survive as an institution. As Peter Jonkers notes in this volume, the Catholic Church has to redefine its self-positioning in the light of the new societal context in advanced modernity.[5] This 'redefining' is well suited for reaching out to young people, who are very much a product of their time. Pope John Paul II played a special part in the movement to evangelize young people. Bishop Samuel Jacobs describes the call for a 'new evangelization' as one of the great legacies of John Paul II and his pontificate.[6]

> "While the message of evangelization is always the same, the audience is different: the world is different; cultures are different; tools of communication are different. Because of these differences there is need to proclaim the same Jesus to all peoples in a new way with great zeal, ardor and clarity, using modern means of communication wherever possible." (Martin & Williamson 2006, p. xviii)

In his encyclical *Redemptoris Missio* (1990), John Paul II emphasizes the great importance for every believer in Christ to put all his or her energy into a new evangelization. He admits this is not an easy task in a society that has changed so much over the last decades. Young people especially are in need of evangelization in order to secure the future of the Church:

> "Speaking of the future, we cannot forget the young, who in many countries comprise more than half the population. How do we bring the message of Christ to non-Christian young people who represent the future of entire continents? Clearly, the ordinary means of pastoral work are not sufficient: what are needed are associations, institutions, special centers and groups, and cultural and social initiatives for young people. This is a field where modern ecclesial movements have ample room for involvement." (John Paul II RM/37b)

---

5   cf. P. Jonkers in this volume.
6   Introduction written by Bishop Samuel Jacobs. 2006. Pp. xvii-xx in R. Martin & P. Williamson (eds.). *John Paul II and the new evangelization.*

Pope John Paul II reached out especially to the youth by telling them:

"In you there is hope, for you belong to the future, just as the future belongs to you. For hope is always linked to the future; it is the expectation of 'future good things'. As a Christian virtue, it is linked to the expectation of those eternal good things which God has promised to man in Jesus Christ. And at the same time, this hope, as both a Christian and a human virtue, is the expectation of the good things which man will build, using the talents given him by Providence." (John Paul II, 1985 DA/1)

He emphasized that new ways of communication were necessary to realize this new evangelization of the youth. A culture itself has to be drenched in a Christian spirit, in the form of music, literature, poetry, and other forms. When a culture remains hostile towards the Gospel, faith cannot express itself fully. Moreover, for youth, music and communication are essential parts of their everyday life; therefore, this new way of communication and transforming cultural expression is very important for reaching them.

One way in which youth have been reached successfully is through the World Youth Days, which were initiated by John Paul II, and started as a response to his call in 1984. Every two or three years many young people from all over the world gather to meet each other, to share their faith, to celebrate, and to meet the pope. It is a very modern way of evangelization that fits in with the world of young people. It incorporates modern music in a 'big event' gathering where today's youth can really *experience* faith.

4. Mobilizing youth: the Catholic Church in the Netherlands

In the Netherlands we see different initiatives undertaken by the Church aimed at reaching the youth. As examples, I will describe and look at large events, special youth officers, the internet usage of young Catholics, and Catholic youth groups. These initiatives have their starting point in the decisions made by the Conference of Bishops, and recorded in their written documentation.[7] In their visit to Rome, the Dutch bishops described the process of secularization amongst the youth in the Roman Catholic Church in the Netherlands and emphasized that it was important to discover the reason for this secularization (1993, p. 20). The bishops reflected on the religious indifference of, or a lack of space for, young people in the Church. Nevertheless, they concluded that there is a positive approachability of young people who authentically long for religious experiences. They suggested that a good, stimulating, and constructive relationship between parishes and schools is important to expand the possibilities of reaching out to youth. Also, the bishops stated that all the efforts of parish, diocese, school, and family are to be directed at bringing the youth

---

7   See *Ad Limina* reports from the Dutch bishops in: *Kerkelijke documentatie* 21 (1993), nr 1 and 26 (1998), nr 6.

back into the Church and making them feel included. What needs to be overcome is the fatal vicious circle that many parishes find themselves in, namely: young people have been openly absent from parishes; therefore, the liturgy, the proclamation, and diaconal activities have become overly focused on those who do attend parish services and events, which is primarily older people. As a result, parishes become places where young people feel excluded and where older parish members become more and more estranged from their youth. The bishops suggested that more financial support should be given to activities that are directed at keeping youth in the parishes, for today's youth are crucial to ensuring future new generations in the Church (1993, p.24).

In addition to this report in the 1990s, a special national policy officer for youth was appointed for the Dutch Catholic community. Young people were encouraged to participate in the World Youth Days, and were invited to become involved in more essential parts of the Church (1998, p. 252). In 2000, about 40,000 young people between the age of 8 and 25 were assembled in all different sorts of groups, which were guided by 14,500 volunteers. In addition, 850 youth choirs were created with a total of 16,000 members, half of whom were below the age of 26. Despite all this, the number of youth pastors has decreased and the number of parishes that do provide activities for young people has also decreased (from 50% to 30% in the last ten years). Also, cooperation between parishes and schools is not at all satisfactory. We will now take a closer look at what the Church in the Netherlands is offering to young people.

The Catholic Church organizes a yearly national event: the Dutch Catholic Youth Day. This event is comparable to other religious events such as the XNOIZZ-Flevofestival (mainly Protestant) and the Ramadan Festival (Muslim). These large events respond to the important role that *experience* plays for the youth of today. The Dutch Catholic Youth Day was held in 2011 for the 7th time. The day is comprised of speeches and workshops, and concludes with a celebration of the Eucharist.

Since 1997, there has existed a National Youth Platform. Here, people between 18 and 30 years old gather once a month to exchange their experiences about the World Youth Days and spread the word, so to speak, to other young people. They have Mass together, eat together, and talk. Since 1978, a foundation (Werkgroep Katholieke Jongeren) has existed that supports activities offered to young people by young Catholics. Such activities have included things like film evenings, summer camps, etc.

The website 'Young Catholic' (http://www.katholieknederland.nl/rkkerk/jongkatholiek/) is a modern communication tool in which all dioceses participate. It contains an agenda of all the events taking place in parishes and dioceses in the Netherlands concerning young people. There is a forum wherein one can react to certain questions and events, special apps can be downloaded, links to several communities are available, and so on. The website lists over 30 groups on the internet spread across the country. These links exist for a long period of time and contain activities and agendas. Of course, there are polls that change about every month as well as rotating new-fashioned theses such as 'Going to church does not make you a Christian any more than going to the garage makes you a car' (L.J. Peter, June 2011). The Young Catholic website looks modern and the agenda is up to date, although the main articles are sometimes from events that happened months ago. The internet has become a place where young Catholic people meet each other to talk about important faith issues and how to integrate these in their everyday life. Because attendance of young people in local parishes is low, the internet is very useful for helping youth meet other believers. Of course, this is not limited to the Netherlands. All over the world Catholic young people meet each other through the internet; there even exists Catholic dating sites. On social media like Facebook, Catholic youth work has its own page. On YouTube, one can find groups like Youth CaFE and Catholic Faith Exploration, where catechesis is offered in a modern way. The diocese of Utrecht has its own website for young people between the age of 10 and 30, called Yougle.

For the Catholic Church, Holy Confirmation provides an important opportunity to reach out to young people because this sacrament usually takes place at the age of 12, before children go to secondary school. A child's primary or elementary school is usually located nearby the family home and, therefore, near the local church. The secondary school is often further away, so children tend to spread further away from home. In secondary school, children also move into adolescence and begin to grow up. As a result, they distance themselves more from their parents. Therefore, the age of 12 is an important moment to reach out to children because they are still close to home and church, and often attached in some way to their local parish. On average, in one year approximately 23,000 people in the Netherlands receive their Holy Confirmation, most of which are between 11 and 16 years of age (Kregting and Massaar, 2010).

Another way of reaching out to youth is to offer them opportunities to 'do' things that help them express their faith. A good example of this is the country-wide project Diaconaction. On one day every year all groups of active Catholic youth participate in diaconal activities to help other people, like visiting elderly people, washing cars, raising money for charity, gardening, etc. During the weekend in which Diaconaction day occurs, many of the participating groups also organize a Eucharist celebration in their parish where they communicate what the project entails. This helps to foster connections with their parish community.

Every diocese in the Netherlands has, as I mentioned before, a special officer for youth, and the officers from all the dioceses together form the *Officium Iuventutis*. Mainly motivated by this group, every diocese has its own way of organizing activities. Much effort is taken to organize Dutch participation to the World Youth Days every two years. Dioceses have groups that try to reach and invite young people to join them. A special Dutch program is set up for traveling to the Word Youth Days and forming the Dutch groups that will take part in the catecheses offered. Dioceses also offer leadership-training programs. For example, the diocese of Haarlem offers education to those who wish to become Catholic youth workers (Duc in Altum).

Furthermore, some of the diocesan youth officers organize holiday camps for young people, and there are different ways in which these officers support the local activities for young people in the parishes. In Rotterdam, for example, there is a large award-winning (Marga Klompé prize 2007) diaconal activity called M25 (which refers to Matthew, chapter 25 verse 40: "And the King will answer and say to them, 'Assuredly, I say to you, inasmuch as you did it to one of the least of these My brethren, you did it to me'".), which has, since 2003, already formed six different groups in different cities to expand this project. Again, when young people can actually *do* something to express their faith, it turns out to be successful.

A successful diocesan example of gathering youth together is 'the Vuurdoop' (baptism of fire) celebration that takes place in the diocese of Rotterdam. During the weekend of Pentecost, all the young people who received their Confirmation in that year gather together (about 1400 in Rotterdam each year). The entire day focuses on what individuals will do as 'adult believers'. Diaconal activities for youth are presented and pastoral youth care is discussed. Also, individuals discuss the initiatives in their own parishes that might be of interest to others. Examples of activities in local parishes are given to young people to provide ideas of things they can 'do' to express their faith. The bishop is always present at this celebration and leads the Mass at the end of the day. During the day there is modern spiritual music and many modern media devices are used to attract young people. Other dioceses also organize similar events to bring together young people who have received their Holy Confirmation (for example, in Haarlem there is BAVO-dag, in Breda there is Lopend vuurtje, in Roermond, there is Christoffeldag). In some parishes, the method known as Rock Solid, which was originally developed for the Youth for Christ but has been appropriated by the Catholic Church, is used to gather small groups of young people.

All through the country in local parishes there are small activities that seem to be successful. Many youth choirs exist (in 2000, there were about 850 choirs made up of about 16,000 members, at least half of whom were below the age of 26), small groups of youth gather weekly for prayer and a meal, youth bible study groups meet, and different Lifeteen groups gather to pray and have mass together. Also in parishes one can find groups that do 'good deeds' (like the M25 group described above). These groups of youth fulfill the diaconal task of the Church, a task that often attracts youth precisely because it involves 'doing' something for someone else – this allows young people to express their faith and thereby be good Christians.

The Brothers of Saint Jean organize weekends and summer camps under the name LVW (meaning Light, Fire, and Truth) for young people in nature where they can explore and discover God. There are also several new charismatic movements in the Netherlands that also offer special activities for young people. Monastic orders and congregations provide programs for young people, (for

example, Ignatiushuis, La Verna, Franciscaans Jongerenwerk Meegen, Domini-
canenklooster Huissen). School groups are invited to come and live with these
congregations for a weekend or midweek term. These 'come-and-live-with-us'
programs tend to be very popular and are fully booked throughout the year.

Many examples given in this section show that the main focus of the
Church with respect to young people has been on those who belong to the type
Fortissimo. Every now and then the Church does offer events and international
meetings that reach beyond this group. In trying to broaden it focus, the Church
has successfully turned its attention to the internet as a useful and important
means of reaching beyond the Fortissimo's.

5. Challenges for churches in the Netherlands

In the previous sections, I described the way the Catholic Church in the
Netherlands is reaching out to young people. Holy Confirmation is a primary
focus for the Church, and large events around this celebration are organized,
because young people at this age are easily reachable. Also, for young people,
the World Youth Days are *the* event to meet other young believers. The local
and dioceses workers put great effort into this event and try to harvest from it by
organizing a nationwide Youth Day and a network of young people who meet
each other during the year.

In doing so, the Church mainly focuses on the "Fortissimo's", i.e., those
youth who already attend church, are highly committed to the Church and its
beliefs, are active, and have a high level of participation. In other words, the
focus is on the 'happy few', the Holy Remains, or the Tough Core ("harde
kern", Kregting en Sanders, 2003). Also, researchers who study the religion and
beliefs of young people tend to look mainly at these Fortissimo's who can be
readily found inside religious institutions. Both the Church and researchers approach youth in the way that *they* (i.e. the Church and researchers) are traditionally used to dealing with religion and the large questions in life. But young people have a different, less traditional way of dealing with life issues *and* with belief, I think. I will explain this later on. First, let us look into the way the Church
deals with youth.

In my view, the Fortissimo's or the Tough Core do not really need much focus in order to gain their attention, for they will find their way to and in the
churches on their own. However, their attention does need to be maintained and
they do need to be served with knowledge and liturgy. This kind of maintenance
takes a lot of the time on the part of priests and other church workers. The use
of modern music and the internet, as in the large events described above, is appreciated by this group but not really necessary to reach them. Modern music
and media can, however, be useful tools to reach out to the *other* three groups of
young people I distinguish. These tools can attract youth who are not familiar
with religious events and activities but who like the music and media used in
them and attend or participate in events as a result. Of course, these less familiar

young people who attend these large events do not all end up in church on the following Sunday; again, only the Fortissimo's will be present in the pews. Here, we see a gap between the efforts church workers make to reach young people with modern means (as John Paul II recommended) and the resulting effects their methods actually have.

Therefore, it is probably *not* wise for the Church to narrow its evangelizing energies to reaching out to the Fortissimo's. Instead, the Church should use modern ways of evangelization with the goal of reaching out to the young people who fall into the other three groups: the Spirituoso's, the Legato's, and the Tranquillo's. These youth are not already attached to the Church; however, at least two of these groups are not completely against interaction with religion. These groups of young people may not necessarily accept the entire identity of the Church with all its demands and dogmatic rules. But there still exists the possibility to foster with these groups a more ad hoc kind of attachment to the Church, which can result in short term participation or small amounts of involvement.

The Legato's still maintain some amount of attachment to the Church due to the old roots of connection that exist in the family. When going to a funeral or to church on Christmas Eve, for example, they re-fresh their connection to the Church and this may lead to further interest.

The Spirituoso's are very active in searching for religious inspiration. With this group in particular, it is important for the Church to be accessible on the internet and to be a part of the social media where these youth are looking for answers in their search for the meaning of life and so on.

The Tranquillo's are not at all interested in religion, but many of them are not really anti-religion or atheists. They, too, are confronted with the big questions in their lives, and it is not really clear where they are looking for answers. There might be opportunities for the Church to connect with them as well, but this is certainly the group that is the hardest to reach.

All the described groups continuously search for answers to essential life issues, so being present in the places they are searching is very important. These may be on the internet, in locations where they gather after school, at big *experience*-promising events, etc. The behavior of young people is continuously characterized by 'choice', and this is true especially in the Legato, Spirituoso, and Tranquillo groups. The Fortissimo's, in contrast, are satisfied with the answers they find inside the Church; for this group, the Church provides the right (and last) choice in their search for the meaning of life, etc. Church workers and volunteers need to focus on reaching the young people who are still searching, hoping, and choosing in order to show them what the Church has to offer.

However, this kind of evangelizing work requires a Church that is less traditional. As S. Hellemans notes: How can the Church reach out to and bind a large audience that has become wayward and increasingly willing to switch to other interesting religious offers?[8] I suggest that the Church does not need to be afraid of young peoples' ability to choose from many different religious offers so long as the Church itself is clear on its own different constituent parts and the specific focus of each of these parts. The Church, as an organization, should be thought of more as a 'network'[9] of religious places where people can meet to further their knowledge, of small communities where people can gather with other people and share their big questions, of big events where people can LIVE their religion and experience it with large groups. The Church should value and pursue these different forms of commitment, and not simply fall back on its 'old-fashioned' offers, which seem only to be relevant to the Fortissimo's.

Above all else, young people need *others* to talk to (digitally or face to face) to help in forming an identity for themselves, and to realize what they really want for their future life, e.g., career, relationship, etc. In forming an identity, one needs to confront oneself with other meanings in order to form one's own opinion. Unlike in the past, young people are no longer engaged in religious groups where questions of self-identity can be addressed and contextualized. In today's world, religion or church is not part of the everyday lives of young people. It is a challenge to reach out to young people in the areas they are already in, and not wait and hope for them to come to the Church on their own. The Church has to enter the communication field of young people in a modern way.

In this communication field, the rule of thumb is to be authentic and not to impose pressure. Young people need to feel free to make their own choices, to find their own answers, but they also need others with whom they can engage in conversations. The Church, and in particular, the workers of the Church, can act as interlocutors for youth if they take the time to meet and really listen to the young people. Using the right language and elucidating their own beliefs are tools of the utmost importance for church workers to connect with young people. It is also crucial to start where young people are already looking for answers, and trust the value of the Church's message. The key, however, to reaching young people is the ability to express the value of this message from the heart.

References

Becker, Jos & Joep De Hart. 2006. *Godsdienstige veranderingen in Nederland. Verschuivingen in de binding met de kerken en de christelijke traditie*. Den Haag: Sociaal en Cultureel Planbureau.

Bernts, Ton, Gerard Dekker & Joep De Hart. 2007. *God in Nederland 1996 - 2006*. Kampen: Ten Have.

Boer, E. de. 2006. *Je bent jong en je wilt anders. 245 jongeren over wat hen bezighoudt en inspireert*. Kampen: Kok.

---

8   cf. S. Hellemans in this volume.
9   cf. K. de Groot in this volume.

Borgman, Erik. 2006. *Metamorfosen: over religie en moderne cultuur*. Kampen-Kapellen: Klement/Pelckmans.

Boschma, Jeroen & Inez Groen. 2006. *Generatie Einstein: slimmer, sneller en socialer. Communiceren met jongeren van de 21e eeuw*. Pearson Education Benelux.

Bucholtz, Mary. 2002. Youth and cultural practice. *Annual Review of Anthropology* 31: 525-552

Collins-Mayo, S. *et al.* 2010. *The Faith of Generation Y*. London: Church House Publishing.

Dijk-Groeneboer, Monique van & Jacques Maas. 2001. *Op zoektocht; levenslang* Utrecht: Katholieke Theologische Universiteit.

Dijk-Groeneboer, Monique & Jacques Maas. 2005. *Geloof? ff checke!* Utrecht: Katholieke Theologische Universiteit.

Dijk-Groeneboer, Monique van, Jacques Maas & Hans van den Bosch. 2008. *Godsdienst? Lekker belangrijk!* Utrecht: Katholieke Theologische Universiteit

Dijk-Groeneboer, M. van (ed.), 2010. *Handboek Jongeren en Religie?!* Almere: Parthenon.

Donk, Wim van de e.a. (eds.). 2006. *Geloven in het publieke domein: verkenningen van een dubbele transformatie*. Den Haag-Amsterdam: WRR/Amsterdam University Press.

John Paul II, 1985. *Dilecti Amici Apostolic Letter to the Youth of the World*. Rome.

John Paul II, 1990. *Redemptoris Missio Encyclical Letter*. Rome: Libreria Editrice Italia

Kerkelijke Documentatie 21 (1993) nr 1 pp. 3-25.

Kerkelijke Documentatie 26 (1998) nr 6 pp. 243-281.

Kregting, J. 2005. *Achtergrond en motieven WJD-gangers 2005*. Nijmegen: Kaski (rapport nr. 539).

Kregting, J. & S. Harperink. 2005. *Doorwerking WJD en bezoek Katholieke Jongeren Dag*. Nijmegen: Kaski (rapport nr. 543).

Kregting, Joris & José Sanders. 2003. *'Waar moeten ze het zoeken?' Vindplaatsen van religie en zingeving bij jongvolwassenen*. Nijmegen: Kaski.

Kregting, Joris & Jolanda Massaar-Remmerswaal. 2010. *Kerncijfers 2009 uit de kerkelijke statistiek van het Rooms-Katholiek Kerkgenootschap in Nederland*. Nijmegen: Kaski (rapport nr. 605).

Martin, R. & P. Williamson (eds.). 2006. *John Paul II and the new evangelization*. Cincinnati Ohio: Servant Books.

Prins, Maerten. 2008. *De deugd van tegenwoordig. Onderzoek naar jongeren en hun grenzen*. Nijmegen: Radboud Universiteit Nijmegen.

Revised King James Bible. *Matthew 25 verse 40*, on the internet: http://www.biblestudytools.com/nkjv/matthew/25.html.

Savage, Sara *et al.* 2006. *Making sense of generation Y. The world view of 15-25-year-olds*. London: Church House.

Smith, Christian & Melinda Lundquist Denton. 2005. *Soul Searching: The Religious and Spiritual Lives of American Teenagers*. Oxford-New York *et al.*: Oxford University Press.

Spangenberg, F. & M. Lampert. 2009. *De grenzeloze generatie*. Amsterdam: Nieuw Amsterdam.

Tuin, Leo van der. 2006. Die jeugd van tegenwoordig ;-). *Praktische Theologie* 33: (3) 290-307.

Ziebertz, H.-G. & W.K. Kay (eds.), 2009. *Youth in Europe*. Berlin: Lit Verlag.

Mission and Modernity:
Reflections on the Mission of the Church in Advanced Modern Society

Jozef Wissink

1. Introduction

Many recent documents of the Catholic Church, written by the last three popes as well as by various national episcopal conferences, speak about the need for the Church to become a missionary church. The main reason for this is the growing awareness of the heavy decline in both membership and participation in the Church, especially in countries of north-western and north-eastern Europe. In this article, I want to reflect, first, on the proper content of the concept of the mission of the Church with special regard to the vision of the Second Vatican Council, some insights of which threaten to be forgotten. I will then reflect on the criteria for engaging in effective ways of mission, or what is also called 'new evangelization': as key criteria, I will propose dialogue and inculturation. Following this, I shall give some examples of new and innovative approaches. I will take my examples especially from the Netherlands primarily because that is the situation I know best and because this situation is probably not well know elsewhere. The approaches of dialogue and inculturation imply that, in mission, our faith is both giving and receiving, teaching and learning. As a result, I will propose a scheme of faith positions in order to sketch the different challenges that need to be met in order to become a missionary church. This scheme can be used to interpret the various initiatives and can also be useful for the development of strategies for new learning processes for missionary agents.

2. The concept of mission

2.1 The old use of the term

In the 1950s when ordinary Catholic people talked about "mission", the word had two meanings. The first association referred to missionary works in the Southern World, where priests brought salvation to pagans by converting and baptizing them, and religious congregations (male and female) took care of hospitals and schools. The numbers of missionaries from France, Italy, Germany, the Netherlands, Belgium, Ireland, and the USA are impressive (Bruls 1977, 165-172). When we add up all the people who were active on the home front for these missionaries, it becomes clear that this missionary movement really was a mass movement. The missions were closely connected to the colonization of the Southern World by European states. In the case of Spain, the popes even confided the missionary task to the Spanish kings, the so-called *padronado real*. But even when political connections were looser, in general, cultural connections were very tight: our missionaries brought the mixed blessings of both the Gospel and Western culture.

The second meaning of the word "mission" concerned the organization of parish retreats. Once every five or ten years, members of religious orders (in the Netherlands, especially the Redemptorists) were invited to preach a mission in a parish. In the course of a week, many religious celebrations were attended by large majorities of parishioners, nearly everyone made confession, and the week was concluded with a great High Mass and other festivities.

2.2. North-west Europe as missionary area

Although traces of these meanings of the word mission still exist in ordinary language today, the actual situation of 'missions' has changed completely. It was considered shocking when French bishops called their country a "*terre de mission*" and founded the institute of the *Mission de France* (1941). Fifty years later, however, the Dutch bishops followed the example of their French colleagues and spoke about the missionary situation of Dutch society and the Church. They were right. In 2008, 58% of the Dutch population stated that they belonged to a church, mosque, or synagogue; however, only 19% of Dutch adults attend church-, mosque-, or synagogue-services at least once a month. Among Dutch Catholics, this figure is 22% (CBS 2009). Most of the big churches have only little contact with 80% of their members; the number of atheists is still growing; and if people find themselves searching for religion, most of these will not end up turning to the great churches for spiritual guidance. The necessity for a new missionary impulse is also reflected in many papal documents. The catchword here is *new evangelization*. This expression specifically refers to the missionary proclamation of faith towards traditionally Christian territories, where people are often baptized but were never introduced to faith and church. With regard to this new evangelization, many questions arise about the legitimacy of this proclamation in a post-modern culture, about possibility and methods, about the requested competencies of missionary leadership, and, last but not least, about the capacity of the existing Catholic Church to welcome new members who were not socialized into the existing climate of church and parish. I shall examine these questions in more detail later on.

3. Mission at the Second Vatican Council

As already indicated, it is no coincidence that the Second Vatican Council started with deep reflection on the mission of the Church. Here, the word "mission" does not refer to the missions towards the Third World (these were the

object of a separate decree entitled *Ad Gentes*), but to the goal God has set for
the Church. What are we intended to do, to attain? To what service is the
Church called? Indeed, the Church, when in power, can forget these questions
because the answer is self-evident: the goal is to ensure her continued existence.
The Church governs the faithful and uses all her influence also to keep the
world of politics, economics, and culture governed by Christian moral principles. One sees in formulations like these that the Church was identified with the
clergy. But was such self-referential arrogance not precisely the cause of the
loss of many members? As the Bishop of Bruge, Mgr. de Smedt, put it in his
famous speech on the Council: "The church suffers from clericalism,
triuphalism, and juridism" (L.Th.K. 1966, E 1, 141). What were the exact asser-
tions of the Council on the mission of the Church and how were they a response
to the new situation?

3.1 The twofold mission of the Church

Vatican II offers characterizations of the mission of the Church in many
places. To approach our subject, I have chosen the text of *Apostolicam
Actuositatem*, nr. 5 because it provides the shortest formulation given by the
Council on this matter: "*Christ's redemptive work, which essentially concerned
the salvation of men, includes also the renewal of the temporal order. Hence the
mission of the Church is not only to bring the message and grace of Christ to
men, but also to penetrate and perfect the temporal order with the spirit of the
Gospel*". Upon analysis of this short formula, one will discover that its content
returns in many places, especially in *Lumen Gentium*.

The first thing we should notice is that this mission is said to be the mission
of the whole Church, of all her members. Within this mission one can distinguish between tasks of the ordained ministry and laypersons, but the mission
itself concerns everyone. This is also the reason why I have chosen the text
from the decree on the lay apostolate. The ecclesiological turn, which was taken
in the dogmatic constitution *Lumen Gentium*, is confirmed: theologically, one
should first speak about the Church as a whole; only afterwards can one distinguish between different positions and tasks. Stated explicitly, "The obligation of
spreading the faith is imposed on every disciple of Christ, according to his
state" (LG 17). The recognition of lay people fully participating in the mission
of the whole Church is the completion of the critical adaptation, which was the
intention of the *aggiornamento* that Vatican II wanted to realize. This means
that Vatican II considered a partnership of our faith and modern culture to be a
possible venture.

The second point requiring our attention is that the mission of the Church is
presented as a duality: it is "not only..., but also". The first part of the mission
of the Church could be said to concern the supernatural dimension, so long as
one understands the word "supernatural" as indicating the atmosphere of grace,
of our final destination to eternal communion with God and all saints, and, fi-

nally, the atmosphere of the theological virtues of faith, hope, and love. [I insist on the right interpretation of *supernatural* here because since the Enlightenment, the word, to many, has become synonymous with miraculous.] The second part of the mission of the Church is characterized by the expression "temporal order". This expression is also susceptible to misunderstanding because, according to our perception, many of the things that belong to the first part of the mission of the Church take place in time, such as preaching of and listening to the Gospel, loving God and your neighbor, etc. We even speak about a salvation history, but, indeed, much of what happens in this salvation history is not considered part of the temporal order. Rather, the expression "temporal order" refers to everything in our human history that is part of human nature as such, with human nature understood as that to which God's grace is directed. The goods of the temporal order include, for example: health, good and just politics, good education, enough leisure time for working people, good relations between men and women, good working conditions in the factories, enough green spaces in urban areas, good science and scholarship at universities, etc. So, we should see the theology of nature and grace behind this text. This theology implies that the natural order is a good order because it is willed and created by God. This natural order is taken up in God's covenant with humankind or, put differently, in the supernatural order (cf. Lash 2004, 44-45, note 1). This implies that God reigns in both orders and that good service in both domains is obedience to God. However, acknowledging that God reigns in the natural order, and understanding that the ultimate meaning of the natural order is to serve the final goal of everything, i.e., the eternal communion of humankind and the angels with God, does not imply that the Church should rule over the natural order. This implication is prevented by the doctrine of the relative autonomy of the natural order (see GS 36). Returning to the formula of the dual mission, we notice that a reduction of Christ's mission to the service of the natural order is forbidden: Christ did not live and die to teach mathematics to us or to improve human health care. But it is equally forbidden for a Christian to neglect the natural goods of this world. A Christian loves the earth and is willing to serve the natural good of humankind (and also the integrity of the rest of creation; however, at the time of Vatican II consciousness of the world's ecological problems was not yet developed).

I have elaborated on this point because the emphasis on the duality of the mission of the Church is very important, and there will always be tendencies to cancel out one of the two parts. Arthur Polhuis, a protestant minister from Rotterdam who had been a well-known diaconal minister, raised a big debate within the Protestant Church in the Netherlands when he claimed that the Christian communities were becoming so small in number that churches should neutralize their diaconal tasks and spend all their energy on core business, i.e., the proclamation of the Gospel. Many right-wing bishops in the Catholic Church would agree. My response to this position is that the Church has two core businesses and cannot give up either of them. The Christian faith that is proclaimed will become too spiritualized and will turn into gnosticism when it is not accompanied by love for our earth, service to the poor, etc. But, of course, the other side should not make the opposite mistake of reducing the mission of the Church to her contribution towards human liberation or welfare. As I said, Christ did not come to improve the world, but to redeem it. If diaconal service is a necessary fruit of faith, and fruits of faith are desired, faith itself should also be desired. In other words, the two dimensions of the mission of the Church belong together: they complement each other and they need each other, but they do not coincide.

The third point I want to comment on is that the Church wants to have an influence in society: "she wants to penetrate and perfect the temporal order with the spirit of the Gospel" (AA n.5). One can read this sentence in different ways. If one states that the Church wants to contribute to a more just and compassionate society, the emphasis is on the Church as a servant church. If one states that the Church wants to have influence in the processes of law-making of the different states because some laws, in her vision, are eroding Christian and/or human values, the emphasis is still on service, but one cannot overlook that the question of power is also entering the scene. In the formula of the Council both aspects are intended. For example, both the way our faith has influenced the care for sick people as well as the attempts to prevent the marriages of homosexual couples can appeal to the text we are commenting on. But, we should note why this text was part of the decree on the lay apostolate. The turn that Vatican II (and, already before this, Pius XII) took was that it recognized democracy as the preferable way of governance for people (cf. GS n. 31 and 75), and it openly declared that the Church, precisely as a church, should not seek political power (GS n.76). Consequently, the Council distinguishes between, on the one hand, the way in which ecclesial hierarchy and members of the Church who officially represent the Church participate in discussions about justice and peace and the like, and, on the other hand, the way Christian lay people are involved in the political and social life of their societies. In the first case, the Church only claims moral power and asserts that other ways of reaching her goal should not be used (GS n.76). Of course, this does not mean that the ways in which the official representatives of the Church are attempting to influence political decisions of nations and international organizations are always impeccable, but it is a declaration of the criteria by which the Church may be judged. In the second case, Christians act on their own authority and according to their own conscience in all domains of society, and realize or do not realize the second part of the mission of the Church. They should do this in ways appropriate to the field of society where they are active. For example, in the medical field, Christian practitioners should act out of love and in just ways, but also with all the professional skills of their professions. The same goes for politicians, scientists and scholars, employers and workers, etc.

3.2 The theological background: A Christian reception of secularization

Against the background of this vision of mission, we can see the works of the great theologians of the *nouvelle théologie*, such as Congar, de Lubac and Chénu, Rahner and von Balthasar. In many spiritual manuals, which were in use during their time, the main task of the Christian was to live as unworldly as possible. The world was seen as a place of temptation. Of course, one could use the goods of the world and should do so, but the main emphasis was on the aversion from the goods of the world. If we apply the opposition of the sacred versus the profane, which is basic in most religions, one could say that people are closer to God in the atmosphere of the sacred than in the atmosphere of the profane. Thus, one can reach God easier in a Church or a monastery than in the "world". In Christian doctrine, however, the opposition between the sacred and the profane is made very relative by the doctrine of creation: both the sacred and the profane in our world belong to the created world. God can be encountered everywhere; no place is void, no place is hopeless. The theologians of the *nouvelle théologie* (and, already before them, Maritain) re-introduced this consciousness into the minds of Catholic believers in their "theology of earthly things". Rahner, for example, spoke about "a faith that loves the earth". By now, this vision has become nearly self-evident, but it must be repeated because it could be forgotten again, especially in a society that is characterized by a functional differentiation and heavily distinguishes different systems of politics, economics, culture, and religion. Under these circumstances, every religion is tempted to withdraw back to its own territory, which then becomes identified with the sacred.

3.3 The new evangelization: Post-conciliar documents

I have shown how the Council formulated its vision on mission with a sharp awareness of the conditions of modern society, such as the secularization of and the changed relations with democratic states. After the Council, the second dimension of the mission of the Church, namely, the care for a just and merciful society, was dealt with in the struggles around liberation theology. The World Church, here, takes on the spotlight (e.g., in *Evangelii Nunitandi*). The first dimension – dealing with faith as it comes into existence and grows – was more in the foreground in the documents on the mission of the Church. Here, Europe was the predominant focus.

The Council discussed the content of this first dimension of the mission of the Church in its many and central texts on the proclamation of the Gospel. However, this was not connected explicitly to the texts on the mission of the Church, perhaps because the semantics of the word "mission" was still strongly associated with proclaiming the Gospel to the non-Christian nations of the Third World. When one reads the decree *Ad Gentes*, we are located more in Africa and Asia than in France or the Netherlands. But, as remarked above, the situation in Europe, too, has become missionary in a new sense. In a series of papal documents, this new missionary challenge is captured in the terminology of "re-evangelization" or "new evangelization". In the encyclical *Redemptoris Missio,* Pope John Paul II mentions three missionary situations. The first is the situation "in which Christ and His Gospel are not known or which lack Christian communities sufficiently mature to incarnate the faith and to proclaim it to others" (RM n.33). Here, we can speak about the mission *ad gentes*, the first proclamation of the Gospel to people who have never heard about Christ. The second situation is where adequate and solid ecclesial structures are present and where Christians are fervent in faith and Christian living. Here, the missionary zeal must be kept alive. The third situation occurs especially, though not exclusively, in countries with ancient Christian roots: "entire groups of the baptized have lost a living sense of the faith or even no longer consider themselves members of the Church. In this case what is needed is a new evangelization or a re-evangelization" (RM n.33). This third situation is often used to describe the actual state of Western Europe, though some find this description to be too negative because it puts the emphasis more on what has been lost rather than on the new cultures of the people living in this area and on what has been maintained of Christian civilization. On the other hand, one cannot deny that the description applies well to the Netherlands, for example. I want to use the concept of new evangelization without implying too pessimistic a view on our culture. This is made possible by conceiving new evangelization essentially in a dialogical manner.

One disadvantage of conceiving new evangelization in this way is that one can forget that evangelization is only one part of the mission of the Church. The diaconal care for the poor and the struggle against the causes of poverty, for example, enter only as a witness that either supports explicit evangelization or is itself a form of evangelization. Therefore, in what follows, I shall sometimes alternate between mission and evangelization and count some activities as missionary (or even as evangelizing) that, according to stricter definitions, would be "only" diaconal because I do not want to lose perspective on the whole of the mission of the Church.

4.   Criteria for sound evangelization

In evangelical circles, the main criterion for evaluating evangelization has always been: growth, growth, growth. A Christian community that does not grow is not a vital community. The emphasis is completely on the quantity of new members. A famous example in the USA is the Willow Creek Community Church. In the Netherlands, we can mention the Bethel Community in Drachten (Brouwer a.o.., 2007, 105-108). This criterion certainly has some validity, but we should not rule out the possibility that negative or bad evangelization could also result in great numerical success: quantity does not equal quality. This insight is gaining ground even in evangelical circles. As a result, the concept of growth is taking on qualitative dimensions as well (Brouwer a.o., 2007, 106-107). From a Catholic point of view, a different missiological starting point is more common.

4.1 Evangelization as dialogue for life

The first insight that I borrow from discussions within the discipline of missiology is that mission is essentially a question of dialogue (cf. Bevans and Schroeder 2004, 348-395). In missiology, the word dialogue is not used in the soft, common sense that we often encounter in liberal, politically correct small-talk, where the word seems to refer to a tolerant conversation between people without opinions or convictions about affairs that do not matter very much. Instead, in missiology, we can gather that the word dialogue has quite a different meaning from the fact that missiologists speak about a prophetic dialogue (Bevans and Schoreder 2004, 352-361; 369-378). The content of the meaning of dialogue is specified in a formula given by the French bishops, namely, that the proclamation of faith is never to be imposed, but proposed (Conférence des Evêques de France 1994; RM n.39). The proclamation of faith is an offer, not a command. Thus, the word dialogue, here, means that when one ('the proposer') offers or proposes the Christian faith to another ('the recipient'), one knows that one is talking to a human person and not to an empty container. The recipient of the offer may or may not start to reflect on what the proposer has said. When the recipient begins to ask questions, the proposer may also start reflecting. If the proposer answers these questions without any reflection, it is a sign that the recipient was seen only as an empty vessel that had to be filled with information, rather than as a thinking human being. However, if answers are given by entering into real, living reflection, a *dialogue* is started in which two people have entered into a learning process. In this dialogue, the Christian proposer also becomes a disciple again and must learn from the recipient. The Gospel also becomes heard in a new way. The questions and remarks of the recipient also *evangelize* the Christian proposer in the dialogue. Actual missiology expresses that no evangelization can happen in an authentic way without a kind of self-evangelization of the Christian proposer or partner too (*Evangelli Nuntiandi* n.14; Sievernich, 2009, 149). What occurs in this kind of dialogue is similar to what happens between a teacher and his or her students. A (good) teacher learns a great deal from the questions and criticisms put forth by his or her students. If students are not engaged with the teacher in this way, the subject matter being offered by the teacher will likely be seen as very dull or uninteresting. Likewise, evangelization has a receptive side for *both* the recipients and the proposers as well; the proposers learn new things, which challenge them to re-formulate and "update" their faith. This mutual, dialogical receptivity is a learning activity of faith. Therefore, care for this kind of self-evangelization of the proposer is an essential part of the evangelization process.

Conceived in this dialogical way, the question about the legitimacy of evangelization is easier to handle. Under the conditions of advanced modernity, forbidding this kind of dialogue puts one in a position where he or she needs legitimation. When dialogue is permitted, a form of inculturation occurs, at least in the culture of the persons who are involved in the dialogue. Here, we have the second important missiological concept, which we should recover for use also in the European context. We have to evangelize not only persons, but cultures as well (*Evangelii Nuntiandi* n.20).

4.2 Evangelization as inculturation

Let us first determine the content of the concept of inculturation. Inculturation of the Christian faith happens when our faith (which always already has a cultural shape because of former inculturations) grows into a new culture in such a way that both our faith and the culture change. Our faith changes because it gets new expressions and a new way of being lived. The culture changes because it undergoes the transforming influence of the Christian tradition. One could call inculturation a process of critical adaptation when one considers the process from the perspective of faith. In fact, a process of critical adaptation is the formative theological law of valid inculturation, which is already valid for each individual: faith has to become personally appropriated by every individual and gets the characteristics of this person; at the same time, every individual is challenged to be transformed by faith. In every person this transformation has the form of a decentralization: the ego is no longer the center of one's world; instead, God takes this place.

The problem is that nowadays many former ways of inculturation are no longer available. When Anglo-Saxon monks evangelized the Netherlands, they were supported by the political power of the Merovingian kings in what is now France. When, in the 19th and 20th centuries, the Church turned itself into a mass organization, she still had control of the people, and transformed the people into Catholic masses. In most countries of Western Europe, the big churches have become a minority and the only way they can influence culture is by using their moral prestige. This leaves the theological law of valid inculturation intact, but application of this law to greater circles of culture becomes more difficult. Another question is whether there are forms of culture into which a creative inculturation is not possible because no mutual transformation is possible.

5. Actual missionary activities

Of course, I will not endeavor to give a complete survey of evangelization activities in the Netherlands and certainly not in the whole of Western Europe. In this section, I simply want to make some observations on what I call the 'carriers' of this movement in the Church and sketch some more or less documented activities.

5.1 Carriers of evangelization

As stated earlier, until 1950 mission referred to the evangelization of people in the Third World who had never heard of the Gospel or parish mission. These missions (*ad gentes*) were mostly carried out by male and female religious orders and congregations. In the parish missions, we see that there was care for the maintenance of faith in ordinary people who belonged to the Church via their parish church.

Who are the actual carriers of evangelization? When we look at the documents of the various dioceses, they talk so often about the missionary parish that we could get the impression that the parishes are the most important carriers of evangelization (DPC-Rotterdam, 2007; Aartsbisdom Utrecht, without year of edition; circa 2004). However, this impression is not completely right empirically speaking. Indeed, there are examples of innovative projects from parishes that have an evangelizing character, and I will look at these in a moment, but most parishes in the Netherlands are so occupied with just surviving and/or organizing themselves anew after many fusions, while mourning the loss of the old parish, that not much energy and time is left for evangelization.

The next candidates of carriers of new evangelization are the religious orders and congregations. Here, we can mention also some new missionary initiatives, especially in the field of pastoral initiatives for young people. In the Netherlands, most activities in this field can be counted as new evangelization because there is a crisis with respect to the tradition of faith for young people in our churches. But most of the congregations are dying and most of the greater orders have very few postulants and novices. In 1950, the Franciscans, for example, had around 1200 friars (priests and brothers). Currently, they have about 130, and only about ten of these are younger than 65 years old. In connection with the religious orders, we should also mention the new movements such as Focolare, the Neocatechumenate, as well as new religious communities like the Frères (and Soeurs) de St. Jean, the Sisters of the Divine Incarnation, and the Sisters of Mother Teresa. In general, they are very active, but their reach (except for the sisters of Mother Teresa) seems to be limited to young people who are already inclined to a form of strict orthodoxy.

There are some new players in the field of missionary activity who were not very active in the past. For example, the papacy and dioceses take it upon themselves to organize many events and meetings with youth, artists, scientists, etc. I do not want to say that, in the past, Rome was not active in the missionary field. The curial congregation of the *Propaganda Fide* shows this was not the case. But Rome's activity then was more on the level of coordinating the missionary activities of the religious orders and congregations. In contrast, today we observe Rome taking on a new role, for example, organizing papal visits to countries or making the pope a central figure on World Youth Days. The same can be said for dioceses: they organize yearly meetings of all the youngsters who have received the sacrament of confirmation, they organize preparatory meetings before World Youth Days, as well as meetings for so-called New Catholics who have joined the Catholic Church in recent years. The results are interesting not so much because of the numbers, but because of the variety of young people that are attracted, and because it gives young believing people support in the sense that they feel, "I am not mad after all".

Finally, individuals can be carriers of evangelization. We see many successful examples of this in the work of priests or (male and female) pastoral workers with a special charism for warm and convincing presentation of the relevance of faith to special situations. Of course, the role of parents should also not be underestimated. Finally, some young people are able to attract other young people.

5.2 Sorts of missionary activities

The Diocesan Pastoral Centre of the diocese of Rotterdam has gathered some examples of innovative and missionary activities (DPC-Rotterdam, 2008). The Dutch Bishops Conference also provided some examples of missionary activities in their pastoral letter *Getuigen van de hoop die in ons leeft* (Witnessing the hope that lives within us, Nederlandse Bisschoppenconferentie, 2006). I shall present some of their examples and add some others I know from experience. My aim is not to give an exhaustive oversight of all activities, but to give some impressions of different types of activities that are considered to be missionary and/or evangelizing activities.

First, in many Protestant communities, the Alpha-Course is quite popular. A Catholic variant of this course has also been developed (Nederlandse Nisschoppenconferentie, 2006, 8/16). The Dutch website of this Catholic variant shows that it is offered in about 36 locations in the Netherlands. The method of this course is now international and well known. Therefore, I will describe it only briefly. An Alpha-Course consists of ten evenings (including a weekend session), which all start with a meal. During the ten evenings about 14 or 15 items of Christian faith are discussed, such as the existence of God, reconciliation by the cross, the meaning of prayer, the Holy Spirit, the Church, discerning God's ways in one's own life, etc. The course is meant to give information, but care is taken to ensure that Christian witness also occurs. Therefore, already-convinced Christians make up half the number of attendants of any given Alpha group.

Second, street evangelization is often characteristic for the evangelical part of Christianity. Although this is rare in Catholicism, members of the Legion of Mary engaged in something similar in the city of Hengelo in the east of the Netherlands. They spoke to people on the street, told them they were Catholic believers in God, and asked people what God meant to them (DPC-Rotterdam, 2008, 26).

Third, in some parishes special attention is given to a well presented website. Such websites offer, e.g., virtual tours of different parish buildings, or texts of sermons given in the past. In the presentation of parish life, the designers of these websites take into account that strangers and newcomers are not familiar with words like diacony, catechesis, or liturgy. As a result, more accessible headings are chosen such as "caring for each other", or "the whole of life" (for information about sacraments and celebrations), or "wanting to believe" (for catechetical activities) (DPC-Rotterdam, 2008, 40-44).

Fourth, in the Netherlands quite a few ministers, priests, and pastoral workers are inspired by the "theory of presence", which was developed by Professor Dr. Andries Baart (Baart, 2001). In his study, Baart analyzed the way some urban mission workers dealt with people in relatively poor quarters of cities in the Netherlands. He discovered that their actions were not directed at solving the problems of these people, after their problems were diagnosed; rather, they encountered these people first as the human beings that they are. These urban mission workers remain in these poor areas and offer their presence, their admiration for what is good, their compassion for what is heavy and difficult. When people tell them their problems, they help them, e.g., by accompanying them to social services and assisting them in telling their own story. In this way, their real problems are not lost to bureaucracy, or because they do not fit the defined categories of the social services. Some priests, deacons, and pastoral workers who work in parishes have adopted some elements of this approach. They take time to enter the quarters of the city without a determined agenda, and they speak to people about how they experience their living situations. When they encounter problems, they take action, often with the help of parishioners who have become interested. In this way, the parish comes into better contact with the people of the area. The result, often, is that, at some moment, inter-religious celebrations are held, or a meeting house is opened where people can drink a cup of tea and gather together, etc. Here, we encounter a more diaconal approach, which turns out to have important consequences for the faith of the parishioners as well (documents on the urban mission workers can be found in Baart's study; the examples of the parish priests and pastoral workers are documented in Breda, see DPC-Rotterdam, 2008, 34-36; from experience I know the way the pastoral team of Utrecht-North has worked in its area).

Fifth, another approach is that churches make an offer to spiritual seekers inside and outside the Church. Often, a connection is sought between artistic expressions and the search for spirituality. Movies are shown and discussed, novels are read in groups, expositions are organized around a spiritual theme or around a hot issue relevant to a particular part of the city. Sometimes, churches that are united in a local Council of Churches manage to present a complete program with many projects, which are published in local and provincial newspapers. In the city of Roosendaal, this type of approach reached a great range of people, most of whom no longer participated in any normal church activities (for Roosendaal, see DPC-Rotterdam, 2008, 12-16; for a parish in Rotterdam itself, 17-22).

Finally, some activities are called missionary because they try to give spiritual and physical space to people within the existing communities who would otherwise perhaps drift away. Some churches organize meetings for their youth or for spiritual seekers on a Sunday afternoon or during the week when there is occasion to have celebrations that are more experimental than would normally be permitted in an official celebration of the Eucharist.

6. Different points of departure

The range of activities considered to be missionary is quite wide. Thus, the question arises as to what aspects these activities have in common and on what aspects they diverge. Over time, I have discovered that the main differences have their origin in a different starting position with regard to how the Christian faith is lived. Here, again, I discern two oppositions as fundamental, namely, whether this faith is inner-directed or looks for contacts with people outside the Christian tradition, and whether one is mainly oriented towards teaching others only or is also oriented towards learning from others as well. Combining these axes, the following schedule results.

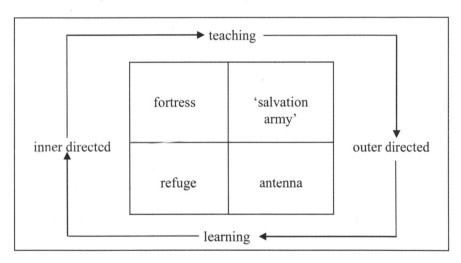

Before I comment on the schedule, I first have to mention its main source. The schedule is based on an idea developed by members of the Diocesan Service Centre of the diocese of Rotterdam (DPC-Rotterdam, 2007). Originally, the schedule was designed to help parishes wanting to become more missionary to discover their starting position. I adopt the schedule because I think it can also be used to analyze the other carriers of evangelizing activity mentioned in paragraph 5.1. I would tend to include even individuals here. I have somewhat modified the original names of the four positions, which result from the combination of the two axes. The position I have called "fortress" was originally called "rock". The term fortress emphasizes better a defensive mode. The position entitled "salvation army" is a renaming of what was originally called "point of departure for attack". The disadvantage of this renaming is that it is difficult to disassociate it from the existing Salvation Army of William Booth. However, the advantage is that the idea of military campaigning is stressed and the name is shorter than the lengthy original. In the original schedule, what I have called "antenna" was previously called "Voice in the Events". I made this change so that the four names appear to be four species of one *genus*.

The *fortress* position represents the active teaching of faith, but this activity is restricted to the happy few who are already members of the community. One could think here of a strictly orthodox community, which is isolated from its context. But one could also imagine a progressive community where any dialogue about what is not "politically correct" is impossible.

The *salvation army* position is a faith position where people take the risk of moving into the surrounding world. One could think of an evangelical community armed with songs, speeches, and speakers.

The *antenna* position is one where faith has moved into the surrounding world and listens actively to the joys and sorrows of the people. In doing this, people also learn much about their own faith. One could think of some forms of urban mission where the emphasis is on pastoral and diaconal presence in the poor areas of our cities. In this presence, the workers develop a new reading of the Scriptures, a down-to-earth spirituality, as it were. In this sense, they develop an interior spiritual dialogue with the culture of the city, and actively use their faith antenna to read the signs of the time. I describe this position in somewhat more detail because, in general, this position is the least known. We recognize this position also in some spirituality centers that enter into dialogue with modern religious seekers.

The *refuge* position sees the community as refuge (or tavern, as the grand old man of Dutch pastoral theology, Jan Hendriks, used to call his ideal Church) (Hendriks, 2001, 53-55). The questions and challenges of our actual culture are fully present, and free discussions on these questions and challenges are not only possible, but even desired. This is a community where people recognize each other and accept each other in their difference. Note that this description does not say that such a community or believer is progressive or theologically liberal. If the community is more traditional, it is at least open. If it is more progressive, questions that are not politically (or religiously) correct may still be asked.

One should also note that the description of these four positions is positive. None of the positions is condemned because none is canonized in itself. In the fortress position there is a consciousness of how precious faith is: it demands some care to preserve it. (When I speak about the orthodox variant, I do not use this term in a derogatory way. I take orthodoxy to mean that a believer orders his or her reason towards the mystery of God's love, and does not attempt the reverse, i.e., to adjust the mystery to fit the categories of his or her philosophical system or interests.)

The proclamation of the evangelicals should also, in principle, be evaluated positively. Most Christians that belong to a major church do not like street evangelization, which they find characteristic of evangelism. But should we not pay respect to the courage and love that is invested in this proclamation? Are we sure that our criticism is not mainly motivated by our own fear to give public witness of our own faith or to be exposed with regard to our lack of faith?

In my more elaborate description of the way some workers in urban mission are present and listen to those around them, a sensitive reader may already notice my respect and sympathy for their spirituality and work.

Finally, is the hospitable and welcoming community where people feel free to reveal their questions and take each other seriously not really mirroring values that are truly theologically valid?

Indeed, all four positions also have weaknesses. Ideally, each position should strive to adopt the positive side of its neighboring position in the diagram. If we move clockwise, we could say that the fortress-people should develop the courage to move out, to *manifest* themselves. In fact, does not the preciousness of their treasure require this? Why not learn from the evangelicals? The Legion of Mary in Hengelo has done this. We see the same in some more or less conservative parishes that offer the Alpha-Course in its Catholic version.

The evangelicals themselves should learn to listen and *empathize* with the people to whom they preach. Does not their own missionary task imply this move? If they are pushed by a real missionary love, that love is interested in the joys and needs of every human being. An interesting example of this move is shown in the missionary activity of the Christian Reformed Church, a small, orthodox Calvinistic church. Their missionary workers did research on the way of life and religious longings of a group of young intellectuals in Amsterdam. At the same time, these missionary workers were active in revitalizing the existing religious community of their church in this city. They discovered that the young intellectuals longed for a community that was open, left one the possibility of being loosely connected, and where all kinds of questions were tolerated, or better, desired. However, the old, existing parish community mainly wished for peace and order. They did not want too many discussions because this would result in too many conflicts. As a result, the missionary workers decided not to ask the young intellectuals into the old religious community, but to start a new project instead. The future will reveal whether these two communities will be able to become one church (Brouwer a.o., 2007, 84-87). But, in this case, we see how evangelicals made a move towards listening to the outside voices. The way some parishes partition their websites with an eye to the religious seeker or the newcomer who is not familiar with the structures of a parish is also an example of this move.

The challenge for the workers of the urban mission is how they share their new faith also with the people of the neighborhood they are working in, to build new communities with a new Christian language. Our account of priests and pastoral workers who, by entering the quarters of the city and taking action on problems, were able to motivate their parish members and get them interested in what was happening around them, is a beautiful example of new ways of gathering people who were already gathered.

The challenge for the refuge position is a renewed concentration. It is really a good thing when we have a receiving and warm community, but the question of whether it still is a Christian community should be asked, even if it is a painful question. My impression is that in many parishes and communities this question is considered to be too threatening.

I have moved clockwise from the fortress-parish to the refuge-parish. Under normal circumstances, it would be recommended that we move counter-clockwise as well. Currently, the problem in the Netherlands is that the dialogue between fortress-church and refuge-church is severely blocked. Perhaps this is one of the reasons why the Church in the Netherlands seems unable, at the moment, really to become a vital missionary church.

When we move through the positions counter-clockwise, the main emphasis is on the receiving role of the Church. The fortress-church, in its conservative variant, should listen to the questions that arise in the context of modern culture. In a culture of individualization, the Church must leave space for free conversation and for experiment, both on the level of reflection as well as on the level of designing life projects. The fortress-church, in its progressive-liberal variant, should be prepared to enter into dialogue with the new religiosity of young people, who sometimes reinvent traditions to which progressives are averse. In both cases, the dialogue is blocked. In fact, the refuge-church consists of mainly elderly people who simply seek some rest. They have to be seduced into the outgoing movement, for example, as in our Breda case. For the workers in urban missions, they are averse to evangelicals.

7. Conclusions

We have seen how the Church is in dialogue with the conditions of advanced modernity when she reflects on her mission. When she defines her mission as the proclamation of faith and service to a just and merciful society, she is aware of her position within actual society, where she is one voice among others (pluralism), and where she, in general, no longer dominates cultures. Within this context we have developed a quadrant of dimensions for the new evangelization, which also gives a matrix of the required competencies for missionary workers of the Church.

When we re-read the two axes in the light of the findings so far, we see that, conceptually, in the diagram, we have implied a vision on mission that is characterized by a double presupposition. On the level of insight, a hermeneutical approach is presupposed. This hermeneutics should be open to the mystery of faith (orthodoxy) and to the values present in modern culture (openness for new learning processes). But there is also another presupposition. On the axis of inner- and outer-directedness, we discovered that openness is not only a question of hermeneutics, but also of courage and curiosity. It is dangerous to confuse these dimensions. Sometimes, a lack of courage to leave the safe refuge of the Church is hiding behind hermeneutical problems and shows an aversion to evangelicalism; on the other side, fear of hermeneutical openings is hiding behind evangelical zeal, which can only repeat more loudly what was not understood before. This is often accompanied by a completely pessimistic view on our culture. To promote the new evangelization, one needs a good diagnosis; and for a good diagnosis, one needs a good set of instruments. I hope to have provided some of these.

Furthermore, our diagram made it possible for us to see more clearly where the main problems of the Church are situated. Too often, convinced believers refuse to enter into a dialogical evangelization because this threatens their certainties. The fortress seems to have become their refuge. On the other hand, the Christians-in-learning too often have a fear of making commitments to what they have learned to be true. There is still much work to do.

References

Aartsbisdom Utrecht (without year of edition; 2003?). *Op weg naar missionaire geloofsgemeenschappen. Samenwerken en profileren in het parochiepastoraat.* Utrecht

Baart, Andries. 2001. *Een theorie van de presentie.* Utrecht: Lemma.

Bevans, Stephen B. & Roger P. Schoreder. 2004. *Constants in context. A theology of mision for today.* Maryknoll-New York: Orbis Books.

Brouwer, R. e.a. 2007. *Levend lichaam. Dynamiek van christelijke geloofsgemeenschappen in Nederland.* Kampen: Kok.

Bruls, J. 1977. Von den Missionen zu den jungen Kirchen. In Aubert, Bruls, Crunican.

Conférence des Évêques de France. 1994. *Proposer la foi dans la société actuelle.* Paris: Cerf.

DPC-Rotterdam 2008?. *Aanstekelijke verhalen. Goed nieuws voor alle mensen deel 2.* Rotterdam: Uitgaven Bisdom Rotterdam.

DPC-Rotterdam. 2007. *Om het missionaire vuur van parochies aan te wakkeren. Goed nieuws voor alle mensen deel 1.* Rotterdam. Uitgaven Bisdom Rotterdam.

Ellis, J. Tracy, J. Hajjar & F.B. Pike. *Geschichte der Kirche.* Band V/2, 165-212. Zürich-Einsiedeln-Köln. Benziger Verlag.

Hellemans, Staf. 2007. *Het tijdperk van de wereldreligies. Religie in agrarische civilisaties en in moderne samenlevingen.* Zoetermeer-Kapellen: Meinema/Pelckmans.

Hendriks, J. 2001[4]. *Gemeente als herberg. Een concrete utopie.* Kampen: Kok.

Lash, Nicholas. 2004. *Holyness, Speech and Silence. Reflection on the question of God.* Aldershot, Ashgate.

Lexikon für Theologie und Kirche. 1966-1968. *Das zweite vatikanische Konzil. Konstitutionen, Dekreten und Erklärungen.* Ergänzungsband I-II-III. Freiburg/Basel/ Wien: Herder.

Nederlandse Bischoppenconferentie. 2006. *Getuigen van de hoop die in ons leeft. Bisschoppelijke Brief over missie in de 21ste eeuw.* www.bidsomhaarlem.nl/docs/2006/ 2006-05-22_missiebrief.doc.

Sievernich, M. 2009. *Die christliche Mission. Geschichte und Gegenwart.* Darmstadt: WBG.

Schulze, Gerhard. 2000[8]. *Die Erlebnisgesellschaft. Kultursoziologie der Gegenwart.* Frankfurt/New York. Campus Verlag.

List of Contributors

Anthony J. Carroll, SJ
Lecturer in Philosophy and Theology, Heythrop College, University of London. Recent publications: The Philosophical Foundations of Catholic Modernism. Pp. 38-55 in O. Rafferty (ed.). *George Tyrrell and Catholic Modernism*. Dublin, 2010; Disenchantment, Rationality, and the Modernity of Max Weber. *Forum Philosophicum* 16/1 (2011) 117-137; The United Kingdom? In *Thinking Faith*, 13 January 2012.

Monique van Dijk-Groeneboer
Assistant Professor in the Sociology of Religion. Recent publication: (ed.). *Handboek Jongeren en Religie*. Almere: Parthenon, 2010.

Stefan Gärtner
Assistant Professor in Practical Theology, Tilburg University. Recent publications: *Zeit, Macht und Sprache. Pastoraltheologische Studien zu Grunddimensionen der Seelsorge*, Freiburg/Br. u.a., 2009; Staying a pastor while talking like a psychologist? A proposal for an integrative model. *Christian Bioethics* 16/1 (2010) 48-60; Prophetic pastoral care. Resistance potential in late modernity? Pp. 23-29 in A. Dillen & A. Vandenhoeck (eds.). *Prophetic witness in world Christianities. Rethinking pastoral care and counseling*. Berlin-Wien, 2011.

Kees de Groot
Assistant Professor in Practical Theology, Tilburg University. Recent publications: Celebrating Mass Via the Television Screen. Pp. 307-213 in P. Post & A.L. Molendijk (eds.). *Sacred Places in Modern Western Culture*. Leuven, 2011; Religion in Liquid Modernity. Collective Manifestations of Religion in Secularizing Dutch Society. In W. Hofstee & A. van der Kooij (eds.). *Religion, public or private?* Leiden, 2012 (in print); Two Alienation Scenarios: Explaining the Distance between Catholics and Roman Catholic Church in the Netherlands. In F.-V. Anthony & H.-G. Ziebertz (eds.), *Religious Identity and National Heritage*. Leiden, 2012 (in print).

Staf Hellemans
Professor in the Sociology of Religion, Tilburg University. Recent publications: *Das Zeitalter der Weltreligionen. Religion in agrarischen Zivilisationen und in modernen Gesellschaften*. Würzburg, 2010; (ed. with W. Damberg). *Die neue Mitte der Kirche. Der Aufstieg der intermediären Instanzen in den europäischen Großkirchen seit 1945*. Stuttgart, 2010; Religious Orthodoxy as a Modality of

'Adaptation'. Pp. 9-32 in B. Becking (ed.). *Orthodoxy, Liberalism, and Adaptation*. Leiden, 2011.

Peter Jonkers
Professor of Philosophy, Tilburg University. Recent publications: (ed. with D.M. Grube). *Religions Challenged by Contingency. Theological and Philosophical Perspectives to the Problem of Contingency,* Leiden, 2008; Religious Truth in a Globalising World. Pp. 176-206 in Ph. Quadrio & C. Besseling (eds.). *Religion and Politics in the New Century: Contemporary Philosophical Perspectives*. Sydney, 2009; Can Freedom of Religion Replace the Virtue of Tolerance? Pp. 73-84 in A. Singh & P. Losonczi (eds.). *From Political Theory to Political Theology. Religious Challenges and the Prospects of Democracy.* London-New York, 2010.

Ton Meijers
Assistant Professor in Canon Law, Tilburg University. Recent publications: The Independence of the Church from the National State. *Bijdragen. International Journal in Philosophy and Theology* 72 (2011) 3-17; Godsdienstvrijheid en waarheid. *Internationaal Katholiek Tijdschrift Communio* 36 (2011) 288-296.

Willem Marie Speelman
Assistant Professor at the Franciscan Study Centre, connected to the Tilburg School of Theology, Tilburg University. Recent publications: The Celebration of the Body. Pp. 166-176 in L. Leijssen (ed.). *Initiation chrétienne et la liturgie.* Peeters, 2008; (co-authored with G.P. Freeman & J. van den Eijnden). *Om de hele wereld. Inleiding in de franciscaanse spiritualiteit*. Nijmegen, 2010; A spiritual method for daily life practices. Pp. 55-71 in E. Hense, F. Maas (eds.). *Towards a Theory of Spirituality*. Leuven, 2011.

James Sweeney, CP
Senior Lecturer in Pastoral Theology, Heythrop College, University of London. Recent publications: (ed. with G. Simmonds & D. Lonsdale). Keeping Faith in Practice: Aspects of Catholic Pastoral Theology. London, 2010; (co-authored with H. Cameron, D. Bhatti, C. Duce & C. Watkins). *Talking about God in Practice: Theological Action Research and Practical Theology*. London, 2010.

Jozef Wissink
Em. Professor in Practical Theology, Tilburg University. Recent Publications: *Toptheologen. Hoofdfiguren uit de theologie van vandaag*. Tielt, 2006; *Begeesterd. Theologische reflecties over God, persoon en gemeenschap*. Heeswijk, 2011; *Christus, missie en theologische cultuurhermeneutiek. Naar nieuwe sporen in de praktische theologie*, Tilburg, 2012.

Henk Witte
Associate Professor of Dogmatic Theology and Xaverius-Professor of Theology and Spirituality in Ignatian Perspective, Tilburg University. Recent publications: Der Diözesanbischof und die Kooperation der Laien in der Seelsorge: Amtstheologische Reflexionen. Pp. 77-92 in B. Kranemann & M. Wijlens (Hgg.). *Gesendet in den Weinberg des Herrn: Laien in der katholischen Kirche heute und morgen*, Würzburg, 2010; Die katholische Kirche in den Niederlanden: Wandlungsprozesse nach dem Zweiten Vatikanischen Konzil. Pp. 139-157 in W. Damberg & S. Hellemans (Hgg.). *Die neue Mitte der Kirche. Der Aufstieg der intermediären Instanzen in den europäischen Großkirchen seit 1945*, Stuttgart, 2010; Reform with the Help of Juxtapositions: A Challenge to the Interpretation of the Documents of Vatican II. *The Jurist* 71 (2011) 20-34.

Tilburg Theological Studies
Tilburger Theologische Studien
edited by/hrsg. von Prof. Dr. Erik Borgman, Dr. Dr. Claudia Mariéle Wulf, Dr. Henk Witte

Harm Goris (ed./Hg.)

Bodiliness and Human Dignity
An Intercultural Approach

Leiblichkeit und Menschenwürde
Interkulturelle Zugänge

Tilburg Theological Studies
LIT

Harm Goris (Ed./Hg.)
Bodiliness and Human Dignity. An Intercultural Approach
Leiblichkeit und Menschenwürde. Interkulturelle Zugänge. Veröffentlichungen des Zentrums für Interkulturelle Ethik 1

In jeder Kultur reflektieren Ideen und Praktiken in Bezug auf den menschlichen Leib wie man den Menschen und dessen Würde versteht. Heutige kulturelle und medizinisch-technische Entwicklungen stellen neue Fragen an traditionelle Auffassungen von Leiblichkeit. Wie können diese Fragen von der Perspektive der interkulturellen Ethik her erörtert werden, insbesondere was die Organspende betrifft?

In every culture, ideas and practices concerning the human body reflect what people think about the human person and his/her dignity. Contemporary cultural and medical-technical developments pose new questions to traditional attitudes to bodiliness. How can these questions be addressed from the perspective of intercultural ethics, in particular with regard to organ donation?

Bd. 2, 2006, 136 S., 16,90 €, br., ISBN 3-8258-9284-0

LIT Verlag Berlin – Münster – Wien – Zürich – London
Auslieferung Deutschland / Österreich / Schweiz: siehe Impressumsseite

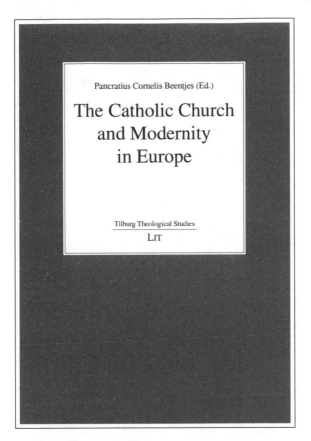

Pancratius Cornelis Beentjes (Ed.)

The Catholic Church and Modernity in Europe

The tense relationship between the Catholic Church and modernity, particularly in Europe, gives rise
to a whole range of questions and analyses which are described and discussed in this volume. It has a
historical overview of the evolution and diversity of the Church after 1945. Also attention is given to the
interaction between theology and contemporary postmodern secular culture, the self-image of the Church
in the wake of Vatican II, the contribution of the Catholic tradition to the contemporary pluralistic world,
and to modern culture influencing Catholic tradition.

Bd. 3, 2012, 248 S., 24,90 €, br., ISBN 978-3-643-90023-4

LIT Verlag Berlin – Münster – Wien – Zürich – London

Auslieferung Deutschland / Österreich / Schweiz: siehe Impressumsseite

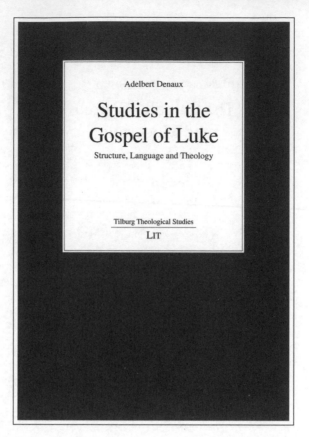

Adelbert Denaux
Studies in the Gospel of Luke

Structure, Language and Theology

Tilburg Theological Studies

LIT

Adelbert Denaux
Studies in the Gospel of Luke
Structure, Language and Theology
This volume offers a collection of Lukan studies by Adelbert Denaux, whose preferred field of studies
has been the Gospel of Luke for many years. The thirteen papers collected in this volume have been de-
livered in different languages and on different occasions. The papers deal with several aspects of Luke's
Gospel: structure, Old Testament influence, theology and christology, Luke and Q, language and style, and
individual passages.
Bd. 4, 2010, 400 S., 69,90 €, br., ISBN 978-3-643-90060-9

LIT Verlag Berlin – Münster – Wien – Zürich – London
Auslieferung Deutschland / Österreich / Schweiz: siehe Impressumsseite